AIRGUN DIGEST

3rd Edition

GW00771304

By J.I. Galan

DBI BOOKS, INC.

Staff

Senior Staff Editors
Harold A. Murtz
Ray Ordorica

Production Manager
John L. Duoba

Editorial/Production Associate
Jamie L. Puffpaff

Editorial/Production Assistant
Holly J. Porter

Electronic Publishing Manager
Nancy J. Mellem

Electronic Publishing Associate
Robert M. Fuentes

Electronic Publishing Assistant
Edward B. Hartigan

Managing Editor
Pamela J. Johnson

Publisher
Sheldon Factor

Acknowledgement

Special thanks to Mrs. Sally Molina, of Quality Typing, Inc., in Miami, Florida, for typing the final manuscripts.

About Our Covers

The world of airguns is filled with both tradition and innovation—tradition in the sense of legendary quality and craftsmanship, and innovation to keep up with our modern times in both design and manufacture. All of these qualities are represented here by two old and respected names, Crosman and Benjamin Sheridan.

Shown at top is the Crosman Silver Series 1008 RepeatAir pistol, one of the most innovative airgun products available. It's styled after one of today's most popular 10mm automatic pistols and uses CO_2 power that delivers reliable semi-automatic performance. It has a rifled 177-caliber steel barrel for accurate shooting of pellets, single/double-action trigger, fully adjustable rear sight, cross-bolt safety, and two eight-shot pellet cylinders. The 1008 RepeatAir is also available with black finish and brown grips.

In the middle is the Benjamin Sheridan H22 pneumatic (pump-up) pistol with gleaming nickel finish and walnut grip and pump handle. The 22-caliber H22 is a bolt-action single shot that features variable pump power for up to 460 fps performance, a rifled brass barrel, solid brass air chamber and receiver, fully adjustable rear sight and cross-bolt safety. It's also available with black finish, as the HB22 model. Traditional hand-craftsmanship and attention to detail make Benjamin Sheridans an American legend.

On the right is the Crosman Auto Air II, a rakish pistol that also replicates a very popular firearm. Said to be the lightest CO_2 pistol at a mere 13 ounces, the Auto Air II shoots BBs as a repeater (seventeen-shot magazine) and 177-caliber pellets as a single shot. Even its gray finish looks like the stainless steel counterpart.

These three modern air pistols combine the best of two worlds to keep our rich airgunning sport alive and well into the next century.

Photo by John Hanusin.

The views and opinions of the authors expressed herein are not necessarily those of the publisher, and no responsibility for such views will be assumed.

Arms and Armour Press, London, G.B., exclusive licensees and distributor in Britain and Europe, India and Pakistan; Media House Publications, Sandton, Transvaal, exclusive distributor in South Africa and Zimbabwe. Lothian Books, Auckland, exclusive distributor in New Zealand.

ISBN 0-87349-154-8   **Library of Congress Catalog Card 76-50750**

Table of Contents

Table of Contents

Foreword

MUCH HAS TRANSPIRED in the world of airguns since the Second Edition of this book was published in the spring of 1988. In a few areas of airgunning, the changes have been nothing short of radical. One prime example—unfortunately, a negative one—was the legislative restrictions placed on replica air-soft guns in the United States. In most areas, however, the changes have been quite positive, though no less dramatic, as broad-based interest in airguns continues to grow at an unprecedented pace.

This tome differs greatly from the Second Edition on several important points. First, it is a totally new book, not merely an updated version of the Second Edition. It is considerably longer than the latter as well, with more chapters on a wide range of topics, including a rather large chapter with Test Reports on some thirty different models from across the broad spectrum of the contemporary airgun. Perhaps the most crucial difference, however, is that this Third Edition of AIRGUN DIGEST includes material from several of the most distinguished airgun writers of our time.

From the early planning stages, I felt that, in order to live up to the word "digest" in its title, this book had to incorporate ideas and perspectives besides my own on a wide variety of airgun topics. That goal, I think, has been accomplished. If I may be permitted a bit of conceit, I am inclined to look at this whole book the same way the conductor of a major symphony orchestra looks at the stellar performance of one of his musical arrangements by all of its players. Thus, to all of those wonderfully talented and knowledgeable individuals who so enthusiastically accepted my invitation to participate in this "airgun symphony," I am forever grateful. You all did a terrific job!

Finally, it is my most fervent hope that this book can contribute, even in a small way, to the survival of the shooting sports in general, encouraging the safety and enjoyment of such activities.

Safe Shooting!
J.I. Galan

Chapter 1

And For Those Who Came In Late...

An introduction to the wonderful and fascinating world of the airgun, from a bit of history to today's bewildering variety of models and their uses.

by J.I. Galan

The ubiquitous Daisy BB gun has served as the first step to the pleasures of shooting to countless generations of youngsters for over 100 years. But even a low-powered BB gun is not a toy and youngsters must be closely supervised during shooting sessions. Eye protection is a must because steel BBs tend to ricochet with force upon striking a solid object.

A BOOK SUCH as this, by necessity, has to cover a lot of ground. It would be easy, perhaps too easy, to simply dedicate each and every chapter to a specialized topic within the broad field of airgunning. Although that has been done to some extent, as we get deeper into this tome, we must not lose sight of the fact that there are countless folks out there just now becoming interested in airguns. It would be grossly unfair to these newcomers to produce a book of this magnitude that does not, at the very least, offer them an opening salvo of what airguns are all about, commencing with a fairly brief historical perspective that can take them from the airgun's obscure beginnings straight into the 1990s.

Thus, in the beginning there was the blowgun. This deceivingly simple, but effective, airgun is the first type of air-powered weapon known to exist. Basic as it is, the blowgun has been in use in various parts of the globe for centuries, and its true origin probably will remain buried forever in the shifting sands of time. Suffice it to say that this silent and—in the hands of a skilled user—rather deadly weapon has been employed by the Jivaro Indians of the deep rain forests of South America, as well as by other Indian tribes inhabiting regions of Central and North America such as the Cherokee. The blowgun also has been used by the peoples of Borneo, and in regions of Southeast Asia as well, as a dedicated hunting weapon. Its employment in warfare, however, appears to have been rather limited, even among the most primitive users, although it was well suited to sniping and other hit-and-run tactics in the jungle.

Surprisingly, the blowgun seems to have been in use also in Central Europe at least as far back as the Middle Ages. However, in this particular region the blowgun was probably more of a novelty than anything else—its use limited to shooting targets and, perhaps, small birds.

Of course, the blowgun is still pretty much with us today. One can hardly read through most popular shooting and outdoor magazines without encountering at least one ad about blowguns. Unlike the blowguns made by natives in some parts of the world today, most commercially made in this country are high-tech all the way, featuring seamless aluminum tubes with all sorts of plastic add-ons to enhance their usefulness. Today, most of the commercially available blowguns are not

The Daisy/Jaycee BB Gun Championship is held every year and attracts a huge number of top young shooters from around the nation, and even from some foreign countries.

toys by any stretch of the imagination. In fact, they are quite capable of causing serious harm, or even death, if used carelessly. Modern darts are usually made of steel wire, sharpened to needle-thin points. A sharp blast of air from one's lungs can fully bury one of those long darts into someone's anatomy at surprisingly long distances. Exercising the proper precautions, however, a blowgun can be a truly cost-effective recreational shooting tool for those seeking to "go native."

Early True Airguns

Leaving the blowgun behind, we are also pretty much in the dark as far as trying to pinpoint the origins of the more conventional airgun. Although some airgun scholars have given tentative dates centered on the late Middle Ages, the fact remains that we are not really certain who invented the airgun and when. We do know there are chronicles from Central Europe in which various types of airguns figure rather prominently, dating back to the 14th century. One name popularly

offered as *the* inventor of the airgun is that of Guter, who supposedly lived in the city of Nuremberg, Germany, sometime between 1430 and 1560. Although this Guter chap may well have developed some type of airgun way back during that time period, no conclusive proof exists regarding this inventor, so we are left with nothing but speculation and a wisp of folklore on which to anchor the birth of the airgun.

We are quite certain, however, that airguns employing the bellows system, as well as some types of pre-charged pneumatics and even the forerunners of today's spring-piston guns, were being used in Central Europe by the mid-1600s. As the name implies, bellows guns used a leather bellows housed in their hollow buttstocks as the means to propel the projectile, usually a tufted dart. By design, the bellows-type airgun was of fairly low power, yet made of the highest quality, and was mostly intended for short-range target shooting. Most surviving specimens display a very high level of workmanship—a further indication that these early airguns were purely recreational in nature and could only be afforded by members of the nobility and others high on the socio-economic strata of the day. Both bellows and early types of spring-piston guns seem to have appeared around the same time, apparently sharing the same recreational/novelty status with the bluebloods of the period.

Enter the Pneumatic

The early pneumatic gun was in a totally different category, at least as far as power capability. Early reports about this type of gun leave no doubt whatsoever as to its lethality. This gave it a fairly ominous reputation as a possible tool for all sorts of devious activities, including poaching and even assassination. In fact, there is a rather well-documented story about an airgun—in all probability a pre-charged pneumatic—that was actually the weapon of choice in a plot to kill Oliver Cromwell, the ruler of England around the mid-1600s. The

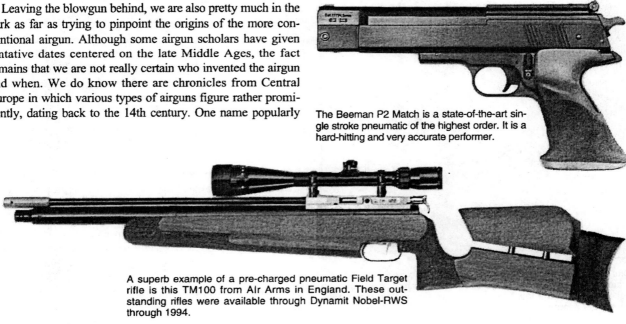

The Beeman P2 Match is a state-of-the-art single stroke pneumatic of the highest order. It is a hard-hitting and very accurate performer.

A superb example of a pre-charged pneumatic Field Target rifle is this TM100 from Air Arms in England. These outstanding rifles were available through Dynamit Nobel-RWS through 1994.

(Left) The Daisy Model 990 rifle is a novel concept incorporating dual power: CO_2 and multi-pump pneumatic. It can also shoot BBs as a repeater or pellets as a single shot.

(Right) The realm of the airgun encompasses a wide variety of models, like these exquisitely made Harper air-cartridge pistols from England. These were available through Beeman's during the late 1980s.

One decidedly unique airgun that never went beyond the working prototype stage was the CO_2-powered Pulse-Matic. This full-auto pellet gun from the late 1980s had a rate of fire of about 2000 rounds per minute. It is now a collector's item.

only thing that prevented Cromwell from taking a large-caliber ball from this potent airgun was the fact that the conspirators' plans were discovered in the nick of time and the key players apparently arrested or scared off.

Some of these powerful pneumatic guns were also used prominently by kings and nobles as hunting arms in those far-off days, as we shall see much later on in this book, particularly in Chapter 21: Modern Airguns and Big Game. Their power was ample enough to kill wild boar and other medium to large game animals in the forests of Europe. Here in America, the pre-charged pneumatic gun also left its mark when it accompanied explorers Lewis and Clark on their famous Northwest Expedition of 1804-1806. There is plenty of written testimony in the journals of these two pioneers regarding the effectiveness of their airgun during their legendary trek through then-uncharted wilderness.

Then, of course, we must not overlook the role of the airgun as a tool of war. Powerful pneumatic guns were used by a select group of Austrian sharpshooters against Napoleon Bonaparte's troops during the Tyrolean Campaign. There is plenty of solid evidence regarding the Austrian airguns' deadliness against the French soldiers. It is reported that those airguns—large caliber repeaters, to boot—were sufficiently potent to kill a man at up to about 150 yards. The Austrian snipers' lethality soon caused great alarm among the French, who decreed that any Austrian soldier captured with an airgun was to be hanged on the spot as an assassin.

Instances such as the above gave the early airgun an aura of nefariousness in some parts of Europe, with the fear and knee-jerk reaction reaching the point where the possession and use of those *evil* airguns was banned in certain places. In any event, airguns managed to survive and eventually their image became more tame as firearms technology evolved and improved, forcing the airgun further into the realm of purely recreational shooting. Airgun calibers also began to shrink until, by the end of the 19th century, they had pretty much set-

One absolutely unique airgun development of recent years was the Air Power Sabot Cannon. It was a precharged (via bicycle air pump), electrically fired pneumatic bazooka of awesome power. It was commercially available for a while, but has been discontinued.

tled into the sizes we now enjoy—.177-, .22- and .25-inch. The fourth major airgun caliber of today, .20-inch or 5mm, would appear shortly after the end of World War II.

BB Guns

Another important chain of events took place during the last quarter of the 19th century that would make airguns as common as...daisies, you might say, while at the same time creating the erroneous image in the minds of millions that airguns had degenerated into little more than children's toys. These trends were initiated by the advent of mass-produced, relatively low-powered spring-piston airguns. Examples of these were produced by the noted American airgun inventor Henry Marcus Quackenbush and, a few years later, by Daisy and several of their competitors, making the tinplate type of BB gun. The introduction of the BB gun was, in many ways, the turning point as far as making the airgun a household word, if not a fixture, here in America. In Europe, airguns were also becoming increasingly popular, but European airguns remained at an adult level for the most part, with performance and workmanship that generally left the American BB gun and its variants in the shadows for decades.

Thus, the BB gun became practically an institution in itself, introducing countless generations of youngsters to the shooting sports. Unfortunately, the perception of the generic BB gun being an inexpensive, low-powered and comparatively crude airgun led many in this country to the erroneous conclusion that all BB guns and, by extension, most airguns were basically in the same category as toys. This perception is still with us to a limited extent, despite the giant strides made by the airgun industry during the last quarter-century or so. All of which brings us to the airgun scene of today.

The Modern Airgun

Today's newcomer to airgunning is faced with a bewildering array of air- and CO_2-powered models. Even seasoned air-

gunners are sometimes overwhelmed just trying to keep up with the huge variety currently available. We are bombarded by new models making their debut practically every month. In fact, during the gestation period of this book, I have been faced with the almost constant problem of having to update several chapters repeatedly, even before sending them off to the publisher, because of new designs reaching the market. That is the nature of things in the extremely fast-paced airgun scene.

So what, then, is the role of the contemporary airgun? The answer is as varied as the guns themselves. Airguns are now used extensively for a wide range of shooting activities, including personal defense, as can be seen in Chapter 18. From simple backyard plinking to world-class competition, hunting, training and even survival, airguns today enjoy a wave of popularity never witnessed before.

For instance, the airgun truly excels in the role of a training tool for those seeking to augment their shooting prowess with firearms. This is hardly news, but it bears repeating for the sake of those who have just joined our swelling ranks. Airguns have been used as firearm trainers from time to time by the military establishments of various nations, including our good ol' U.S.A. During the bleak early days of World War II, aerial gunnery instructors relied heavily upon air-powered BB-firing machine guns such as the MacGlashan. These amazingly realistic guns saved a great deal of time and cost in teaching recruits certain basic concepts before moving on to the real thing.

During our involvement in the Vietnam conflict, the U.S. Army once again relied upon the airgun—a Daisy BB gun—to teach soldiers the basics of the snap-shooting techniques so crucial to short-range jungle warfare. A regular Daisy lever-action BB repeater with a full-size wood stock was chosen. The only other modification was that these guns did not have any sights, in order to force the trainees to rely exclusively on instinctive point-and-shoot techniques. These techniques enabled recruits who had never fired a gun before to hit dime-sized targets thrown in the air after only a few hours of practice. This type of training undoubtedly helped save many of our GIs' lives when they engaged the VC and NVA regulars in the up-close-and-quick firefights of that nasty war.

Airguns and the Law

The law enforcement community has also seen the advantages offered by the airgun as a training tool for a number of years. Air or CO_2 handguns can be used effectively to provide remedial training to those recruits who encounter serious difficulties qualifying with the service sidearm. Often, the muzzle-blast and anticipated recoil of a 38 Special revolver or 9mm pistol can be hard to overcome for police recruits who have never fired a handgun before—something that is encountered with greater frequency these days. In such cases, several hours of quiet practice with a suitable air or CO_2-powered handgun closely resembling the actual service sidearm can be sufficient to raise the confidence level of the recruit to the point where he or she can shoot qualifying scores with the duty gun.

Perhaps a more dramatic and highly useful application of the airgun in the law enforcement field is in training scenarios involving units such as SWAT teams, dignitary protection teams and others who are routinely exposed to highly specialized and dangerous duties. By necessity, these elite units must train almost constantly in all facets of hostage-rescue operations, drug house raids, VIP protection, etc. Their training should include a variety of situations in which they are actually facing people who can shoot back with something that can add a certain degree of excitement, without causing serious injury.

Enter the paintball gun.

These CO_2-powered guns have blossomed into a giant industry during the last dozen years or so. In addition to being a ton of fun, they can also be utilized most effectively in certain kinds of extremely realistic police/para-military training where the bad guys can shoot back and splatter you with paint if you don't stay sharp. There is nothing that can add more motivation to those participating in this type of training than the prospect of being hit one or more times with those big—usually .68-inch—paint balls. You can feel it, too! In Chapter 14, we will take an in-depth look at the paintball gun scene. For now, let me just say that this is another facet of the modern airgun that is not only fun, but has a great deal of value when applied to training.

One comparatively new development within the field of airguns which appeared rather suddenly here in the U.S. during the mid-1980s—and disappeared almost as quickly—was that of the air-soft gun. In fact, in the Second Edition of this book, published back in 1988, I devoted an entire chapter to this rather unusual type of airgun. For those who just joined us, let me simply say that air-soft guns are a direct by-product of the firearm laws of Japan. Since practically all firearms and many regular airguns are banned in Japan, the air-soft gun got around that problem by sort of killing two birds with one stone. The Japanese began to produce an increasing variety of exact firearm replicas—mostly made out of plastic and some metal parts—that could shoot 6mm *plastic* BBs at velocities in the 150 to 300 fps or so bracket.

Currently, the variety and sophistication of air-soft guns is truly incredible. There are air-soft replicas of nearly all popular firearms in most of the main groups: handguns, modern mili-

(Left) Paintball guns have become a giant industry within the overall field of airguns in little more than a decade.

(Below) Paintball guns are a natural for law enforcement training. The wise players use face masks and, in some cases, ballistic vests for added protection against paintball hits.

tary rifles, submachine guns and even some shotguns and full-size machine guns. Beside their amazing realism, they are incredibly fun to shoot, even indoors. Their light, low-velocity plastic projectiles are non-lethal, although they can sting a bit if they hit an exposed part of the body. The maximum effective range of air-soft guns hovers around the 20-yard mark—and that's for the peppier models—with most being hard-pressed to have any effectiveness knocking down lightweight targets at more than 10 yards. Mind you, just about all of these air-soft guns are repeaters, using either manually cocked spring-piston systems or gas. The latter allows semi- and full-auto operation as well. The latest trend is the use of a spring-piston power plant driven by a battery-powered motor. Selective-fire replicas of the M-16, H&K MP5 subgun and the French FAMAS assault rifle are currently made using this

ingenious power plant. They work extremely well and can sure rip out those plastic BBs with gusto when their selectors are set on "rock 'n roll."

Unfortunately, realistic looking air-soft guns were basically legislated out of existence here in the U.S. a few years ago, when some of them were involved in mistaken identity shooting incidents. So now, any air-soft gun imported for domestic sale has to have the same red or orange color markings that apply to toy guns, to avoid confusion. The Japanese manufacturers of air-soft guns apparently decided not to comply with the color markings—primarily, it seems, because of their relatively limited share of the U.S. market at the time. The net result is that air-soft guns basically have become collectors' items in this country.

Organized sport-shooting activities are another important area where airguns play an increasingly crucial role. In addition to the formal 10-meter shooting events and going all the way up to the Olympics for both air rifle and air pistol, there is metallic silhouette, Field Target shooting and the bikathlon. All of these will be covered in detail later in this book.

The modern airgun has also earned a good reputation as a viable hunting arm for small game in recent years. The increasing popularity of magnum-power air rifles has made it possible to lawfully hunt popular small game quarry such as rabbit and squirrel in areas where the use of any firearm—even a 22 rimfire—would be extremely dangerous, illegal, or both. Although the magnum-class airgun has remained basically well below the power level of firearms, there have been some exciting developments in recent years that have produced airguns that *do* compete with some firearms, at least within a relatively short distance. Some of these guns have already proven

(Below) These air-soft replicas of the Beretta 92FS (left) and Glock 17 are exact in every detail. They shoot 6mm plastic BBs and use the spring-piston system.

(Above) Talk about a collectible piece—this air-soft copy of the legendary Mauser KAR.98K features a spring-piston power plant and real wood stock.

An increasing number of sportsmen are discovering the suitability of the adult air rifle as a small game hunting tool.

The Airrow A-8S1P Stealth is capable of taking deer and other medium-sized game with its compressed air- or CO_2-propelled bolts.

they are quite capable of killing medium-sized animals such as deer and wild boar very efficiently indeed. We will take a close look at these developments in upcoming chapters.

American Airgun Growth

Our domestic airgun industry is now light-years ahead of where it was barely a couple of decades ago. While American airguns have generally remained in the easily affordable price range and have not been regarded as being in the same league as the more adult-oriented airguns of Europe, that situation is changing rapidly. In recent years, giants such as Crosman and Daisy have launched a growing variety of both pellet and BB guns that replicate in almost every detail the looks of real firearms. Their training value is obvious, but they are also first-class fun guns for limited-area recreational shooting. Even the traditional smoothbore BB long gun that we grew up with is still produced in large numbers, and continues to be the first step into the world of shooting for countless youngsters.

American airgun manufacturers have also turned out some truly impressive guns that could compete toe to toe against some of the best world-class match airguns that the Europeans—mainly the Germans—have to offer. The Daisy Model 777 single-stroke pneumatic pistol was the first of these, and it is still in production. Unfortunately, this match-class air pistol never reached its full potential in international matches, but it is, nonetheless, a worthy effort to take on some of the big names from Europe. Crosman, for its part, developed a world-class match rifle and pistol in the mid-1980s, both powered by CO_2. These superb models used state-of-the-art technology, but despite their very real potential, they were eventually discontinued. I am confident that, in due time, the concept of an American-made, world-class match airgun will be resurrected.

In the meantime, the healthy growth of the American airgun industry continues to signal good tidings for airgunning, in general, for the foreseeable future. There are quite a few exciting new models coming down the pike that are sure to boost people's interest in airgunning, even if it's just for casual plinking. Also, there has been quite a reshuffling of the major players in this field in recent years as a result of buyouts and the like, so the airgun industry in this country now looks rather different that it did even when the Second Edition of the book was published. For instance, Crosman Air Guns bought Benjamin/Sheridan in 1992, and shortly thereafter moved the entire Benjamin/Sheridan operation from Racine, Wisconsin, to Crosman's home base in East Bloomfield, New York. Benjamin and Sheridan guns continue to pour forth, however, under their traditional names, as they have for decades. Then, in 1993, S/R Industries, owners of Marksman Products, rocked the domestic airgun scene by announcing the purchase of Beeman Precision Arms, Inc. Beeman, one of the two largest importers and distributors of some of the top names in European airguns, had a huge influence on the growth in popularity that adult airguns have enjoyed for over two decades here in the U.S. So now, S/R Industries has a wide range of the airgun spectrum covered: At the low-to-medium price range Marksman takes care of things, while Beeman Precision Airguns can cater to the needs of shooters at the higher levels.

Another giant importer and distributor of top-brand airguns from overseas is Dynamit Nobel-RWS, Inc. While this company does not sell directly to the general public, their airguns are widely available through many retail outlets. Dynamit Nobel-RWS imports most of the models produced by the world-renowned Dianawerk firm in Germany. In addition, in recent years they have brought in a variety of El Gamo airguns

In terms of world-class state-of-the-art in a CO_2 competition pistol, the Beeman/FWB C55 says it all. It works both as a five-shot semi-auto or as a single shot.

The Daisy Model 93 closely replicates the looks of an S&W 9mm "wondernine." This fast-shooting BB repeater is another excellent firearms trainer and a ton of fun to boot!

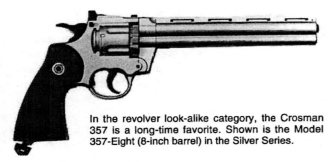

In the revolver look-alike category, the Crosman 357 is a long-time favorite. Shown is the Model 357-Eight (8-inch barrel) in the Silver Series.

from Spain, and currently they also have added top-of-the-line air rifles from BSA in England and some superb pre-charged pneumatic rifles from Air Arms, another widely known British airgun manufacturer.

The so-called collapse of the Soviet bloc nations of Eastern Europe has opened up a whole new market for the airguns produced by several of those countries. Many of those airguns are now coming into the United States in large numbers, and their prices are, for the most part, comparatively lower than airguns from Germany and other parts of Western Europe. There are quite a few airguns currently on the market from Hungary, the Czech Republic and even Russia. Some of the guns are of decidedly high quality. Others seem quite interesting, although I did not have the opportunity to test them at length in time for this book.

Then, there are the products from Red China. Although practically all the Chinese airguns available in this country fall in the low-price category, most are quite sturdy and shootable. Their finish is fairly crude by our standards, but they are

decent performers for the most part and will give you a lot of shooting for the money. So far, all of the Chinese airguns that I have seen imported here use the spring-piston power plant, although there is at least one multi-pump pneumatic repeating rifle that is not currently available on these shores.

Of course, there is also a bird's eye view of the British airgun scene in Chapter 22. So many exciting things are happening with regard to airgun design in Albion that this book would be incomplete without one chapter on what's going on over there.

Finally, besides all the talk of models, types, power plant designs, competitive games and serious uses for airguns, we have actual test reports on some of what's currently available to the airgun buyer. We have given some thirty models a thorough workout, and the results are interesting to say the least. See Chapter 23 for the latest information, and check the catalog at the end of this book for all currently available models.

So there we are. Hopefully, all of the foregoing has presented an overview of what airguns are all about, from a necessarily brief historical perspective to the present. Whether you just joined us or are a veteran, dyed-in-the-wool airgunner—even an airgun collector—the rest of this book is sure to contain something of interest for you.

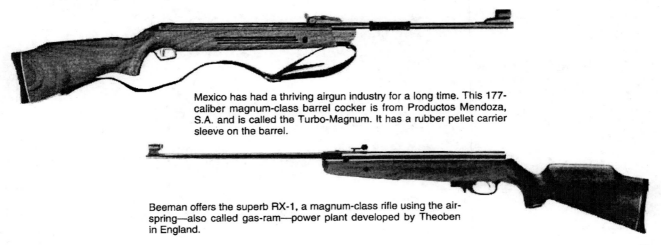

Mexico has had a thriving airgun industry for a long time. This 177-caliber magnum-class barrel cocker is from Productos Mendoza, S.A. and is called the Turbo-Magnum. It has a rubber pellet carrier sleeve on the barrel.

Beeman offers the superb RX-1, a magnum-class rifle using the air-spring—also called gas-ram—power plant developed by Theoben in England.

Chapter 2

Airgun Power Systems

An overview of all the different power plants used in today's airguns.

by J.I. Galan

MODERN AIRGUNS CAN be lumped into three distinct categories according to their respective power plants: spring-piston, pneumatic and CO_2. However, within each major category there are important subdivisions that further assist us to distinguish and evaluate different airguns. Even within these subdivisions we find airguns that vary considerably from each other in terms of applied design, performance and, ultimately, cost. To complicate matters even more, we are now beginning to see hybrids that can function in two of the three basic categories, as we will see later when we look at specific models.

The Spring-Piston

As the name implies, the spring-piston power plant consists of two basic components in order to generate the necessary air pressure to push a projectile out of the barrel. A relatively heavy piston with a suitable sealing cup or washer on its front surface is driven inside an air chamber by the pressure of a rather massive helical spring that has been compressed and then released by the trigger/sear mechanism. As the piston surges forward in a fraction of a second, the air in front of it is instantly pressurized to extremely high levels, with a correspondingly high rise in temperature. This air, under enormous pressure, has to go somewhere, and fast, following the path that offers the least resistance: the pellet—or BB or dart in some guns—sitting in the barrel breech. Therefore, the pellet

Benjamin Sheridan airguns currently cover all of the three basic power plants. From the top, the spring-piston Sterling HR83, CO_2-powered Model GS392 and the potent Model HB17 multi-pump pneumatic pistol. These are just a few of their models.

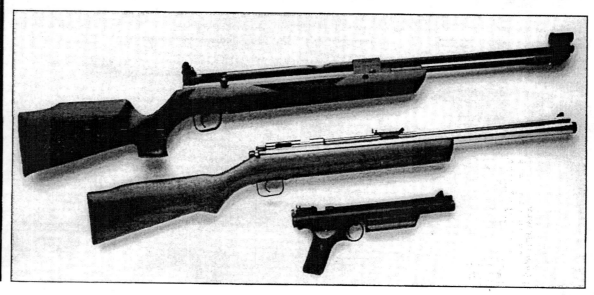

This Russian air pistol, the IJ-53, is a spring-piston barrel cocker in 177-caliber that's quite sturdy, accurate and budget priced.

is driven down the bore with tremendous force as the firing sequence unfolds. This type of air compression, incidentally, is sometimes referred to as "sequence compression" because there is a chain of mechanical actions taking place that result in practically instantaneous air compression during the firing sequence.

Simple enough. In fact, the spring-piston can be both extremely basic as well as incredibly sophisticated, depending upon the type of airgun in which it is used. The vast majority of the traditional, inexpensive BB guns that have been an inseparable part of this country's airgun industry for over 100 years are a prime example of the spring-piston power plant in its most basic expression. At the opposite end we find the "dream machines," virtual marvels of spring-piston power plant design incorporated into a wide variety of world-class competition airguns with price tags of well over $1000. In between those extremes there are countless air rifles and air pistols at various levels of sophistication, intended for everything from plinking to small game hunting. Most of them offer a pretty good return for the money, although the occasional "lemon"—though rather rare these days—can still show up unexpectedly.

Spring-piston air rifles and air pistols fall into three different groups regarding their cocking mechanisms: barrel cockers, sidelever and underlever types. The names are really self-explanatory.

The Barrel Cockers

Among spring-piston air rifles, barrel cockers remain the most popular, as well as the most plentiful. Their relative simplicity no doubt has a lot to do with their longstanding popularity. The action of breaking open the barrel not only cocks the action, but also automatically exposes the breech for easy pellet insertion directly into the bore. Barrel cockers are usually less expensive than either sidelever or underlever types of comparable quality because they have fewer parts and are, therefore, cheaper to manufacture.

The Sidelever

The sidelever cocking mechanism first became popular in the 1960s with the introduction of the European recoilless match air rifle. This cocking method permits the use of a solid stock, unlike most barrel cockers and many underlever air rifles which must have some part of the forend cut away in order to allow the cocking linkage or lever to operate freely. Like the underlever rifle, the sidelever type has the advantage of a rigid barrel, which is often considered a decisive advantage in accuracy. Such is not necessarily the case, however. If barrel-cocking and fixed-barrel models are made to similarly high standards, *both* should be about equally accurate for all practical purposes. For example, comparing an expensive fixed-barrel recoilless match air rifle to a high-quality sporter-class barrel cocker (which may be priced hundreds of dollars below the match rifle) is not a valid comparison. The finely tuned, super-accurate match rifle should also outshoot any underlever rifle in the sporter class as well.

Recoilless match air rifles using the spring-piston system reigned supreme for about two decades. German airgun manufacturers such as Dianawerk, Feinwerkbau and Anschütz pioneered the concept of a spring-piston power plant that could remain totally still during the firing sequence; no small achievement when you are dealing with the unleashing of a powerful spring pushing a fairly massive piston. Each of those companies dealt with the problem successfully in different ways. Dianawerk incorporated the Giss contra-piston

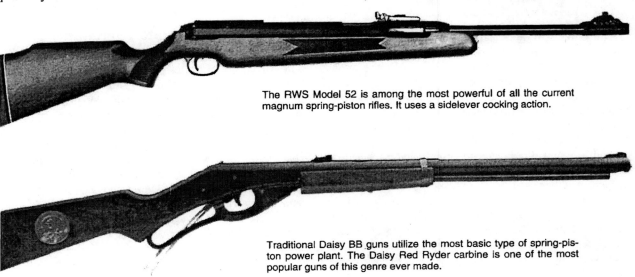

The RWS Model 52 is among the most powerful of all the current magnum spring-piston rifles. It uses a sidelever cocking action.

Traditional Daisy BB guns utilize the most basic type of spring-piston power plant. The Daisy Red Ryder carbine is one of the most popular guns of this genre ever made.

15

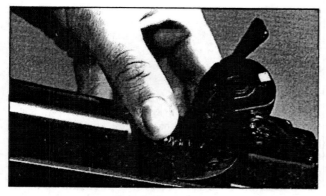

(Above) Whiscombe air rifles are underlever cockers of very high quality that incorporate a double-piston recoilless action. Some models are also extremely powerful.

(Left) Some single shot underlevers, like the elegant but powerful Webley Eclipse, feature a flip-up breech cover that allows fast and easy pellet loading directly into the barrel.

LG220, the LG250 was still terribly complicated and was soon eclipsed by the simpler and more efficient Diana and Feinwerkbau designs. In the early 1980s, however, Anschütz introduced the superb LG380, a sidelever-cocking spring-piston match rifle that neutralizes recoil by having its barrel/action unit slide rearward within a fixed receiver and stopped by a spring brake.

The Underlever

The underlever air rifle has enjoyed great popularity in Europe since its appearance shortly after the turn of the century. This type originated in Great Britain when Birmingham Small Arms (BSA) bought the Lincoln-Jeffries patent and, with some modifications, marketed it as the BSA No. 1 air rifle. In those days, there was an abundance of airguns whose quality and performance left a lot to be desired. The powerful, accurate and solidly built BSA underlever model with its fixed steel barrel was a novel and welcome departure from the norm. German airgun makers also jumped on the bandwagon. Faced with increasing competition from the British, the Germans began producing their own versions of the type and, as has happened in other instances with different products, the copy was sometimes better than the original.

Spring-Piston Variants

The Air/Gas-Spring Design

One exciting and fairly popular variation of the spring-piston power plant is the air- or gas-spring (originally referred to as gas ram) system. This extremely interesting power plant works just like the spring-piston system, except the helical spring is replaced by a sealed air—or some other inert gas—chamber that acts as the "spring" that propels the piston. This design was created in the early 1980s by the British company Theoben Engineering, founded by two dedicated airgunners named Dave Theobald and Ben Taylor.

The Theoben air-spring is cocked just like a regular spring-piston gun. The difference is that the air in the sealed chamber, which is similar to a sealed pneumatic shock absorber, is compressed in much the same fashion as with a regular

One of the author's favorite underlever air rifles in current production is the BSA Goldstar. This potent, yet extremely accurate sporter has a rotary ten-round magazine that allows quick follow-up shots.

system in their world-class match air rifles, as well as in a couple of match-grade air pistols. The Giss system basically utilizes an opposing second piston of equal mass moving rearward during the firing sequence in order to cancel out any movement imparted to the gun by the forward-moving piston that produces air compression.

Feinwerkbau devised a clever system that has the entire action of the gun moving during the firing cycle. The action/barrel unit slides rearward on precision-machined rails for about 1/4-inch within the stock, in order to cancel out the movement of the piston.

Anschütz initially utilized a pneumatic braking system to neutralize the recoil of their Model LG220 match rifle. This was not entirely satisfactory, however, and was eventually superseded by a much improved model, the Anschütz LG250, employing a hydraulic brake instead. Although superior to the

Beeman's RX-1 Magnum uses the gas-spring power plant and can reach 20 foot pounds of muzzle energy in 25-caliber.

Marksman Products imports the super-accurate Anschütz LG380 match rifle. This world-class spring-piston rifle has a totally recoilless firing sequence.

spring. When the trigger is pulled, that air is suddenly able to expand once again, driving the piston forward to compress the air ahead of it in order to push the projectile out of the gun. Cleverly simple and marvelously engineered, the Theoben system offers some important advantages over regular spring-piston guns. The lack of spring fatigue is a definite plus. Unlike spring-piston guns, Theoben guns can be left cocked for very long periods without any loss in power whatsoever, since there is no steel spring inside. The elastic properties of air or similar gases ensure the same shot-to-shot consistency for many thousands of shots. In addition, air-spring guns usually have a faster lock time than their spring-piston counterparts.

The power of many of these guns can also be adjusted up or down by the owner. Releasing some of the air out of the "air spring" reduces the power, while a few pump strokes from a special pump—much like a bicycle pump—will increase the power of the air-spring. Some Theoben air-spring guns are imported by Air Rifle Specialists, while Beeman distributes the affordable RX-1, a Theoben power plant adapted to a Weihrauch rifle, as well as the ultra-powerful Crow Magnum II, which is basically a Beeman-marketed version of the superb Theoben "Eliminator."

Recoilless and Other Systems

The saga of the modern spring-piston gun is by no means over. There are some extremely interesting variations of the recoilless opposing pistons system that have been adapted to magnum-class air rifles. For example, the potent (and expensive) Whiscombe models utilize two *converging* pistons of equal mass in order to do away with recoil. These exquisitely engineered air rifles require either two or three strokes—

Ben Taylor (holding rifle) and Dave Theobald are the creators of the superb Theoben gas-spring series of air rifles.

The Beeman Crow Magnum II has a magnum-class gas-spring power plant. This superb barrel cocker can have its gas-spring power increased by means of the hand pump shown.

depending upon the model in question—of their underlevers in order to fully cock their twin pistons.

Another similar British design that depends on two pistons rushing toward each other to neutralize recoil is the Park rifle. Unlike the Whiscombe, however, the Park's pistons are of unequal mass, driven by springs of different strength and with different travel lengths. If you think that concept is complicated, the two pistons are cocked by an underlever mechanism that utilizes a bicycle chain to pull the pistons apart. Despite this apparent engineering nightmare, the Park rifle works beautifully and exhibits a very high standard of workmanship throughout. Mind you, this is not the first time that a chain has been used in an airgun. There are reports of an early type of spring-piston gun, possibly made in Italy during the late 1500s, that utilized some sort of chain in its cocking mechanism.

Rubber bands instead of springs? Yep, we've had that, too. Henry Quackenbush, noted airgun genius of the 19th century, designed and built such a gun called the Lightning, although it was a commercial flop. The concept was revived a few years ago when a Texas company marketed an airgun that shot blowgun darts powered by the air pressure generated from a piston driven with slingshot-type tubular elastic bands. The Mega-Dart company produced various models, including a pistol, but was in business for only about two years.

The absolute latest in the field of spring-piston guns is the use of an electric motor to cock the mechanism. Called the Airstar, it's made by Rutten Airguns in Herstal, Belgium, and depends on a rechargeable Ni-Cad battery in order to operate the cocking motor. The Japanese, by the way, have been using this system for some time in an increasing variety of air-soft guns. These electrically operated spring-piston systems enable exact replicas of famous subguns and assault rifles to fire 6mm plastic BBs in full- and semi-auto modes, just like the real items.

The Pneumatic

The pneumatic gun differs vastly from the spring-piston type. In the latter, air is compressed in fractions of a second by the action of a spring-driven piston. With the pneumatic gun, however, air compression is the result of a much slower process that stores compressed air in the gun *before* the shot is fired. When the trigger of a pneumatic gun is pulled, a valve is opened by one of various means, allowing all or some of the compressed air stored in the gun to escape in order to expel a projectile. This system is sometimes called "staged compression," usually referring to pneumatic guns utilizing the multi-pump power plant. Clearly in a gun of this type, one achieves the desired level of power in stages—i.e., the number of pump strokes required to compress the air up to that level.

The Multi-Pump

Pneumatic guns are also divided into different sub-groups. We have, of course, the aforementioned multi-pump types which have been mostly the province of American airgun manufacturers for a very long time. Famous names such as Benjamin, Crosman, Daisy and Sheridan have all been heavy hitters here. To their credit, all of those companies have quite a variety of immensely popular multi-pump air rifles and, with the exception of Daisy, air pistols as well.

One of the most unusual pneumatic guns ever produced falls rather loosely in the category of multi-pumps. The Air Power Sabot Cannon, as this most unconventional airgun was called, looked more like a bazooka than anything else. Its fearsome appearance was enhanced even more by the gaping 2-inch bore, huge length and all-black finish. Rather amazingly,

Daisy's PowerLine Models 970 and 920 (177 and 22, respectively) are top-of-the-line multi-pump pneumatics featuring adult-sized hardwood stocks and centerfire rifle styling.

The ARS/Magnum 6 is a Korean-made precharged pneumatic of tremendous power and interesting design. It's imported by Air Rifle Specialists.

In recent years, Daisy has marketed a couple of "spittin' image" guns, such as the Youth Line 914, using the single-pump pneumatic system. This model closely resembles the popular Ruger Mini-14.

this air bazooka was made almost entirely of PVC piping of the type commonly found at plumbing supply stores!

The Air Power Sabot Cannon could shoot a 50-caliber steel ball with sufficient velocity to punch through a couple sheets of 1/2-inch plywood at 50 yards. It could also shoot special fin-stabilized steel projectiles of various sizes with an effective range of over 100 yards. A charge of small shot could also be launched from this gun with an effective range of about 40 yards. Air pressure was provided by an ordinary foot pump of the type used to inflate bicycle tires, while the firing mechanism was a battery-operated solenoid valve. All the air in the reservoir was exhausted with the shot, hence the reason that I loosely call this airgun a multi-pump pneumatic. Originally marketed by a company from Las Vegas, Nevada, in 1989, the Air Power Sabot Cannon disappeared from the market after about two years and surviving specimens must surely rank as valuable collectors' pieces.

The Single-Pump

In addition to multi-pump pneumatics, we also have quite a selection of *single-pump* pneumatic guns these days. In this area, Daisy has been the heavyweight among American manufacturers, with seven different models—three pistols and four long guns—in their 1994 lineup. Currently, Crosman's only entry in this category is the Model 781, a BB/pellet repeater with a smoothbore barrel. Neither Benjamin nor Sheridan have ever marketed a single-pump pneumatic.

For all practical purposes, the first company to produce a viable single-pump pneumatic gun was Walther, way back in the 1960s. Walther's first try in this area was a match pistol, the LP2 (LP for *Luftpistole* or air pistol). Improvements to the power plant and other areas of the gun eventually led to the introduc-

tion of the LP3 around 1971. In 1974, the company marketed the first single-stroke match rifle, the Walther Model LGR (*Luft Gewehr Ruckstossfrei* or recoilless air rifle), a true world-class gun that has won its fair share of medals in international competition. Unlike the LGR, however, the Walther LP3 air pistol never met with great success in international events despite a technically sound design and satisfactory performance.

Single-pump pneumatics caught on big with other German airgun giants during the 1980s. Feinwerkbau has produced both match rifles and pistols that use this power plant with huge success. Dianawerk and Anschütz have also made world-class match rifles of this type for a few years, trying to catch up to the ever-progressive Feinwerkbau. Currently, the single-pump pneumatic is trying to break new ground by venturing into the realm of magnum airguns. A prime example of this is the Parker-Hale Dragon, a beautifully engineered single-pump pneumatic rifle capable of producing respectable power. This superb airgun is offered in Sporter and Field Target versions.

The Precharged Pneumatic

Going back in time more than a century, precharged pneumatic guns were the only truly powerful airguns in existence. Their power was such that they could kill deer and other game animals of similar size with ease, even at surprisingly long range. It is also a well-documented historical fact that powerful precharged pneumatic rifles were used by Austrian sharpshooters to quietly pick off a fair number of French soldiers during Napoleon Bonaparte's military campaign in the Tyrol.

Eventually, the precharged pneumatic gun faded into almost total oblivion, replaced by cheaper mass-produced power plants such as the spring-piston system. In fact, the only pneumatic guns available for nearly the last 100 years have been

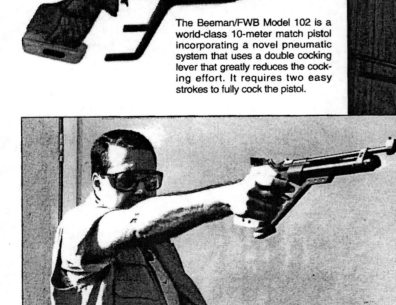

The Beeman/FWB Model 102 is a world-class 10-meter match pistol incorporating a novel pneumatic system that uses a double cocking lever that greatly reduces the cocking effort. It requires two easy strokes to fully cock the pistol.

(Above) One unusual BB gun that became popular during the late 1970s and early 1980s was the LARC M19-A. It was a freon-powered BB subgun that was lots of fun to shoot. These guns are now prized collectors' items.

(Left) The Baikal IZH-46 match air pistol from Russia uses the single-pump pneumatic system. It is a top performer, very attractively priced, and distributed by Mandall's and others.

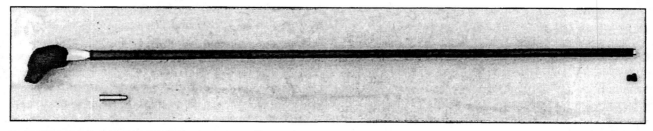

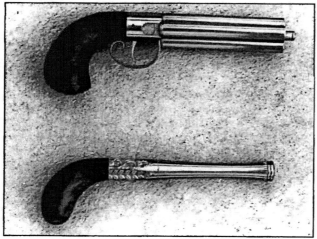

(Above) Harper air canes use precharged air cartridges and are of the highest quality. They were imported by Beeman during the late 1980s.

(Left) These beautifully crafted Harper pistols were designed to handle precharged air cartridges. The four-barreled pepperbox on top, in particular, is a joy to shoot.

those using a built-in pumping mechanism, such as the afore-mentioned multi-pump guns and, in recent years, the single-pump pneumatics. It was the British, led by companies such as Daystate, Sportsmatch, Air Arms, Titan and others, who resurrected the concept of the precharged pneumatic power plant during the 1980s, developing it to such a degree that it now occupies a prominent place among serious adult airguns.

Unlike the precharged pneumatic guns of centuries gone by, modern precharged guns do not require laborious pumping of their air reservoirs by means of manual labor. Today's guns are a real breeze to pressurize, if you'll pardon the pun, generally using a scuba tank for their air supply. Depending upon the specific model and its power setting, each refill of the gun's air reservoir from the scuba tank can give anywhere from a few dozen shots to well over a hundred. Thus, a standard scuba air tank at around 3000 psi can supply enough power for literally thousands of shots.

As we will see in subsequent chapters, just about all of the precharged pneumatic guns made until early 1994 fell squarely in the "magnum" or high-power category. However, there are some new precharged pneumatic guns being introduced that are specifically designed for 10-meter competition. The new Feinwerkbau P30 pistol is one, as is the Hammerli 480, another match air pistol of the highest quality. This one can be considered a hybrid because it will also work with CO_2. One of the most potent precharged pneumatic guns available—and a hybrid as well, capable of working with CO_2 also—is the Airrow Stealth, an awesome machine that can shoot crossbow-style bolts or more airgun-oriented projectiles when fitted with a rifled barrel. A pistol-sized version of the Stealth, called the Model A-6, can also work with either CO_2 or compressed air and is included in the Test Reports in Chapter 23.

The Air Cartridge

A most interesting twist to the precharged pneumatic concept, the pneumatic air cartridge, also originated in England during the 1980s. Guns using this system generally look and operate just like many firearms, because they merely chamber

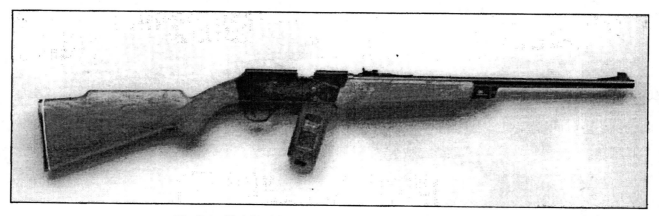

The Daisy Model 990 is the most versatile of all the hybrid airguns. It works as a multi-pump pneumatic or as a CO_2 gun, shooting BBs as a repeater or pellets as a single shot.

and fire special air cartridges resembling modern firearm cartridges. The air cartridges are miniature air reservoirs that are pressurized by means of either a hand-operated air pump or by a scuba tank via a special adapter. Of course, the scuba charging method saves the shooter quite a bit of elbow grease! A British firm called Saxby-Palmer was the first to market this concept during the mid-1980s. Following much-needed development work of the original concept, the tandem air cartridge system is currently produced by Brocock, while another British company called WASP produces a somewhat different air cartridge called the Crown, the brainchild of Mike Saxby, the original developer of the air cartridge. Brocock also offers a pretty good selection of guns that use this fairly unique power plant. For its part, WASP also offers a fair choice of firearm replicas for the Crown air cartridge, including a recently unveiled copy of the Browning Hi-Power that uses a newly developed cartridge capable of cycling the semi-auto action like the real McCoy.

This life-size archery target of a wild boar took two bolts in the lethal zone from a CO_2-powered (7-ounce bottle) Airrow A-6111. The range was 25 yards.

The Familiar CO_2

The CO_2 gun, unlike the pneumatic and spring-powered airgun, is a comparatively recent development with clearly defined origins. While pneumatic and spring-powered airguns have their emergence pretty well obscured by the swirling fog of centuries, there is ample documentation available to tell us exactly who developed the CO_2 gun, as well as when, where and why.

The first three Ws (who, when and where) take us to Paris, France, in 1889, where an already successful inventor named Paul Giffard obtained a patent for a gun using carbon dioxide as propellant. Although Giffard's creative genius had already produced other useful gadgets like the pneumatic mail tubes widely used in Paris for many years, his major claim to fame rests primarily with the development of the CO_2 gun. Early commercial versions of the Giffard CO_2 guns manufactured in France came in calibers 8mm, 6mm and 4.5mm. In the first caliber, the shooter had a choice between a smooth-bored gun for use as a shotgun or a rifled bore for bullets. The 6mm and 4.5mm versions apparently were produced with rifled barrels

only. Giffard also made CO_2 pistols in both 4.5mm and 8mm calibers. A bit later, after moving to London, his CO_2 rifles were made in .295-inch caliber and were designed to shoot a conical bullet.

When Giffard's CO_2 gun first appeared, it was hailed by some overzealous French journalists as some sort of superweapon, destined to revolutionize warfare or even to do away with it completely due to the gun's presumed deadliness! It is hard to comprehend how, in light of the CO_2 design's power limitations, such obviously overly optimistic pronouncements could have been made. While it is true that Giffard's CO_2 gun was a remarkable technological feat for its time, its power and range were not even close to those of the military rifles in use during the final years of the 19th century.

Giffard's gun did create a fair amount of interest among civilian shooters on both sides of the Atlantic. This was due to its novel design, which allowed the firing of up to 300 shots from a single charge of CO_2. The fact that the gun did not require any pumping, combined with clean and odorless operation, translated into good selling points, which gives us the why for this creation. Interestingly, Giffard's original CO_2 gun was one of his early pneumatic gun designs modified to work with carbon dioxide instead of compressed air.

Crosman has put out quite a variety of guns in recent years, such as the Model 262, a neat CO_2-powered carbine in 177-caliber.

The exquisite Feinwerkbau C5 was the first world-class rapid-fire pellet pistol. This slick semi-auto is powered by CO_2.

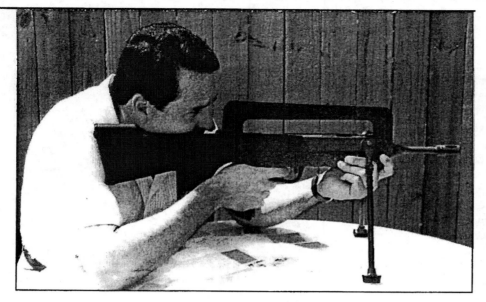

CO2 guns traditionally have been marvelously adapted to replicate firearms, like this almost exact pellet-firing copy of the French FAMAS assault rifle.

The Pulse-Matic CO2-powered pellet machine gun disappeared almost as soon as it was unveiled in the late 1980s. It was an interesting design.

Reportedly, the Colt family of Hartford paid a million dollars for the American rights to Giffard's CO_2 gun, although there is absolutely no evidence that this gun was ever produced in this country. The "Colt connection" sounds a bit farfetched, however, and is the one area in the saga of the CO_2 gun where there are some empty gaps. Paul Giffard died in 1897, and production of his guns ended shortly thereafter. Following Giffard's death, the only significant CO_2 gun produced in Europe was the Excellent, a Swedish design from the early 1900s.

The concept of the CO_2 gun eventually took hold in America, but not before several decades had passed since the heyday of Giffard's guns. However, there was a big difference. While the Frenchman's models were exquisitely made and sold for correspondingly high prices, American CO_2 guns were aimed at a mass market rather than at those shooters of considerable financial means. As in the case of multi-pump pneumatic and some types of spring-piston airguns before, it took good ol' Yankee know-how to make the CO_2 gun a viable reality that the shooter of average economic means could afford.

CO_2 guns have some very definite advantages over spring-piston and pneumatic guns. The most obvious is the lack of sometimes strenuous physical effort, since there is no powerful spring to cock or pneumatic pump to operate in preparation for the shot. Once a CO_2 gun is charged with gas, a more or less constant number of shots can be had with ease. Another advantage is that CO_2 operation lends itself admirably to repeating mechanisms. The result of this is the wide variety of CO_2 models, particularly handguns, that are almost exact replicas of various repeating firearms. This makes the CO_2 gun an extremely valuable training tool for basic marksmanship and firearms safety instruction.

A few years ago, the Europeans rediscovered the CO_2 power plant and began adapting it quite successfully to world-class match guns. This has resulted in a steadily expanding array of ultra-sophisticated 10-meter competition guns from some of the top names in European airguns, such as Feinwerkbau and Walther.

In the United States, the CO_2 gun has also had a huge revival following a slump that lasted through most of the 1970s and early 1980s, with a wide selection of models cur-

rently available from the American airgun manufacturers. The incredibly successful paintball gun industry relies solely on the CO_2 power plant, and there is no end in sight, as increasingly sophisticated paint splatterers intended for use in the popular tag games hit the market. All of this suggests that the future of the CO_2 gun looks very bright indeed.

The Daisy Mfg. Co. launched what is undoubtedly the most versatile of all the hybrid airguns produced in recent memory. The Model 990 Dual Power rifle can work as a CO_2 gun or as a multi-pump pneumatic with the simple flick of a switch. This incredibly practical rifle also shoots BBs as a repeater or 177-caliber pellets as a single shot. In the Model 990, Daisy may well have the ideal all-round plinker/trainer and we may well see similar models appearing before too long.

In light of all of the tremendous developments in the area of airgun power plants that have taken place during the last ten to fifteen years, there is every reason to expect this trend to continue for some time. The competition is fierce among airgun manufacturers at all levels because there is a growing demand for just about all types of airguns. This is healthy. Strong competition in most instances leads to a greater, and usually better, variety of airguns at competitive prices. Let's hope it remains so.

Chapter 3

Safety With Airguns

Safety is a crucial aspect of any airgunning activity. In this chapter, Dr. Robert Beeman assists in driving home the point in a convincing and incisive manner.

by Dr. Robert Beeman
Introduction by J.I. Galan

Father and son sharing an afternoon's plinking session with air pistols. Such an activity also serves to reinforce gun safety practices.

GUNS AND SHOOTING quite often become a lifelong source of legitimate enjoyment for millions of youngsters as well as adults. The common denominator that serves as the key to that enjoyment is *safety*, pure and simple. Safe handling practices and common sense are crucial to all types of activities in which firearms and airguns play a part. For that to happen, however, the individual, whether youngster or adult, must be taught properly and effectively that safety comes first and foremost when guns are being handled. The consequences of an instant of carelessness may well bring a lifetime of grief. This is of particular importance with young shooters, because they usually start out with airguns, and whatever gun-handling practices they learn—good or bad—may carry over to firearms later on.

I speak from personal experience, because I was introduced to shooting at an early age by my father, to whom guns and marksmanship were always important pursuits. It wasn't all fun and games for me, however. My dad set down some pretty stern rules before I was even permitted to shoot my first BB gun. Among them, he made it quite clear that I could shoot that BB gun *only* under his direct supervision. When not in use, the BB gun was to be kept safely stored—with BBs unloaded—in his gun cabinet, under lock and key. Ditto for the BBs, which would be locked away in a separate drawer. I was also drilled extensively on all matters pertaining to safe gun handling.

My old man very carefully explained to me that even low-power BB guns are not toys; they could inflict a serious eye injury if misused and/or mishandled. He went on to say that, with more powerful airguns, the result of carelessness could be death.

Of course, my dad was right on target on all of the above, and what he taught me about gun safety served as a rock-solid foundation to my endeavors in later years as a shooting enthusiast, forensic firearms examiner, police instructor and gun safety/marksmanship instructor. My two oldest boys have received the same teachings from me regarding gun safety practices. I know they follow the rules and am confident that their children will also receive a solid foundation on gun safety when their time comes. Their younger brother is just now reaching the age where he, too, will commence receiving basic gun safety instruction with a suitably sized airgun.

Unfortunately, there are still a lot of people out there who believe that BB guns—perhaps even all airguns—are mere

An air rifle that's simply too big or too heavy may well discourage a new young shooter, as well as distract him from learning the fundamentals properly.

Paintball guns, even when used in plinking or other activities against inanimate targets, require safety eyewear for the shooter as well as bystanders.

Using the Crosman 1077 rifle on a firing range at their booth, Crosman raised more than $3,200 for the Hunter Education Association during the 1994 SHOT Show. Olympic gold medalist and Crosman spokesperson Launi Meili (second from left) and Crosman marketing manager Ted Horrocks (holding rifle) were on hand during most of the action.

toys. Many of these individuals let their kids handle and shoot airguns totally unsupervised by any adult, often without any instructions regarding the basics of safe gun handling. Under those conditions, sometimes it doesn't take long for something tragic—and totally preventable—to occur when the carelessness and horseplay with the airgun(s) start. This is most unfortunate because airguns are ideal for training youngsters and grownups alike in both safety and marksmanship. Those misguided individuals who say that airguns have no value as training tools are either ignorant or deliberately trying to mislead others.

A few comments are required at this point regarding American airgun manufacturers, many of whose products are intended for young shooters under adult supervision. These companies bend over backwards in order to market thorough-

ly safe products. Their airguns carry an abundance of safety instructions in the form of comprehensive and highly detailed owners' manuals. But there's a lot more, because the packaging for these guns also carries highly visible and easy-to-read warnings and cautions that the gun inside is not a toy, as well as the minimum recommended user's age for which the specific model is intended, plus other pertinent safety information. As a matter of fact, just about all domestically produced airguns carry plainly visible warnings somewhere—usually on the receiver area—the user can't miss regarding safety and operation of the gun. And yet, despite all of those efforts by the airgun makers, there are some folks who are prone to ignore any and all warnings, instructions and cautions, blundering on to perhaps injure others with their carelessly handled guns.

More and more, girls are becoming a very important part of airgun shooting nationwide, as evidenced by these top shooters at the Daisy/Jaycees BB gun championship match.

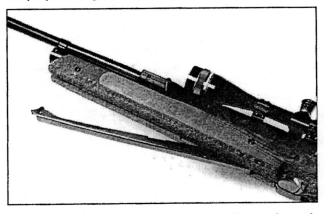

No matter how refined and expensive the airgun, the manufacturer's operation procedure must be followed, paying particular attention to possible pinch points, safeties, etc.

Because airgun safety is such a crucially important subject, I asked Dr. Robert Beeman, founder—along with his wife Toshiko—of Beeman Precision Airguns over two decades ago, to give us an in-depth look at all of the key aspects surrounding this topic. The Beemans, who are now in semi-retirement, sold their company in 1993 to S/R Industries. However, they are still quite active in several pursuits, including the operation of their ranch in California. Dr. Beeman recently received the Lifetime Achievement Award from the shooting industry, a significant feat which also for the first time clearly indicates that the firearms fraternity has openly recognized their airgun brothers as important participants of the gun industry in general.

When it comes to airgun safety, Dr. Beeman and I are in complete agreement. I said it clearly in the Second Edition

of this book, on page 120, to be exact: "...the best safety device of all is not on the gun itself, but inside the shooter's own head."

Following, then, is his interesting and timely dissertation on this vitally important topic.

• • • •

Considering the many millions of airguns in the United States and the billions of airgun projectiles fired every year, airgunning has a remarkable safety record. The U.S. government's Consumer Product Safety Commission listed bicycles as the most dangerous product on the American market, but put airguns far down the list, even behind such things as bedroom furniture, fishing equipment and paper money! However, any injury that you receive, or cause, becomes a very significant matter indeed.

Safety, Safety, Safety

Virtually all of the accidental injuries that have ever occurred with airguns are the result of violations of the various rules of safe gun handling. One commonsense rule stands out as the Golden Rule: "See that all guns are pointed in a safe direction!" Some might argue that the basic rule should be to treat all guns as if loaded, and while that is certainly true, it is just a less sweeping form of the Golden Rule. Note that this admonition applies not only to the person handling the gun, but to all those around that person. The matter of safety always overrides the matter of courtesy—one should never hesitate to object when another person is handling any gun in an unsafe manner.

Fortunately, the rules of safe gun handling are simple and few, and upon close reflection, it can be seen that almost all of them are just subsections of the Golden Rule. The key rules of gun handling include:

1. See that all guns are pointed in a safe direction!
2. Treat all guns as if loaded.
3. Be aware of what your projectile may hit if it misses or ricochets.
4. Wear eye protection and, if appropriate, ear protection.
5. Never handle a gun while under the influence of any substance that may impair judgement or safe handling.
6. Store guns safely.
7. Read, and be sure that you understand, the gun's instruction manual.
8. Know how to competently and safely handle guns. A local gun club and/or the National Rifle Association can help you.

While many of these cautions are the same for firearms and airguns, there are some very significant differences. Airguns almost always have their power plants within the mechanism of the gun rather than packaged with the projectile. Airgun projectiles also don't have rims, grooves, belts or cases for easy extraction if you don't plan to shoot right away. This means an airgun may have a pellet (or BB) in the chamber or,

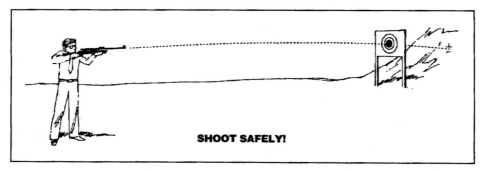

SHOOT SAFELY!

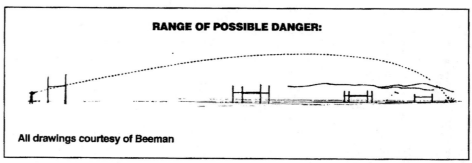

RANGE OF POSSIBLE DANGER:

All drawings courtesy of Beeman

The shooter must always know what lies beyond his intended target. Even an air shotgun, such as the CO_2-powered Farco, can send a load of small lead shot quite a ways.

Airguns are tremendously well adapted to pest control. Even in this pursuit the shooter must be well aware of what lies beyond the critter should his shot miss.

even more dangerous, a deformed, reused or improper one stuck in the bore, not readily seen. Thus the shooter may be unaware the gun is loaded. With a firearm, it's easy to see a cartridge in the chamber, whether it's "live" or not and this should send up a red flag of caution.

Considering the hazard of a projectile in the barrel, it is clear you should not attempt to shoot damaged or previously fired projectiles or any unauthorized projectile. If you cannot see through the bore of your airgun, from the rear to the front, you cannot consider it to be unloaded and simply must always treat it accordingly.

Always Be Sure of Your Backstop

Be sure that the entire path of your airgun projectile, even beyond the target, is safe. Do not shoot at glass or hard surfaces. Avoid ricochets; when shooting over water, use only flat-head or hollowpoint pellets. Hollowpoints are generally the safest type of pellet, as they are the most resistant to ricochet. Remember that an airgun pellet may travel over 500 yards—more than the length of five football fields. Inspect your target backstop for wear before and after each use. Replace the surface if it shows signs of failure or if projectiles rebound or ricochet. Since many backstop surfaces eventually fail, always place a backstop in a location that will be safe in the event the backstop fails or that you miss the backstop entirely.

What About Automatic Safeties?

Few parts of a gun are as ineptly named as the "safety." No mechanical device can make any gun safe. Safeties, like any mechanical device, are subject to failure, and they may fail at the most inappropriate moment. Furthermore, safeties can

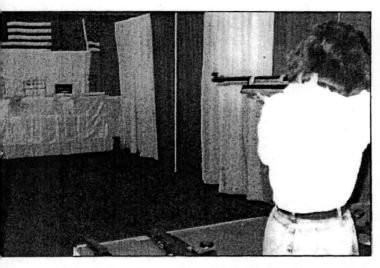

Although many airguns can be safely fired indoors, the proper backstop must be used in order to catch pellets and/or BBs safely.

The reason many spring-piston airguns carry automatic safeties is to reduce the possibility of the so-called "beartrap" mishap. This can happen when the gun is fired accidentally while the barrel or cocking lever is in the open position during the loading cycle.

even contribute to the unsafe handling of guns by promoting a dependency on the device rather than on safe handling practices. No experienced shooting instructor would ever suggest that pointing a loaded gun at someone with the safety on and pulling the trigger is a good idea. However, this is exactly what some people, particularly those accustomed to automatic safeties, will do.

Many airguns, especially spring-piston types, have no safety latch at all. Basically, this is because these guns are intended to be fired immediately after cocking. Having a safety on spring-piston airguns could encourage the user to leave the gun cocked, adding to cumulative fatigue of the mainspring, which is compressed in the ready-to-fire mode. Several long periods of total compression may cause a deterioration of function. Thus, the presence of a safety on such guns could defeat the very function for which such guns were designed, i.e., firing a projectile.

Many airguns, and some firearms (including double-action handguns), have an extremely long, or two-stage, trigger pull which some feel serves as a safety system of sorts. In fact, some firearms have been designed with this in mind, and it does help ensure that the gun is fired only when firing is intended.

The safety latches on some spring-piston adult airguns have been designed to be automatic, engaging when the gun is cocked. This feature is meant to reduce the possibility of damage to the gun, injury to the shooter, or any bystanders in close proximity, during an accidental snapping shut of the barrel or cocking lever during the cocking cycle. It's possible to crack the stock, bend the barrel and break or bend the cocking lever of the gun when this happens. And it is possible for a person to be painfully hit by a part of the gun or to be pinched when the action snaps shut. There are certain other mechanisms that are also sometimes used to prevent this so-called "beartrap" action, usually more complex and expensive than just making the safe-

ty automatic. Ultimately, safety from accidental discharge was not the primary purpose of any of these safety mechanisms.

A wide variety of automatic safety mechanisms have been devised during the centuries-long development of guns. However, although some firearm and airgun makers have offered automatic safeties, the lack of them on the vast majority of modern firearms and most airguns attests to their undesirability and unpopularity.

The very nature of an automatic safety can also defeat its own purpose. That is, most users of guns with automatic safeties soon develop the habit of taking off the safety automatically, without even thinking or realizing that they have done so. The user becomes as "automatic" as the safety. It's hard to fire many shots, especially in target practice or extended shooting, through a gun with an automatic safety without getting into the habit of automatically moving the safety to its off position.

The acquisition of lower-cost gas and pump pneumatic guns is, more often than not, the prelude to the use of firearms. New shooters, particularly the young, have traditionally been taught shooting skills and safety with airguns before being introduced to firearms. The habits formed during this preliminary training generally serve as the basis for a lifetime of habits in handling other guns. Thus, most manufacturers of gas and pump pneumatic airguns have avoided the introduction of automatic safety mechanisms on almost all of their guns. Shooters who have come to rely on their airgun being automatically "safe," or who automatically move the safety off, could transfer those habits with tragic results when they begin using firearms.

Firearms, as already noted, rarely have automatic safety mechanisms. Revolvers typically have no safety latch of any kind. Among the few firearms with automatic safeties are double-barrel shotguns. Puzzled by this anomaly, I asked Bob Brister, shooting editor for *Field and Stream* magazine and one of the deans of American shotgunning, for the reason. He said the addition of safeties to double-barrel shotguns

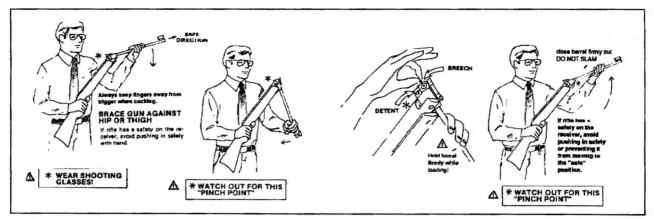

was an historical accident brought about because it "seemed" like a good idea, coupled with the fact that designing automatic safety mechanisms into such guns is quite easy. Brister feels that this safety feature is most undesirable, an abomination that is removed or defeated by many shooters. In some cases, an automatic safety could cost a firearms shooter his life in situations where he is under stress with dangerous animals or persons.

Largely as a bow to those who do not understand this concept and to the American market, with its sometimes misguided concepts of safety, safety latches began to appear on spring-piston airguns, even single shot airguns. Many airgun experts consider this to be an undesirable addition.

Some training instructors feel so strongly about not letting shooters develop a dependency on any sort of safety-latch mechanism that they insist that any guns used during the training period have no safety latches. Throughout the shooting sports it is generally accepted that the only true gun safety is in the mind of the gun handler.

The matter of automatic safeties now presents a moral, legal and marketing dilemma for airgun manufacturers, especially in the United States. They are often under great pressure to bend to the will of the technically poorly informed on the issue of auto safeties. Unfortunately, in these times of "political correctness," complex technical issues sometimes lead to expedient situations that do not necessarily solve the problem in a satisfactory manner.

Trigger Cautions

From a safety standpoint, the trigger certainly is one of the key points of a gun. Airgunners should be aware that the very nature of some airguns will allow them to go off without action of the trigger. That is, hard falls or impacts can cause a piston or valve hammer to jump off the sear and discharge the gun. Never lean or put an airgun where it might fall. Of course, the best plan is to be sure that you never let go of an airgun while it is still loaded.

It is very tempting to adjust airgun triggers. This is something that must be approached with great caution and care. Adjustments, except on the specialized match guns, should generally be held to a pull weight of more than 2 or 3 pounds, and if there is a first stage in the trigger pull, it should be left intact. That first stage is an intentional "safety" factor, not

"creep." Modifying, smoothing and lubricating airgun trigger mechanisms generally should be left to competent airgunsmiths or the factory.

Remember that a dangerously low trigger pull weight, trigger lubrication, etc., may lead to severe injury or death of those involved, but also, because of the powerful mainspring mechanism of many airguns, to painful injuries inflicted directly by the mechanism of the gun. That is, the barrel may fly up, the action may slam shut, or the cocking lever may close on your fingers or knock out a tooth. Fortunately, such accidents are rare, but there is absolutely no excuse for them, as virtually all such injuries are due to foolish or stupid actions by the shooter and could easily have been avoided.

Keep Your Finger Off the Muzzle

Never put a finger or any other part of your anatomy in front of the muzzle of a gun or any release point of air reservoirs, tanks or filling devices where compressed air is released. Astonishingly enough, some airgunners and tinkerers test their guns by holding a finger over the muzzle while discharging the unloaded gun. Not only can an unnoticed projectile be fired, but high-pressure air itself, perhaps carrying oil or debris, can pen-

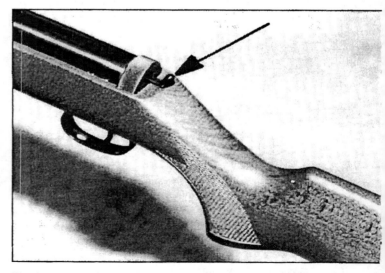

The shooter must learn early on that to rely solely on an airgun's safety catch is to court disaster! The best safety of all is to use common sense and adhere strictly to the rules of safe gun handling at all times.

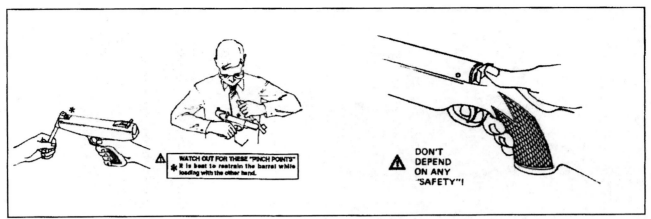

etrate your skin, even through clothing, with serious medical implications. If air penetration occurs, seek emergency medical attention at once.

CO_2 and Compressed Air—Special Cautions

Some airgunners have been concerned about the safety of using compressed air or CO_2. In addition to the hazards of high-pressure air previously mentioned, the biggest potential concern would be the scuba tanks themselves. If you decide to use one of these tanks, be assured that, while reasonable care is advised, hundreds of thousands of these tanks have been used for decades by divers all over the world with an excellent safety record. The air chambers in the guns, or the separate quick-change bottles, generally are designed with a safety factor of several hundred percent. Even in the unlikely event of a failure, they are more likely to rip open rather than explode and shatter. However, there are some obvious and not so obvious cautions.

● Do not alter such cylinders in any way, and be sure that the threads are protected from damage.
● Do not overpressurize. Filling too rapidly will ruin the valves and seals. Filling *must* take at least 1 minute.

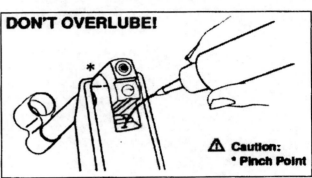

● Be careful not to expose pressurized air cylinders, CO_2 bottles or even disposable CO_2 cartridges to temperatures in excess of 130 degrees Fahrenheit. Such high temperatures are most commonly reached within closed parked cars in full sunlight and near heating devices. Also, the tanks or reservoirs of precharged pneumatic airguns may become dangerously overheated if incorrectly filled.
● Oiling or spraying the gun or filler devices with lubricant or other materials can cause contamination to find its way into the air tanks or reservoirs, with dangerous results.

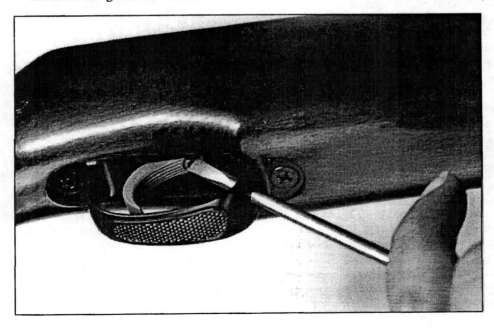

Trigger adjustments should be carried out with great caution, lest the airgun be rendered unsafe due to an excessively light trigger pull.

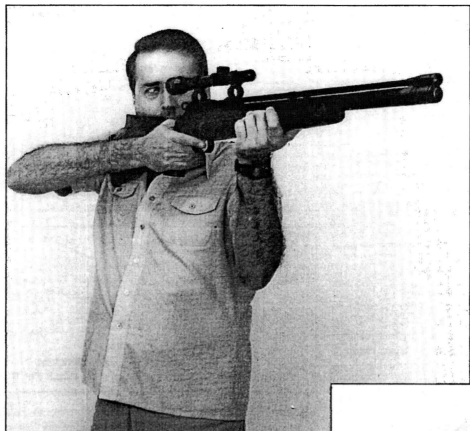

Precharged pneumatic guns must not be overpressurized. Likewise, great care must be taken to keep lubricants away from the air tank and the gun's air intake areas.

CO_2 and compressed air tanks must never be left where they are exposed to direct sunlight or high temperatures because they could burst.

- The use of industrial compressors to charge the tanks or reservoirs can result in contamination with oil or dust particles. Only pure, clean, dry diving-grade air should be used. No gas or gas mixture other than normal air or CO_2 should ever be used!
- Ensure that your air storage bottles and master scuba cylinders are kept in a cool, safe location. Scuba tanks should either be laid on their side or firmly secured in a vertical position.
- Excessively fast firing from a semi-automatic CO_2 gun can cause the gun's mechanism to frost up and operate in a potentially dangerous manner.

Finally, while it is high power and high pressure that are usually the caution concerns, you must be careful not to operate any airgun at very low power. Excessively low charging in gas-spring airguns, low pressure near the end of the charge in CO_2 cylinders, and excessively low pressures in precharged pneumatics, even spring-piston guns with weak mainsprings, may cause a pellet to lodge partway up the barrel. This could cause a jammed barrel or lead a careless person to believe that the gun is unloaded—a potentially dangerous situation. Again, if you cannot see all the way through the bore, it may contain a projectile. Sliding a cleaning rod (a flexible, roll-up rod is especially handy) or dropping a match or toothpick through the bore is also effective in determining if the bore is clear. If you cannot effectively complete this test, you must assume that the gun is loaded.

Virtually all airgun safety considerations are simple, common sense. You owe it to yourself, to others and to the future of the airgun sport to be safe. Again, only the brain of the shooter is the real safety of any gun.

Chapter 4

The Magnum Airgun

An update on the pneumo-blasters, their power systems and practical applications.

by J.I. Galan

Although generally too powerful for repeated use in suburban settings, a magnum air rifle can still come in handy in a variety of situations calling for extra punch.

MAGNUM-CLASS AIR rifles constitute, without any doubt, one of the fastest growing groups among all airguns. Although the term "magnum air rifle" has been applied rather liberally at times, particularly in advertising hype, in general terms it refers to air rifles whose muzzle velocity exceeds 820 fps in 177-caliber and about 630 fps in 22-caliber. These figures are certainly not engraved in stone, but they have served well since the early 1980s as a general guide concerning the minimum muzzle velocities for air rifles to qualify as magnums. In the last few years, however, we have seen the power curve of magnum air rifles begin a slow but fairly steady climb. This has been particularly evident since the appearance of some of the newest Theoben gas-spring rifles, as well as an increasing number of precharged pneumatics also produced in the U.K. In fact, for a number of years the British have had a leading role in the field of magnum air rifles in general. The Germans, although producing some respectable powerhouses of their own—the RWS 48, 52 and 54, the HW80/Beeman R1, R10, etc.—have for the most part concentrated their magnum efforts in the area of spring-piston systems.

Ironically, what we call magnum air rifles are, in most cases, considered the same as firearms in Britain and thus pretty well restricted. Over there, any air rifle exceeding 12 foot pounds of muzzle energy—approximately 5 foot pounds for air pistols—requires the buyer to obtain an FAC (Firearms Acquisition Certificate or "ticket") from the police and is subject to the same restrictions that apply to regular shotguns. In Germany, the situation is worse, with airguns that even approach magnum power levels being severely restricted. Therefore, the production of magnum air rifles from those two nations is, generally speaking, intended for export to the United States where we still have the freedom to enjoy these high-powered airguns.

Magnum Rifles

There are literally dozens of magnum-class air rifles currently on the market, with new models surfacing on a regular basis. Most magnum air rifles still utilize the spring-piston power plant, although precharged pneumatics are certainly catching up.

Gas-Spring Magnums

Gas-spring-powered models are still in the minority, even though the Theoben power plant design has been most successfully adopted by Weihrauch, one of Germany's top airgun

Author is quite partial to the BSA Goldstar. This magnum sporter features a clever ten-shot rotary magazine that really works.

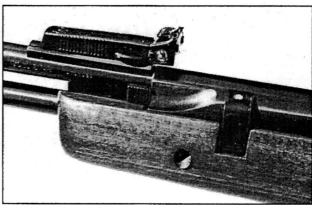

The Goldstar's rotary magazine automatically advances and loads one pellet each time the rifle is cocked.

makers. For instance, the Weihrauch HW90 was that firm's first model incorporating the gas-spring system. This potent air rifle is available in the U.S. as the Beeman RX-1, in all four airgun calibers from 177 through 25. Another gas-spring magnum rifle available from Beeman is the Crow Magnum II. This pricey powerhouse, based on the famous Theoben Eliminator, can be had in a choice of 20- or 25-caliber, with 22-caliber available on special order only. In 25-caliber, it can produce up to 32 foot pounds of muzzle energy, depending upon the pellet weight used. Air Rifle Specialists, by the way, imports several Theoben models, all of them in the magnum class.

CO$_2$ Magnums

As for CO$_2$, only a couple of models are currently available in this country that fall squarely in the magnum class. Coincidentally, both of them are imported from the Philippines by Air Rifle Specialists. The Farco shotgun, which is covered in a test report in Chapter 23, and in Chapter 21's discussion of big game hunting, is one of those CO$_2$-powered blasters and I won't dwell on it here. The other model is also made by Farco, but it is a stainless steel rifle available in a choice of 22- or 25-

caliber. This CO$_2$ gun is not only potent, but quite elegant and reasonably priced, retailing for around $395, which includes a 10-ounce CO$_2$ bottle. An additional CO$_2$ rifle that could be included in the magnum group is the QB22. This modern clone of the venerable Crosman 160 can top 12 foot pounds of muzzle energy, depending upon the 22-caliber pellet used. The QB22 is covered in great detail in a test report in Chapter 23, as well.

Spring-Piston Magnums

With the largest of all the magnum groups, the spring-piston types, it is difficult to decide where to begin, given the huge variety of models now available. Therefore, I will start with one of my personal favorites, the Beeman Kodiak. To be sure, this gun quite probably represents the quintessence of the barrel-cocking, spring-piston system in the area of power output. This decidedly man-sized air rifle—made by Webley and dubbed the Patriot in the U.K.—is available here from Beeman in 22- or 25-caliber, generating 25-plus foot pounds of muzzle energy in the 1/4-inch bore. Apparently, there has been a slight reduction in the energy figures for this rifle, because when it was introduced in 1992, Beeman rated it at over 30 foot pounds of muz-

Another magnum blaster that ranks among the author's top choices is the Beeman Kodiak. In 25-caliber, this barrel cocker can generate over 25 foot pounds right out of the box.

Author testing a rare version of the Beeman R1 with a fancy Tyrolean-style stock.

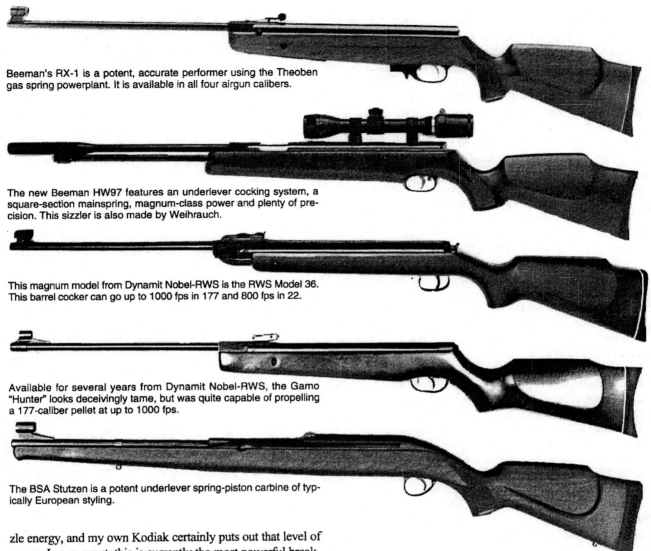

Beeman's RX-1 is a potent, accurate performer using the Theoben gas spring powerplant. It is available in all four airgun calibers.

The new Beeman HW97 features an underlever cocking system, a square-section mainspring, magnum-class power and plenty of precision. This sizzler is also made by Weihrauch.

This magnum model from Dynamit Nobel-RWS is the RWS Model 36. This barrel cocker can go up to 1000 fps in 177 and 800 fps in 22.

Available for several years from Dynamit Nobel-RWS, the Gamo "Hunter" looks deceivingly tame, but was quite capable of propelling a 177-caliber pellet at up to 1000 fps.

The BSA Stutzen is a potent underlever spring-piston carbine of typically European styling.

zle energy, and my own Kodiak certainly puts out that level of power. In any event, this is currently the most powerful break-barrel spring-piston rifle available anywhere as it comes from the factory.

Another classic barrel cocker in the magnum group from Beeman is the R1. Introduced in 1981, this hot-rod is currently offered in all four airgun calibers. In 25-caliber, for instance, the R1 can reach a respectable 17 foot pounds of ME. This rather substantial and highly popular model is also offered in carbine version—in 177, 20 and 25—as well as in a specially tuned version called the Laser. In this guise, the R1 sports a beautiful laminated stock and its power is boosted by several foot pounds in all calibers. A lighter, slightly less powerful cousin of the R1 is the Beeman R10, but this one is only available in 177 and 20 calibers. Early in 1994, Beeman introduced the Model R11, a 177-caliber barrel cocker that generates a still respectable 875 fps.

Beeman also offers a couple of powerful underlever cocking models that deliver a healthy wallop to the target. The Webley Eclipse, for instance, is rated at 12.6 foot pounds in 177-caliber, while the 22 version will surpass 15 foot pounds. Beeman's latest underlever, however, is the Weihrauch HW97, a direct descendant of the famous HW77 underlever, a borderline mag-

num that deserves mention here as well and is still in production. The HW97, however, boasts a number of refinements that should make it quite popular in a very short time. Internally, it features a square-section mainspring that is more efficient than standard coil springs, while at the same time being easier to compress during the cocking stroke.

Dynamit Nobel-RWS offers an impressive line-up of magnum spring-piston air rifles. In the barrel-cocking group, we find the RWS Models 34, 34C, 36, 36C and 45. (The "C" indicates a carbine version of a specific model.) All of these models, except the 45 (in 177 only), are available in 177- and 22-caliber, producing muzzle velocities of about 1000 and 800 fps, respectively. The company also offered the Hunter model for a number of years. Made by El Gamo in Spain, it was available in 177-caliber only and also produced a muzzle velocity of 1000 fps.

Besides barrel cockers, Dynamit Nobel-RWS has offered a good selection of both sidelever and underlever magnum rifles for quite some time. In the sidelever department, the RWS Models 48 and 52 have already earned a well-deserved reputation for high quality and rugged dependability. Differing only in the degree of refinement of their stocks—the 52 is a fancier version—these two hard-hitting and accurate magnums are excellent choices for field use. They have been available only in 177 and 22, with velocity ratings of 1100 fps and 900 fps, respectively. In 1994, 25-caliber was added to the list, something that will make these two top sellers even more popular with a lot of folks. Then, there is the RWS Model 54. This is a *recoilless* rendition of the Model 52, available in 177 and 22 only thus far, with the same MV ratings as the Models 48 and 52. Imagine all that power in a spring-piston rifle that remains totally motionless during the firing sequence!

As far as underlever-cocking magnum rifles are concerned, the only models available from Dynamit Nobel-RWS during 1994 were the Stutzen, the Superstar and the Goldstar. All three are products of the world-famous BSA firm in England. BSA's trademark in the world of airguns for almost a century has been the production of powerful underlever rifles, and the previously mentioned trio are merely among the newest this company has to offer. The Stutzen is really a carbine with a full-length stock in the best European tradition. Although compact—it is only 39 inches overall and weighs 7 1/4 pounds—this model packs a respectable punch in both 177- and 22-caliber. The Superstar is a full-size rifle (43 inches long) with the same MV specs as the Stutzen: 1000 fps in 177, 800 in 22. The newest member of the tribe is the Goldstar, which resembles the Superstar in many ways. The main difference between the two lies in the fact that the Goldstar has a ten-shot rotary magazine that advances automatically when the rifle is cocked, while the Superstar and Stutzen are single shots. Imagine the tremendous advantage of not having to fumble with loading a pellet every time you fire a shot. Repeating spring-piston rifles have not had the best reputation for feeding reliability, but I can tell you without reservation that the rotary magazine system of this rifle really works! The Goldstar, by the way, shares the same MV specs as the other two. Despite their full-blown magnum status, these three rifles all have a rather breezy cocking effort in the neighborhood of 28

pounds. Unfortunately, they are no longer distributed by Dynamit Nobel-RWS.

Marksman Products is another outfit that offers several magnum-class spring-piston rifles, all of them barrel cockers, at truly competitive prices. The Models 45, 55, 59 and 70 are available in 177-caliber and all boast MVs of 900 fps and above. The Model 71 comes in 22-caliber and generates an MV in the 740 to 780 fps range, while its 20-caliber cousin, the Model 72, produces up to 840 fps. Then, there are the more refined Models 56-FTS and 58-S, two 177-caliber sizzlers in the neighborhood of 940 fps.

Moving way up in the price scale of magnum spring-piston rifles, we find such terrific dream machines as the Whiscombe series, which are delightful, albeit expensive, powerhouses. The Whiscombe's claim to fame is its novel use of two converging pistons in order to create sufficient air pressure during the firing sequence to push out some of the heaviest pellets at magnum velocities. In the process, these twin pistons cancel each other's inertia, with the net result that they are also recoilless. These superbly engineered air rifles are the brainchild of John Whiscombe, a Britisher with a stable full of talents in a wide variety of engineering and scientific areas. At this time, Whiscombe offers three basic models, the JW-50, JW-60 and JW-75, all of which can be had in a choice of calibers— although the super-potent JW-75 is *not* recommended in 177— and stock grades.

By the time you read this, however, Whiscombe will probably have a new model available, the JW-70. This one, like the JW-75, requires three easy strokes of the underlever in order to fully cock the rifle. The other models require only two strokes. All of the tilting barrel models were being phased out by mid-1994, so all Whiscombe models currently utilize only fixed barrels. Whiscombe offers so many options that the guns are practically custom-made. They are available from Pelaire Products of West Palm Beach, Florida.

There is still another series of magnum-class spring-piston rifles available with recoilless actions. The Park Rifle Compa-

Author checks out a Whiscombe rifle. The powerful JW-75 and the new JW-70 require three strokes of the underlever in order to fully cock the twin pistons.

The Park RH93 air rifle has a rather interesting cocking system incorporating a bicycle chain. It is fairly powerful and recoilless in operation. (Stephen Gibbons photo)

ny, Ltd. of London, England, is the maker of the Series RH91 and RH93 rifles, two rather interesting models utilizing a converging double-piston action. Unlike the aforementioned Whiscombe rifles, however, Park rifles use a bicycle chain as part of the cocking mechanism in order to pull apart the two pistons. The Park RH91 and RH93 differ in certain points such as the level of refinement of their respective stocks (each offers two stock options), safety mechanisms, etc. They are all offered in a choice of 177- or 22-caliber, and although by no means cheap, their quality is first-rate. These air rifles are available from Air Werks International Shooting Sports in Norfolk, Virginia.

Air Werks International also sells the Rutten air rifles made in Herstal, Belgium. The Winstar D.E. Mach 1, for instance, has an MV rating of 1000 fps in 177-caliber, while the Winstar D.E. 250 produces around 860 fps in the same caliber. These are underlever cockers. The Winstar 300 HS is a barrel cocker capable of 1000 fps in 177 and 760 fps in 22-caliber.

Precharged Pneumatic Magnums

In the realm of magnum air rifles utilizing the pre-charged pneumatic system, there is also a wide and growing selection available at this time. I think we should begin with some of the super powerful models being imported from the Far East. That region is no stranger to high-power airguns, to be sure. In fact, long before the British began developing their modern precharged pneumatics, there were some rather potent airguns being produced in places like the Philippines and South Korea. The latter nation produced the tremendously powerful Yewha 3B Dynamite, a 25-caliber smoothbore that could be used to shoot either a charge of shot or a standard 25-caliber

lead pellet. The Yewha was a multi-pump pneumatic that required up to 150 pump strokes in order to make it flex its muscle—not to mention those of the shooter! Once that number of pumps was achieved, however, the gun could fire several shots until all the air pressure was depleted. The Yewha 3B was, by our standards, a crudely made airgun that, although powerful and reliable, did not win any prizes for beauty, elegance or precision. It was available commercially in this country in the mid-1970s and is now a highly sought-after specimen to add to any serious collection of adult airguns.

One interesting pneumatic rifle using a multi-pump power plant similar to that of the old Yewha is the new Farco FP (for Foot Pump) survival rifle. Imported by Air Rifle Specialists, this is a powerful rifle made by Farco in the Philippines and available in either 22- or 25-caliber. The FP features a bolt-action pellet-loading system and a no-frills hardwood stock. Another plus is its retail price of around $295.

Currently, there are several magnum airguns from South Korea available to American shooters. All of these are far ahead of the old Yewha in every way. The ARS AR6, for instance, is imported and distributed by Air Rifle Specialists, which explains the first three letters of its monicker. The second half of the name indicates that this is an air rifle with a six-shot repeating mechanism. Far from being an over complicated repeating rifle, the AR6 incorporates a single-action/double-action mechanism similar to that found in most modern revolvers. There is a removable, fluted stainless steel cylinder with six chambers for 22-caliber pellets, with 177-caliber available on special order only. The large, exposed hammer can be easily cocked to fire in the single-action mode, or, if desired, rapid fire can be

Marksman's Model 56-FTS is available in 177-caliber only, but can produce a muzzle velocity of up to 940 fps. This barrel cocker is intended mainly for Field Target use.

The Marksman Model 59 is a carbine-size barrel cocker that can generate up to 940 fps muzzle velocity in 177-caliber.

Air Rifle Specialists imports the Farco FP (Foot Pump) Survival Rifle in a choice of 22- or 25-caliber. This multi-pump pneumatic is rugged and affordable.

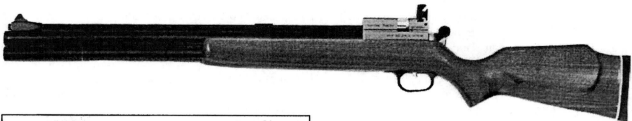

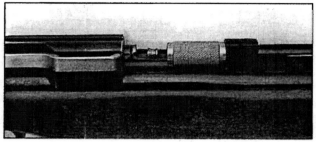

The most popular of all the precharged magnums offered by ARS is the AR6, a 22-caliber six-shot repeater capable of generating over 1000 fps with ultra-heavy 32-grain pellets.

The ARS/Hunting Master 900 is a single shot. Notice special 9mm pellet in the open breech.

had by simply pulling the trigger all the way through in the double-action mode. Imagine the tremendous advantage of an air rifle like this in a hunting situation, where quick follow-up shots may be required.

For looks alone, the AR6 gets high marks. The rifle measures a well-proportioned 41¼ inches overall, tipping the scale at a comfortable 7 pounds. This compactness is a direct result of using the precharged pneumatic power plant, which requires no heavy internal parts and no built-in pumping mechanism. In profile, the AR6 bears a strong resemblance to the old Sheridan Super Grade, a classic among vintage pneumatic rifles. In keeping with such looks, the AR6 is equipped with a nicely shaped, oil-finished Indonesian walnut stock.

The powerful AR6 is not the only precharged magnum rifle imported by ARS. There are also the King Hunting Master and Magnum 6—both 22-caliber repeaters—as well as the Hunting Master 900. The latter is a 9mm single shot that can fire a special 52-grain pellet—also made in South Korea—at an amazing MV of about 1100 fps. That, friends, translates into a muzzle energy of just under 140 foot pounds.

One of the best examples of British precharged pneumatic technology of recent years was the Series 100 magnum rifles from Air Arms. Dynamit Nobel-RWS made these available to American shooters for about three years, but that came to an end during 1994 when Air Arms phased out these particular models. The Series 100 had four models, the SM 100, XM 100, TM 100 and the top-of-the-line NJR 100. The latter was a Field Target shooter's delight in every way, and its retail price of around $2600 reflected that fact. Depending upon the power desired, both the SM 100 and XM 100 were capable of muzzle energies of between 12 and 22-plus foot pounds and were available in 177- and 22-caliber.

One decidedly outstanding precharged pneumatic that is a repeater to boot is the Beeman Super 7, which is made by none other than Theoben. It has a rather unconventional appearance with its slender, free-floating barrel, short forend and 400cc air bottle located horizontally below the barrel, but it reeks of quality and is a first-class performer besides. Like most precharged pneumatics in its class, the Super 7 is intended for use only with a telescopic sight and comes without any iron sights. Available

only in 22-caliber, the Super 7 has a seven-pellet rotary magazine that advances automatically whenever the bolt is worked. As for power, this rifle can top the 30 foot pound mark when set at maximum. All of this costs money, of course, and the gun will set you back about $1600 as of mid-1994. Taking the concept of the Super 7 one giant step forward, we now also have the Beeman Super 12, a *twelve*-shot repeater that looks like a bigger brother of the Super 7, both in terms of overall length as well as caliber. That's right, the Beeman Super 12 comes in 25-caliber only and is capable of producing a muzzle energy of about 40 foot pounds. The retail price of this powerhouse is also quite steep, but for the airgunner who wants the best and is not shy about spending big coin, the Super 12—as well as the Super 7—can be regarded as a "must have" magnum.

There are many other outstanding precharged pneumatics out there. Some that come readily to mind are those models made by the Falcon and List companies in Great Britain. Falcon, in particular, has taken over the now-defunct Titan company and seems to be making a nice attempt at keeping up production of their line. The Falcon Model FN12TW appears to be the same as the Titan Monitor MPT—available until recently in this country as the Beeman Wolf Pup Deluxe—with a different name. Then, there is the Skan, a bullpup-style precharged pneumatic that has that "assault rifle" look that drives the gun-hating crowd bananas. The Skan bullpup is amply covered in a test report in Chapter 23. The Skan is a gorgeous example of British precharged magnum rifle technology.

Magnum Pistols

How about magnum air pistols? Sure, there are a few, and the Beeman P1 is probably one of the best-known examples. This Weihrauch-made spring-piston model is available in 177- and 20-caliber and produces enough MV in both calibers to easily qualify as a magnum—which for air pistols means reaching or exceeding 5 foot pounds of muzzle energy. Two absolutely awesome magnum air pistols which, unfortunately, may not be available by the time this book goes to press are the Beeman Wolverine and Adder—the same gun, really, except for the choice of wood used in the grip: walnut for the

In precharged pneumatics capable of producing respectable power, the Air Arms XM 100 ranks high indeed!

The Air Arms TM 100 was designed as a field-target rifle first and foremost. Like most precharged magnums, it was supplied without sights.

The Beeman Super 12 is an upgraded Super 7, featuring a twelve-shot rotary magazine for 25-caliber pellets and a beefier walnut stock. This is a truly awesome precharged pneumatic.

The Beeman Adder was a full-fledged magnum air pistol, capable of generating 20 foot pounds of muzzle energy in 25-caliber. This precharged pneumatic was made in the U.K. by Titan.

Wolverine and hardwood for the Adder. Either pistol can produce up to 20 foot pounds in 25-caliber. They were also available in 177 and 20 calibers, but the 1/4-inch bore was my top choice. These guns were made by Titan in the U.K. and employed the precharged pneumatic system. Hopefully, ultrapotent air pistols such as these will continue to be made by other companies because I feel there is a real market for them here in America.

A lot of people, however, ask why we need airguns that are so powerful. Well, why does anyone need a souped-up sports car capable of doing nearly three times the posted speed limit on most of our highways? Variety is, some say, the spice of life, and in airguns, as in so many other areas, there certainly is room for the high-powered models. I guess a lot of it has to do with plain old human nature. We all have different tastes and there are many shooters who simply like the idea of owning a truly powerful airgun.

Magnum airguns are intended primarily for field use, given their relatively high power output. That does not mean that they cannot be used safely in more confined areas, such as in a suburban backyard, as long as the proper safety precautions are followed, of course. The problem is that a great many of these truly powerful airguns have a louder than normal discharge report that can upset neighbors, and that's not good public relations at all. So, make sure that your neighbors are not going to protest, or, worse, call the local gendarmes, before you go out in the yard and start shooting that pneumo-blaster. Naturally, that applies to *all* airguns, but even more so to the ones that are really loud and extra powerful.

Field Target, metallic silhouette and small-game—and sometimes not so small—hunting are the primary uses for a magnum-class airgun. Hunting, in particular, is one of those activities in which these potent airguns excel. Closely related to hunting, survival is another area in which many of the air rifles mentioned in this chapter would come in handy, and you can read more about that specific topic in Chapter 13.

The bottom line is that high-powered airguns such as those discussed here can be just as much fun as their more sedate cousins. As for practicality, there is no question that these comparatively powerful airguns have a lot to offer as well for more serious applications. Although power levels have been creeping upward for some time, in all likelihood the present levels will remain the norm for a while, at least as long as our well-established small calibers are used. Bigger airgun calibers undoubtedly open up all sorts of new possibilities; a tantalizing prospect for sure, but one fraught with the risk of government intervention (regulation). So let's take it easy and enjoy those wonderful magnum airguns.

Chapter 5

Some Thoughts on Match Air Rifles

A peek at the exciting field of high-tech, hair-splitting precision air rifles.

by J.I. Galan

The reduced size of the FWB C60 Mini enables small-statured folks to compete on equal footing in any 10-meter event, all the way to the Olympics!

MANY SHOOTERS STILL cling to the erroneous belief that match air rifles are intended mostly for those who compete in Olympic-style 10-meter matches. The reasoning behind this opinion stems from the fact that match air rifles are highly specialized, low-powered and terribly expensive. Therefore, many folks conclude these guns have little to offer when it comes to more mundane uses away from the formal, controlled environs of the international firing line.

Such mental convolutions may, at first, appear sound. After all, most people will agree that the European world-class match air rifle of today is a mechanical marvel designed for the specific purpose of neatly obliterating the pinhead-sized center of international-style 10-meter targets, shot after shot. These rifles are so accurate that, for all practical purposes, the shooter must blame only himself for printing anything less than a perfect score. It is a pure case of man against himself, if we allow ourselves a brief philosophical contemplation. In fact, the razor-sharp precision that match air rifles deliver constitutes their main suitability for certain applications which would make a dedicated match shooter cringe.

Take pest control, for instance. I can't think of a deadlier rat killer than a top-notch match air rifle topped with a good scope and a handful of good quality pointed pellets. Even at fairly long range—up to 35 yards or so—the pinpoint accuracy of these rifles will enable the shooter to place his shots exactly where he wants them.

I still recall when a colony of grasshoppers invaded my backyard some years back, intent on devouring the carefully tended flowers and decorative shrubbery. Rather than use a hazardous pesticide, I decided to turn the situation into a scaled-down version of a varmint hunt. Out came my RWS Model 75HV fitted with a 3-9x variable scope with parallax adjustment ring. From a distance of about 25 yards, the hungry little critters were literally blown up by the wadcutter match pellets quietly spit out by this fine air rifle.

Of course, match air rifles fall way behind magnum air rifles in terms of kinetic energy delivered to the target. Remember that the top muzzle velocities produced by match rifles lie in the 600 to 640 fps range. Some models, like the famous Walther LGR and the Gamo 126, both single-stroke pneumatics, generate only around 580 fps. My 1970-vintage Anschütz Model 250, for instance, has never surpassed 570 fps of MV, but even today it is quite capable of trimming the whiskers off a mouse at any distance up to 30 yards. Two of my RWS match air rifles from the early 1980s, the Model 75U and the Running Target Model 75K, are so accurate that I have been able to pick off large carpenter ants, consistently, at ranges of up to 15 yards, shooting from a benchrest with carefully zeroed scopes. Yet, those two models generate only around 600 fps of MV. Power, in terms of foot pounds of muzzle energy, is basically of academic interest when dealing with one of these tackdrivers.

Since all true match air rifles come only in 177-caliber, the average muzzle energy they generate is in the area of 5 to 6 foot pounds. This is not exactly the kind of *oomph* pneumo gun buffs like to brag about, but is more than sufficient to do the job when you send a 7- to 8-grain piece of lead down the ear canal of a nasty rodent.

For plinking and pest control, I always replace the micrometer aperture sights common to these guns with a good high-power telescopic sight. Since just about all of the rifles in this exclusive group are recoilless, the problem of scope creep is of no real concern. Although a 4x glass will suffice for most plinking, a higher power sight is a definite advantage for pest control. At the risk of being accused of overkill, I must admit that my 11-year-old Feinwerkbau 300S Running Target model carries a huge 3-9x 40mm scope. To say that this $10^3/_4$-pound combo is accurate would be a gross understatement. The same applies to my RWS Model 100 single-stroke pneumatic with its 4-12x scope. With such a setup, even the fleas on a rat aren't safe. Although all of these rifles are a bit on the heavy side, I can get far more satisfaction from one afternoon of plinking or long-range benchrest shooting with them than with many of the more common air rifles. Their high order of craftsmanship, flawless performance and dead-on precision provide a great source of enjoyment and pride of ownership.

The now-discontinued RWS Model 72 is an ideal junior rifle for serious 10-meter target work. It is a recoilless model with many of the features found on full-fledged match rifles.

The author found the novel top-lever pump mechanism of the Hammerli 450 quite pleasant to use.

The Beeman/Feinwerkbau C60 Running Target is powered by CO_2 and hosts a long list of refinements, including a removable barrel sleeve to assist in balancing the rifle through the swing.

The RWS Model 75K TO1 Running Target ranks high among the author's all-time favorite match rifles; its stock is fully adjustable.

The Anschütz LG380 has been around for more than a decade. It is another proven performer utilizing a recoilless spring-piston system.

The Daisy 853 is an ideal entry-level match-grade rifle utilizing the single-stroke pneumatic system.

For aspiring biathlon shooters, the Marksman #1790 is a fine home training air rifle. It uses the spring-piston break-barrel system.

The match air rifle market has been dominated primarily by German manufacturers. Firms such as Dianawerk, Feinwerkbau, Walther and Anschütz have been on the cutting edge of match airgun technology for several decades, producing an impressive array of models capable of outshooting all other types of airguns. Back in the mid-1980s, the lone American challenger to the West German hair-splitters was the Crosman Model 84 Match, a CO_2-powered beauty that was truly in the world-class club.

The Spanish firm of El Gamo has produced two excellent match air rifles, the Models 126 and 128. The former is distributed in the U.S. by Daisy. Both models utilize the increasingly popular single-stroke pneumatic power plant, which has caused the recoilless spring-piston system to fade rather quickly from international match circles in recent years. CO_2 has also become a viable power plant for match guns, with Feinwerkbau and Walther currently offering their own gas-powered tackdrivers.

World-class match air rifles are for anyone who can appreciate fine craftsmanship and pinpoint precision. You don't have to be an aspiring Olympic shooter, either, to reap the pleasure derived from owning one of these marvelous shooting instruments. All sorts of wonderful possibilities open up when you discover that with match air rifles, practically anything that the eye can see these rifles can hit, time after time.

Chapter 6

Air Pistols: An Update

Here we check out the latest in the world of air pistols, with a comprehensive review of the field by a well-known authority.

by David Wayland
Introduction by J.I. Galan

The Daisy Power Line 400 is a BB-shooting semi-auto that looks and functions like the famous Desert Eagle pistol.

If you are looking for a Glock look-alike for backyard plinking, the Daisy Model 1700 is just the ticket. It is a sixty-shot BB repeater powered by CO_2.

LIKE ALL OTHER areas of the airgun scene, air pistols have experienced a rather substantial upsurge since the Second Edition of this book in 1988. In fact, the field of air pistols seems to be growing at an unprecedented rate, given the slew of models that have appeared during the last three or four years. Just about every airgun manufacturer, it seems, is bent on expanding its air pistol offerings, with the result that the consumer now has a bewildering array of models and prices from which to choose.

One good example of this is the Daisy Mfg. Co. In 1994 alone, this company unveiled four new handguns, of which at least two models, the Power Line 400 and 1700, are quite likely to become big sellers. The other two pistols are the Models 1410 Stingray and 1420 Tiger Shark, two economy-class paintball shooters powered by CO_2 that incorporate some very advanced features. The Stingray is a semi-auto, while the Tiger Shark has a pump action. In this chapter, however, we shall concern ourselves with more traditional air- and gas-powered handguns rather than with those that shoot paintballs.

The Daisy Power Line 400 features a semi-automatic action and a twenty-shot BB magazine. This model is a spittin' image of the awesome Desert Eagle autoloader, a handful of a pistol any way you look at it. The Daisy look-alike is powered by CO_2 and spits out BBs at a muzzle velocity of 420 fps from a smoothbore barrel. A unique—though not entirely new—feature is its reciprocating slide that cycles back and forth whenever the gun is fired, just like the real thing. Of course, many shooters may remember the famous Crosman 451, a Colt 1911 look-alike powered by CO_2 that also featured a blowback slide as part of its operation. Unlike the short-lived Crosman—a complex and costly gun to produce back in the late 1960s—the new Daisy 400 looks like a sure-fire fun gun of the first magnitude.

The other Daisy BB pistol recently introduced is the Model 1700, another spittin' image of a famous handgun. This time, Daisy chose to replicate the looks of the Glock 17L, the long slide or target version of the hugely popular Glock 17 combat autoloader. The Daisy is also a repeater, powered by CO_2, producing an MV of 420 fps. Its ammo reservoir has capacity for sixty BBs.

For the remainder of the chapter, I asked fellow airgun scribe David Wayland to give us a bird's-eye view of the air pistol scene; no small task given the sheer size of the field, as well as the almost constant changes taking place on it. Wayland is the author of many fine articles on airguns going back quite a few years, appearing in popular firearm publications such as *Gun World* magazine, the *Gun World Annual* and others. In addition, David's business as a custom stock and pistol grip maker—Precision Wood Products in Mill Valley, California—has earned him a well-deserved reputation in the world of guns and shooting among those who appreciate top-notch workmanship and elegance in a special piece of wood for a prized firearm or airgun. He is also an accomplished knifemaker, hunter and self-confessed gun nut extraordinaire. Here is his report:

• • • •

Air pistols are not nearly as well known to the average American as their shoulder-fired counterparts. Like most Americans over fifty, I began my shooting life with a lever-action Daisy BB gun. I am, however, hard put to remember the first air pistol I ever fired. I recall neighborhood youths, an arrogant bunch of teenagers, firing a Benjamin pump pistol in their garage. It was charged by pushing in a piston that protruded from beneath the muzzle. Still being in short pants, they would not let me shoot it, and I've never forgiven them. That was in the 1930s, and air pistols continued to be unusual items for some time.

I recall owning a sheet metal pistol that fired small shot powered by rubber bands. It came with some colorful celluloid birds on a wire that spun if you hit them. I also recall a later gift of a Daisy that fired shot with equally unsatisfying results. So much for the dark ages. Today, the world of airguns offers an almost stupefying array of air pistols for every possible budget and need. There are the low-powered spring pistols for the neophyte, magnum-level field pistols, and Olympic quality match pistols to test the skill of the most demanding marksman. In these next pages, we shall try to give you a brief look at the cream of the crop.

But first, safety mention here is in order: There is a real danger of ricochet or bounce back from hard surfaces with BBs; this means careful selection of targets and backstops. Since most shooting with air pistols of this sort is done in basements or backyards, a backstop can be an earthen bank or a piece of old carpeting large enough to catch misses as well as hits. Don't use the back fence, since weathered boards tend to bounce BBs with enthusiasm. And, not to nag, but safety glasses are a must.

Air Pistols

Daisy

A beginner of any age would do well to get a Daisy Model 288. Made of moulded polymer with a smoothbore steel 177-caliber barrel, it features easy underlever cocking and a twenty-four-shot magazine for steel BBs. Velocity is a modest 215 fps. The Daisy 288 has a full-size grip and simple, positive action. It is not easy to tell if there is a BB in the magazine, but that won't present problems if the shooter obeys the rules. Sights are fixed, and while light in weight, the gun has the feel and looks of a more sophisticated pistol. This is definitely not a toy.

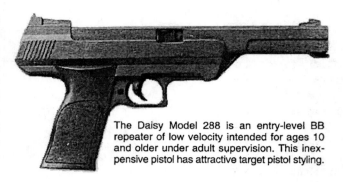

The Daisy Model 288 is an entry-level BB repeater of low velocity intended for ages 10 and older under adult supervision. This inexpensive pistol has attractive target pistol styling.

Daisy's Model 93 is a spittin' image of the 9mm S&W autoloader, but shoots a whole bunch of BBs at an MV of around 400 fps.

The Daisy Power Line Model 1200 is a step up in firepower from the 288. It uses 12-gram CO_2 cylinders for power and lets you squeeze off up to sixty shots without reloading, but does require cocking for each shot. Also a smoothbore steel barrel, the Model 1200 nearly doubles the muzzle velocity to 420 fps. A bit heftier than the Model 288, it would suit the more advanced shooter. Daisy recommends this pistol for shooters age sixteen and over, but this is strictly arbitrary and conservative in the extreme. My youngest son had shot two deer with a high-powered rifle by age sixteen, but not all shooters are that advanced...or fortunate.

For best performance from CO_2 guns, it is best not to get too trigger happy and engage in rapid-fire. Expanding CO_2 tends to cool the metal parts of the gun, and the lowering of temperature reduces both the pressure of the gas and the number of shots. It's a study in the practical application of high school physics.

The Daisy Power Line Model 44 is a realistic shooting replica of the Smith & Wesson Model 29 44 Magnum revolver and one of my favorite plinkers. A true revolver, it uses round disc pellet magazines that can be loaded ahead of time and kept handy for speedy reloads. The CO_2 cylinder hides in the butt under the left grip panel. The Model 44 is large and well proportioned with a good feel. The rifled barrel stabilizes pellets so a more demanding shooter has the satisfaction of hitting smaller targets than with a smoothbore. Muzzle velocity is a snappy

Another big success story from Daisy in the 1990s is the Model 645, a spittin' image of the legendary Colt Model 1911 autoloader. This one is a 177-caliber pellet repeater powered by CO_2.

The Daisy Model 91 is a superb 10-meter match pistol imported from Hungary. It comes in a fitted attaché case with all accessories and retails for around $400!

400 fps. You can fire this dandy gun by double action (just pulling the trigger) or single action (cock the hammer and squeeze off your shot).

There is a push safety located just below the rear sight and clearly visible when you aim. The sights are adjustable, and the cylinder swings out just like its magnum counterpart. This is an excellent choice for training and practice before and after acquiring a large-bore firearm. Select between 4-, 6- or 8-inch barrel lengths. You can get an extra barrel of a different length and switch anytime you want. I like the 6-inch myself. Not a spectacular pistolero, I can still perforate an empty matchbox at 50 feet with ease using my Model 44.

Daisy has a large selection of firearm look-alikes in addition to the above revolver. The current popularity of automatics has brought forth an equally large population of CO_2 clones of the best-known firearms.

The Daisy Power Line Model 93 is a copy of the Smith & Wesson Model 59, one of the first of the large-capacity 9mms made in this country. A smoothbore BB repeater, the Model 93 uses a CO_2 cylinder in the grip area and a fifteen-shot BB magazine that slips into a slot on top of the barrel. Strictly double-action, the hammer on this pistol is just for looks. The sights are fixed, and there is a manual safety located on the slide, plus a grip safety. A real handful, the Model 93 shoots BBs at 400 fps. Daisy makes a dual-tone black and nickel-plated version called the Model 693. Same specs, just a bit spiffier.

Colt 1911 fans will take to the Daisy Power Line Model 45. It is also CO_2-powered, but has a rifled steel barrel and shoots only pellets. The hammer works, but the trigger pull is long, giving a double-action feel whether the hammer is cocked or not, which makes it a bit safer in operation. The manual safety is very positive and requires both hands to disengage. The rear sight is adjustable for elevation only. This is a first-rate trainer and plinker. A dressier version with two-tone nickel-plating is called the 645. Same pistol, just fancier.

The Daisy Model 500 Raven was introduced in 1993 and is a dead ringer for the Beretta 92FS, the 9mm that is standard issue for the U.S. armed forces. The Raven is another outstanding look-alike, but has several important differences in function. First, while the Raven has a rifled barrel (this makes lead pellets mandatory), it is *not* a repeater. The rear of the barrel lifts up, exposing the breech, a pellet is manually inserted and the barrel returned to the closed position. While the Beretta offers a double-action option, the Raven requires that the hammer be cocked for each shot. Both these features—breech pellet seating and single-action mechanism—allow more accurate shooting. It isn't match-grade accuracy, but it's light-years ahead of the smoothbore BB guns. An interesting concept.

For those shooters who have gotten to the point where they want to really test their abilities, Daisy has produced an excellent series of three pneumatic target pistols. Some versions are being used to win in U.S. competition. They give the American shooter equipment that is much more affordable than the Olympic-grade models. These pistols are in a special category of airguns, the single-stroke pneumatics. A precision piston is compressed just once and its compression head forms the end of a compression chamber. In turn, the trigger releases the air compressed in that chamber. Such systems are inherently accurate when properly constructed and are used in match-grade rifles with considerable success.

This series begins with the Daisy Power Line Model 717. A single shot match-style pistol, it has a 9.6-inch rifled steel barrel, thumbrest plastic grips for right-handers and micrometer rear sight adjustable for elevation and windage. Muzzle velocity is a modest 360 fps, but remember, this series of pistols is designed to put pellets through the scoring rings of 10-meter paper targets with great repeatability. It's a good idea to use the best flat-nose match pellets available and to try as many different brands as you can get your hands on. This is a good idea for any serious airgun shooting, but it really makes sense for target guns. You will be surprised at the variations in groups, even between high-quality pellets. Each pistol (and rifle, too) is unique.

Next in the series is the Daisy Model 747. The finish is a non-reflective matte black, and the barrel is made in Germany

Jess Galan puts a Benjamin Sheridan Model E17 CO_2 pistol through its paces. This is a compact, yet hard-hitting and accurate CO_2 pistol with nickel finish and smooth walnut grips.

The Crosman 1389 Backpacker is a versatile multi-pump pneumatic pellet pistol that can easily be converted into a mini-carbine. Available in 177 only, its top velocity is 560 fps.

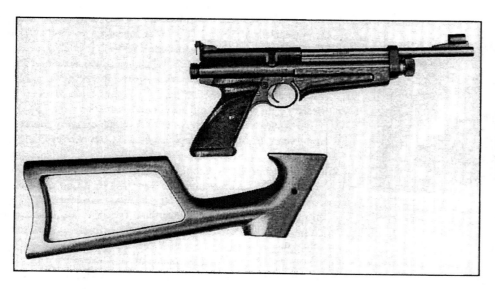

The Crosman SSP 250 comes in 177-caliber, but has optional 20- and 22-caliber barrels available. This potent single shot CO_2 pellet pistol can also be fitted with Crosman's #1399 Shoulder Stock.

by Lothar Walther. There is a trigger-pull adjustment, but the manual does not recommend a pull setting of less than 2 pounds.

The top of the Daisy line is the Model 777. It features the same power plant as the 717, but has other refinements, such as form-fitting walnut grips that can be modified to fit your hand—you file, carve and sand them to your heart's delight. Left-hand versions are also available. The sights are more sophisticated, being micro-adjustable for elevation and windage, and the rear notch is adjustable for width.

For the shooter striving for an Olympic medal, the Daisy Model 91, a European import utilizing the latest CO_2 technology, would be a good start. It takes refillable CO_2 cylinders, has adjustable anatomical wood grips, uses an adjustable trigger for pull weight and length, and sports match-grade adjustable sights. An adapter is available to allow the use of precharged 8- and 12-gram CO_2 cylinders. The muzzle velocity is higher than the 777, with the pellets zipping along at 476 fps, a speed that

reduces barrel time a bit. Everything is designed to squeeze out the last bit of advantage.

Benjamin Sheridan

A company that also had its roots planted early in the history of American airguns is that of Benjamin Sheridan. Benjamin began making pneumatic airguns in 1882. The Sheridan firm was acquired much later and in 1992 Benjamin Sheridan became part of Crosman.

The Benjamin Sheridan H9 Series of pneumatic pistols are the descendants of that pump-up pneumatic of my youth. Available in 177-, 20- and 22-caliber, they are well-made, solid pistols ideally suited to plinking and pest control. The barrels are rifled brass, and the grips and pump handle are solid walnut. The sights are simple and screw-adjustable for windage and elevation. To operate, just engage the safety, twist open the breech, pull back to cock the striker, insert a pellet, pump the handle three to eight times and you're ready. Top velocity is around 525 fps for the

The Crosman/Skanaker Model 88 CO₂ match pistol is no longer in production, but samples of this fine competition gun still surface from time to time in the used airgun market.

The BSA Model 240 magnum air pistol uses a top-cocking spring-piston system. This fairly potent pistol has the overall look and feel of a combat autoloader.

Jess Galan likes the Crosman Silver Series 1008 a lot. It features both single- and double-action operation and is accurate enough to dispatch small rodents at short range.

177 version and will vary with pellet weight and number of pumps. Available blued or nickel-plated, these are tough and reliable, great camp guns. If you don't like pumping, Benjamin Sheridan E9 Series Model E pistols feature CO₂ power. Barrels are a bit shorter than the pneumatic models, but except for the absence of the pumping lever, they are nearly identical. A knurled filler cap knob just below the muzzle unscrews, allowing you to change CO₂ cylinders. You'll get about forty shots per cylinder, and they claim velocity is on a par with the pump-up version, about 500 fps in 177. You can choose among 177-, 20- or 22-caliber, but it's best to buy the same caliber as your rifles to simplify pellet inventory. These pistols are straightforward in design and well made.

Crosman

Crosman Air Guns produces an extensive line of pneumatic and CO₂ pistols. The SSP 250 Super Sport Pistol is a large and interesting gun offered in 177-caliber, with 20- and 22-caliber

barrels available. It is unique among CO₂ pistols because you can select between two power settings very easily. The pistol is loaded by rotating a loading lever to expose the pellet chamber, seating a pellet and closing the lever. Pulling back the cocking knob two clicks gives you the lower "economy" velocity (in 177) of about 525 fps. Pulling it back all the way (three clicks) gets the maximum velocity of 560 fps. Velocities for larger calibers will be lower. The grips are wood-grained polymer with thumb-memory grooves to fit either hand. The receiver is grooved to take a long eye relief pistol scope. If you install an optional shoulder stock, you can mount a rifle scope. This is a versatile pistol designed for the typical American who likes to plink and engage in informal target shooting, including airgun silhouettes.

The Crosman 1389 Backpacker is a pneumatic version of the SSP 250. Made in 177-caliber with a muzzle velocity of up to 560 fps, this gun has a detachable stock—a wilderness plinker.

The Crosman Model 1377 American Classic and Model 1322 Medalist are two versions of the same gun. Long-barreled pneumatics, the 1377 is in 177-caliber and the 1322—you guessed it—a 22. Both have rifled steel barrels and come with ambidextrous polymer grips and pump forends. The sights are screw-adjustable, and their operation is simple and straightforward. The grips can be replaced with a shoulder stock to convert the pistols into short-barreled carbines. The factory recommends a minimum of two pumps and a maximum of ten. Six to eight pumps are usually sufficient for most uses. Don't think you can turn a pneumatic into an instant magnum by trying to pump more than the recommended maximum number of times, because the pressure curve flattens quickly and you will only manage to strain the gun...and yourself.

In the look-alike category, Crosman offers the 1008 Repeat Air, a repeater with an interesting system. On the outside, the 1008 Repeat Air looks like a Third-Generation Smith & Wesson automatic. On the inside, it is a revolver with a removable rotary magazine "cylinder" that holds eight pellets and is easily replaced when exhausted. CO₂-powered, it pumps out 177-

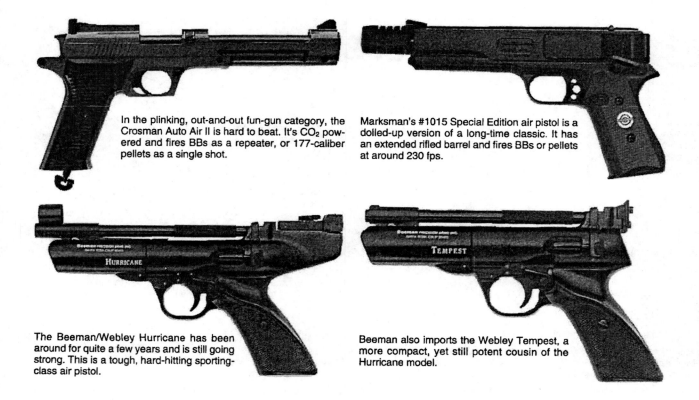

In the plinking, out-and-out fun-gun category, the Crosman Auto Air II is hard to beat. It's CO_2 powered and fires BBs as a repeater, or 177-caliber pellets as a single shot.

Marksman's #1015 Special Edition air pistol is a dolled-up version of a long-time classic. It has an extended rifled barrel and fires BBs or pellets at around 230 fps.

The Beeman/Webley Hurricane has been around for quite a few years and is still going strong. This is a tough, hard-hitting sporting-class air pistol.

Beeman also imports the Webley Tempest, a more compact, yet still potent cousin of the Hurricane model.

caliber pellets at 430 fps and accepts wadcutters, domed and pointed pellets. It's a clever and reliable system.

The Crosman Auto Air II is a visual clone of the AMT Automag II pistols, but instead of shooting 22 WMR ammo, the Auto Air II shoots BBs from a magazine or pellets loaded singly. Extremely light, it should be easy for young shooters to hold for prolonged shooting sessions. It is surprisingly accurate for a smoothbore at short range (10 yards or so).

One of my favorite look-alikes is the Crosman 357. Not one, but a series of CO_2 revolvers, these handguns replicate the Colt Python and feature 4-, 6- or 8-inch barrels that are interchangeable. I don't know why, but the 4- and 6-inch barrels are rifled steel while the 8-inch is rifled brass. Small matter, they all shoot well for informal target shooting and plinking. The interchangeable pellet cylinders are made in six- and ten-shot versions. Blued guns come with brown grips; nickel-plated versions sport black grips. The CO_2 cylinder hides under the left grip. Sights are adjustable, and a push safety is readily visible below the rear sight while aiming. A version called the Model 1357 is identical except it shoots BBs through a smooth barrel. My vote goes to the pellet versions.

Marksman

Now for a quick quiz! Name the world's most popular air pistol. Daisy? Crosman? Benjamin? Sorry, time's up. It is the Marksman 1010. Yup, over the years more of these handy little plinkers have been made and sold than any other air pistol. I've even seen them advertised in auto parts catalogs. They are simple and reliable and, best of all, fun. Not strictly a look-alike, the lines are reminiscent of the 1911 Colt 45. They fire

pellets, darts and BBs out of a short smoothbore barrel at about 200 fps. It's scarcely a magnum, but great for dancing beverage cans and blowing away styrofoam cups. Extras include a dart board and a large variety of fun target games. Marksman understands that airgun shooting is, first and foremost, *entertainment*. They also understand that most folks are not died-in-the-wool, steely-eyed target shooters whose ambitions are gold medals. The Model 1010 is available in a deluxe nickel-plated version and in a Special Edition that has an extended rifled barrel and medallion grips. Like the original, the action is spring-powered and is cocked by working the slide just like an old Colt 1911.

Beeman

The Beeman/Webley Hurricane and Tempest are classic British air pistols using the spring-piston system. The Webleys are interesting because the compression chamber is placed *beneath* the barrel and the piston moves to the rear when fired. This gives the Webleys a slight recoil that is reminiscent of a firearm. It also makes them shorter and handier than most spring-piston pistols, so they fit nicely into a tackle box or backpack.

The Hurricane and the Tempest are essentially the same pistol with a few minor differences. The Hurricane has a hooded front sight mounted on a barrel extension. The rifled steel barrel isn't longer than the Tempest's, it just looks that way. The rear sight is mounted on an extension of the receiver, giving the Hurricane a longer sight radius. Tempest sights are screw-adjustable, while the Hurricane's are micrometer-adjustable. To operate, push forward the typically Webley stirrup latch, lift up the barrel and muscle it all the way forward until the piston

The Beeman/Webley Nemesis is a single-stroke pneumatic pistol capable of delivering very good accuracy at medium power in a recoilless package.

The Beeman P2 Match is outwardly almost identical to the P1, but uses a single-stroke pneumatic power plant instead.

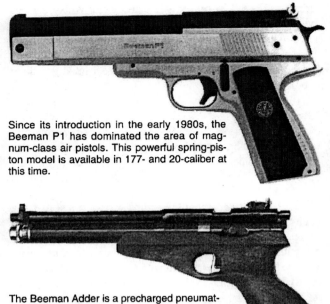

Since its introduction in the early 1980s, the Beeman P1 has dominated the area of magnum-class air pistols. This powerful spring-piston model is available in 177- and 20-caliber at this time.

The Beeman Adder is a precharged pneumatic pistol that could be had in a choice of 177-, 20- or 25-caliber. In the latter, this model produces an awesome 20 foot pounds of muzzle energy! Sadly, this gun is no longer available.

latches on the sear. Seat a pellet in the breech and snap shut. The safety is a handy lever operated by the right thumb, while the grips are black plastic with a right-handed thumbrest. Velocities for the two are 500 fps for the 177 version and 400 fps for the 22. I recall once testing a Tempest over a chronograph and was amazed at the consistency of the readings. They seldom varied more than one or two fps with that particular pistol. This would be unheard of with any firearm, no matter how good the ammo.

The Beeman HW70A is a simple spring-piston pistol made in Germany by Weihrauch. The barrel is in front of the piston and cocking is accomplished by breaking the barrel and pushing it down until it clicks. Then, seat the pellet in the breech and snap it shut. While there is no manual on-off safety, there is a built-in safety that prevents the barrel from snapping shut while in the open, cocked position. It is my opinion that manual safeties are dangerous, especially if shooters expect to substitute them for safe handling techniques. Muzzle velocity is around 440 fps, and accuracy is .32-inch center to center at 10 meters, quite respectable for a moderately priced air pistol. The grip is of one-piece checkered polymer with ambidextrous thumb grooves. A good intermediate target pistol.

The Beeman P1 Magnum is a remarkable airgun that offers accuracy and power only equaled by air rifles. It looks a bit like the Colt 1911 except for a massive slide/barrel assembly. The grip geometry is identical to the 1911; in fact, it accepts 1911 grip panels. The design is a sophisticated barrel-over-piston Webley-like arrangement. The barrel is unlatched by pulling back on the hammer, which really isn't a hammer, then swung upward and forward. However, there are two cocked positions. The first click gives about 380 fps in 177-caliber. The full-for-

ward (and fully cocked) position gives the maximum power, about 600 fps in the 177. The gun is also available in 20-caliber, producing 500 fps. This gives the 177- and 20-caliber P1 the versatility of a pneumatic—low power for plinking and less effort, full power for pest control. Accuracy is .30-inch center to center in 177, and the sights are micrometer-adjustable. The trigger is a two-stage, with very light let-off (28 ounces) and adjustability. A shoulder stock is optional, and receiver grooves accept scopes and electronic sights. This is an engineering tour de force and top-of-the-line field gun.

The Beeman P2 Match is a kissin' cousin to the P1, but very different in principle and mission. The lines are the same and cocking is accomplished in a similar fashion. However, this is not a spring-piston magnum field pistol, but a single-stroke pneumatic *target* pistol. And being a single-stroke pneumatic, it is recoilless. Accuracy is .20-inch center to center with a velocity of 435 fps. The sights are micrometer adjustable; walnut match grips are optional. This is a good choice for the upwardly mobile target shooter or the plinker who wants something a bit more elegant than most.

With the Beeman Adder and Wolverine, we entered—though rather briefly—the world of the magnum precharged pneumatic pistol in the U.S. Designed with power in mind, these two gave new meaning to the word "magnum." While the Beeman P1 produces 600 fps (and that is significant for a spring-piston handgun), the Adder and Wolverine developed over fifty percent higher velocity. As for energy, just compare the 6 foot pounds or so of ME in the P1 to the 18 to 20 foot pounds of these two. The air supply was charged from a scuba tank and provided ten to thirty shots per charge, depending on how high you turned up the power setting. The Adder was offered in 20- and 25-caliber, while the fancier Wolverine was available in 177-, 20- and 25-caliber. Maximum velocities: 177/940 fps, 20/850 fps, 25/630 fps. If varmints are your thing, these two pistols could do the job handsomely. Unfortunately, just as this chapter was being finalized, we learned that these two potent pistols are no longer available, due to the fact that their British manufacturer, Titan, went out of business late in 1993.

A magnificent match-grade pistol that has been around in one form or another for a long time is the Beeman/Feinwerkbau 65 MKII. A sidelever spring-piston design, this gun has an optional recoil feature that allows you to switch from recoilless target mode to recoiling mode for firearm practice. As a devotee of bucking, roaring, magnum handguns, I don't feel that any airgun recoils much, but to be quite honest, when you get into serious practice sessions, recoil can be distracting. And remember, you will fire a 177 *many* more times than a 445 Supermag. The FWB 65 MKII is equipped with ergonomic Olympic-style adjustable wood grips; a trigger that is adjustable four ways with pull ranging from 39 to 17.6 ounces; and click micrometer, fully adjustable rear sight and interchangeable-width front blades. Barrel weights are optional, as is a shorter barrel model. The muzzle velocity has increased to 525 fps over the years since it was discovered that shorter barrel time and reduced wind drift were an advantage. An American firing an FWB 65

MKI won the gold at the Second World Airgun Championships. The FWB 65 MKII is a good choice for a serious target shooter or someone who just craves sheer elegance in plinking. Accuracy? How about .04-inch center to center at 10 meters!

New on the air pistol scene is the Beeman/Feinwerkbau Model 102, a two-stroke pneumatic. The design is similar to a single-stroke except it breaks down into two strokes to make the effort of each stroke easier. You must remember that your heartbeat has an important effect on concentrated target shooting, and anything that can reduce the effort is a plus. This 2.5-pound master-puncher groups .04-inch at 10 meters and features all the grip, trigger and sighting adjustments any medal-craving shooter would want. A nice feature is the automatic opening of the breech when the cocking lever is actuated. This blocks the sight path, reminding the shooter to load a pellet. The sight line is close to the bore, and the pistol sits very low in the hand, all combining to improve sighting. Weight distribution can be fine tuned to the shooter's needs by means of a sliding weight. The only thing this pistol lacks is Muzak!

To totally remove the pumping or stroking effort, you must rely on compressed gas, namely CO_2. Feinwerkbau overcame the many engineering problems inherent in achieving true match-grade accuracy with a CO_2 pistol, and the result was more airgun shooters using their models than any other for serious competition. An FWB shooter won Olympic Gold, and

The Beeman/FWB Model 102 is a state-of-the-art pneumatic match pistol using a two-stroke pump system that demands very little effort.

One of the modern classics in the field of German spring-piston air pistols is the RWS Model 5G. It's a hard-hitting, accurate air pistol that has been around for decades, undergoing periodic upgrades.

The Beeman/FWB Model C20 is another CO_2 match pistol incorporating a host of advanced features.

The Gamo Compact is another match-grade single-pump pneumatic with several outstanding features. (Ben Saltzman photo)

The Beeman/FWB C25 utilizes a vertical CO_2 canister and a weight rail below the barrel. This outstanding tack-driver is also intended for world-class 10-meter events.

If you thought the Beeman/FWB C5 was advanced, the newer Model C55 will blow your mind. This pricey, yet outstanding CO_2 pistol features both rapid-fire and single shot operation.

since then a trend was set. The Beeman/Feinwerkbau Models C20 and C25 are among the latest refinements in this line. They are different only in that the C25 has a vertical CO_2 cylinder with a rail that carries a sliding weight for weight distribution control. The internal feature that distinguishes these pistols from others (outside of superb precision and sophistication) is the separate gas staging chamber. It is easy to understand that as gas in a cylinder is used up, the pressure is reduced. This would mean that the one-hundredth shot might not have the same velocity as the first. The staging chamber regulates the pressure so that each shot is identical. Accuracy is on the order of .04-inch; velocity is 510 fps. The trigger has a dry-firing feature and is fully adjustable. The sights are also fully adjustable, including the rear notch for width. The CO_2 cylinder is good for 200 shots and is recharged from a 5-pound storage tank. The cylinders have a special seal that prevents overcharging.

Now, suppose you like the CO_2 match format, but you want to shoot in *rapid-fire* matches. You had better check out the Beeman/Feinwerkbau C55. As sophisticated as the C20, the C55 can shoot pellets singly or five shots from a magazine as fast as you can pull the trigger! The other CO_2 repeaters we have been talking about are fine for informal paper punching or tormenting an empty soft-drink can, but to get in there with the big boys and really compete, you'd better get state-of-the-art equipment. The C55 is it. It even has a muzzlebrake to reduce

the minor recoil produced when the CO_2 leaves the barrel. Trigger, grip and sights are of the multiple adjustable match features you find in other FWBs of this grade. The velocity is 510 fps, and accuracy is .05-inch center to center. That means you can use a C55 for slow-fire matches as well. The 225-shot CO_2 cylinder is charged from a separate tank.

Dynamit Nobel-RWS

The firm of Dianawerk has long provided a wide range of spring-piston air pistols to the American market. They were marketed under the Winchester, Original, Hy-Score and Beeman brand names at one time or another. For some time, they have been sold under the RWS label from the Dynamit Nobel-RWS, Inc., firm that produces and markets rimfire and center-fire ammo, as well as airgun pellets. Dynamit Nobel-RWS, until recently, offered five air pistols to the American market, three spring-piston models and two single-stroke pneumatics.

The RWS PR-45 is one of the pneumatics. The receiver containing the barrel lifts for loading and cocking. There is no recoil, and the 177-caliber rifled steel barrel delivers pellets with satisfying accuracy. Muzzle velocity is 430 fps and trigger pull is a clean 2.2 pounds. The design of the Spanish-made PR-45 is very compact for a handgun with an 8.3-inch barrel. This gun is a good choice for keeping the eye and hand in shape for firearm shooting. A slightly more elegant version of

Another Jess Galan favorite is the Gamo PR-45. This accurate single-pump pneumatic has the looks and feel of a combat autoloader.

The first world-class rapid-fire 10-meter CO_2 pistol was the Beeman/FWB C5. This precision shooting machine has now been superseded by the FWB Model C55.

A staple among traditional Beeman offerings is the excellent FWB 65 MKII, a recoilless spring-piston match pistol that has won countless world-class matches.

The current top-of-the-line RWS Model 6M is also a recoilless spring-piston pistol with a rotating barrel sleeve/weight that also offers a firm grasp during cocking.

The RWS Model 6G is a recoilless spring-piston match-grade pistol with a distinguished track record. This latest version has an adjustable match grip.

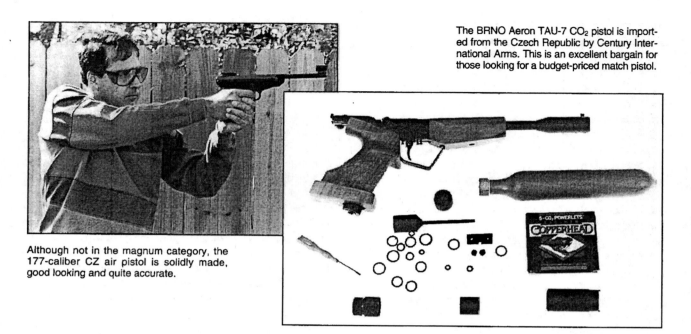

The BRNO Aeron TAU-7 CO_2 pistol is imported from the Czech Republic by Century International Arms. This is an excellent bargain for those looking for a budget-priced match pistol.

Although not in the magnum category, the 177-caliber CZ air pistol is solidly made, good looking and quite accurate.

the PR-45 is the RWS Compact. It uses the same power plant and adjustable sights, but has adjustable wood target grips and a two-stage adjustable trigger with a swiveling shoe. The trigger can be tweaked down to 1.65 pounds. This one makes a good choice for the target shooter on a budget. Unfortunately, these two pistols are no longer carried by Dynamit Nobel-RWS.

The RWS Model 5G is a reasonably priced Diana-made target and plinking pistol. It is of the barrel-cocking variety and has an adjustable trigger, adjustable rear sight and hooded post front sight. It has an automatic safety that prevents pulling the trigger while the barrel is in the cocked position. A large pistol, it measures 15 inches in length and requires nearly 40 pounds of cocking effort. The reward is good accuracy and a muzzle velocity of 450 fps.

A step up in refinement is the RWS Model 6G, a recoilless version of the 5G. To achieve this lack of vibration, it uses not one but two pistons that move in opposite directions and are regulated by a rack-and-gear system. When firing this pistol, it is hard to believe that a piston has slammed forward, firing a pellet at 450 fps. It has an adjustable wood grip, adjustable trigger and a hooded front sight with interchangeable inserts. Cocking effort is a bit less than the 5G.

Last on the list is the RWS Model 6M. As far as I can tell, it is identical to the 6G except for a front sight adjustable for width. To accomplish this and still permit easy cocking, a rotating barrel shroud is part of the barrel assembly.

Miscellaneous Pistols

For the shooter on a tight budget, Century International Arms is marketing an import from the Czech Republic. The BRNO Aeron TAU-7 CO_2 is a match pistol with adjustable sights, trigger and grips. Century claims it surpasses all the U.I.T. (International Shooting Union) requirements. It has a 10.3-inch barrel and is unique because it uses 12-gram CO_2 cylinders as well as a large, refillable cylinder, which makes it easy for the average

shooter to keep it powered. Velocity is adjustable. What makes this pistol attractive to a match shooter wannabe is the price. It is a fraction of that charged for the top-of-the-line European entries. Czech this one out.

We can't cover *every* air pistol available to the dedicated shooter today. Many firms are offering a variety of models, including low-cost plinkers from Mainland China and the Czech Republic, and interesting designs from Hungary, Russia and Italy are showing up as well. Two outstanding Olympic-quality pistols are currently being imported by Nygord Precision Products. The Steyr Match LP1C is one that is as sophisticated as they come. A CO_2 pistol, it uses rechargeable cylinders with integrated safety valves that prevent excessive pressure, whether on or off the pistol. Muzzle velocity is not quoted but can be varied, a useful feature in a CO_2 arm. Another good feature is a dry-firing mode that lets you practice without actually shooting. Grips are the accepted ergonomic walnut adjustable variety. An interesting option from Steyr is that you can order the LP1C in white, red, green or blue. How about that? Now you can match your pistol to your outfit instead of the other way around! A handsome as well as efficient target pistol.

Also offered by Nygord is the Morini 162 E air pistol. Made in Switzerland, it uses a precharged air cylinder you recharge from a scuba tank and is good for about 180 shots. A preset valve prevents shooting when the pressure drops below the necessary minimum. The trigger is electronic and adjustable from 50 to 400 grams. If you're worried that the battery might go dead in the middle of a match, don't. Morini says the battery is good for 10,000 shots, including dry-firing. Sights are micro-adjustable, the rear and front both adjustable for width. As a former four-position smallbore target shooter, I appreciate all these "adjustables." No two people are exactly alike. Hands, eyes and shooting styles have infinite variations, and when you concentrate as hard on every facet of a sport as a serious match shooter, you want to get a perfect fit. If you have to compensate for a

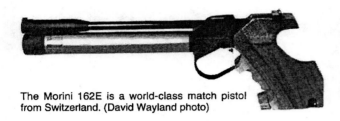

The Morini 162E is a world-class match pistol from Switzerland. (David Wayland photo)

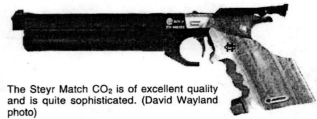

The Steyr Match CO_2 is of excellent quality and is quite sophisticated. (David Wayland photo)

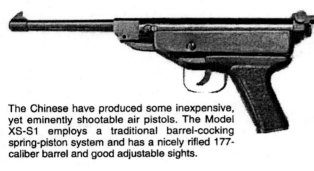

The Chinese have produced some inexpensive, yet eminently shootable air pistols. The Model XS-S1 employs a traditional barrel-cocking spring-piston system and has a nicely rifled 177-caliber barrel and good adjustable sights.

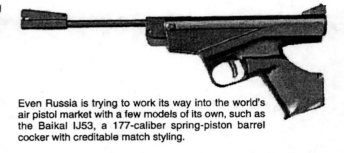

Even Russia is trying to work its way into the world's air pistol market with a few models of its own, such as the Baikal IJ53, a 177-caliber spring-piston barrel cocker with creditable match styling.

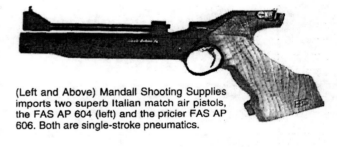

(Left and Above) Mandall Shooting Supplies imports two superb Italian match air pistols, the FAS AP 604 (left) and the pricier FAS AP 606. Both are single-stroke pneumatics.

stock that's a bit too small or a trigger that doesn't allow for a natural-feeling let-off, you aren't going to shoot as well. It just makes sense.

The first free-pistol I ever saw was a Hammerli. That fine old firm is still producing quality arms, and their Model 480 is a honey. A precharged pneumatic, the gun has a large-capacity carbon-fiber-wrapped alloy air cartridge that delivers up to 320 shots with each filling from a scuba-type air bottle. It has all the sight, trigger and grip adjustments you would expect from a top-of-the-line Swiss handgun. The grip adds a 7-degree rake adjustment as well as the other adjustments.

If you want to take on the world of air pistol target competition, you have plenty of choices in the pistols to use. But a word of caution: You'd better have a fat checkbook handy because these beauties are not cheap.

Let's depart the thin air of the purist target shooters and talk about some of the "oldies but goodies" out there in airgunland. I have some favorites that are typical of the excellent air pistols you may find on the used market. Walk through a gun show and you may very well find a few attractively priced jewels. Many firearms fanatics turn up their noses at airguns and don't recognize the worth of an old classic.

I will admit to being a shameless Webley fan. I love their old top-break 455-caliber revolvers and their top-cocking air pistols. I have an old Webley MKII, one of the ancestors of the current Tempest and Hurricane. It's well made and solid, a joy to shoot. A pistol I would like to see back in production is the 177-caliber Webley Jr. MKII. It is the smallest of the Webleys, but is just plain fun. I have sat in many a hunting camp after the day's trudging was over and tormented countless empty beverage cans with one of these guns. That compact little Webley amazes all with its inherent accuracy. Not as exotic, I have a Benjamin 137 that accompanied me on an ocean kayak trip some years back. The brass parts weren't a bit fazed by the salt air. I'm not particularly interested in repeaters; it's probably the result of too much target shooting, but I'm very fond of a Crosman 600 CO_2 repeater. I even have a collector's item I haven't shot yet that I picked up last year at a gun show (probably paid too much). It's a clean Benjamin Model 250 smoothbore CO_2 in the original box. I'll shoot it someday, but for now I'll just admire it. There's another gun I don't shoot much these days, maybe because it's intimidating to have an air pistol that is capable of a much higher degree of accuracy than I am. It's a like-new Beeman "Original" Model 6, the predecessor to the RWS Model 6G, a recoilless dandy that puts 'em where you aim 'em. Now if I can just aim 'em better!

All of the foregoing may be more than you wanted to know about air pistols. But you have to admit, there is something for everyone, whether they're going for the gold or just an afternoon of fun.

Chapter 7

A Look at Air-Powered Scatterguns

Air and CO$_2$ shotguns have been the least understood of all airguns. Here, fellow airgunner Larry Hannusch sheds much needed light upon the history of this rather unusual airgun.

by Larry Hannusch
Introduction by J.I. Galan

MY FIRST EXPOSURE to air-powered shotguns occurred in a very subtle way a great many years ago with the flea-market purchase of a small, humble-looking cardboard box bearing the name Plainsman. The box contained about two dozen short and rather plain cardboard tubes, each of which contained a ridiculously small amount of tiny lead shot. These tubes were, in fact, shotshells for the Plainsman 28-S pneumatic shotgun that was marketed in the late 1940s and early 1950s, without a great deal of commercial success. Intrigued by all this, I did not rest until I eventually found a specimen of the Plainsman shotgun in fairly acceptable shape to add to my airgun collection.

Since then, several other air and CO$_2$ shotguns have joined that old Plainsman. With each new addition, however, my interest and admiration for these rather unique airguns grows.

Given the somewhat nebulous—if not outright elusive—status of the air shotgun in the overall airgun scene, I felt that an entire chapter ought to be dedicated to this subject and asked top-notch airgun collector and connoisseur Larry Hannusch to tell us about it. Of course, those of you who were acquainted with the now-defunct *American Airgunner* magazine no doubt remember Larry's eminently erudite articles dealing with rare and exotic airguns. I have had the privilege

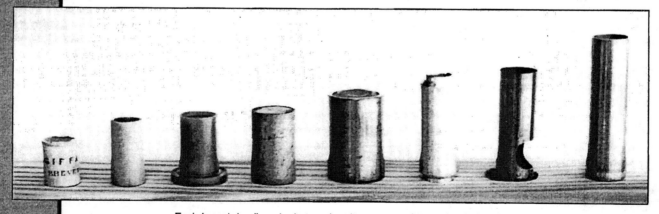

Each breech-loading air shotgun has its own proprietary shotshell. From left to right: Giffard 8mm, Plainsman 28-S, Crosman 1100, Paul 420, Farco, Yewha/National, Vincent and LD 380 shotgun. (L. Hannusch photo)

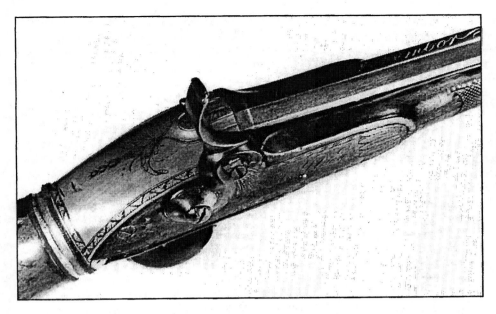

This butt-reservoir 44-caliber air-gun is a powerful muzzle-loading shotgun built by Joseph Schembor of Vienna, Austria, in the early 1800s. (L. Hannusch photo)

of admiring firsthand Larry's impressive airgun collection, spending in the process a few hours discussing many facets of airgun history. A truly memorable experience that I shall not soon forget.

Here is what Hannusch has to say about the realm of the air shotgun.

• • • •

For some unexplainable reason, the obscure world of the air shotgun seems to lie in a perpetual state of suspended misinformation. While most airgunners openly acknowledge the existence of the Crosman Trapmaster and the Yewha 3B, further discussion on the subject will usually elicit strong reprimands about the unsuitability of such talk in mixed company. Heaven forbid should someone actually collect them!

Perhaps this less-than-enthusiastic acceptance of this field of airgunning stems from a lack of understanding about the great diversity of specimens that have originated from all corners of the globe. This type is certainly not a recently developed pattern of airgun, as we shall soon discover upon closer examination.

Air Scattergun History

The Earliest Designs

To begin the story of the pneumatic scattergun, we must back up our calendars to over 300 years ago. A barrel-reservoir airgun in the Tøjhusmuseum in Copenhagen features a dual-barrel system in which a smaller liner is fitted into the larger outer bore. While this possibly was for the firing of two different balls, it seems quite probable that the outer bore was actually designed for use with shot. Other smoothbore examples of this barrel-reservoir design in air shotguns are also documented.

The next design that presumably saw use in shotgun form was the butt-reservoir, outside-lock type. Many of these smoothbore airguns have barrels that are removable, allowing

for the breech-loading of balls or shot. Though perhaps not developed exclusively as shotguns, it is logical to assume that the smoothbore feature of the outside-lock airgun naturally lent itself to early fowling and small game shotgunning.

Outside-lock airguns appeared in the last quarter of the 17th century and enjoyed continued production well into the third quarter of the 1700s. Generally speaking, they are among the most primitively constructed airguns of the antique pneumatic period. On occasion, however, specimens will show a higher level of refinement and quality.

As the airgun developed into the more refined forms of the ball- and butt-reservoir guns, the air shotgun remained a prominent type. Collectors encounter a number of specimens that were designed specifically for fowling and other sporting tasks. The earliest of the "new" breed of butt-reservoir guns can be traced to the Girandoni Austrian Model 1779 military air rifle.

Bartolomeo Girandoni is famous to collectors as the inventor of the Model 1779. This is one of the few historically documented airguns that was produced as a true military weapon. This 51-caliber repeater was indeed potent, but design and construction weaknesses led to its ultimate demise from the ranks of the Austrian army.

After Girandoni's death in 1799, many of his apprentices from his military contract days began to produce airguns based upon this repeater design. Many of these same gunsmiths also made single shot versions, some of which were smoothbore shotguns. Both breech- and muzzle-loading variations are known by such makers as J. Lowenz, J. Schembor and A. Wolf. Calibers usually ranged from 42 to 47. Such shotguns can be easily identified by observing the sight system, consisting of a bead front only.

19th Century Progress

An interesting and extremely rare variation of this butt-reservoir type is a double-barrel, side-by-side gun made by Joseph Mladek of Vienna, Austria, in the early 1800s. On this specimen, one barrel is a rifled repeater which is fed from an internal magazine; the other barrel is a smoothbore shotgun of about 410-bore. The gun is fitted with a shared single trigger and hammer. A selector switch located on the receiver determines which barrel is fired.

Another relatively rare form of air shotgun is the early British ball-reservoir type in which the rifled barrel was actually a removable liner. When the liner was removed, a larger smoothbore shotgun barrel was revealed. Among the examples encountered have been specimens made by London gunsmiths Thomas Bate, William Parker and John Utting.

The British pneumatics from the 1800-1850 period took the air shotgun to a new pinnacle of refinement. Both ball- and butt-reservoir types were made in which the maker supplied an interchangeable barrel system. In this way, the avid sportsman could change from a rifled bore, medium game airgun to a fowling piece in a matter of moments. Many two-barreled cased sets from this Golden Age of the Pneumatic Era are among the finest examples of airguns known today.

During this period, we also find the emergence of the air canes. Although they were made since the mid-1700s in various forms and countries, the English took the design to a new level of performance and compactness, which continued throughout the late 1800s and well into the first quarter of the next century.

Many of these air canes had both a rifled barrel liner and a smoothbore barrel designed for shot. These, too, can be considered air shotguns. A brochure from Edward Reilly, one of the most prolific British air cane makers of the 1850-1900 period, explained how to determine the proper amount of shot to be used for best results. His written explanation leaves no doubt that one of the air cane's intended purposes was that of a shotgun.

But the English were not the only game in town. A Frenchman named Paul Giffard was busy developing several airgun designs about this time. His earliest airguns date from the 1860s and were straight-rod pump pneumatics. Later, in the 1890s, he designed CO_2 gas airguns that used a refillable steel reservoir. Giffard had rifles, shotguns and pistols made to his specifications by Manufacture Francaise D'Armes et Cycles de Saint in St. Etienne, France.

All the Giffard CO_2 airguns used a turn-bolt tap-loading system. As the bolt was raised to the vertical position, a round hole in the top of the receiver was exposed to accept the ball. The Giffard shotguns were made very similarly, but instead had an elongated hole to accept the 8mm cardboard shotshell. The Giffard shotguns are much more rare than his rifles and comparable in rarity to his pistols. All were made for only a few years and were discontinued before the turn of the century.

20th Century Technology

The next shotgun to make a major impact was from an American named William Paul of Beecher, Illinois. He invented an air shotgun and was granted two patents in 1924 to protect the design.

The original patent called for an airgun that had the internal hammer cocking rod placed in the pistol grip of the stock. Pro-duction models, including the two different known variations, are made to the design of the second patent which has the cocking rod lying parallel to the barrel. Paul called his shotgun the Paul Model 420, which is interesting because it was actually a 410-bore gun.

The construction of the Paul shotgun involved a nickel-plated brass action and barrel (later versions were blued) which was fitted to a large, plain walnut stock. Knurled steel caps were threaded to both ends of the large-diameter air chamber which formed the receiver. To charge, the cocking rod is pushed back toward the shooter until the sear engages. The folding tab attached to the front end of the straight-rod pump is placed under the shooter's foot, and the entire gun is then moved in an up-and-down pumping motion for at least 100-150 pumps. The smoothbore barrel is then slid forward to allow breech-loading of the cardboard shotshells that Paul sold for his airgun. Several shots could then be fired before it was necessary to repump the gun.

The Paul Model 420 is a quite powerful airgun, capable of energy levels up to 80 foot pounds. Unfortunately, it was a rather complex gun and had a valve system that, though efficient, was especially complicated. It was a real labor of love for Paul to continue to produce and repair his shotguns from around 1923 through the mid-1930s. The Paul shotgun is known as one of the loudest firing airguns on the block—definitely too much report for use around the neighborhood.

Perhaps it was the Paul shotgun that inspired another American to produce his own air shotgun a few years later. Perry Franklin Vincent was an avid trapshooter from Hillsdale, Michigan, and received two U.S. patents for his airgun—the first in 1942 and the second in 1950. In addition to the air shotgun, Vincent also made some of his airguns in 177 and 25 calibers.

The Vincent shotgun used a more conventional pumping arrangement with the underlever-style pump arm. However, the Vincent's novel design was in using an extra tubular chamber between the barrel and the pump tube. This gave such extra reservoir capacity that multiple firings could be made from a single charging session, generally consisting of 150-200 pump strokes.

Vincent realized that perhaps the shooter may not want to take the time to pump the gun to full capacity. Consequently, he made a removable end cap for the middle tube which allowed the insertion of a wooden dowel. Because of the displacement afforded by this dowel, the total number of pumps needed to achieve full power were reduced, though at the expense of a reduced number of total shots as well.

The Vincent shotgun used a strange, bottom-ported, 410-bore, brass shotshell. It had a choked barrel and loaded via a bolt that could also cock the gun if desired. The guns had blued steel actions and barrels fitted to nice walnut stocks.

The Vincent shotgun is not quite as powerful as the Paul Model 420, though it is perhaps a bit more aesthetically pleasing to the eye. It was designed more as an economical training arm for the active trapshooter rather than for the hunter. But with energy levels in the 60+ foot pound range, it is no wimp. Its production period is thought to have been circa 1942-1955.

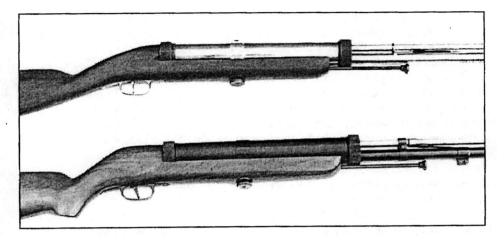

The Paul Model 420 shotgun was made in at least two major variations, the older model at the top. The brass pump tube supplies air to a large-diameter air reservoir. (L. Hannusch photo)

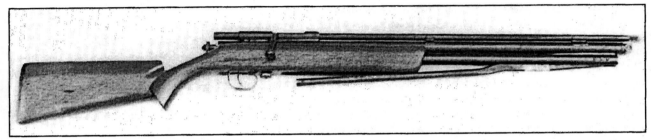

The Vincent air shotgun is a bolt-action-loading gun which uses the more familiar swing-arm pump lever. The large air-storage capacity is achieved by use of a double tube reservoir below the barrel. (L. Hannusch photo)

The Plainsman 28-S is basically a standard pump airgun chambered in a smoothbore 28-caliber. The cardboard shotshells sold with the gun came twenty-five to a box. (L. Hannusch photo)

Meanwhile, back in Europe during the 1930s, an air shotgun made in Italy was being produced. Called the Setter, this 28-gauge gun strongly resembled the Browning Auto 5. Although imported into England, it apparently was never offered for sale in the U.S.

The Setter used a pump system in which the barrel became the pump handle. By releasing the barrel at the breech, it would pivot at its midpoint, forming a "T" arrangement. The barrel thus became the handle for the pumping action to charge the gun.

After manually setting the blow-off valve, about 10-15 pumps were necessary to bring the Setter to full charge. The barrel could then be loaded with a brass shotshell filled with the shooter's favorite shot. Reloading the shells was a simple mat-ter of filling the brass tubes with loose shot and capping both ends with wads.

The Setter was a decent, full-size airgun, but valve problems (and probably numerous bent barrels) led to its demise. It is a difficult air shotgun to locate on today's collector market.

Post-War Developments

Just a few years after this, in 1948, an American firm began to make their own version of an air shotgun. This was Challenger Arms Co. of Eagle Rock, California, a division of the National Cart Co. (The National Cart Co. is well known as the makers of the Apache line of airguns.) The Challenger gun was sold as the Plainsman 28-S, which identified this airgun as a 28-caliber shotgun.

A standard underlever pump pneumatic with a choked smoothbore barrel, the Plainsman used a bolt-action loading design with a separate cocking action to strike the valve. The gun was adequately built and had a blued steel barrel and tube with an alloy frame. Stocks were usually beech, though walnut is sometimes encountered. Small cardboard tubes were loaded with #7 1/2 shot and formed the shotshell for the 28-S. Later marketing of the gun was handled by Healthways of Los Angeles.

Although the 28-S had lofty aspirations, it simply was not powerful enough to be much of a formidable contender. The relatively small bore (for a shotgun), coupled with stresses involved in the pumping mechanism, caused its limited sales and production. But today, these factors are some of the reasons for its popularity as a collector's item.

The Japanese were taking notice of the increased demand for CO_2 airguns. They copied Crosman's gas rifles and sold them under the tradename Taiyo Juki. Amid the various Taiyo Juki airguns, there is a model believed to be a gas shotgun that is marked "7mm Gas Gun Model 380." (The Model 380 is deceptive because this designation is used on several of their smaller caliber gas rifles.) It has an overall length of 44 1/4 inches and uses a two-cartridge gas system for power. Its classification as a shotgun has not been positively ascertained, though several clues lead to this possibility. First, it is a larger (.265-inch) caliber smoothbore, whereas all other Taiyo Juki airguns have rifled, smaller-bore barrels. Second, it is fitted with what appears to be a screw-on reducing choke, though it could be a thread protector for a missing silencer. The extended breech opening would allow for seating a short shotshell of some sort. However, the presence of a rear aperture sight remains a mystery, as does the full purpose of this unusual airgun.

There is no mistaking Crosman's entry in the world of the air shotgun with their Trapmaster 1100 in 1968. Built to resemble the Remington 1100 autoloading shotgun, Crosman deftly used the same numeric designation. It was a full-sized airgun with an overall length of 46 1/2 inches and a smoothbore 380-caliber barrel.

Two CO_2 gas cartridges were placed back-to-back within the lower gas tube. After puncturing the cartridges using the toggle device, the power level could be chosen from a low or high setting. The high setting would yield factory muzzle energies around 25 foot pounds.

The Trapmaster was designed as part of a Skeet-shooting set which consisted of an 1100, a target thrower, plastic break-apart targets and reloadable plastic shotshells. The shotshells were color-coded to easily identify the size of shot they contained.

The Trapmaster 1100 was one of the most thoroughly designed air shotguns ever made. Certainly not one of the most powerful, it was nonetheless easy to use and very functional for its intended purpose. It is unfortunate that Crosman discontinued the design in the early 1970s amid sales disappointments.

The decade of the 1970s brought a new wave of foreign-made air shotguns. Among the most famous of the Korean efforts was the 25-caliber Yewha 3B Dynamite. It was a solid, though plain, gun with a hardwood stock and Parkerized metalwork. The heart of its famed power was the straight-rod pump mechanism.

There's no denying this simple, yet effective pump system is capable of putting up the big numbers. The Paul 420 is an excellent example of its potential. The Yewha 3B is also powerful,

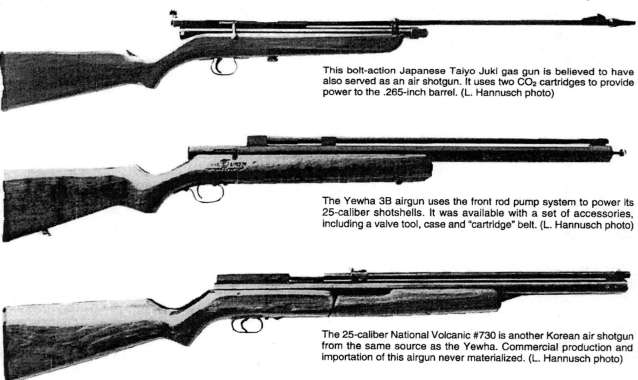

This bolt-action Japanese Taiyo Juki gas gun is believed to have also served as an air shotgun. It uses two CO_2 cartridges to provide power to the .265-inch barrel. (L. Hannusch photo)

The Yewha 3B airgun uses the front rod pump system to power its 25-caliber shotshells. It was available with a set of accessories, including a valve tool, case and "cartridge" belt. (L. Hannusch photo)

The 25-caliber National Volcanic #730 is another Korean air shotgun from the same source as the Yewha. Commercial production and importation of this airgun never materialized. (L. Hannusch photo)

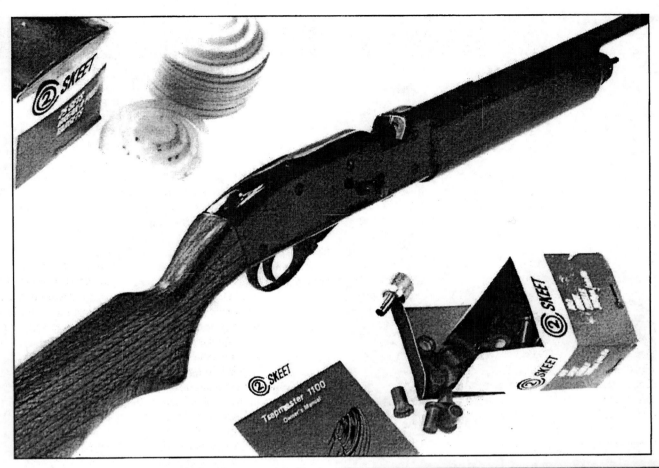

The Crosman Trapmaster 1100 was designed as a complete Skeet-shooting outfit. This 38-caliber gas gun has both low and high power settings. (L. Hannusch photo)

The Crosman 1100 is peppy enough to be used successfully against suburban mice and even rats at fairly close range. The trick is getting close enough to blast them!

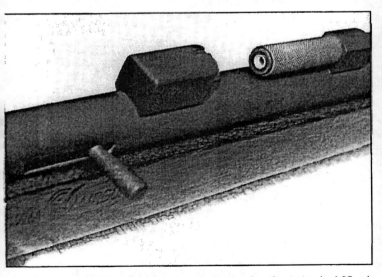

The Korean-made Yewha shotgun can also shoot standard 25-caliber diabolo pellets, delivering quite a hefty punch in the process.

Larry Hannusch, much to his chagrin, discovers that the big Farco gas shotgun is much too powerful for the Crosman plastic aerial targets. This 51-caliber brute can generate over 100 foot pounds of muzzle energy. (L. Hannusch photo)

especially when using a single 25-caliber projectile which can yield 40+ foot pounds of energy. The energy achieved with a shotshell loading would be greatly reduced, of course.

The problem with its effectiveness as a shotgun lies with its 1-inch shotshell, relatively long compared to its .25-inch bore. This has a tendency to reduce the efficiency of the power plant, yet it is still no slouch and evidently has been successfully used for years by muscular Koreans for hunting their native pheasants.

Another air shotgun that appeared about this same time from the same Korean source was the National Volcanic #730. This 25-caliber smoothbore airgun used the conventional underlever pump system and was solidly built with nicely blued, machined steel components. A blow-off valve formed the basis of the power plant, but the shotshells were identical to the Yewha shotshells. The National never reached the commercial U.S. market, and only a few prototypes are known to exist.

Today's Air Shotguns

Since the late 1970s, more air shotguns have appeared on the market than in all previous years combined. Most of these models have originated in the Philippines, where airguns have played a major role in the sporting arms scene because firearms have been prohibited for years.

Today, one of the most popular air shotguns is the Farco Air Shotgun—a powerful, bulk-filled CO_2 design currently imported by Air Rifle Specialists. The Farco is made by Giron Metal Craft of Manila, which also produces several different air rifles as well.

The Farco is a very large airgun, measuring over 48 inches in overall length. Its high power is achieved by the use of a long 30-inch barrel, coupled with a huge bore of .51-inch—com-

Jess Galan during tests with the powerful Farco CO_2-powered shotgun. This piece packs a real wallop!

The Daisy "Critter Gitter" shotgun pistol was unveiled in 1988, but, strangely, it was never marketed in the U.S., despite its obvious sales appeal and seeming practicality.

monly known as 28-gauge. The Farco uses a bolt-action system to cock and breech-load the brass shells. These 1-inch shells can hold nearly ¾-ounce of lead shot.

The Farco is realistically one of the most practical hunting air shotguns to come along in years. Experimentation with a variety of different loads consistently yields muzzle energies hovering around 100 foot pounds. Though not likely to win any local beauty contests, the Farco remains one of the truly popular air shotguns available on the market today.

A close cousin of the Farco is the Garco, a front rod pump type reportedly made by family relatives of the Farco clan. The Garco smoothbores are usually in 380-caliber, though other bore sizes apparently are available. The general fit and finish of this half-stock pneumatic appears to be a bit nicer than that seen on its cousin, the Farco.

Another innovative line of Filipino airguns is made by LD. Among a host of air rifles and pistols, LD also produces a line of "convertible" Model 380 air shotguns. In this type, a removable rifled liner is placed inside the shotgun barrel. This option permits rifle shooting until the liner is removed from the gun. At this point, the LD becomes a breech-loading 380-caliber shotgun.

LD shotguns use a standard, bulk-filled CO_2 design which has the gas storage reservoir placed below the barrel. The breech is pivoted and swings to one side to facilitate loading of the long brass shotshell. The external hammer is drawn back to cock the gun, which, in turn, allows the hammer to strike the exposed valve stem of the exhaust valve. The power is adequate, but a far cry from the Farco's sonic boom. The exception is the tremendous report from one of the scarce LD air shotguns chambered in a whopping 20-gauge configuration.

Many LD airguns are beautifully stocked with Filipino mahogany in a variety of configurations. In addition, LD's typical use of metal engraving, albeit rather coarse, is a nice touch for the airgunner who appreciates gas guns that are a bit unusual.

Numerous Filipino convertible air shotguns have been made which are very similar to the LD 380 swing-out breech designs. Among the multitudes listed are specimens known as Harlie's Apollo, Koffmanz Dakota and Rogunz Hawk. All of these are

bulk-filled CO_2 gas shotguns that use a rifled 22-caliber liner within a 38-caliber smoothbore shotgun barrel. However, several smaller makers have made powerful air shotguns that share the same 20-gauge caliber as the big LD shotguns.

There has even been a recent British air shotgun made by the famous Daystate airgun firm. This bolt-action cocking, precharged pneumatic used 3000+ psi air to propel the shot. The reloadable aluminum shotshells hold about 120 grains of lead shot, and the Daystate is capable of firing this heavy load to the tune of about 85 foot pounds. This all-blued steel wonder was reportedly part of a small batch run of only six shotguns made in the early 1980s.

Though not a long gun, no history of air shotgunning would be complete without mention of another semi-prototype from Daisy. This shotshell-shooting CO_2 pistol was called the Critter Gitter Model 807, made in 1988. It was chambered for a 38-caliber, non-reloadable cardboard shotshell to be offered in #1, #4 and #8 shot.

The purpose of this imported gun was for a "tackle box pistol" that could be used to dispatch snakes and other small animals at close range. With an overall length of 12 inches and a weight of just over 2 pounds, it was indeed a handy size. To the best of my recollection, the Critter Gitter is unique because it was the only shotshell-firing air pistol ever made.

The gas cartridge fits into the grip frame under the brown plastic grips. A bolt-action lever on the left side cocked the action in addition to sealing the chambered shotshell. Although not considered powerful, it nonetheless was respectable, considering the compact package. Most of the few prototypes that were made are now safely in the hands of collectors. No doubt, rogue snakes around the world rejoiced when Daisy dropped the project before commercial production actually began.

In this overview, we have only briefly highlighted air shotgun developments seen through the years. It is a vast subject covering a field of airgunning that is often misunderstood and rarely appreciated. Perhaps we can now begin to acknowledge that air shotguns do, indeed, deserve our respect, as they have continued to play a major role in the building of our richly diverse airgun heritage.

Chapter 8

Tracking The Trends in Airgun Ammunition

An overview of airgun ammo with special emphasis on pellet development, current trends and designs.

by J.I. Galan

Match-style flat-head pellets punch neat, easily scored holes in paper targets.

THE DEVELOPMENT OF airgun ammunition is a rather wide and sometimes complex topic that has been largely ignored by a good many airgun scribes, and I certainly must include myself among those guilty of that charge. This fairly widespread avoidance of the topic may be due, in part, to the fact that airgun ammo has not had the radical impact upon the course of human events that firearms ammunition has enjoyed. Another plausible reason for the sporadic coverage of this field may stem from the rather widespread perception that the airgun/ammunition relationship is heavily stacked in favor of the gun. After all, most airguns are self-contained, incorporating their own sources of power; the pellet, BB or dart is simply propelled by the mechanical force imparted by the gun itself. Whereas with firearms, the cartridge, not the gun, is what contains the power required to launch the bullet.

Of the three basic types of airgun ammo—BBs, darts and pellets—the latter are almost exclusively the type used these days in adult airguns. BBs and darts, while still immensely popular, are intended primarily for use in youth-oriented and fairly inexpensive general-purpose airguns having smooth bores. Darts, in particular, being made of steel, should *never* be used in airguns with rifled bores, because the rifling would be ruined in a very short time.

Pellet Origins

The hourglass-shaped airgun pellet, popularly known as the diabolo, is the most common and popular pellet design currently used around the world. As is so often the case in matters of airgun history, not much in the way of solid evidence has survived regarding the true origins of this projectile. Incidentally, the term diabolo is derived from the pellet's resemblance to the spool-shaped device used in an old European throwing game called Diabolo. Apparently originating in ancient Greece, the game was probably adopted by the Romans in due course, and as the Roman Empire spread out over much of Europe, so did this game with its strangely shaped projectile.

The diabolo-style pellet first made its appearance in England shortly after the turn of the century, although there is no hard evidence to credit one single individual or company with its adaptation to airguns. This pellet design was preceded by the

Careful testing from the bench with a variety of pellets will reveal an air rifle's favorite diet for peak performance.

parallel-side, felt-base airgun slug. Then, a hollow-base airgun slug was patented in the mid-1870s by the famous American airgun inventor Henry Marcus Quackenbush. These slugs gained a great deal of popularity and were made in several sizes between 177 and 22 calibers. They were a vast improvement over the much less accurate ball projectiles in general use prior to the mid-19th century.

As airgun shooting spread and gained in popularity, calibers began to standardize in the U.S., England and Germany during the late 1800s. As a result, the market for airgun pellets became a fairly lucrative business, and all sorts of variations—often nothing more than gimmicks of little practical value—began to appear. The standardized calibers fit into three major sizes: 177 (4.5mm) or No. 1 bore, 22 (5.5mm) or No. 2 bore, and 25 (6.35mm) or No. 3 bore. Some variations of these, particularly in the No. 1 bore range, became popular for certain guns—especially in Germany, where 4.4mm and 4.45mm guns were being manufactured. As a point of interest, 4.45mm translates into .175-inch, which is the nominal diameter of the steel BB gun so prevalent in the U.S. for many years. Shortly after World War II, the 20-caliber (5mm) was adopted and refined in the U.S. by Sheridan of Racine, Wisconsin. This caliber was confined to Sheridan guns for decades, until the early 1980s when European airgun manufacturers "discovered" the inherent ballistic advantages of the 20 and began to produce an ever-increasing variety of spring-piston guns in that caliber.

The Modern Airgun Pellet

The widespread use of rifling in adult-oriented airguns by the turn of the century was probably the most important factor leading to the adoption of the diabolo pellet. Straight-sided airgun slugs required far too much pressure behind them in order to move efficiently through a rifled bore and still produce acceptable velocities. The fairly large bearing surface of the slug against the rifling tended to cause too much friction, resulting in rather inferior performance. The diabolo pellet solved all that by providing an absolute minimum of contact between the pellet and the rifling due to its slim-waisted shape. With the diabolo pellet, the bottom section of the relatively thin, hollow base or skirt is the only part that engages the rifling, while at the same time providing an effective air seal. The head of the pellet is a few thousandths of an inch smaller in diameter than the base and merely rides the rifling lands with an absolute minimum of friction, acting as a guide in the process. In a properly designed diabolo pellet, most of the weight is up front in the head. This gives the pellet excellent stability in flight, even when shot out of a smoothbore airgun. It is also very important that the distance between the head and the bearing surface of the base be as long as possible—within reason—in order to provide stability.

Most airgun pellets are made of lead alloy. The manufacturing processes used these days usually involve swaging by computerized machinery. The dies used in these machines are generally the key to quality control. Batches of pellets punched by well-worn dies will not be as dimensionally consistent as those made in newer dies, and the differences in performance can be considerable, even when the same gun is used. Pellet manufacturers are aware of this problem and are extremely careful for the most part. However, the possibility of a bad batch of pellets falling through the cracks cannot be eliminated completely. This is one of the reasons why many serious target shooters and experimenters resize their pellets, in order to ensure dimensional uniformity and consistent performance.

Uniformity, Tolerance, Sizing

Uniformity, particularly in the skirt area, is the single most important factor affecting the pellet's behavior in flight. In the case of bulk-packed pellets, their usually thin, hollow bases can be easily deformed due to the softness of the lead. This is unavoidable and can occur even in the top brands. Incidentally, 177-caliber pellets are particularly sensitive to distortion, far more so than 22s. The 177 pellet has a greater surface area

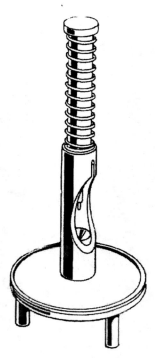

Spring-piston guns are particularly pellet sensitive, so optimum performance can only be obtained by trying a wide variety of good quality pellets.

The Beeman Automatic Pell Sizer has at its core the basic Pell Size unit. Both are ideal for precision resizing of pellets.

relative to weight than the 22, so any deformation of the smaller size will have a more pronounced influence on its performance.

Of course, pellets are sized to a particular set of tolerances at the factory. However, there can be very subtle, but significant, differences in the fit of them in a given airgun bore. Optimum accuracy, therefore, will not be realized unless pellets are custom-sized to the individual gun. There are other considerations as well. For instance, many British airgun bores and pellets are slightly oversized compared to their German counterparts. This means that British pellets often have a rather tight fit in most German airguns, while German pellets may have a relatively loose fit in the bores of British guns. American pellets, until fairly recently, have varied a great deal, depending upon the manufacturer, with some brands usually running a bit oversize, while others went in the opposite direction.

In the case of spring-piston guns, the relationship between pellet fit in the breech and peak pressure is of critical importance, because if the pellet is either too tight or too loose, optimum muzzle velocity and accuracy will not be achieved. Furthermore, if the pellet is grossly undersized, the gun itself can be damaged because there may not be enough air cushioning to slow down the piston at the end of its compression stroke.

Fortunately, pellet sizers offer a way to squeeze every possible micron of precision out of most airgun pellets, even economy-class pellets. A pellet sizer is simply a device incorporating a die made to highly precise tolerances. The pellets are run through the die, resizing the outside diameters of their skirts to a uniform diameter and eliminating, in the process, minor distortions which may be present due to bulk-packing and other factors. The accuracy obtained with resized pellets is often nothing short of outstanding. Groups fired with resized pellets are sometimes up to fifty percent smaller than those fired with the same, unsized pellets, from the same gun. Another advantage offered by these sizers is that they allow shooters to buy economy-class pellets—sometimes notorious for their distortion and fluctuation in tolerances—for plinking and general use, and still be able to shoot with accuracy that at times exceeds that of unsized top-brand pellets.

One of the best pellet sizers I have ever tried is the Beeman Automatic Pell Size Assembly. This handy, spring-loaded unit comes with a stand that allows fast and easy resizing of pellets, even while watching television. It's available in four calibers: 177, 20, 22 and 25. There are dies in several sizes—in .0010- and .0005-inch increments—available for each caliber, giving the shooter the opportunity to custom-fit each pellet type to a wide variety of airguns. The dies are made from solid graphite tool steel heat-treated to 60 Rockwell, while the plunger is made of Du Pont Delrin. The spring-loaded plunger automatically opens the feed trough after each sizing stroke.

Airguns are highly particular when it comes to their ammo diet. Spring-piston guns especially seem to be the most finicky in this area. To obtain the highest level of performance from a given airgun, the shooter should do a bit of experimenting with several brands and types of pellets to determine which ones give the best results. Resizing can further fine-tune the performance of that gun.

Pellet Styles

There is no question that the boom in airgun popularity of recent years has brought forth a veritable flood of pellets, many of which are intended for specific applications. The round-head or so-called English-style pellet has been the most popular design since the diabolo pellet appeared nearly a hundred years ago. The round-head pellet is ideal for general use in both rifles as well as pistols and is available in a huge variety of brands and prices. Another widely used pellet is the match or flat-head type, which is really a highly specialized style. This type was designed for cutting neat, clean holes in paper targets that can be scored easily, just like wadcutter bullets. Therefore, the match pellet is universally used in all kinds of serious paper-punching airgun competition.

In addition to the above types, there are also pointed, hollow-point, ogival or bullet-shaped pellets, as well as combinations of all of the above head shapes. Most of them are intended for field use, such as small game hunting, Field Target and metallic silhouette shooting. All of the major airgun importers in the U.S. offer a rather wide selection of quality pellets in the various calibers, affording the dedicated airgunner quite an array of ammo for different applications.

As for hollowpoints, there are some truly outstanding performers out there. The Beeman Crow Magnum is one of these, offering a heavier pellet with a gaping cavity up front that permits truly impressive expansion when used against live targets. In fact, it is not unusual for these pellets to turn themselves almost inside out upon impact with the animal, transferring a great deal of kinetic energy. Beeman Crow Magnums, as well as the Beeman Silver Bear (another hollowpoint design), are currently available in all four calibers.

Dynamit Nobel-RWS offers a wonderful hollowpoint pellet, the RWS Super-H-Point. This fairly lightweight pellet is available in 177 and 22, and is also a proven stopper. In addition, it delivers near-match accuracy, another important consideration in a pellet intended for hunting applications.

Another real shocker among hollowpoint pellets is the Lamprey MAXI-SHOK hollow-head from Vortek Products. As their description suggests, these pellets have a huge cavity up front that causes them to mushroom tremendously upon entering an animal. In fact, these pellets appear to be made backward—with the apparent base actually being the head—so the shooter must be careful to insert them correctly in the gun. Furthering this impression is the Lamprey's solid concave base, which tends to limit this pellet's undeniable effectiveness to fairly short range.

Unleaded Pellets

The last dozen years or so have also witnessed the introduction of composite pellets from England, made of materials other than lead. The first of these was the Prometheus, which is still

Dynamit Nobel-RWS has carried a comprehensive variety of top-notch RWS pellets from the world-renowned German maker over the years.

Daisy's five-shot Pellet Clips are a neat idea. They can be used in some highly popular Power Line multi-pump pneumatics in 177- and 22-caliber.

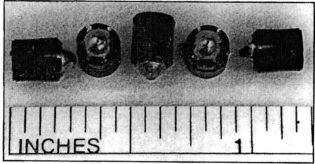

The SABO consisted of a sub-caliber, bullet-shaped projectile encased in a synthetic sabot that engaged the rifling.

The Sussex SABO pellet was a great idea, initially marketed around the mid-1980s in England.

available and consists of a straight-sided—in 177-caliber—synthetic skirt mated to a bullet-shaped head made of zinc alloy. The now-discontinued Titan Black pellet utilized a similar design, except it was heavier than the rather light Prometheus. Due precisely to their relatively light weight, Prometheus pellets develop much higher muzzle velocities than regular lead pellets of the same caliber. That, coupled with the hard zinc alloy and head shape, also renders them capable of impressive penetration at short to moderate distances. Heavier pellets, however, perform better than the Prometheus at longer ranges due to superior velocity retention and less wind drift. Incidentally, Prometheus pellets are also offered with truncated heads in 177-caliber, for those who prefer a semi-flat-head configuration in this particular brand.

Another remarkable composite pellet to come out of England during the mid-1980s was the SABO. This highly intriguing projectile was really a sub-caliber, copper-coated lead *bullet* carried in a synthetic sabot—shades of the Remington Accelerator bullet—capable of developing tremendous velocity and

penetration, particularly when shot out of magnum-class air rifles. By virtue of its weight/shape ratio, the SABO had a comparatively high ballistic coefficient that ensured good performance even at extended ranges. Unfortunately, the SABO is no longer made, which is a real pity given its impressive ballistics. Its high cost, compared to most other airgun pellets, was one of the main causes of its demise.

One of the latest composite designs introduced by the British is called Paragon, initially made in 22-caliber, with 177 slated to follow a bit later. By the way, the Paragon pellet is also made by the same manufacturer of Prometheus pellets. The Paragon Z2, the most popular of three versions offered, has a dome-shaped zinc alloy head coupled to a synthetic body and an average weight of just 11.5 grains, all of which translates into much greater muzzle velocities than with conventional pellets of the same caliber. Thus, the Paragon pellet seems to be ideally suited to hunting applications, because it offers increased velocity, good penetration and shock—the latter due to its flattened dome head. On the downside, how-

The 22-caliber Paragon Z2 has a zinc alloy dome head and weighs just 11.5 grains.

Paragon's Z1 and C1 pellets have bullet-shaped heads of zinc and copper, respectively.

The British Champion Fireball has a straight-walled antimony/lead body with a zinc-plated steel ball up front.

Champion also offers the Ballistic pellet, another super-penetrator that hides a steel ball bearing at its head. Notice this pellet's peculiar four-ring design.

European repeating air pistols, like this 4.5mm Gamo AF-10, traditionally use lead shot instead of steel BBs.

The 22-caliber Cobra Magnum pellet, distributed by Air Rifle Specialists, is a real heavyweight at 26.4 grains. It is, of course, intended mainly for high-power airsporters.

ever, are Paragon's relatively high cost and the fact that, like all pellets having a synthetic bearing surface, this one should be shot only in lead-free barrels. To do otherwise may seriously impair performance. Incidentally, Paragon's Z1 and C1 pellets have bullet-shaped heads, with the Z1 made of zinc, the C1 of copper. Their weights vary considerably, with the 22-caliber Z1 at 14.5 grains, the C1 17.5 grains. These pellets are available from John Groenewold in Illinois and from Pelaire Products. Besides their obvious ballistic properties, all of these composite, non-lead pellets offer an environmentally friendly alternative for airgunners.

Pelaire also carries the 22-caliber Champion Fireball, a most unusual straight-sided British pellet. It weighs 20 grains and is touted as being "armour-piercing," given its zinc-plated steel ball head atop an antimony/lead alloy body. A slightly different variation on this theme is the Champion Ballistic pellet, which carries a small steel ball bearing within its lead alloy head.

The variety in pellet offerings these days has spread to all of the standard airgun calibers as well. Whereas barely a dozen years ago most pellet designs concentrated around 177-caliber, the current proliferation includes 20 and 22 calibers. Even the big No. 3 Bore (25-caliber), long regarded as obsolete by some folks in the airgun industry, has now been resurrected, with an ever-increasing number of airguns currently offered in the 1/4-inch bore. Among the most prominent of these are the potent Beeman Kodiak, Beeman RX-1 and the RWS models 48 and 52; all extremely potent and ideally suited to small game hunting.

Worldwide Variety

No one pellet, however, is ideal for all uses, and research goes on at a fast pace in the U.S. and Europe. Even the Japanese have long been recognized for their top-quality pellets, such as the excellent Jet and Silver Jet, made by Hasuike Seisakusho KK and available for many years in the U.S. under the Beeman label. Beeman also imports other world-class pellets, such as those made by H&N in Germany. Dynamit Nobel-RWS also imports a comprehensive selection of top-

World-class 10-meter shooters use only individually packaged match pellets of the highest quality. RWS has been one of the top names in this demanding field.

quality RWS pellets, including the superb 177-caliber R10 Match, available in two weights and *four* different head diameters!

For their part, American pellet manufacturers realized some time back that mediocre pellets in top-notch airguns usually give mediocre results. Domestic makers, therefore, have moved effectively in recent years to produce a variety of truly outstanding home-grown fodder. In some cases, these pellets rival the quality and performance of some of the best field-grade offerings from overseas. One prime example is the superb Crosman Premier. This domed pellet was designed from the ground up and is intended for Field Target shooting, an area where it has already earned an enviable reputation for hard-hitting precision. The Premier is available in a choice of 7.9 and 10.5 grains for 177 caliber, as well as in 20 and 22 calibers, both at 14.3 grains.

(Right) The Crosman Premier is a truly outstanding Field Target pellet. It is available (left to right) in 20, 22 and two different weights in 177-caliber.

(Below) RWS R10 Match pellets are world-class and come in individually packaged foam sheets that protect them against the slightest deformation.

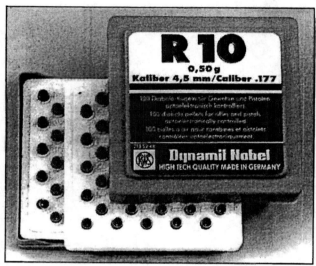

The Marksman Field Target Special pellet comes in 177-, 20- and 22-caliber.

To give an idea of the variances in performance among some of the many different pellets available, I asked Harry Steiber, owner of Pelaire Products, to submit a ballistic performance table of many of the pellets he sells. Pelaire Products carries a huge selection of airgun pellets in all four main calibers from around the world. So wide is the selection that they even carry various types of 30-caliber pellets, for those lucky enough to have a custom airgun in this esoteric caliber.

The rifle used in Steiber's tests was a Whiscombe JW75, a magnum-class, high-performance rifle of impeccable quality. His tests were fired over a period of six weeks, with weather conditions naturally differing among the various sessions and having a slight effect upon the results. All of the velocities listed in the Ballistic Performance Table reflect the averages obtained from ten-shot strings.

"It is interesting to note," writes Steiber, "that the 20-caliber Crosman Premier retains more of its downrange velocity than any other pellet tested. This can be attributed to three things: the pellet's high weight (14.3 grains), its small frontal area and the sleek aerodynamic shape given it by its creator, Robert Holtz of the Crosman Corporation." The much-talked-about efficiency of a larger caliber, however, can also be clearly seen in the table. Using the same action and just changing the caliber, we find the 22-caliber Premier is leaving the muzzle 55 fps *faster* than the smaller 20-caliber Premier of equal weight.

Steiber further states: "It is also interesting to point out that the 25-caliber pellets retained a large amount of their muzzle energy, due to their great weight, out to the 10 yards tested, but rapidly shed energy downrange due to a larger frontal area and their often poor wind-cheating designs. This fact can play havoc with some of those computerized trajectory programs that have become popular, rendering them virtually useless."

Although the Table gives an excellent bird's-eye view of the basic performances given by several popular pellets in the main calibers, it is only a rough guide to this vast area of experimentation. The truly dedicated airgun ballistician can now take advantage of a complete set of airgun ballistic tables published by FSI (Firearms & Supplies, Inc.). These extremely comprehensive tables come in a three-ring binder and are computer-generated, giving all sorts of useful data on the trajectories of various pellet designs and calibers at different velocities, according to their specific ballistic coefficients. Although not cheap, the FSI Airgun Ballistic Tables are a virtual must for anyone with a scientific interest in the topic of airgun pellets and their ballistics.

As the variety and sophistication of airgun pellets continues to increase, there is no doubt that the sport of airgun shooting in general is bound to benefit. They say that variety is the spice of life, and in the area of airgun ammo, there certainly is enough variety to keep us busy for a very long time.

BALLISTIC PERFORMANCE TABLE

	Wgt. Grs.	@Muzzle MV	Ft. Lbs.	@10 yds. MV	Ft. Lbs.	%MV Ret.	Loss (fps)
177-Caliber							
Prometheus	6.0	1255	20.9	1080	15.5	86.0	175
Beeman Silver Bear	6.8	1180	21.0	1020	15.7	86.4	160
Crosman Premier	7.9	1100	21.2	995	17.3	90.4	110
Beeman Silver Jet	8.1	1090	21.3	970	16.9	88.9	120
H&N Match	8.2	1070	20.8	940	16.2	87.8	130
Bisley Superfield	8.5	1045	20.6	940	16.6	89.9	105
Beeman Silver Sting	8.8	1030	20.7	910	16.1	88.3	120
Beeman Crow Magnum	8.8	1025	20.5	885	15.3	86.3	140
Marksman F.T.S.	8.8	1025	20.5	915	16.3	89.2	110
Lamprey Maxi-Shok	8.9	1010	20.1	875	15.1	86.6	135
RWS Supermag	9.3	985	20.0	860	15.2	87.3	125
Crosman Premier	10.5	920	19.7	875	17.8	95.1	45
Bisley Premier	10.6	920	19.9	830	16.2	90.2	90
Beeman Kodiak Match	10.6	915	19.7	850	17.0	93.2	65
Beeman Silver Arrow	11.9	850	19.0	780	15.4	91.7	70
20-Caliber							
Beeman Laser	8.8	1100	23.6	945	17.4	85.9	155
Beeman Bear	9.6	1050	23.5	905	17.8	86.1	145
Beeman Silver Bear	10.1	1030	23.7	920	18.9	89.3	110
Beeman Silver Jet	10.7	1005	24.0	915	19.8	91.0	90
H&N Ultra Match	10.8	1000	23.9	885	18.7	88.5	115
Beeman Silver Sting	10.5	1000	23.3	895	18.6	89.5	105
Marksman F.T.S.	11.1	975	23.4	910	20.4	93.3	65
Bisley Superfield	11.5	965	23.7	885	20.0	91.7	80
Beeman Crow Magnum	12.6	925	23.9	835	19.5	90.2	90
Champion Exorcet	12.2	915	22.6	845	19.3	92.3	70
Beeman Kodiak	13.3	880	22.8	835	20.5	94.8	45
Crosman Premier	14.3	835	22.1	810	20.8	97.0	25
Sheridan Aero-Jet	14.3	830	21.8	800	20.3	96.3	30
Sheridan Cylindrical	15.1	815	22.2	755	19.1	92.6	50
Beeman Silver Arrow	16.0	790	22.1	710	17.9	89.8	80
22-Caliber							
Prometheus	8.8	1150	25.8	980	18.7	85.2	170
H&N Hollow Point	12.9	955	26.2	820	19.2	85.8	135
H&N Match	13.8	920	25.9	805	19.8	87.5	115
RWS Superdome	14.4	900	25.9	810	20.9	90.0	90
Crosman Premier	14.3	890	25.1	850	22.9	95.5	40
Bisley Bullet	14.4	890	25.3	830	22.0	93.2	60
Bisley Superfield	15.0	875	25.5	800	21.3	91.4	75
Marksman F.T.S.	15.0	870	25.2	815	22.1	93.6	55
Beeman Silver Jet	15.2	860	24.9	790	21.0	91.8	70
Beeman Silver Sting	15.8	855	25.6	780	21.3	91.2	75
Beeman Ram Jet	16.1	840	25.2	770	21.2	91.6	70
Lamprey Maxi-Shok	16.5	830	25.2	760	21.1	91.5	70
Beeman Silver Arrow	16.8	825	25.3	760	21.5	92.1	65
Beeman Crow Magnum	18.6	775	24.8	700	20.2	90.3	75
25-Caliber							
Beeman Laser	17.7	840	27.7	715	20.0	85.1	125
Lincoln Jeffries	18.8	830	28.7	720	21.6	86.7	110
BSA Pylarm	18.8	825	28.4	725	21.9	87.8	100
Milbro Rhino	19.1	820	28.5	735	22.9	89.6	85
Beeman Ultra Match	21.1	780	28.5	685	21.9	87.8	95
Champion Apollo	21.4	765	27.8	695	22.9	90.8	70
Beeman Silver Ace	22.4	740	27.2	685	23.3	92.5	55
Beeman Ram Jet	24.3	710	27.2	650	22.8	91.5	60
Beeman Silver Arrow	24.6	700	26.7	655	23.4	93.5	45
Bisley Superfield	24.6	695	26.4	660	23.8	94.9	35
Beeman Silver Sting	25.1	685	26.1	640	22.8	93.4	45
Beeman Crow Magnum	26.0	665	25.5	615	21.8	92.4	50
Beeman Silver Bear	26.7	655	25.4	610	22.0	93.1	45
Beeman Ram Point	27.2	645	25.1	625	23.5	96.8	20

Dynamit Nobel-RWS also distributes three other outstanding pellets of moderate cost. From left: RWS Club, RWS Hobby and RWS Superpoint.

Beeman's Ram Point pellet is available in 25-caliber only and weighs a whopping 27.1 grains.

The Vortek Lamprey has a solid concave base and a gaping cavity up front (arrow). It comes in calibers 177, 20 and 22.

The Beeman Silver Jet is a proven performer afield. It was available in all four main airgun calibers until very recently.

Chapter 9

Pneumatic Guns: The Inside Story

A unique glimpse inside the world of pneumatic gun engineering by a veteran airgun designer.

by Sig Liepins
Introduction by J.I. Galan

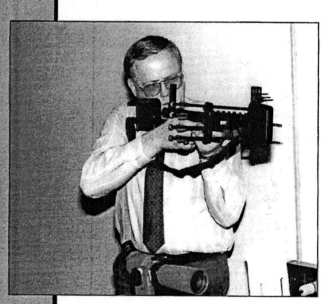

The master designer himself testing a most intriguing prototype airgun. Sigurds Liepins has had a highly successful engineering career with America's two largest airgun manufacturers.

TALK TO ANY hard-core airgun enthusiast and, chances are, sooner or later, he will confess to toying with the idea of designing at least one airgun at some point in his life. I know, because I have been there myself, devoting quite a few hours to the design—or so I thought—of a real airgun masterpiece. But that was many, many years ago.

Designing a good, solid airgun capable of consistently performing a task takes far more, however, than a set of fancy-looking sketches or renderings. A great deal of barebones math and physics is irrevocably linked to the design of any airgun capable of producing reliable performance, regardless of its type of power plant. In the specific case of pump-up pneumatic guns, for instance, a great deal of engineering know-how must be delicately balanced in order to make that pellet or BB do such a seemingly simple thing as leave the barrel when the trigger is pulled.

Thus, when the idea for this tome began to take shape, I thought that it would be absolutely nifty to go right to the source—an honest-to-goodness airgun engineer who would, in his own words, give us an insight into the many details affecting the design of a multi-pump pneumatic rifle.

The fellow whom I tapped for the task is one of those largely unknown, unsung heroes who labor behind the scenes—in this case, at the drawing boards—of the American airgun industry. He is responsible nonetheless in a more or less direct manner for some of the most popular airguns that this country has produced during the last quarter of a century.

His name is Sigurds Liepins, a graduate in mechanical engineering from the Rochester Institute of Technology who spent over twenty years at Crosman Air Guns, both as chief engineer and vice president of engineering until the late 1980s. Following that, Mr. Liepins was director of engineering at Daisy Mfg. Co., Crosman's long-time competitor. He has also been active on many airgun committees and projects, including the voluntary airgun safety standards committee formed under the auspices of the American Society for Testing and Materials. Mr. Liepins is not only a charter member, but past chairman and current active member of the subcommittee on airgun industry standards, in which yours truly has also served for a number of years. Here he gives us a rather

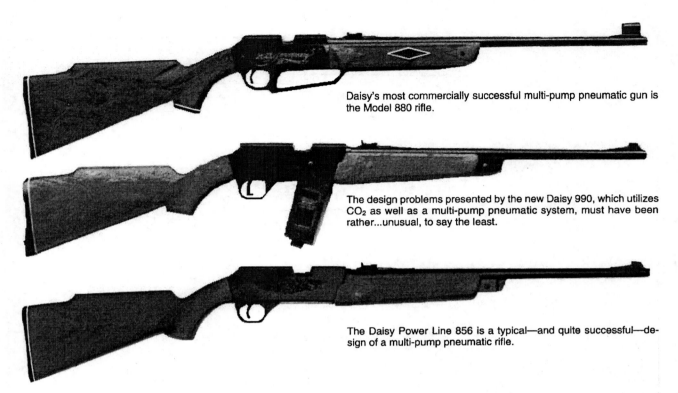

Daisy's most commercially successful multi-pump pneumatic gun is the Model 880 rifle.

The design problems presented by the new Daisy 990, which utilizes CO_2 as well as a multi-pump pneumatic system, must have been rather...unusual, to say the least.

The Daisy Power Line 856 is a typical—and quite successful—design of a multi-pump pneumatic rifle.

unique look at the complexities of the pneumatic power plant from an engineer's perspective.

• • • •

The pump or pneumatic airgun has a rich history. The often acknowledged father of the airgun, Guter of Nurenberg, supposedly designed and built the first modern airgun way back around 1560, according to some. Since that time, airguns in calibers from .12- to .775-inch have been built. These have ranged from low-velocity "toy plinkers" to the high-powered military rifles used by the Austrians against Napoleon in the late 1700s and early 1800s.

Today's airguns are designed to satisfy three basic shooters' needs: 1) informal target shooting or plinking; 2) competition target shooting; 3) pest control and/or small game hunting. Within this spectrum, airgun prices vary from a low of around $30 for a low-velocity plinker to $1300 or more for a competition-grade target rifle. Ammunition, too, is as varied as the calibers and the desired uses by the shooter. The most popular ammunition includes steel or lead balls (BBs), pellets of both hard and soft lead in calibers ranging from 177 all the way to 25, and even larger in some special custom-made guns.

Pneumatic airguns come in a variety of sizes and configurations. The complexities of operation are too numerous to mention, but most of them utilize a piston which pushes air into a reservoir valve containing a smaller volume than that of the pump stroke. In this dissertation, for purposes of illustration, I picked a currently popular pneumatic airgun made in the United States by Daisy, the Model 856 Power Line. The internal components and functions are typical of many pneumatics on the market today.

Starting with the pump (see Figure 1), this mechanism can be broken down into four main parts: *pump assembly, pump tube, piston* and *oil wiper*. By opening and closing the forearm, the piston is moved back and forth along the pump tube. In the open position, air is allowed to enter the pump tube. When the

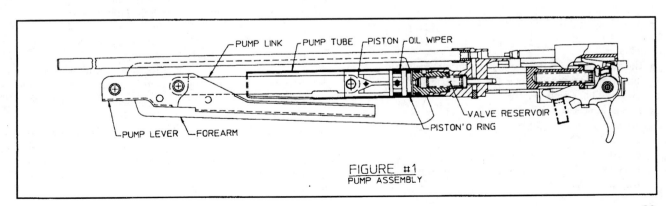

FIGURE #1
PUMP ASSEMBLY

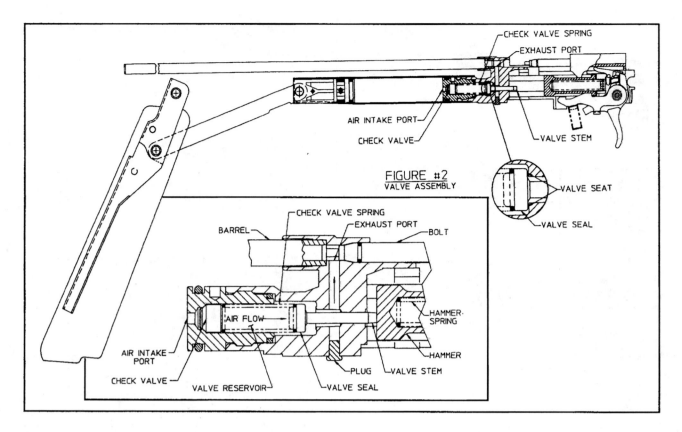

FIGURE #2
VALVE ASSEMBLY

forearm is in the closed position, compressed air is pushed into the valve reservoir.

With a multiple-pump air gun, the force required to move the piston back and forth increases with each stroke. As the pressure in the valve reservoir rises, so does the velocity of the shot to be fired.

The pump mechanism is an extremely rugged and efficient unit. This ruggedness is built into the pump assembly, and the efficiency is derived from the piston's O-ring, oil wipe and pump tube areas. Because efficiency dictates higher pressures, which translate to higher velocities, a few comments on efficiency are necessary.

Efficiency is best described as the ability of the piston O-ring to seal against the inside wall of the pump tube, thus trapping air and compressing it into the valve reservoir.

In a pump-up pneumatic gun, there are a number of variables that affect efficiency:

- The inside finish of the pump tube. The finer the finish, the less dirt and rust, therefore, the higher the efficiency obtained.
- The piston O-ring's finish and material. Proper size, excellent finish on the outer diameter and good material selection also allow higher efficiency.
- Proper lubrication. When everything else is at its optimum efficiency, the lubricant plays the most important part. Selection and application of a good lubricant can mean a difference of over 150 fps on your pneumatic gun's peak velocity. In other words, at ten pumps, an increase of from 500 all the way up to 650 fps.

At this point, the oil wiper plays an extremely important part, too, as it insures proper lubricant distribution in the tube through which the pump cup passes. Daisy recommends two to three drops of oil on the oil wiper only every 250 shots. Over-oiling will not help as much as hinder, because it will gum up the valve reservoir. Under-oiling will decrease pump efficiency and prematurely wear out the piston O-ring and pump assembly.

A word of caution, however. Never put oil in front of the piston O-ring, as it may cause extremely hard pumping and the eventual failure of the pump mechanism.

The next area to cover is the heart of the pneumatic system— the valve (see Figure 2).

The valve is simply a high-pressure storage tank which is capable of storing more pressure with each pump stroke and then instantly releasing this air when the trigger is pulled. The valve is designed in harmony with the rest of the system in order to obtain maximum performance or velocity.

The valve consists of seven basic parts:

Air intake port: the passage through which air compressed by the pump assembly enters the valve body.

Check valve: the unit which allows the compressed air to enter the valve body during the compression pump stroke. It then closes to trap the air inside while the pump is returned to the open position.

Check valve spring: closes the check valve to trap the compressed air.

Valve stem assembly: consists of a valve seal which is usually a tough, pliable seal material. It keeps the compressed air from escaping until the trigger is pulled.

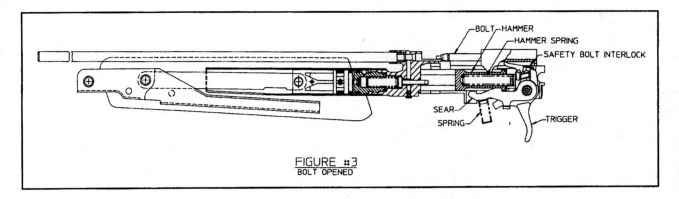

FIGURE #3
BOLT OPENED

Valve stem: retains the seal. Pulling the trigger releases a force which moves the seal inward and allows the compressed air to escape.

Valve seat: a finely machined or precision die-cast piece against which the seal is allowed to push in order to trap the air under pressure.

Exhaust port: the passage through which compressed air is directed from the valve into the barrel of the gun.

Putting this all together, as the piston compresses the air, the force of the compressed air will eventually exceed the force of the check valve spring. This allows the check valve to open and the compressed air to enter the valve reservoir. When the pump stroke is completed, the piston is moved to the open position, and the check valve will then close, trapping the compressed air in the valve.

As the gun is pumped repeatedly, more air is compressed into the valve and higher and higher pressure is created. However, as the pressure increases in the valve reservoir, the piston loses its efficiency to compress more air because of seal limitations and the pressure will peak out. This is why most manufacturers recommend a maximum number of pumps, as further pumping will not significantly increase the performance of the gun.

Once the valve is charged, the gun can be loaded and fired. To accomplish this (see Figure 3), the bolt is opened so a BB or pellet can be fed into the barrel chamber. In most pneumatic guns, this backward travel of the bolt also cocks the gun by pulling the hammer (striker) back against a spring. At the extreme rear position, a sear pops up in front of the hammer, holding it firmly in place.

The Daisy 856 has a safety bolt interlock. This unique device will lock the trigger when the bolt is in the rear or load position, thus making the gun inoperable until the bolt is closed. At this point, the safety bolt interlock swings free, so the trigger can be pulled.

The sear is an independent member of the trigger, which allows the gun to be cocked while the trigger is locked by the safety. When the trigger is pulled, the sear moves downward, releasing the spring-loaded hammer. Upon striking the valve stem (see Figure 4), the hammer releases the compressed air by pushing the valve seal momentarily out of position. The compressed air rushes out of the valve and is channeled by the exhaust port to the BB or pellet, pushing it out of the barrel.

A delicate balance exists between the pump and the valve assemblies in order to obtain maximum efficiency. The right amount of pressure and volume must exist in order to ensure the maximum velocity out of any given pneumatic system. Hence, the very simple formula $P_1V_1 = P_2V_2$, or pressure times volume of the pump assembly equals pressure times volume of the valve assembly. In other words, the more you put into the system, the more you will get from the system. As previously mentioned, the major obstacles to achieving higher velocities are pump efficiency, shooter strength to pump higher pressures, and the flow of released high-pressure air to propel the projectile out of the barrel. The shortest, most direct air path from the valve to the barrel will result in more efficient, higher-velocity shots. Again, bends and obstructions in the path of the air flow will reduce efficiency, making the high-pressure air react in a turbulent flow. Therefore, eliminating as many of the restrictions the air has to go through and around will create a more laminar flow, resulting in increased efficiency.

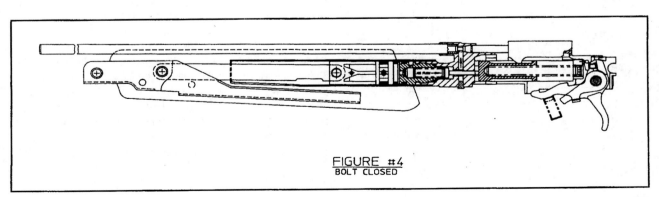

FIGURE #4
BOLT CLOSED

Chapter 10

Budget-Priced Airguns And Accessories

You don't necessarily have to spend a small fortune to enjoy the rewards of airgunning.

by J.I. Galan

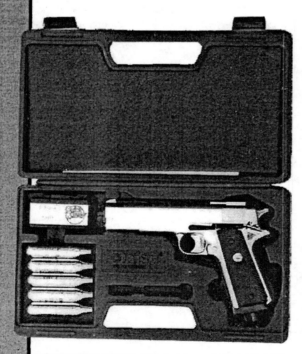

Daisy offers several of its handguns in Pistol Pak kits, complete with ammo, CO₂ and other goodies, all in a convenient moulded carrying case.

PART OF THE appeal of airguns stems from their huge practicality under various circumstances and in many places where firearms would be totally out of the question. Indeed, airguns are ideal for a wide variety of limited-area shooting applications such as target practice, safety and marksmanship training, plinking, pest control and small game hunting. Cost effectiveness is an important factor, too. Compared to the operational cost of firearms, airguns really make the most of your hard-earned dollars, giving you far more bang for your buck, one might say.

As we have seen thus far in this tome, however, airguns come in all types and, quite often, with price tags that can do some serious damage even to a well-stocked pocketbook. In fact, during the last few years, the prices of many airguns—particularly the adult-oriented types—have soared to levels that were hard to imagine as recently as a decade ago. While inflation and other economic factors surely have played a part in this dramatic escalation, a big share of the blame must go to the super-sophisticated technology that seems to have taken over entire sectors of the airgun industry. This is certainly the case in the area of precharged pneumatic guns, particularly those made in the U.K., although a similar situation also applies in the field of world-class match airguns produced in Germany, which often retail for shockingly steep figures.

Simply perusing current issues of airgun-related publications, as well as the latest catalogs dealing with many super high-tech airguns from overseas, will give you a good idea of how much you can expect to pay for many of those fancy pellet blasters. In the field of British precharged pneumatic rifles, for example, even the most basic model can set you back around $1000—and that's without any accessories and/or sights, since most of these precharged pneumatics are intended for use with telescopic sights only. The more refined models among the precharged genre can retail for well over $2000—again, without any accessories and devoid of sights. By the time you throw in the cost of a good scope, air tank, regulator, special charging connector, etc., your bankroll can be seriously depleted, even before the first shot is fired.

World-class match airguns from Germany can also punch big holes in one's wallet. Most of these super-accurate, totally recoilless rifles and pistols start in the $1200 price range and

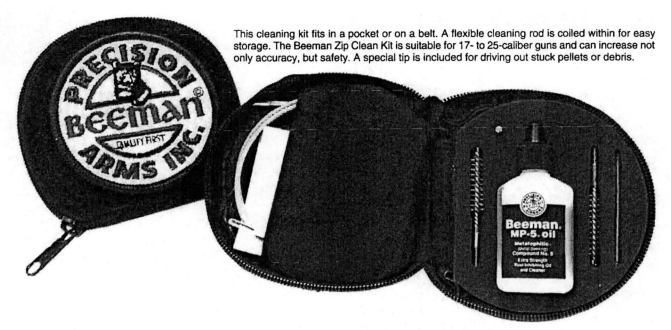

This cleaning kit fits in a pocket or on a belt. A flexible cleaning rod is coiled within for easy storage. The Beeman Zip Clean Kit is suitable for 17- to 25-caliber guns and can increase not only accuracy, but safety. A special tip is included for driving out stuck pellets or debris.

the muzzle, the rod must have a barrel bushing to prevent rubbing of the extremely critical barrel crown area. Also, flexible cleaning rods are now available which may be rolled up into a small pouch. These are especially handy because they are easily taken into the field and encourage cleaning when it is most needed. And these devices may also be used in the field to clear out debris or a stuck pellet. Whatever rod is used, it must be very thoroughly wiped between each stroke. Use only an approved cleaner/degreaser, never a regular firearm bore cleaner (such as Hoppe's #9, etc.), as such solvents may damage seals and cause dangerous dieseling. Follow the moist patches with dry ones until no trace of oil is seen. When cleaning the bore, use only damp patches, not wet; avoid getting fluids into the action.

For storage, clean the bore as above and leave it with a light coating of polarizing oil such as Beeman MP-5, WD-40, etc. Do not use polarizing oils on airguns made of brass; binding may result. A few regular or felt cleaning pellets will have to be shot through a cleaned bore before it can be expected to return

to its zero. Felt cleaning pellets may be used, particularly between strings of target shots, to keep a bore impeccably clean. However, it is my conviction that felt cleaning pellets alone are not sufficient for cleaning an airgun bore.

The release of compressed CO_2 or compressed air, in guns using such gas as a propellant, can cause condensation in bores. This will eventually pit and rust steel barrels, effectively ruining the accuracy and much of the value of the gun. To prevent this, fire two felt cleaning pellets or draw a cleaning patch, moistened with *polarizing* oil, through the steel bore *after every shooting session*. It is advisable to do this before shooting any pellets from your new gun. This will leave a protective coating of oil in the barrel before any condensation touches it.

Performing General Maintenance

Proper accuracy and power are impossible to obtain without a properly functioning breech seal. The breech seal is the washer or O-ring that seals the space between the compression

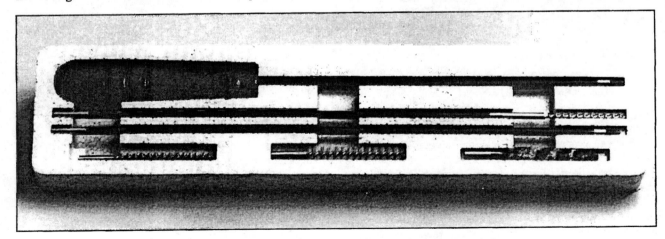

The RWS 22-caliber Deluxe Cleaning Kit has a three-piece coated rod, plus suitable tip accessories. This kit can be used on 22 airguns as well as rimfires, but the brass brush is intended only for the latter.

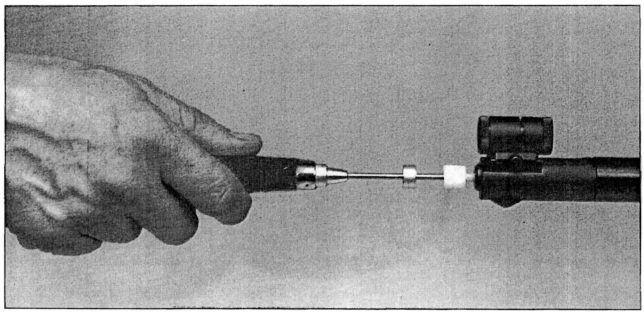

A proper muzzle-end cleaning in progress shows a nylon muzzle guard and locking depth-stop.

(Right) A top-quality polarizing oil is essential for the bores and external metal surfaces of airguns.

Hard felt cleaning pellets can keep an airgun bore accurate between regular cleanings. And they can do double duty for chasing away animal pests without wounding them.

chamber's air vent and the bore after the action is closed. Low power should lead you to suspect a missing, defective, worn or damaged breech seal. To test for proper breech seal function, ·cock and load the airgun. Hold the palm of your hand about ¹/₂-inch (15mm) above the location of the breech seal, but be very careful not to let it touch the gun. Then, fire the gun in a safe direction. If there is a seal leak, you will feel a strong blast of air. On the other hand, a slight leak is normal blow-off of excess pressure in some models. It is usually a simple matter to pop out

the inexpensive breech seal and replace it. However, don't disturb even an ugly, blemished seal if it works well.

Loose screws are another major cause of complaints concerning airgun accuracy, both in new and old airguns. One-quarter of a turn may affect accuracy by as much as 2 inches (50mm) at 33 feet (10m). This is especially a problem with front and rear stock screws and scope mount screws. At first, just try tightening the screws very firmly. (Please note that over-tightening of the rear trigger screw on some airguns will pre-

Any pounding on an airgun should be carried out only with a suitable mallet that won't mar the surface and finish of the gun. (From left) Leather, synthetic/brass and plastic mallets can be used for such tasks.

vent operation of the trigger mechanism.) If the problem recurs rather soon, remove the screws, degrease them and apply a light grade of Loc-Tite sealant. Do not use the industrial grade or you may never be able to move the screws again! If the screws in the forend seem to be burrowing into the wood, a special screw cup should be installed on each side. These are available at nominal cost from airgun supply catalogs and are easily installed.

Some shooters may believe they have a gun quality or maintenance problem because they are getting poor accuracy, when there is actually no problem. Because of the relatively long time that pellets remain in an airgun after the trigger is pulled, as compared to bullets in a firearm, and the motion of major internal parts, airguns are much more sensitive to shooter motion and support of the gun. This is one of the reasons why airguns are so good for teaching shooting technique to firearms shooters. Many *excellent* firearms marksmen do *not* do well with airguns until they have improved techniques that were not so critical with firearms. Many benchrest or other techniques, which are excellent for firearms, may cause oversized groups. Give yourself time to become accustomed to each airgun that you use. Don't rest the barrel on anything while shooting. Use consistent gripping pressure and replace the gun to the same, well-secured position for each shot. For air pistols, use a firm two-handed grip and do not touch any part of the pistol to a rest.

The surface of well-blued gun metal is a delight to behold. However, it can be rather easily rusted if not properly protected. If possible, the first thing to do after aquiring any gun with a blued surface is to remove it from the stock and thoroughly wipe it down with a similar cleaner/degreaser as used for bore cleaning. Then after wiping dry with a clean cloth, apply a top grade of polarizing gun oil. The active material in such special oils is so attracted to metal that its molecules slip right through surface moisture films and join beneath them to form a protective barrier to the metal. These modern substances can provide as much protection, almost invisible, as an old-time coating of

heavy grease and, most important, will not trap any invisible moisture. The polarizing oil will neutralize sweat and salt, and also very effectively lubricate by penetrating into the smallest crevices and finally drying into a thin, non-gumming film which lasts through almost indefinite storage. As with all oils not approved for airgun compression chambers, these polarizing oils should be kept away from the compression or air storage chambers of airguns.

Powder rust on the blueing of a used or improperly stored gun, as well as spots and "blooming" on factory bluing, may be removed by gently wiping the affected area with 0000 steel wool, wiping it clean, and then lightly burnishing the area with polarizing oil. This can make a dramatic difference and prevent further deterioration of the surface.

Oil-finished stocks, or those stripped and refinished with oil, should be rubbed with a little Tru-Oil from time to time. A good stock finish polish or wax can aid the appearance and life of your stock. Whenever a gun has been handled, it should be wiped gently with a good grade of silicone cloth. Even a fingerprint can leave a rust mark. If you have never noticed such a problem when handling your own guns, be especially careful to wipe the guns down when they are handled by someone else because the sweat from some people can have a far more corrosive effect. (Gunsmiths refer to such people as "rusters.")

Rusting is particularly insidious because it generally occurs after the gun has been put away. This is particularly a problem in winter, when a cold gun is put into a case, especially if that case is then taken into a warm vehicle or building. The cold surface of the metal will draw moisture from the surrounding air or even from the lining of the case itself. Then, sometime later, the disappointed gun owner may blame his innocent gun case for the rusting of his favorite airgun.

Proper maintenance of high-quality airguns, once understood and made a habit, takes little time or effort and adds a great deal to the longevity, performance and pleasure of owning these fine instruments.

Chapter 12

Using Airgun Scopes

Telesights are practically a must for many of today's air rifles—and some air pistols as well. Here, with the assistance of Ben Saltzman, we explore this seldom discussed area.

by Ben Saltzman
Introduction by J.I. Galan

A powerful, yet accurate air rifle mated to a good-quality airgun scope with the proper mount is hard to beat for sheer shooting pleasure.

WITH THE GROWING popularity and variety of air rifles, it is only natural to expect many of their accessories to become just as sophisticated as the guns themselves. In the case of telescopic sights, incredible advances have taken place in recent years, with a steadily increasing number of scope manufacturers now catering to the optical magnification needs of airgunners. The current state of affairs is certainly a far cry from the days when the only airgun scopes available were barely one step above the toy level. In those days, the mere idea of mounting a regular scope on an airgun was generally dismissed by all but the most dedicated airgunners. Such a poor attitude was fostered mainly by ignorance; however, the largely unsophisticated types of airguns in vogue back then helped fuel the belief that scoping any airgun was a waste of time, effort and money.

The fact is, most of the reasons for using scopes on firearms also apply to air rifles—and some air pistols—as well. To go one step further, it can be stated rather categorically that for small game hunting, for instance, a scope is practically a must on an air rifle. Air rifles—even the magnums—generate but a fraction of the power delivered by even 22 rimfires. Therefore, every advantage must be squeezed to the utmost when air rifles are used against live targets in order to ensure a quick, humane kill. With an air rifle, this means precise shot placement.

Any solid hit in the body of, say, a squirrel with a 22 rimfire at up to around 50 yards is almost guaranteed to kill the animal quickly. With an air rifle, the same squirrel would have to be hit squarely in the head or, at the very least, in the center of the thorax area for a humane kill. Open sights simply can't deliver that kind of accuracy under most field conditions, where distances fluctuate and the target may be partially obscured by shadow, vegetation, or both. Peep sights are superb for bullseye target shooting, but their advantage over open sights can be somewhat limited under hunting conditions. It is the telescopic sight that gives the air rifleman a distinct edge in utilizing the precision inherent in his gun.

In choosing a scope for an air rifle, certain important factors should be kept in mind. First, scopes that are designed for centerfire rifles seldom work satisfactorily when mounted on an air rifle. This is due mainly to that optical phenomenon called parallax. Simply put, parallax results in the apparent shift of the target image in relation to the scope's reticle when the eye is not exactly lined up with the axis of the scope. This misalign-

(Left) A telescopic sight is a virtual necessity for any hunting activity involving air rifles.

(Below) Pneumatic rifles, like the ARS AR6 shown, have no recoil or vibration problems to affect a scope.

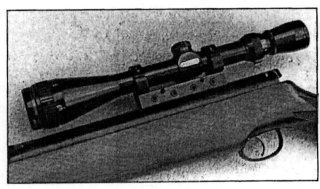

For maximum staying power, the one-piece scope mount is hard to beat, particularly on an air rifle with heavy recoil.

ment—caused by the target image being on a different plane from that of the reticle—can make a miss of even the most carefully executed shot. Firearm scopes are generally designed so that parallax is not a problem except at very short range—airgun range—usually at less than 30 or so yards.

There is another key factor to consider regarding telescopic sights, and it surfaces only when they are mounted on spring-piston guns. An often-forgotten fact regarding these guns is they can be a lot harder on scopes than even big caliber centerfire rifles. This is due to the "double recoil" typical of most spring-piston airguns. As the airgun goes off, the heavy piston used to create air compression surges forward, forcing the gun to move rearward. No problem so far; however, the piston stops rather abruptly on a cushion of compressed air just before it can crash against the front end of the cylinder. This cushion of air forces the piston to rebound somewhat. The sudden stop-and-rebound makes the gun literally halt in mid-recoil and then snap forward. This entire sequence takes place in a fraction of a second. In the process, terrific punishment can be inflicted on any telescopic sight mounted on the gun. Vibration, to a greater or lesser degree, is also present in the spring-piston gun and can add its

share of damage to the scope. Even expensive scopes for centerfire rifles can be seriously damaged in a short time when exposed to the pounding from a magnum-class spring-piston rifle. These problems do not apply, of course, to pneumatic and CO_2 guns, which for all practical purposes are free of vibration and recoil.

Another direct result of the spring-piston's double recoil and vibration is scope creep. This is an extremely annoying problem which sometimes calls for fairly drastic measures in order to solve it. The double recoil can force the scope, mounts and all, to slide rearward a bit with each shot, making it almost impossible to maintain zero. Fortunately, some scope manufacturers, prodded by airgun makers and consumers, have come up with various ways of solving this problem.

Shooters now have a wide array of scopes designed specifically for airguns. These are corrected for parallax at short range and, in many cases, have objective focusing that allows the shooter to correct for parallax error at practically any airgun distance. The lenses used in these scopes have special bracings that can withstand the peculiar recoil of even the most powerful spring-piston rifles. Also, scope mounts are now available that have been specially designed for airgun use. B-Square, for instance, has offered a special scope mount for several years that will fit some RWS, Beeman and Walther rifle models. Furthermore, many airgun companies offer scope-stop blocks and other devices that prevent the scope base from sliding rearward with repeated shooting.

All the major importers of European airguns (Dynamit Nobel-RWS, Beeman and Marksman) currently offer an extensive array of telescopic sights and mounts to fit just about any air rifle with receiver grooves. Tasco, for instance, has for several years marketed a line of airgun scopes. Other major scope companies have also seen the light, adding suitable airgun scope models of their own. Mind you, many of the airgun scopes currently offered are the equals of those intended for firearms. Moreover, a growing number of airgun scopes feature

variable power, reaching up to 24x and even higher in some cases, with big 40mm (and larger) objective lenses. Now that air rifles are taken much more seriously for hunting, Field Target and metallic silhouette shooting, it is not uncommon to find glasses of 24x with 50mm objectives mounted atop highly accurate and powerful rifles.

Of course, that's not the end of the story, by a long shot. I invited one of airgundom's foremost scope experts to share his extensive knowledge on this subject, as well as to give us his impressions and opinions on some of these highly sophisticated sighting devices.

I initially got acquainted—and quite impressed, by the way—with Ben Saltzman's articles several years ago through his writings for the now-defunct *American Airgunner* magazine—on which yours truly served as Technical Advisor. Eventually I got to meet him in person and exchange views on many aspects of the airgun scene. Ben Saltzman is not only a tremendously dedicated airgunner and Field Target competitor, but a highly successful professional photographer as well. Let's see, then, what Ben Saltzman has to say regarding airgun scopes.

• • • •

Since airguns are so accurate, it seems a shame to use one with open sights. I know there are folks out there who get along just fine without optics on top of their favorite rifle, but I felt the same way until I put my first scope on an airgun.

What a scope gives you is the ability to make a safer, more accurately placed shot. Whether you are hunting, plinking or shooting metal targets, you will have an advantage using a scope. To make an informed decision about which scope to

B-Square's scope mount is shown atop an RWS air rifle. This mount effectively negates "scope creep."

The Marksman 56-FTS is supplied without sights, or with the optional 4-12x40mm scope and mount combo shown.

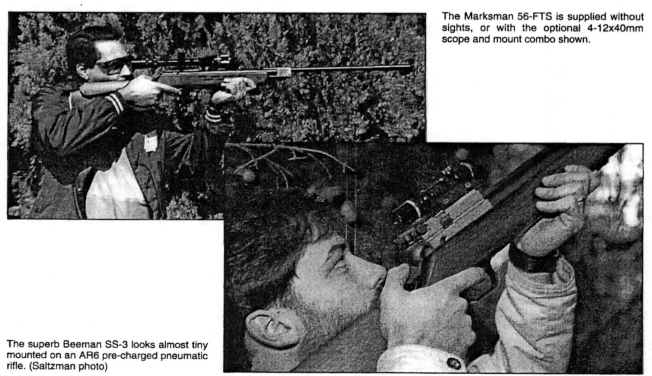

The superb Beeman SS-3 looks almost tiny mounted on an AR6 pre-charged pneumatic rifle. (Saltzman photo)

(Below) A short, super-compact scope like the Beeman SS-2 is ideally mated to the big, potent Beeman R10 air rifle.

The regular Beeman SS-2 scope has other impressive features such as objective focusing and extra-wide field of view.

The Beeman Short Scope 1 or SS-1 was once billed as the world's smallest riflescope. It is 2.5x, has a 16mm objective lens and razor-sharp optics.

Featuring an illuminated reticle by means of ambient light, via a "skylight," the Model 5066RL is the top scope offering in the Beeman line.

buy, you'll need to know a few things, once you decide what you are going to do with your airgun. Here are my rules of thumb. For hunting, I like to use a fixed-power scope of moderate magnification for snap-shooting and a slightly more powerful fixed or variable for still-hunting. For metallic silhouettes, I would go with the most magnification you can hold without making yourself nauseous. For Field Target, you need a scope that can be used for rangefinding—the more magnification, the better. But watch out: the more magnification, the less brightness, and those targets in the deep woods will be elusive. No matter what type of shooting you do with an airgun, you will want a scope that has an adjustable objective lens to allow parallax adjustments for the reduced airgun ranges. Everyone except possibly the low-magnification airgun hunter will require a scope with an adjustable objective so the target can be focused on sharply.

Now that I have expressed some blatant opinions, let's get down to some tech stuff you'll need to know about scopes so we are both speaking the same language.

- Magnification or power or X: a measure of how much closer you seem to be to your target. The nomenclature of a scope will say 3-7x32. This means it is a variable magnification scope that zooms from 3x power to 7x power utilizing a 32mm objective lens.
- Field of view: how much you see right to left and up and down at a certain magnification. A greater field of view will make target acquisition easier, especially for hunters.
- Transmission: the ability of the scope's optical system to allow light to pass through it. The more light a scope can transmit to your eye, the brighter the image will be.
- Objective size (front): the diameter of the front element (lens) of the scope. Like a funnel, the bigger the opening, the more light can enter.
- Exit pupil: the size of the light dot that contains the image you see in the scope. A smaller exit pupil makes it more difficult to acquire the image, and a larger one is better up to a point.
- Saddles: the protrusions on the body of the scope that house the adjusters. Some scopes have partial saddles; some have full ones.
- Adjusters: the little knobs that get you confused. What they

The Bushnell 3-9x32mm scope (top) is dwarfed by the huge and powerful Bushnell 6-18x40mm glass below. Both are superb choices for a hunting air rifle. (Saltzman photo)

really do is move the optical system around inside of your scope to change the point of impact up or down, left or right.

- Reticle: the crosshairs (or dot, or other type) you see in the scope and use for aiming.
- Depth of focus: how much front-to-back apparent sharpness you see. Photographers call this depth of field.

All of these are important if you have unlimited funds. If you are like me, you have to make compromises, and the scope manufacturers are no different. There is no point in their making a perfect scope, because what is important to me might be window dressing to you.

Light enters into the scope through the objective (front) lens. It is then focused and transmitted through a series of lenses and then eventually out the rear element and into your eye, if your head is placed correctly behind the scope. The internal lenses are part of the optical designer's plan of how he or she wants the scope to work. The clarity, brightness and sharpness of the image the shooter sees depends upon how well the lenses are ground, polished and coated; the quality of the glass itself; and how precisely the lenses are mounted in the tube. The construction and choice of materials also have an effect on the quality and longevity of the scope. What you have to decide is how much quality you can afford, then spend your money on what you really need.

Airgun hunting scopes come in all shapes and sizes. The common wisdom is that a hunter only needs 4x to shoot game, but this comes from the 22 rimfire experience, where a body shot is good enough. Airguns are so accurate, but quite a bit less powerful than 22s, so with a scope stronger than 4x, you can choose where you want to place your pellet to make a clean, one-shot kill. I recommend that tyros get a 2-7x or 3-9x as minimum, but a 4-12x or 6-18x would probably be best.

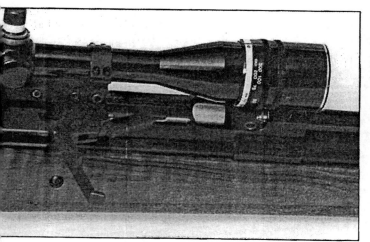

Just about all of the top-notch variable-power airgun scopes feature objective focusing.

Shooter takes careful aim through his Bushnell 6-18x40mm mounted atop an Air Arms TX200SR spring-piston rifle. (Saltzman photo)

The fixed-power (4x) RWS 300 air rifle scope also has objective focus. This is an outstanding scope with razor-sharp optics.

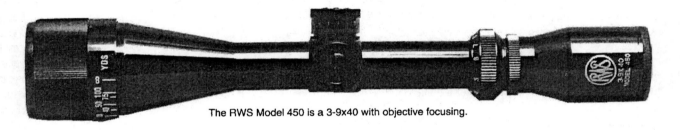

The RWS Model 400 from Dynamit Nobel-RWS is a superb air rifle scope in 2-7x with a 32mm adjustable objective lens.

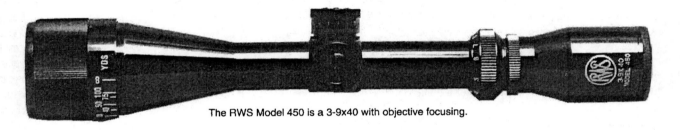

The RWS Model 450 is a 3-9x40 with objective focusing.

Everyone seems to be afraid of magnification at first, because they think they will get lost in the woods, but I'd bet there are few 2-7x scopes that live with their power ring on any number other than 7x. I know terrain and light can change, but many airgunners will be glad they can zoom out and still see the little critter they're after. Whatever the magnification you choose, get a scope that has a decent field of view. This will make target acquisition easier, especially when the game is moving.

The final group of scopes are long, figuratively and literally. In the early days of shooting optics, the longer the scope, the more magnification it had, due to prehistoric optical designs. These scopes are mostly used by silhouette, benchrest and Field Target shooters. The types include 6.5-20x, 6-24x, 8-32x, 8-40x, and fixed-power 30x, 24x, plus the whole gamut of optically boosted scopes that turn 6.5-20x Leupolds into a 13.5-35x or 18-40x, along with the reticle of your dreams.

The more magnification, the more critical the construction and quality of the optics become. It is not easy to build a scope that will rangefind accurately and consistently, and adjust for windage and elevation over and over again. Silhouette shooters have a huge selection of good scopes, because their targets are at known distances. For benchrest shooters, whatever you can lift onto the shooting bench that can transmit light will work—the more magnification, the better. Our Field Target shooting friends have a lot more to worry about when it comes to scope selection. To compete at

the highest level, you need a scope with lots of magnification so you can rangefind accurately, especially at the extreme pellet drop ranges between 40 and 55 yards. If you can tell a target is 47 yards away instead of 45 or 50, you stand a better chance of scoring a point. You'll also need a scope with great light transmission so you are able to find targets in the bright, bright sun or really deep shade. You have a tall order to fill, not to mention the scope must have very accurate, repeatable, and long-lived windage and, most importantly, elevation adjusters. Whew!

There are potentially more important things to consider than magnification and objective size. Transmission of light is high on my priority list. All things being equal, a scope that can bring more light in and then magnify the image, producing a bright image for my eye, is preferable. This is easier to do and/or overdo with scopes in the under-12x range. This becomes much harder to do as the magnification increases. Optical design and quality of the glass are paramount to this cause.

I see some head scratchers wondering about reticles. Well, the scope has to have one unless you opt for a red dot instead. For snap-shooting, red dots are the ticket. They are quick and easy to get on the target. Lighted reticles are good, too. If you are an old reactionary like me, you will choose a good, reliable duplex reticle. The different types of reticles available will boggle your mind.

Picking the right airgun scope is not hard if you accept the limitations of the device. In most cases, one scope cannot do

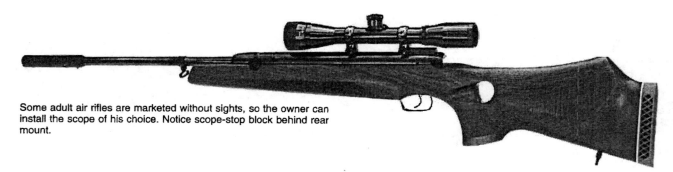

Some adult air rifles are marketed without sights, so the owner can install the scope of his choice. Notice scope-stop block behind rear mount.

everything, just like one airgun cannot do everything. My advice is to talk to other airgunners who do the same sort of shooting you do, and look through their scopes. Go to a local dealer, if you have one, and look *through* the scopes, not just at them. Twist the adjusters respectfully from lock to lock. How do they feel? Crisp? Wonderful. Look inside from the front side. Is it black in there? Good. Can you afford to own it? Better. The marketing hype on scopes is wide and deep. Your eyes, wallet and common sense are all you really need to choose a good scope. If the scope looks well made and finished to you, it probably is, and if it comes with a lifetime warranty, that's even better.

"Oh, my gosh, will I break the reticle with my super-magnum's sharp recoil?" Probably yes. I've seen it done many times with "airgun-proof" scopes. If you are into optic abuse,

make sure you get a scope with a lifetime warranty against said breakage and a UPS account so it will be convenient for you to ship your scope back to the maker. If you are shooting an airspring (gas-ram) airgun, please let some air out of it so you don't pull a muscle or bend the barrel trying to cock it. Anyway, you don't need all that power now that you have a scope to guide you in placing your shot.

Following last year's SHOT Show, I scanned all the scope manufacturers' catalogs I could find trying to locate American-made scopes that would focus down to 10 yards. Many high-quality "airgun" scopes could be had, but almost all of them came from the Pacific Rim.

Wading through all of the literature, I noticed two of the U.S. scope manufacturing biggies had been paying attention. They both looked at the market and saw a need for high-quality

Leupold 3x9 EFR shown on a Skan Bullpup air rifle. (Saltzman photo)

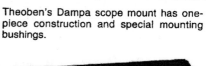

Theoben's Dampa scope mount has one-piece construction and special mounting bushings.

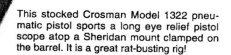

This stocked Crosman Model 1322 pneumatic pistol sports a long eye relief pistol scope atop a Sheridan mount clamped on the barrel. It is a great rat-busting rig!

Above is the Burris 4x Mini. Below is the somewhat larger Burris 4-12x Mini. Both are especially designed for airguns. (Saltzman photo)

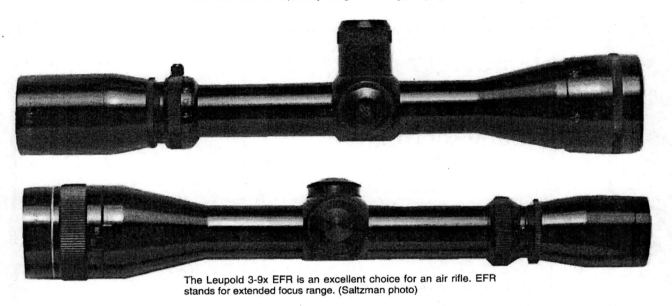

The Leupold 3-9x EFR is an excellent choice for an air rifle. EFR stands for extended focus range. (Saltzman photo)

scopes that airgun shooters could use. Because of them, we now have lots of world-class, if not superior, airgun scopes made right here in America.

For a number of years, Burris has been making their 4x and 6x Mini scopes especially for airguns. The 6x Mini is one of my favorites for a hunting scope. It is small, sturdy and handsome. The two Minis are bright and sharp, have good color, focus down to 10 yards and are as airgun-proof as the more highly touted imports. The fit and finish of the Burris scopes are first class. The problem is that not many people know about them.

The Leupold 6.5-20x has been used for years as an airgun scope by Field Target shooters worldwide. A 6.5-20x suitably modified to a 14-35x or 18-40x by Dick Thomas at Premiere Reticle was *the* scope to own. These Leupolds were modified to make them more precise rangefinders in Field Target games. The problem with the old model 6.5-20x was that it could not focus down to 10 yards without using Leupold's 50-foot adaptor. This was inconvenient, at best, and left a spot at about 17-21 yards where you just could not get in focus. The new 6.5-20x Leupold EFR will focus down to 10 yards without the need for an adaptor. If you haven't figured it out yet, EFR stands for "Extended Focus Range."

The Burris 6-24x is an adaptation of their Signature series. They took the same excellent housing and optics, added a 1/4-minute target adjuster for elevation and a 1/4-minute coin-slot adjuster for windage. They got rid of the bright light iris they

use on their centerfire scopes and replaced it with an adjustable yardage ring. The adjustable ring seems like a gimmick at first, but it works great.

If it were a perfect Field Target world, Burris would build a scope that could zoom up to 30x and Leupold would have a 50mm objective. But until we arrive in Utopia, which scope would I buy? It is a hard question to answer. The Leupold EFR has one option open to its owner that the Burris does not. His name is Dick Thomas at Premiere Reticle. Dick will boost the power of the EFR from 6.5-20x to a 14-35x or an 18-40x and build you a custom reticle. Boosted scopes get a bit dark for me at maximum magnification, but everyone tells me to just back off the power for those dark corners. The Burris, on the other hand, comes straight from the factory ready to knock down field targets. With careful focusing at the ever critical distances from 40 to 50 yards, you can do quite well with the Burris. But I am still left wanting for more magnification than 24x.

Both are great all-round air rifle scopes right out of their respective boxes. You could hunt, shoot Field Targets or silhouettes with either one. Please don't make me pick one! I like them both for different reasons.

Remember that Leupold also makes a 3-9x EFR scope just for airgunners, as well as the 6.5-20x. Burris builds their magnificent 4x and 6x Minis and a 4-12x Mini, too. So what are you waiting for? Go out and spur the economy. Show some consumer confidence. Buy a U.S.-made airgun scope today.

Chapter 13

The Survival Airgun

The right airgun can be a useful tool for staying alive in a hostile environment.

by J.I. Galan

An air rifle could be an invaluable tool in survival situations to get meat for the pot with a minimum of noise and expenditure.

ONE TOPIC OF conversation that rarely fails to elicit a swift and sharp response among shooting enthusiasts is that of survival guns. Just about anybody who claims to know anything about guns has at least some idea about the best combination of guns to have on hand if and when a major social breakdown befalls us.

The scenario in question could entail urban survival in the aftermath of a major war or a complete economic collapse. The Los Angeles riots of 1992 are a prime example of the terror and helplessness accompanying such a rupture in the social stability of urban America. Another excellent example of the incredible value of guns as survival tools when the chips are *really* down also takes us back to 1992 and the aftermath of Hurricane Andrew in South Florida. This is a scenario with which I am personally familiar because I was there before, during and after the storm. As a law enforcement officer I saw firsthand the value of armed citizens living in totally devastated areas and protecting what remained of their belongings. These folks knew that they could not count on help from the authorities—many police officers were also victims of the storm—most of whom were stretched to the limit in trying to marshal vital supplies to the worst hit areas. Many homeowners were seen standing guard with their rifles, shotguns or handguns over whatever remained of their homes, and as a result, looting was practically nonexistent in most residential areas. All categories of serious crime, in fact, went down drastically in the weeks after the hurricane.

Survival could also be applied to long-term situations in a remote wilderness area. The scenarios can vary, but the basic idea is to keep body and soul together when faced with such dire predicaments—not an easy task in many instances.

Of course, firearms are of paramount importance in any situation where there is a real possibility of being physically attacked by other human beings. This is a worst-case scenario which, unfortunately, could occur in the midst of a complete breakdown of society, when one's ability to stay alive may depend mainly on heavy firepower. A basic survival battery for such purposes could include one or two semi-auto centerfire rifles, a pump shotgun, a couple of 22 rimfire rifles, a brace of reliable large-bore combat handguns and *at least a couple* of top-quality adult air rifles.

Although I am not even remotely suggesting that air rifles be used for purposes of self-defense—except in the most extreme emergency, when nothing else is available—their

The author does a bit of hard-hitting plinking with the Sterling HR83 in 22-caliber, a good choice for survival. This underlever-cocker was made by Benjamin Sheridan until 1994, but is now discontinued.

place in the survival battery is quite legitimate and should not be regarded casually at all. Any air rifle chosen for survival purposes must meet certain criteria. Reliability and ruggedness are at the top of the list. The survival air rifle must be capable of operating reliably under adverse conditions with minimal maintenance. This just about rules out most pneumatic and CO_2 guns. These types are more prone to serious trouble or outright breakage than spring-piston or gas-spring

(gas-ram) guns if used under less than ideal conditions on a regular basis. Dirt, humidity and even drastic temperature changes can have adverse effects on the often delicate valving mechanisms of pneumatic and CO_2 guns. In addition, these types are generally trickier to repair than the typical spring-piston airsporter. Should something go wrong with the latter's power plant—such as a weak or broken mainspring, or perhaps a defective piston seal—the gun can be put back into

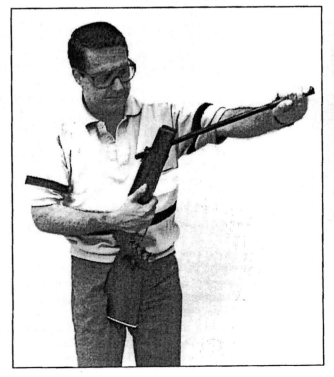

Don't overlook air-spring (gas-ram) guns like the Beeman RX-1 being tested by author. These Theoben-design airguns are also sturdy and quite powerful.

Spring-piston airsporters in the magnum class are the top choice when it comes to survival airguns. Barrel cockers are generally the most rugged of the genre.

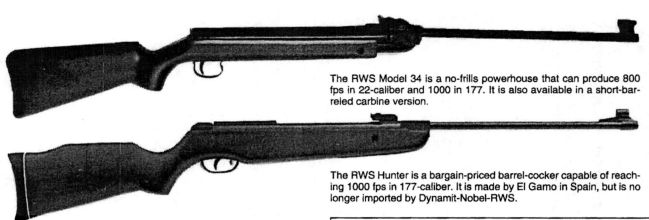

The RWS Model 34 is a no-frills powerhouse that can produce 800 fps in 22-caliber and 1000 in 177. It is also available in a short-barreled carbine version.

The RWS Hunter is a bargain-priced barrel-cocker capable of reaching 1000 fps in 177-caliber. It is made by El Gamo in Spain, but is no longer imported by Dynamit-Nobel-RWS.

A telescopic sight is always useful, but the survival air rifle should also have iron sights, just in case the scope is damaged.

The Beeman R1 Carbine in 25-caliber packs a real wallop and is plenty accurate out to 30 or 35 yards.

proper working order by anyone having a modicum of skill with common tools. Storing compressed air, as in the case of precharged pneumatic guns, could present a serious problem, as would be the case also with CO_2 guns that depend on a good supply of bulk-fill tanks or 12-gram cartridges. This could definitely be a major problem in a long-term survival scenario.

Accuracy and power are close behind reliability and ruggedness on the list of requirements for the survival air rifle. Magnum models naturally fill the top slots, but medium-power airsporters can also be considered serious contenders, as long as they are consistently accurate within their practical range. There is no room for borderline or iffy accuracy here. It must be kept in mind that a 177-caliber air rifle in the 600 to 750 fps range of muzzle velocity can still kill rabbits and other edible small game animals at up to 30 yards or so. Beyond that, a magnum air rifle should be used.

Caliber is a matter of personal choice. Keep in mind that 22-caliber pellets hit harder at any practical distance. In recent years, the proliferation of 25-caliber airguns has added a new dimension to the concept of small-game hunting. In fact, most, if not all, of the currently available air rifles in 25-caliber are marketed primarily with hunting as their main application. There are definitely some real powerhouses in this group, with the Webley-made Beeman Kodiak—known in the UK as the

Patriot—being one of the most potent of the current crop. There is also a lot to be said about the killing effectiveness of the 20-caliber pellet, a fact that's not lost on a lot of folks who swear by this size for field use.

Don't forget, however, that 177 pellets have a flatter trajectory—which usually means better shot placement—and also tend to penetrate a bit deeper than pellets of larger calibers. But there are other trade-offs. For instance, if extreme power and range are not absolute requirements, an accurate spring-piston rifle of medium power may be preferable because of its generally lower discharge report. This could be an important consideration in some survival situations in which one's presence in an area must remain unnoticed. Many of the really hot magnum air rifles produce a fairly loud "crack" upon discharge. They're not really as loud as a 22 Long Rifle round, to be sure, but enough to perhaps attract unwelcome attention at an uncomfortably long distance.

The survival air rifle should be equipped with both a good-quality scope made to withstand the "double recoil" of a spring-piston rifle as well as sturdy iron sights. It is not very smart to have a so-called survival rifle (and this applies to firearms as well) equipped with only a telescopic sight. If something happens to the scope, the survivalist had better be prepared to do a lot of guessing if he has to shoot at anything. When you are shooting to protect your life, or to get some-

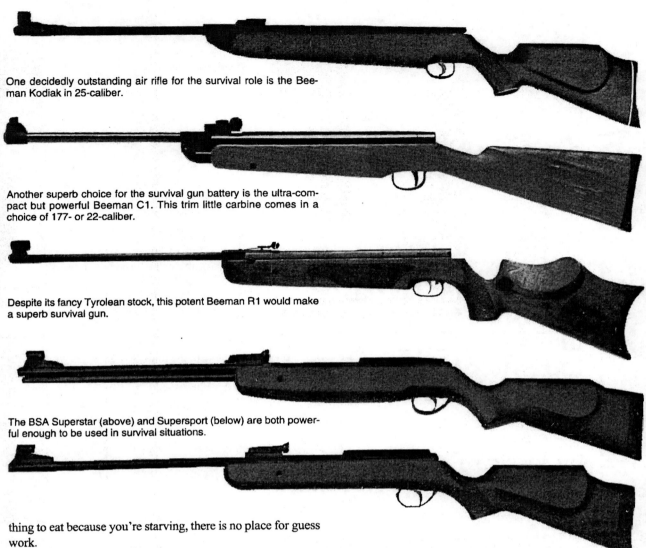

One decidedly outstanding air rifle for the survival role is the Beeman Kodiak in 25-caliber.

Another superb choice for the survival gun battery is the ultra-compact but powerful Beeman C1. This trim little carbine comes in a choice of 177- or 22-caliber.

Despite its fancy Tyrolean stock, this potent Beeman R1 would make a superb survival gun.

The BSA Superstar (above) and Supersport (below) are both powerful enough to be used in survival situations.

thing to eat because you're starving, there is no place for guess work.

Along with a sizable supply of top-brand pellets, any airgun used for survival should have at least two or three extra sets of spare mainsprings and piston seals put away in a safe place. Also, don't forget the highly important breech seal in barrel-cocking models. A lot of premature mainspring failure can be traced directly to a leaking breech seal. A handful of these should be stashed away for each air rifle. Several bottles of the lubricants recommended by the importer or manufacturer of the air rifle should also be stored away. Spring-piston air rifles require very sparing but careful lubrication, so several bottles of the proper lubricants should last for a very long time.

The economy of the air rifle is another important factor in a long-term survival situation. In addition to hunting edible game, an air rifle can dispatch a wide variety of pests around the house or farm, quietly and at a fraction of the cost of even 22 rimfire ammo. Several thousand airgun pellets can be safely stored in a couple of metal tins or boxes—for instance, large, resealable coffee cans are ideal. Firearms ammo, on the other hand, occupies far more space, and storing cartridges securely can present problems, particularly over a long period of time. Cartridges stored for a long time can deteriorate and become unreliable, prone to misfiring at a critical moment. Airgun pellets are not so affected, of course.

The type of pellet chosen for the survival air rifle is mostly a matter of trial and error; however, in this area, economy definitely does not pay. Buying cheap pellets will usually yield poor results when you have to shoot in order to eat. Quality pellets are really inexpensive when compared to 22 rimfire ammo, so there is no need to buy inferior pellets. My personal choices for small game are pointed pellets such as RWS Superpoint, Beeman Silver Jet, Beeman Ram Point (in 25 only), as well as a few others that I have used with telling results. Hollowpoint pellets are real stoppers at up to 25 or 30 yards, while some of the latest heavyweight field pellets can be quite deadly on larger prey, like raccoons and jackrabbits. Again, the trick is to learn which pellets work best in your survival air rifle(s) and stick with them.

Used judiciously, an air rifle can play an important part in many survival situations. Common sense and a sound understanding of the gun's limitations will dictate what's possible—and what isn't—when the chips are really down and every shot must count.

Chapter 14

Paintball Hits The Mark

Hailed by many, vilified by some, the sport of paintball has flourished for more than a decade, and top writer Jessica Sparks tells us why.

by Jessica J. Sparks
Introduction by J.I. Galan

Players wear camouflage for protection from the brush and to hide from their opponents. These two members of the California Bushwackers tournament team are shooting constant air guns with 200-ball bulk loaders. (Photo courtesy of Ron Kilbourne)

I MUST ADMIT the sport of paintball has always held a remarkable fascination for me. Beyond that, there is also my longstanding interest in the paintball guns themselves. The paintball industry, however, has grown so much over the last few years that, in order to do justice to the sport, I asked one of the top professionals in that field, Jessica J. Sparks, to write this chapter.

Sparks is one of paintball's most respected writers. Since she began playing the game in the mid-1980s, she has written and photo-illustrated hundreds of articles on all aspects of the game, its equipment and the industry. She is co-founder and member of the board of directors of the International Paintball Players Association (IPPA) and five-year editor of the monthly *IPPA News*. Sparks is also the field editor of *Action Pursuit Games* magazine and former editor of *Paintball* magazine. As an attorney, she regularly deals with legal and legislative matters affecting the game worldwide. So, then, let's enter the exciting world of paintball.

• • • •

In your hand you hold a paintgun, freshly loaded with bright orange paintballs. Ahead of you, your best friend's shadow quietly moves through the pines. Slowly, you advance. Ahead in the dark forest, somewhere, your opponents guard their flag station. Your mission: Find them; capture their flag; take the flag back to your team's flag station to win the game.

Every tree and bush holds safe danger. Sweating, adrenaline pumping, you press every sense to full alert for anything out of place. There—something changes. Dry leaves crunch. Freeze! Your eyes dart left, right, forward. A shape...a movement! "Down!" you warn, "Down!"

Splat! Too late. Your friend raises his hand. "Hit! I'm out!" he shouts. A broad blue splatmark decorates his goggles.

Welcome to paintball!

The Game

Paintball is a fast-action airgun shooting sport. What makes it special? Your target tries to out-think, out-maneuver and out-shoot you. Adventure, excitement and competition await those who accept this game's challenge.

A day of paintball takes you back to childhood days when you played hide-and-seek, tag, and capture the flag—and adds shooting-sport thrills. Paintball offers players an escape from

Scenarios at paintball playsites often include mock towns. This player shoots a modified class constant air pumpgun. (Photo by J. Sparks)

The object of the game is to capture your opponents' flag—if you can. Every tree and bush holds safe danger!

day-to-day responsibilities and a special way to rekindle their spirit of adventure. Once the adrenaline starts pumping, you can't help but love the thrill of the game.

Paintball officially began in June, 1981, when twelve people played the first game. Today, playsites operate in more than three dozen countries. About a million people per year play paintball in the United States alone.

The game is a sophisticated, distant cousin of tag and hide-and-seek. Players enter a real-life video game full of safe danger. Heart-pumping excitement drives players from tree to tree, and building to building. You try to tag your opponents by shooting them with a paintball—before they can do the same to you. What shooting sport can be more challenging than one where the opponents shoot back at you?

The Game Plan

Two teams play a typical paintball game. Each team starts the game at its own flag station (home base). The object of the game is to capture your opponents' flag from their flag station and return it to your home base. The team that completes this mission, before game time expires, wins. Of course, your team has to protect its own flag from being captured. If neither team hangs the flag before game time ends, the game is a draw.

The game's time limit differs according to the size of the teams and the field. Most games run between twenty minutes

and one hour, and several games are usually played each day. Referees start and stop games, and enforce the safety and playing rules.

During the game, you try to eliminate your opponents by shooting them with paintballs. Simply put, the more opponents your team eliminates, the easier it will be to capture their flag. When a paintball marks an opponent with a quarter-sized splatmark, he or she is out of that game. An eliminated player must raise a hand or paintgun overhead and loudly shout "I'm hit!" or "I'm out!" or "Dead man!" and

Using his Tippmann semi-auto and a large bulk loader lets this player create his own "cover fire" to advance. (Photo by J. Sparks)

Scott paintball-approved goggles with extended face and head protection go a long way in preventing injury.

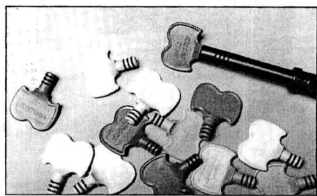

Barrel plugs like these are an additional safety device. The plugs are inserted into the barrel to help keep an accidental discharge safely inside the barrel.

leave the field. A tagged player cannot talk or pass equipment to active players.

The non-toxic, water-soluble "paint" is rubbed with a little dirt or water between games so a player will not be called out from a prior game's mark. Fortunately, paintsplats wash off skin and clothing with soap and water.

Team sizes vary and may have from two to ten or more players. Teams are kept approximately equal in size for recreational ball and even for tournament play. In singles matches, individuals square off to see who is the better shot and can make the better moves. "Big games," scenario games and re-enactments draw hundreds of players who are divided into large teams of approximately equal numbers. The largest game on record drew over 3000 players to a Pennsylvania playsite about three years ago.

Game tactics depend on the experience level of the players. Corporate and recreational players usually just do whatever they feel like doing—play defense and guard the flag, sneak out and try to pick off one or two unwary opponents, or join the main offense for a "let's rush 'em!— power play.

To play tournament ball, players must join a team. These teams develop actual game plans and plays, as in other sports. Their strategy will give squads or players specific assignments like "set up at the fallen log and pour paint at their wire man" or "hold in the trees, and when the middle squad makes contact, everyone push hard along the ridge for their flag station."

Between games, players check their equipment, reload paintballs, have a soda—and swap stories on winning tactics or how I got splatted this time. Win or lose, another game is just a few minutes away.

Safety

Most importantly, because players shoot paintballs at each other, and because a paintball can damage the unprotected eye, paintball-approved eye protection is mandatory for the game. Not allowed for paintball play are shop goggles, motorcycle goggles, shooting glasses, sunglasses or anything other than *paintball-approved* eye protection. Everyone on the playing field must wear these special goggles, as well as anytime a person is in a shooting area—meaning the playing field, target range or chronograph area.

Paintball follows the basic rules of airgun safety: Keep your finger off the trigger until you are ready to shoot; keep the barrel pointed in a safe direction at all times; and be certain of your target before you shoot. Players also use the paintgun's mechanical safety and a barrel plug when not shooting. Used worldwide, barrel plugs are special safety devices for paintball that are inserted firmly into the barrel whenever the player is outside an authorized shooting area. These colorful plastic or metal plugs are designed to stop an accidental discharge from getting out of the barrel. They're also easy for the staff to spot, so anyone without a barrel plug can be reminded to put one in.

Safe paintball also demands regular chronographing during the day, a pre-game rules orientation, clearly designated boundaries for playing fields and safe CO_2 handling. The Safety Guidelines of the International Paintball Players Association (IPPA) are the currently followed industry safety rules. See the Airgun Directory at the back of this edition for their address.

Sometimes people think paintball is not a safe sport because players are shooting at each other. However, this unfounded fear simply is not supported by insurance safety records, which show paintball is a very safe sport *as long as safety rules are followed*. Insurance statistics show that paintball is much safer than golf, jogging, tennis, swimming and many other sports. No one has ever been killed by being hit with a paintball.

The Players

Paintball players come in all shapes and sizes. Men and women compete equally, and the game is not dominated by youth. Physical size, speed and strength do not guarantee victory. Those with limiting handicaps, the differently abled, can play paintball. As in chess, anyone who can think quickly and decisively, and who can evaluate changing situations on the playing field, will become an excellent player. Intelligence and determination, coupled with good teamwork and straight shooting, are the most valuable skills for a player.

Since the game teaches teamwork, many companies invite their employees, suppliers or competitors out for a day of confidence-building, leadership-training paintball. Regardless of age or lifestyle, whether homemakers or high-school students, professionals or retirees, all paintball players share a love for adventure and a strong competitive spirit.

Tournament players compete in amateur and semi-pro events worldwide, but competition at the tournament level adds a special edge to the sport. It drives manufacturers toward better products and players toward ever-better on-field performance. Every year, the world's leading paintball events happen in the U.S., Canada, the U.K., France, Australia, Brazil and the Netherlands, with more events added every year. Prize purses can top $50,000 per event.

In Japan, where guns are banned except for law enforcement purposes, thousands play a game like paintball using "air-soft" airguns. These very closely resemble firearms and currently are banned from commercial importation in the U.S. They shoot tiny plastic "BB-like" projectiles, so the players also wear eye protection. In the air-soft game, when you feel the ball tag you, you call yourself out. There is no "paint" mark. Japanese air-soft players and U.S. paintball players began in 1993 to exchange invitations to each other's tournaments. Players and industry members in each country would like to change the laws so competitions could be held in each form of the sport.

Women compete equally with men on the paintball field. This Arizona tournament-level player wears Tiger Stripe cammies and shoots a semi-auto F-1 Illustrator from Direct Connect. (Photo by J. Sparks)

Elaborate scenarios at playsites may include very real props that add to the fun. Photographed at S.C. Village, Southern California.

This Worr Game Products Auto-Cocker semi-auto paintgun has a vertical-style constant air bottle, often chosen because it sends paint flying with more consistent velocity. (Photo courtesy of Team Fatal Swoop)

Beginnings

Paintball is related to the childhood games of hide-and-seek and tag. Add the Boy Scout game "capture the flag," marking equipment and safety gear, imagination, and it's 1981—paintball is born.

Here's the story, in a nutshell. For several years, three friends and businessmen, Robert Gurnsey, Hayes Noel and Charles Gaines, looked for a competitive challenge that would prove who could "survive" better in the woods—a person from the concrete jungle of a city or someone raised in the country. A friend found the Nel-Spot 007 Color Marking Gun and its oil-base paintballs in a farm equipment catalog, and after a bit of testing, it was time to take the challenge.

The three men invited nine other friends to come to New Hampshire for a day, at a cost of $275 each for guns, goggles and food. That day in June, 1981, each individual adventurer played the game. The goal? To capture several flags that had been set around a wooded area on Charles Gaines' land without getting shot with a paintball. Who won? Ritchie White, a New Hampshire forester who captured all the flags without ever shooting his Nel-Spot. The guys had a great time running around in the woods.

Robert Gurnsey, now known as the father of paintball, saw the opportunity to develop a business and a new sport. He quickly founded the National Survival Game, Inc. (now NSG, Inc.), in 1981, to market the game and its equipment. Early feature articles about paintball appeared in *People, Playboy, Time, Sports Illustrated, Business Week, The Wall Street Journal*, and many other magazines and newspapers. "The Today Show," "Nightline," "Donahue" and many local television shows covered the game. Principally through Gurnsey's marketing efforts, paintball spread across the U.S., and a few years later moved into Europe.

In the very early days, executives came out to play just as they do today. "I thought it was silly at first," said a Hyatt executive. "It was 110 degrees, and when I saw the gun and the camouflage, I said, 'This is nuts.' But once I got started, it was a fantastic experience. I never thought it was so much fun shooting people."[1]

Growing, Growing

Today, paintball is a multi-million-dollar worldwide industry selling thousands of paintguns and hundreds of millions of paintballs every year. Estimates put the paintball industry at $500 million worldwide, with continued growth projected through the 1990s.

[1]Lionel Atwill, *The New, Official Survival Game Manual*, 2nd ed., 1987, p. 150, NSG, Inc., New London, NH.

Players sometimes go all out with the heavy camouflage look. This shooter is using a Benjamin Sheridan VM-68 semi-auto paintgun with 200-ball Viewloader bulk loader. (Photo by J. Sparks)

The ultimate in high-tech, perhaps? This is the author's custom pink anodized Benjamin Sheridan VM-68 Magnum with Emerging Technologies red dot sight.

National and international tournaments helped paintball grow during the past decade. Why? Players and manufacturers exchange ideas and information, and showcase new products. First to run tournaments was NSG, starting with the 1983 North American Championship. NSG stopped its sponsorship in 1989, leaving the arena to Jim Lively of Nashville, Tennessee. Today, Lively Productions' World Championship Masters series draws participants and exhibitors from around the world. Additional high-profile international tournament and trade shows include Jerry Braun's World Cup in New York, Debra Dion-Krischke's World Amateur Championship in Pittsburgh, and Paul Wilson's European Championship at Mayhem, U.K.

Developing its own media also brought new life and new players into the game. Today, the U.S. has five magazines and three newspapers with national distribution covering the game. This media-generated growth began in 1987 with the first internationally distributed magazine, *Action Pursuit Games* (APG), published by CFW Enterprises, Inc., Burbank, California. APG's founding editor, Russell Maynard, and CFW's distribution system opened many doors so paintball could grow.

The nonprofit International Paintball Players Association (IPPA), founded early in 1988, is dedicated to growth of the sport and works to standardize safety and playing rules worldwide. Joining the IPPA on the list of paintball organizations are the North American Paintball Referees Association (NAPRA), the International Paintball Field Operators Association (IPOA), the National Professional Paintball League (NPPL), the American Paintball League (APL), the European Paintball Sports Federation (EPSF), the Dutch Paintball Federation, and many other associations large and small. See the Airgun Association and Publication Directory for their locations.

Paintgun Development

Swarm, a team from Illinois, raised many an eyebrow in the fall of 1990 by winning paintball's prized Line SI International Masters. Swarm already had a national reputation, so what, then, was different? Swarm shot Airgun Designs' 68 Automag semi-automatic paintguns. Back then, only a few players had semi-autos, and pump-gun shooters dominated tournament winner's circles. Swarm's victory escalated a semi-auto trickle into an avalanche, even though California's Navarone team with pump-guns won Lively Productions' overall World Championship that year.

Then, 1991 became the "Year of the Semi-Auto," and manufacturers scrambled to put new semi-autos into the tournament players' hands. From this point, semi-auto shooters dominated the U.S. tournaments. California's Ironmen swept the 1991 World Championship shooting Worr Game Products' Sniper Auto-Cockers. Pennsylvania's All-Americans won the 1991 Line SI International Masters title with semi-automatic Benjamin Sheridan PMI-IIIs (VM-68s). Today, Aftershock, Tour de Force, the Bushwackers—along with other leading teams in the world—shoot semi-autos. Semi-autos became the choice of recreational players and playsite operators, too. New players found it easier to learn the game when they didn't have to learn how to shoot a pump-gun at the same time.

103

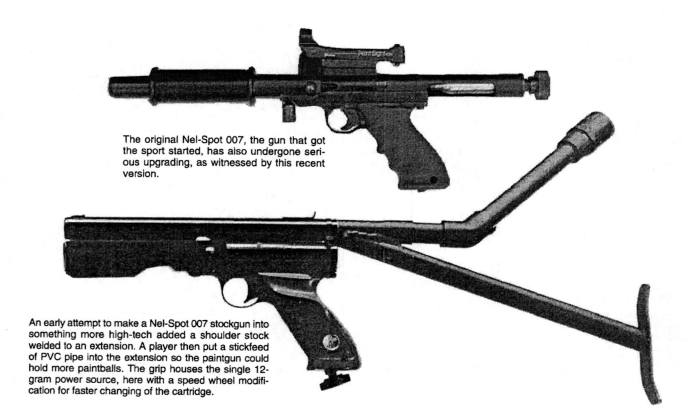

The original Nel-Spot 007, the gun that got the sport started, has also undergone serious upgrading, as witnessed by this recent version.

An early attempt to make a Nel-Spot 007 stockgun into something more high-tech added a shoulder stock welded to an extension. A player then put a stickfeed of PVC pipe into the extension so the paintgun could hold more paintballs. The grip houses the single 12-gram power source, here with a speed wheel modification for faster changing of the cartridge.

Early Guns

Things weren't always this fast-paced on the field. When paintball began in 1981, the Nel-Spot 007 paint pistol from the Nelson Paint Company was the only gun around. The 007 is a single 12-gram CO_2 cartridge-powered gun designed in the mid-1960s to mark trees and cattle with oil-base paintballs. It holds ten balls in a metal tube attached above and parallel to the barrel. The shooter must pull back a short cocking rod, tip the gun forward so a ball can roll into the chamber, push the rod forward and squeeze the trigger. The lone predecessor to the Nel-Spot 007 is the Crosman 707, but only a very few of these were made for the Nelson Paint Company.

In 1983, NSG, Inc., produced the first paintgun designed exclusively for paintball, the Splatmaster. The single-12-gram-powered Splatmaster holds ten balls in a tube integral to the gun and above the barrel. The shooter must push a rear cocking knob forward while tipping the Splatmaster back so a ball can roll into the chamber to be shot. Both the Nel-Spot 007 and Splatmaster stockguns are in production today.

As the sport grew through the mid-'80s, so did the family of 12-gram paintguns, to include Benjamin's PG Sideloader (out of production) and PGP (currently manufactured), the Canadian-built Mark I Uzi that held thirty-eight paintballs (replaced by today's Mark II Uzi of similar design) and Jim Riley's undercocking Puma (out of production). The power systems and basic designs of nearly every pump-style paintball gun today are variations on these early models.

Innovation

By the late '80s, innovation drove the sport wild. You had to visit the field every weekend just to see what someone invented during the week. Airgunsmiths customized existing factory production paintguns. Their goals? More shots, smoother action, more efficient use of CO_2, less need to reload paint or air, more comfortable shooting and better cosmetics. Extended barrels, pumps, adjustable shoulder stocks, auto-triggers, velocity adjusters, quick-changers, direct feed, bulk loaders, constant air and other changes took paintguns beyond anyone's earliest imagination. Magazine ads and feature stories publicized innovative products. Several new makers entered the market because they had seen opportunities for profit.

Today, most paintguns and accessories are made in the U.S., but many companies worldwide are entering the marketplace. Some twenty-five U.S. paintgun manufacturers now compete with those making guns in England, Korea, Taiwan and Brazil, with designs expected from Russia soon. Currently, more than 100 models can be purchased. Custom and small-production run models nearly double that number.

Power and Accuracy

Paintguns range from simple to sophisticated, all sharing the industry-accepted limitations on power and range. Speed? The accepted maximum velocity for a paintball shot from any paintgun, regardless of caliber, is a chronographed 300 feet per second (fps). With this limit, even at maximum elevation and velocity, a paintgun can lob a paintball not much more than 50 yards before the ball will plop rather gently to the ground. Accuracy? At 50 feet, a paintgun should group within 6 inches. That may not seem very accurate by quality airgun standards, but paintguns shoot large, liquid-filled gelatin capsules. Differences in individual paintballs, atmospheric

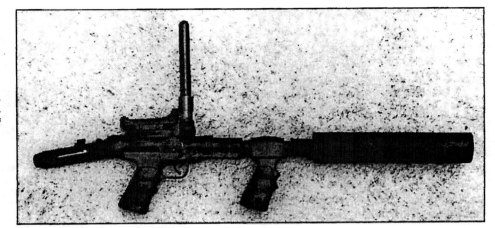

Some paintball accessory companies supply *fully legal* sound moderators to fit a wide array of paintguns.

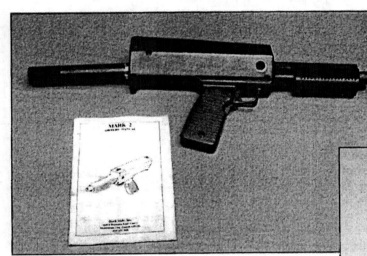

(Left) The pump-style Mark 2 Uzi from Dark Side (Canada) holds thirty-eight paintballs in its integral bulk loader. The 12-gram power source extends behind the receiver.

(Below) Paintballs load into the Mark 2 Uzi through this slide opening on top of the gun.

conditions and many other variables can throw a paintball off target.

Paintguns use two basic power sources. One is the standard 12-gram CO_2 cartridge so familiar to BB-gun shooters. A 12-gram cartridges will shoot from ten to perhaps thirty paintballs before it needs to be changed. The other, larger paintgun power source is called "constant air." This term refers to the large, refillable carbon dioxide (CO_2) cylinders (also called bottles or tanks) that attach to the guns. Practically all the semi-autos and nearly all pumps today use constant air, though all can operate on 12-gram power.

A constant air bottle has enough CO_2 for hundreds of shots before it must be refilled. Exactly how many shots a bottle gives will depend largely on the bottle capacity by weight, with sizes used ranging from 3.5 to 20 ounces. The number of shots per bottle also depends on the paintgun's gas efficiency and the velocity at which it is shooting, as well as atmospheric conditions that affect the CO_2. The size of the power source does not determine the velocity of the paintgun.

A constant air bottle can be attached to the front, rear, side or below the paintgun. It becomes a shoulder stock when attached to the rear of the gun as a back bottle. When attached to the base of the grip and pointed backward, the bottle also can serve as a shoulder stock, but is called a "bottom line" style.

The accepted worldwide industry standard power source for paintguns is carbon dioxide (CO_2). Compressed air has been used now and then, principally in the U.K. One reason for using compressed air was, at one time, the need to avoid stringent U.K. regulations regarding CO_2-powered airguns. As the regulations changed to accommodate paintball, players returned to CO_2 power. Use of other compressed gases, particularly nitrogen, may be part of paintball's future, but at present such use is experimental and not generally allowed. A paintgun power system designed for lower-pressure CO_2 can become unsafe when subjected to the higher pressures of different gases such as nitrogen.

Chronographing

The paintball industry adopted chronographing as a safety measure in the late 1980s. The velocity of a paintball is measured by shooting it over a chronograph. Speed and weight of the projectile affect impact velocity in foot pounds (meaning, how much will it sting?). Keeping the game fun and keeping

105

players from getting hurt are the reasons paintball imposes a safety limit on speed. As previously mentioned, the maximum allowable velocity is 300 fps for all paintballs of generally available commercial manufacture, regardless of caliber. Paintball-approved goggles are engineered according to this safety limit. A paintgun that is shooting over the speed limit is referred to as a "hot gun," and a player with one of these is not allowed to go onto the playing field. If a player is found to be using one, he will be ejected from a game and will be penalized in tournament play.

A player needs to be able to adjust a paintgun's velocity. Not only do speed limits vary between playsites, but also a change in temperature, humidity or paintgun components can cause a velocity change. Thus, nearly every paintgun today has a velocity adjuster built in, so with a special tool or dialing rod a player can change the speed. Players are not allowed to take adjusting tools onto the playing field.

Current Paintguns

Paintguns may be broadly classified into three main categories based on their power systems and features: stockguns, modifieds and semi-automatics.

Modified paintguns are more high-tech than stockguns, with semi-autos considered the most highly developed of the three categories. Playsite operators and tournament producers generally run separate events according to the class of paintgun allowed. A player can take his or her paintgun up to a more high-tech category, but cannot move down into a more basic category. For example, a player could not shoot a semi-auto in a pumpgun event. However, a player with a stockgun would be free to shoot it in a modified or in a semi-auto game.

Semi-Automatic Paintguns

The fastest-shooting semi-auto paintguns today can send up to twelve balls a second flying. Nearly all today's semi-autos are single action, though there are a few double-action models. The hot-selling single-action, semi-automatic paintguns are almost all blowback semi-autos, such as Daisy's Stingray, Direct Connect's F-2 Illustrator and Tippmann's Pro/Am.

A few manufacturers offer semi-autos with unique operating systems. For example, Airgun Designs' 68 Automag uses a pressure regulator rather than a blowback design. Those using a pneumatic valve system include the Sniper Auto-Cocker and Mini-Cocker from Worr Game Products, and custom paintguns from Palmer's Pursuit.

Semi-automatics cost anywhere from about $150 up to $600 for a factory production semi-auto. Customized semi-autos such as those from Carter Machine can cost up to $1000. Yes, there is a fully automatic paintgun. Tippmann Pneumatics brought to market the first and only full-auto paintguns over five years ago, but has since virtually discontinued production. Tippmann's SMG-60 fired 62-caliber paintballs and its companion, the SMG-68, shot standard 68-caliber paint. Both guns shoot as either a full- or semi-automatic. Paint was fed through the guns on reloadable stripper clips.

Paintguns must be chronographed regularly to see that they shoot under the speed limit. Here, a referee at S.C. Village in Southern California checks this player's paintgun on the field during a game. (Photo by J. Sparks)

Stock Paintguns

A stock paintgun (stockgun) is the simplest in terms of features. A stockgun must be powered by no more than a single 12-gram CO_2 powerlet, and the feed tube must run parallel to the barrel and cannot hold more than twenty paintballs. Players carry extra paint in ten-ball plastic tubes. Stockguns are configured so the player must tip the gun in order to roll each paintball into the chamber to be shot and are often called a "rock-'n-cock." Quick-change CO_2-holders are too high-tech, so they are disallowed; a stockgun player must have a CO_2-changer that requires the use of two hands.

Generally permitted stockgun options include a pump, shoulder stock, sight or scope, any length smoothbore barrel, and other items that do not change the basic limits on the gun. Examples include Nelson's Nel-Spot 007; Brass Eagle's Nightmare 68; Benjamin Sheridan's P-12, PGP, P68-SC and the KP1 paintrifle; NSG's Splatmaster; and the custom David Loo-designed Desert Duck. Stockguns cost from $100 to about $300, while custom units can run $600 and more.

About two years ago, a group of players in Southern California went back to stock. They wanted to emphasize the individual skills and tactics required to succeed as a single shot paintball player and escape the high paint bills associated with semi-auto play. This trend led to the founding of the Stock Gun Players Association (SGPA) in the spring of 1992. Their address can be found in the Airgun Directory.

Modified Paintguns

The modified paintgun category broadly includes all pump guns that are neither stockguns nor semi-automatics. Modified paintguns must be pumped or cocked manually each time the player wants to shoot. Adding certain high tech features to a stockgun moves it into the modified class.

Among the newest of the high-tech semi-auto paintguns is Tippmann's Pro/Am, shown here with accessories, including an instructional videotape and the fitted carrying case included with each gun.

(Below) This customized Airgun Designs 68 Automag has a vertical CO_2-bottle power source designed by Carter Machine in Hawthorne, California.

A modified-class paintgun usually is powered by some size constant air bottle and can also accept a single 12-gram cartridge like a stockgun, but may have a 12-gram quick change for fast 12-gram replacement. Quick-changers can be lever-action, screw-action or push-action. Some, like PMI's revolving Turret changer, contain multiple cartridges for faster changing action.

Like a semi-auto, a modified may have any large-capacity bulk loader holding hundreds of paintballs. The balls are poured into the loader, from which gravity pulls them down into the gun through a direct feed spout. This replaces the slower "rock-'n-cock" feature of a stockgun. A modified-class pumpgun with an auto-trigger lets the shooter squeeze and hold down the trigger, and then just pump and shoot. Each pump sends a ball flying at full velocity with no need for indi-

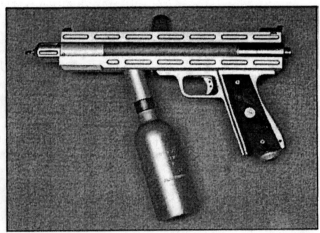

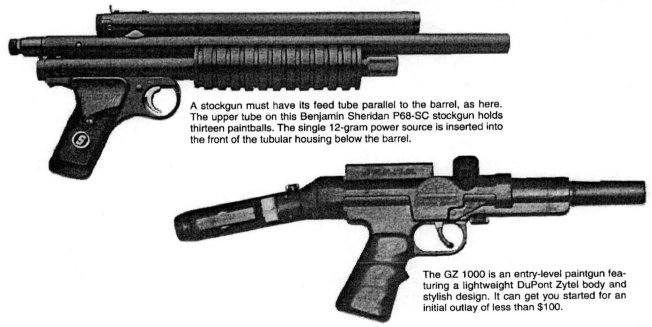

A stockgun must have its feed tube parallel to the barrel, as here. The upper tube on this Benjamin Sheridan P68-SC stockgun holds thirteen paintballs. The single 12-gram power source is inserted into the front of the tubular housing below the barrel.

The GZ 1000 is an entry-level paintgun featuring a lightweight DuPont Zytel body and stylish design. It can get you started for an initial outlay of less than $100.

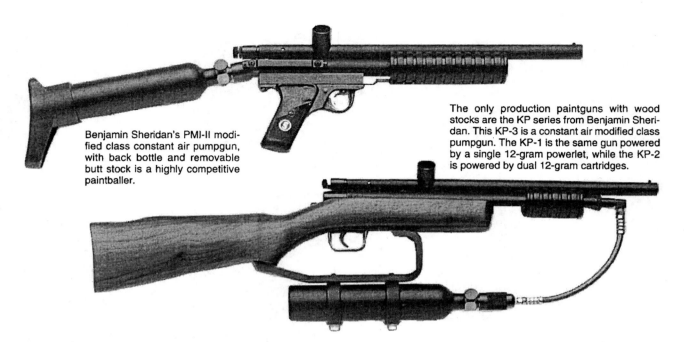

Benjamin Sheridan's PMI-II modified class constant air pumpgun, with back bottle and removable butt stock is a highly competitive paintballer.

The only production paintguns with wood stocks are the KP series from Benjamin Sheridan. This KP-3 is a constant air modified class pumpgun. The KP-1 is the same gun powered by a single 12-gram powerlet, while the KP-2 is powered by dual 12-gram cartridges.

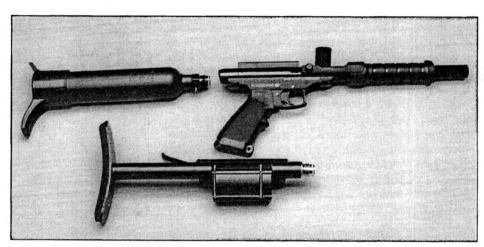

PMI's Trracer modified class pumpgun can be powered by a constant air bottle (left of gun), a PMI Turret changer holding several 12-gram cartridges (below gun) or by a single 12-gram powerlet (not shown).

Players may choose from a variety of bulk loaders, holding dozens or hundreds of paintballs. These loaders are used on guns in the modified and semi-auto classes.

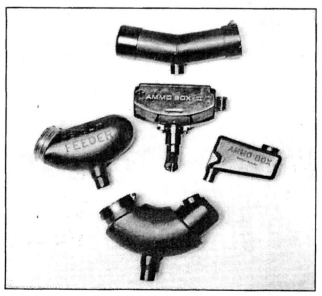

vidual trigger pulls. A practiced player can auto-trigger as fast as many semi-autos shoot. Auto-triggering is not allowed for stockgun play.

Modifieds are available under dozens of brand names. Examples include Air Power's Elite, PMI's Trracer, TASO's Spartan and Worr Game Products' Sniper. Costs range from under $100 to about $300 for a modified-class paintgun.

Barrels

Paintgun barrels reflect the hottest new area in paintgun innovation. Players change barrels for better performance under varying playing conditions and with different brands of paint. Barrels are made of aluminum, brass, steel or special polymers, and come in silver, black, red, blue, green, gold, camo-patterns, etc. Ads for the high-tech, futuristic-looking vented or ported barrels mention better accuracy and more silent shooting.

Nearly all barrels run between 7 and 14 inches from the ball drop to the muzzle. The inside diameters vary, usually

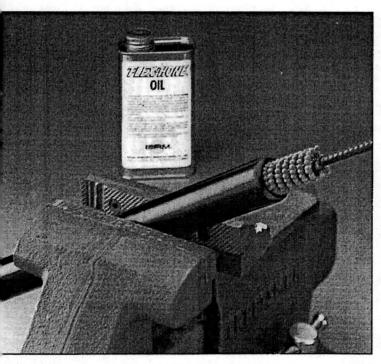

Players often use a Flex-Hone® to smooth and polish the barrel and chamber area. This gives more consistent velocities and straighter shots. (Photo courtesy Brush Research Co.)

between .687- and .693-inch. Barrels generally are smoothbore, but a few companies offer rifled versions. Nearly all smoothbore barrels are stone honed, Flex-Hone® finished, or roller-burnished.

Paintballs

A paintball is a round, thin-skinned gelatin capsule with colored liquid inside and comes in a rainbow of colors including blue, pink, white, silver, orange, red and yellow. When a paintball tags a player, the thin gelatin skin splits open and the liquid inside leaves a bright paint mark. A marked player is eliminated from the game. The paintball fill is a colored liquid that is non-toxic, non-caustic, water-soluble and biodegradable. It rinses out of clothing and off skin with mild soap and water. In the early years, paintballs really were made of oil-base paint, but these are not allowed in the game today.

The industry standard paintball is about .68-inch in diameter (68-caliber), with a weight of about 48 grains. Being gelatin capsules, the balls have a seam and are neither exactly round nor exactly .68-inch in diameter. Very few paintguns shoot the smaller 62- or 50-caliber balls.

Soft-gel encapsulating machines making paintballs cost over $1 million each. The leading paintball encapsulators today are Bullseye, near New York City; R. P. Scherer, with nearly a dozen plants worldwide and U.S. production in Florida; Sobel, Inc., with several plants worldwide including a California facility formerly known as Banner Gelatin (whose engineers designed and manufactured the first water-soluble paintball for NSG, Inc., in the early 1980s); and Zap, a Canadian encapsulator that is quickly taking market share.

Law enforcement and the military use paintball equipment for training exercises such as prison escapes, ships' security, vehicle stops and building-to-building clearings. Besides using recreational paintball equipment, they use other types of primer-powered "paint marking" devices and a "paint marker" ammunition shot from firearms—neither of which is allowed in the sport of paintball for safety reasons.

The Future

For paintball's first ten years, companies headed by long-range planners weathered the ups-and-downs of the new industry. Those with superior skill and foresight continued to grow and lead the industry today. Attesting to the industry's growth in the last three years, two airgun giants have put their marketing might into the paintball business. Crosman Corp. purchased the Benjamin Air Rifle Company, with its Sheridan Division, in 1992, and continues aggressive paintgun marketing and engineering through Benjamin Sheridan. In 1993, the Daisy Manufacturing Corp. moved ahead with mass merchandising plans for its Stingray semi-auto paintgun.

The multi-million-dollar deal that pulled Schwinn bicycles from the clutches of bankruptcy was made during paintball games called "War at Four," played at venture capitalist Sam Zell's place in Ketchum, Idaho. Bob McGuire's "Outdoor World" television show on SportsChannel America has included paintball for nearly three years. The 1993 Charlton Heston Celebrity Shoot included a paintgun shooting booth with PMI Trracers and Direct Connect F-2 Illustrators, located next to Marksman's airgun shooting booth. Retail dealers and distributors flocked to the '92 and '93 IWA international gun shows in Germany, buying paintball products to meet consumer demand. Paintguns and products are displayed at the National Rifle Association's annual meeting and trade show.

On the other hand, paintball is not always welcome and still suffers growing pains. In the U.S., paintball products are banned from the largest outdoor shooting sports show in the world, the SHOT Show. According to Robert Delfay, spokesman for the National Shooting Sports Foundation that sponsors SHOT, the ban that began in 1988 is caused by the fact that paintball players point "guns" at other people. Similarly, some folks feel playing paintball glorifies war and desensitizes players to violence and war.

As more people, especially corporate executives, play paintball, the game's negative image continues to fade. Talk to any new player coming off the field with a big blue splat square on his goggles and you're going to hear, "If this were real, I'd be dead." Players easily recognize the difference between paint and bullets. The more people that play the game, the more the public will learn that comparing a paintball game to real war is as unrealistic as comparing fencing to a knife fight in a back alley. Someday, paintball will be widely recognized for its ability to promote non-violent conflict resolutions.

The next time you're looking for a new thrill, a new way to shoot and a game that will challenge your skills to the max, try paintball. Good luck, and happy painting!

Chapter 15

The Bikathlon Event

A once unlikely combination of airguns and mountain bikes has become one of the hottest shooting/riding sports for the younger set.

by John Clark
Introduction by J.I. Galan

YOU MAY HAVE your own opinions on the subject, but it sure looks like kids nowadays have more ways of having fun—and I am referring only to *clean*, wholesome recreation—than the kids of my generation. Take such simple, seemingly unrelated devices as bicycles and airguns, for example. Back in the long-ago days of my childhood, no one apparently gave even a fleeting thought to the possibility of combining cross-country biking and airgun shooting as an organized activity in order to keep us little devils out of mischief.

That was, of course, long before the advent of those beefy mountain or off-road bikes. Those were also the days when most airguns, particularly those deemed suitable for a young lad just reaching his teens, were about as specialized as a 2x4 plank. Hey, I hope I'm not being overly critical. It's just that I honestly wish that there had been a sporting event like the bikathlon back when I was a kid!

So what, exactly, is this bikathlon thing? Well, read on, for all the facts surrounding this exciting new sport from John Clark, former public relations and advertising manager for Marksman Products. John has been General Manager of Beeman Precision Airguns since S/R Industries—which owns Marksman—bought Beeman in 1993. He was instrumental in

The finish line never looked so good when panting from an all-out bike ride.

110

the successful implementation of the bikathlon program for Marksman and, thus, has a unique perspective on this fairly new twist to make competitive airgun shooting even more attractive for the young.

• • • •

Out of breath, young Amy stood at the firing line wiping the sweat out of her eyes. "I've got to concentrate," she thought to herself as the sights of her airgun wavered all around the target. Two hits, and then a miss. Another miss. "I can do it!" Amy thought to herself. And she slowly squeezed the trigger and the final target dropped. Quickly putting the airgun down, Amy jumped on her bicycle to continue racing around the course.

Her bicycle? And shooting? Yes, off-road biking and airgun shooting are now combined in a fast-paced new sport called the bikathlon. Designed as a way to keep young shooters involved in the shooting sports, the bikathlon is modeled after the grueling biathlon event seen during the Winter Olympics. In the biathlon, the competitors cross-country ski while stopping at various points to shoot small metal targets with a 22 rimfire rifle. Since many areas of the country do not get enough snow, and to offer a year-round sport, this event was modified to use off-road bikes instead of skis and 177-caliber airguns in place of rimfire rifles.

The bikathlon is a fast-paced event for the participants as well as the spectators. The competitors race around a small track, stop and dismount from the bikes to shoot metal targets which fall over when struck, and then continue along the course. The track is normally small enough (about 1/3-mile around), so the spectators are able to watch all the action as the participants square off against each other. While the sport does require a certain amount of strength for the biking portions, the shooting is the key to the event; it takes real skill and control to hold the airgun sights steady and shoot while puff-

Bikathlon competitors must make every shot count, but speed is also essential.

(Above) The water crossings are always exciting as the competitors splash their way through the race.

(Left) A range officer oversees each shooter to make sure that gun safety is followed, as well as to score the shooting portion.

Marksman product manager, Jim Bishop, presents awards to a pair of female finalists at a recent bikathlon event.

Mountain bikes are preferred, as their wide tires and strong design make them suitable for the off-road biking that takes place in a bikathlon event.

ing from an all-out bike ride. Both Crosman Airguns and Marksman Products actively support the bikathlon and host several events around the country each year. A first-time activity at the 1993 National Boy Scout Jamboree, more than 18,000 Scouts had an opportunity to try out the bikathlon at Fort AP Hill in Virginia.

The sport was designed for both boys and girls between the ages of eight and sixteen years. Competitors usually race in heats of five with the boys and girls racing together, and with the girls winning more often than you might imagine. Of the fifteen finalists at a recent Masters Bikathlon National Championship, five were females, and at least one female made the finals in each age bracket.

Typically, there are three age brackets for the competitors, which are based on the age of the competitor on the first day of the match. Ages eight through ten fall into the "Novice" bracket. "Juniors" are eleven to thirteen years. The "Senior" division holds racers aged fourteen through sixteen. As there are no official rules for the sport, only guidelines, the match director is free to modify, add or change the age groups as he or she sees fit for a particular event.

The age divisions are important, as the older the competitor, the longer the race will be. A Senior competitor will ride the course three times (for a total of one mile) while stopping to shoot three different times. Junior racers make two laps and shoot twice, while the younger, Novice division participants go around the track once and stop to shoot only once.

The biking course is set up as a loop so the start line is also the finish line. The course usually travels along trails or is marked with cones or rope so the racers know which way to

The Marksman #1790 Biathlon Trainer air rifle is an ideal choice for the bikathlon.

The Crosman 357 CO_2 revolver has been the favored handgun model used in the bikathlon. Shown here is the 8-inch-barrelled version with optional scope.

The Daisy Model 44 CO_2-powered revolver also would be a good handgun choice for the bikathlon.

head. Dirt tracks are preferred, as they are not as dangerous should a participant fall while riding, and there are always the natural obstacles to go over or around. Water crossings always make exciting photographs when the rider splashes through, and many of the shooters proudly wear their mud-covered shirts as badges of honor. Hills, mounds and other natural terrain can also add to the racer's challenge.

Safety is *always* the foremost concern during the bikathlon. Therefore, the participants must wear helmets while riding, and it is strongly suggested that they also don knee and elbow pads. The best type of bikes to use are mountain bikes or BMX bikes; with most bikathlons run on an off-road course, the wide tires and sturdy design of these bikes make them the most appropriate.

There is at least one point along the course where a firing line is set up with a bank of targets for each competitor. While nearly any type of target can be used, the best consists of a bank of five metal discs, about 2 inches in diameter, that fall when struck with a pellet. No BBs are allowed, due to the possibility of dangerous ricochets. Available through Crosman, these targets can be reset with the pull of a string and should be painted a high-visibility color so the shooter can easily see them. The targets can be set at any reasonable distance from the firing line, typically between 5 and 10 yards. During the shooting portions, all competitors are required to wear protective eye wear.

While speed on the bike is important, a steady aim and cool nerves on the firing line are even more vital to success in the bikathlon. A missed target adds a time penalty to the competitor's score, often up to 30 seconds for each missed shot. The

competitor fires as many shots as necessary to drop all the targets, but some races allow only a maximum of twenty-four shots, with time penalties for targets left standing. Either way, the lowest overall time (after all penalties are tallied) is declared the winner. So while some competitors may be quick on the pedals, if they cannot also shoot competently, they will not do too well in the overall event.

It should be noted that the participants are not allowed to ride the course with the airguns—they are always at the firing points. The match director can set up the shooting portions of the event as he or she chooses. Some events have been run using only air pistols, others with air rifles exclusively, while still others have used a combination of the two. Considering all the airguns on the market, the most favored air pistol is the Crosman 357 revolver because of the CO_2 power and multi-shot capability which allows fast shooting. The Marksman #1790 Biathlon Trainer air rifle is a favorite of many due to

The targets are small, round discs that fall when struck to indicate a hit.

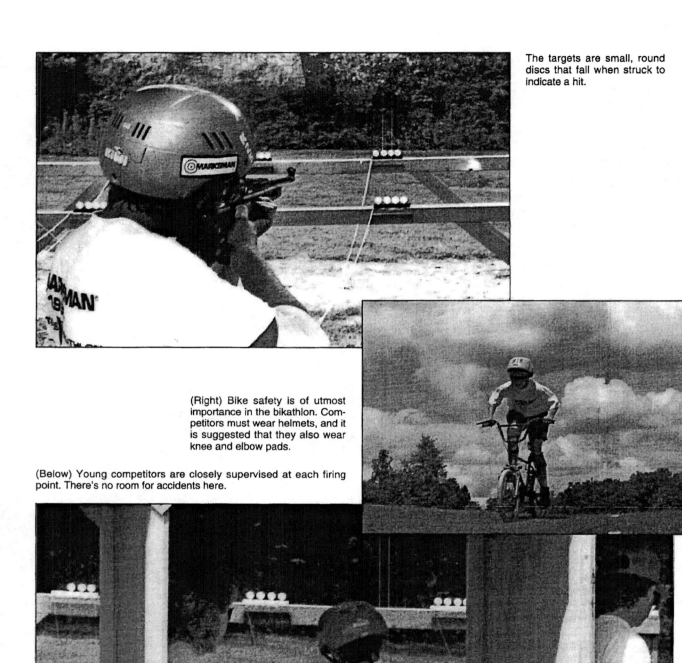

(Right) Bike safety is of utmost importance in the bikathlon. Competitors must wear helmets, and it is suggested that they also wear knee and elbow pads.

(Below) Young competitors are closely supervised at each firing point. There's no room for accidents here.

Depending upon the age group, the bike portion of the race involves one to three laps around a 1/3-mile course.

Competitors must load their own airguns. Note that during shooting each shooter must wear the proper protective goggles.

the accuracy of the gun and the diopter sight, which makes it easy to quickly get on target while puffing from an all-out bike ride.

During most events, before racers are allowed the chance to participate, they are required to complete a ten- to fifteen-minute lecture on safe bike- and gun-handling techniques. The topics covered include how to operate the airguns, shooting safety and proper gun handling, the correct sight picture with the airguns, proper bicycle use and riding safety, plus specific details relating to the match. If space and time allow, it is also recommended that there be a practice range available for those competitors who may not have a lot of shooting experience.

There is not much equipment needed for the bikathlon, basically just airguns, bicycles, targets, stop watch, safety pads and bike helmets. Competitors are usually allowed to bring their own equipment, so long as it is not deemed by the officials to give anyone an unfair advantage. For those who want to give this new sport a try, there are usually both bikes and airguns available, as well as the necessary protective equipment, right at the match site.

Interested in finding out more about the bikathlon, or even how to set up your own event? Both Crosman Airguns and Marksman Products put on events each year around the country and can give you more information on the sport. They will also send you a catalog full of airguns suitable for the bikathlon.

For those looking for a new challenge that combines physical stamina and great discipline, give the new bikathlon a try. It is not always the fastest individual on the bike who wins, nor even the best shot, but the racer who is able to blend both biking speed and accurate shooting is the one who will finish with the gold medal. And as young Amy learned, it is not easy to concentrate on shooting a 2-inch target with sweat trickling down into your eyes and your legs weak from a tough ride.

Chapter 16

Airguns and the U.S. Olympic Shooting Team

This chapter includes an exclusive report from Karen Mutka, former Public Relations Director of the U.S. Olympic Shooting Center, that gives unique insights into world-class training with airguns.

by Karen Mutka
Introduction by J.I. Galan

MOST OF US mere mortals who love the shooting sports have, at one time or another, participated in some type of formal competitive shooting event. In fact, drawing from my personal experience over the course of many years, I would guess that at least one-fourth of all the people who own guns of all types (firearms as well as airguns) participate more or less regularly in some form of competition. As for pure airgunners, however, I would estimate the proportion of competitive shooters among their ranks to be even higher than with firearm shooters.

I base guesstimates upon the fact that airguns offer far greater flexibility and adaptability than firearms when it comes to any kind of competitive setup. Have you ever heard of a formal target shooting match, with any kind of firearm, being conducted at the local school gym, or perhaps on the back lot of some civic club in the middle of a populated area? I think you get my drift; when it comes to limited-area competitive shooting of any kind, airguns can be used almost anywhere with complete safety and minimal alterations to the locale.

The only physical requirement, as far as space is concerned, consists of some 40 to 45 feet that includes the regulation 10-meter firing distance and enough room for the

Any large room or hall having at least 40 to 45 feet in length can be adapted, safely and quickly, to accommodate a 10-meter airgun match. These young ladies show tremendous concentration as they go through the course of fire. (Photo courtesy Shooting Federation of Canada)

State-of-the-art training facilities greet top shooters at the U.S. Olympic Shooting Center.

Competitive shooting with airguns can be just as exciting and rewarding as with firearms. In fact, it could be argued most convincingly, I believe, that 10-meter airgun events offer even more of a challenge to the individual, because the pellets fired by match airguns move far slower than bullets. Therefore, the shooter must exert greater control over the gun during the entire firing sequence, lest the pellet be disturbed in any way while it is still moving up the bore. Although the time differences involved are, in mundane perceptions, infinitesimal, we are dealing with a world-class sport in which the most minute variances can easily mean the difference between coming home with a gold medal, a lesser medal, or nothing at all except disappointment.

Considering all of the above, and in order to bring you an in-depth look at what it *really* takes to excel in world-class airgun shooting, I thought it would be best to contact one of the top sources in the world for this sport: the Shooting Center at the U.S. Olympic Training Center in Colorado Springs, Colorado. Thus, I asked Karen Mutka, former public relations director of the Center, to bring us the story of what it is really like to train for Olympic airgun events, to go, as she put it, "straight to the top—airguns can take you to the Olympics." Her story is chock-full of information, not only on the various 10-meter disciplines, but also with lots of valuable tips and comments from some of the world's top coaches and shooters themselves.

• • • •

It happened in 1984. The International Olympic Committee waved its magic wand, and air rifle shooting gained Olympic status.

American athletes rejoiced. "Right from the start, we took the air rifle events very seriously," said U.S. Shooting Team (USST) Director Lones Wigger, a two-time Olympic gold medalist. "Our women, in particular, have always been among the best in the world in airgun, so we knew this could increase our medal potential in a big way."

Eighteen-year-old Pat Spurgin was quick to prove him right,

shooters up front, plus the pellet traps and backstop at the opposite end. The backstop itself can be fashioned from a row of large cardboard boxes stuffed with old newspapers or magazines. These are placed behind the pellet traps in order to catch any stray shot that somehow misses the trap. Another excellent, yet simple and economical backstop consists of a section of heavy canvas or blanket(s) hung behind the traps. Although 10-meter matches are shot exclusively with 177-caliber pellets, the guns typically used produce muzzle velocities in the 450 to 600 fps range, so a thick, heavy blanket or canvas is usually enough to safely stop a wadcutter-style flat-head pellet. Cork panels also work very well as backstop material, by the way.

Olympic team shooters train on the ultra-modern air pistol range at the U.S. Olympic Training Center in Colorado Springs. (Photo by Casey B. Gibson)

Seoul World Cup bronze medalist Lonn Saunders stands in the running target ready position. (Photo by Casey B. Gibson)

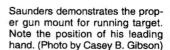

Saunders demonstrates the proper gun mount for running target. Note the position of his leading hand. (Photo by Casey B. Gibson)

earning her place in history as the first female Olympic air rifle champion. Four years later, men's and women's air pistol events joined the Olympic program, and the USA's Erich Buljung took the men's silver medal after shooting's equivalent of a photo finish.

"Airgun is a big sport in Europe, and the fact that Erich had that fabulous score in the Olympics was a big shot in the arm for us," said U.S. National Pistol Coach Arnie Vitarbo. "Today I'd say ninety-five percent of our people shoot air pistol. It's one more chance for a medal, and they know it helps with their other guns. The fundamentals are exactly the same."

Olympic running target "went airgun" in 1992, as international officials converted the sport from 50 to 10 meters. The new game suited twenty-one-year-old Rusty Hill's style, and the young talent led the nation with his eleventh-place Olympic finish that summer in Spain.

"Changing Olympic running target to 10 meters has built our

participant base unbelievably. Ten-meter ranges can be installed anywhere, the airguns and pellets are relatively inexpensive, and people are now saying 'Yeah, we can afford this sport. Let's give it a try,'" said U.S. National Running Target Coach Martin Edmondson. "We've got a new generation of shooters like Rusty, Lonn Saunders and Adam Saathoff with the confidence and expertise it takes to win. They know that if you've got the drive and motivation, then, yes, you can do it."

Different people have different views on training methods, but world-class athletes learn what works for them and use it to optimize their strengths. This article will give you the perspectives of several U.S. Olympic Training Center coaches and athletes about how to launch an international shooting career in running target, air rifle and air pistol. While they aren't the only authorities on this subject, and sometimes their opinions conflict, they've all used their knowledge of equipment and training to win medals at the world and Olympic level.

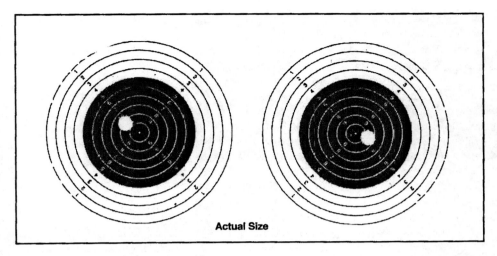

Actual Size

In 10-meter Running Target, scoring "10s" is a most elusive proposition. On the left target, the shot barely touched the 10-ring, but that's good enough for a top score.

Running Target

In Olympic running target, athletes shoot sixty shots from the standing position at paper targets moving across an opening in a wall 10 meters downrange. A match is divided into thirty slow runs and thirty fast runs. In slow runs, athletes have 5 seconds to bring the rifle up from the waist area and track, aim, and fire at the target. Fast runs allow 2.5 seconds for the same process.

Currently, the Olympic event is open only to men, but more and more women are now competing on the national and international level (Olympics and World Cups excluded). "In 1994, we'll be sending qualified female running target shooters everywhere that there's an event for them," said Edmondson, at the beginning of that year.

Equipment

For both men and women, choosing the right equipment is critical. Edmondson recommends that beginners start with a Daisy air rifle, while intermediate shooters may modify the heavier Diana and RWS guns. In international competition, most elites shoot the Feinwerkbau C-60 or 601, while a small percentage use the Steyr Match. Running target guns have adjustable buttplates and cheekpieces to elevate and align the shooter's head with his scope.

International rules dictate that scopes must be fixed 4x and no more than 300mm in length. Beginners might want to consider a Burris or Leupold single-post reticle for their training. More experienced shooters should choose a modified scope like the Nickel or Premier, which is available in both the large post (21mm) for shooting at the target bull or the small post (13-15mm) for aiming at the aiming dot. For mounts, he recommends Premier Reticles or the European-made EAW.

Clothing is another concern for most shooters, but Edmondson cautions beginning and intermediate competitors not to spend too much money too soon. "For less experienced running target shooters, equipment can become a crutch," he notes. "We'd rather see them learn and perfect the fundamentals instead of getting in the equipment race and paying lots of money they don't need to pay at that stage in their career."

For the advanced, Edmondson recommends flat-soled, stabi-lizing shoes—like AHG, Sauer, or Kustermann—and a Mouche leather jacket over a Mouche sweater. "The jacket and sweater basically act as a corset to keep your torso turning as a single unit over your hips," he notes. There are no international restrictions on running target clothing.

For beginners, the USST recommends Crosman pellets or a low grade of H&N or RWS. Intermediate and advanced shooters should train and compete with RWS, H&N Finale Match, or any other pellet with which they feel comfortable.

Early in their training, new shooters simply need a place to shoot static air rifle until they can consistently hit the 8-ring or better. Then it's time to shop for a 10-meter running target machine. Two good bets are the OMTM or a used Daisy. The OMTM is self-contained with its own pellet trap and illumination system, while the Daisy requires a separate trap and lighting. In both cases, the user needs a 46-inch-high table and enough space to set up and shoot.

Edmondson tells new running target shooters to concentrate on learning to accurately fire an air rifle, generally by shooting from a supported position on a bench. (His recommendation on a guide to the fundamentals is the NRA's *The Basics of Rifle Shooting*.) Start by shooting from 10 meters at a bigger target—like the air pistol target, for example—then advance to the static air rifle target. "We don't transfer anybody to the running target until they've spent enough time learning how to get in the ready position, how to mount and rotate, how to adjust the sights—in essence the basic fundamentals of shooting a perfect shot," said Edmondson. "And our elites don't do anything different. They reinforce those basics every single day."

Position and Practice

Running target is fired entirely from the standing position. Assuming the shooter is right-handed, the left arm and hand hold the rifle near the end of the forend of the stock, elevating the gun to target height. The right hand holds the pistol grip, lifting the buttplate roughly two centimeters above the hip bone. From this position, the shooter waits for the target to appear, then mounts the rifle to the shooting position.

"The key to the mount is being consistent," notes Edmondson. The left hand moves only a small amount as the right

(Left) Competitive airgun shooting is a discipline that allows women to become just as involved as men. (Photo courtesy of Shooting Federation of Canada)

(Below) Many handicapped individuals can easily participate in formal 10-meter airgun events, as witnessed by this air pistol match. (Photo courtesy Shooting Federation of Canada)

hand lifts the butt of the rifle to the shooter's shoulder and cheek. "You have to bring the rifle up until it hits your cheek," he emphasizes. "If you do this, it creates a pivot point at the muzzle which allows the rifle to be pointed directly at the target."

Perfect your mounting technique by doing exercises in front of a mirror or with a wall bracket, which supports the muzzle and assures that it's the pivot point.

Learn the proper ready position and mount, then practice dry firing at a stationary target. When you've mastered this, you'll need to begin working on rotating and tracking targets. "Basically, from your pelvis up through your head should be one, still unit. Like a platform," said Edmondson. "Most people want to rotate with the arms and shoulders, but that's not correct. The rotation should come at the ankles, knees and hip joints as you pivot in the direction the target is moving. You have to be able to keep the rifle pointed at a target crossing the track in either 2.5 or 5 seconds."

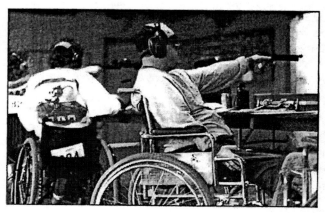

To practice proper rotation technique, Edmondson recommends cradling the gun in the crook of your left arm, with the butt under your right arm. "As you rotate your torso using your ankles, knees and hips, it teaches you the movement without being tempted to move your arms." Beginners may find it helpful to practice by following a line on the wall with the gun cradled, then in the mounted shooting position.

Next, begin tracking the moving target. Once again, Edmondson believes the best practice is in dry firing. "It allows you to learn the technique correctly without getting discouraged by less than perfect results," he said. "A beginning shooter should dry fire seventy-five percent of the time; an intermediate should do it about fifty percent of the time. Most of our elites mount and dry fire (on stationary targets) for 10-15 minutes every day, then shoot on stationary targets for 10-15 minutes, then dry fire thirty-four times (equivalent to one slow or fast run) before live firing on a moving target for fifty or more shots."

"Above all, you don't want to get wrapped up in the score. Then you're thinking about the end result and lose sight of the job at hand. Concentrate on shooting a perfect shot, then learn how to repeat that performance over and over, and the score will take care of itself."

Edmondson encourages his shooters to build their overall aerobic fitness, as well as upper body and back strength. Mental training is also critical. "It's important that you spend some time on visualization, whether it's before you shoot or between strings in a practice," he said. "Visualize yourself mounting the rifle, being on the aim point, tracking correctly with the correct sight picture, and then shooting a 10. Once you're proficient with your technique, visualizing yourself doing it correctly can be more effective than actually shooting the shot in many cases. It leaves a very powerful imprint on the mind."

Set goals and monitor your progress by keeping a training diary. "You need to have a written plan with realistic and obtainable goals. If you write it and review it daily, you'll be more likely to follow it," said Edmondson. "Our shooters have a plan for what they expect to do each day for the coming month, and bigger goals for the years ahead."

For more detailed explanations and demonstrations, consider purchasing the USST's thirty-two-minute video on Olympic running target. It's available for $25 plus postage and handling by calling USST Sales Inc.

(Right) This young lady is shooting an Anschütz 380 match air rifle at a recent Crosman-sponsored match conducted by the Shooting Federation of Canada. (Photo courtesy Shooting Federation of Canada)

(Below) This 10-meter group fired with the Anschütz 380 and Beeman H&N Match pellets forms one single, slightly elongated hole.

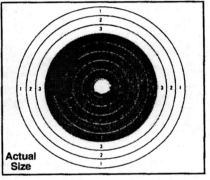

The perfect "10" shot on an official, UIT-approved 10-meter rifle target.

Olympic Air Rifle

Perhaps the greatest test of the trigger finger is Olympic air rifle, in which athletes stand and shoot at pin-sized bullseyes from 10 meters. It's the tiniest target in the Olympics, and men and women fire sixty and forty shots at it, respectively.

Guns and Gear of Choice

Few rifle modifications are permitted, and with a half-millimeter ten-ring (more like a dot) having accurate equipment is a must in this game. The 1992 Olympic rifle silver medalist, Bob Foth, recommends shooters start with the Daisy or El Gamo, but move up to the Feinwerkbau 300S, Walther LGR, or Anschütz 380 as soon as possible. These guns are available used from several dealers across the country. "As soon as possible after that you should try to move up to the Feinwerkbau 600, 601, or C60; the Anschütz 2002; the Hammerli; or the Steyr," he said, adding that, "Ninety percent of the people at the big international matches are using a Feinwerkbau."

Start out with RWS Meisterkugeln pellets in bulk. Because price differences are modest, Foth recommends moving up quickly to the best label you can get, preferably H&N Finale Match or RWS R10. "The sooner you have the good equipment and are using good pellets, the sooner you can start to learn

what it takes to shoot a ten," he said. "Your learning curve is much slower with lesser equipment."

Shooting jackets and pants made of canvas or leather are governed by strict rules for fit and thickness, as outlined in the NRA International Rule Book. The USST recommends beginners start with a cloth coat, then pick up used European gear or an inexpensive American brand. Intermediate and advanced shooters should consider Korean, Mouche or Thune—all labels worn by world-class shooters. Also, wear the jacket over at least one sweatshirt or sweater to absorb the motion caused by your heartbeat and pulse, adds Foth.

A glove on your non-shooting hand will give you protection and a better grip on the gun, while high-topped shooting boots will support your ankles during these lengthy contests (75 minutes for women, 105 minutes for men). A beginner might go with a Korean glove and high tops or tennis shoes. More advanced shooters should consider gloves by AHG, Gehmann, Kustermann or Thune, and boots by Kustermann, AHG or Korean.

"Most people can get their hands on used rifles and equipment through their club or a dealer who specializes in new and used international equipment like Neal Johnson/Gunsmithing Inc.," notes Foth. "Most of the rifles hold their market value, especially the better ones, so you should be able to get your money back when you decide to upgrade."

With the proper equipment, you're ready to begin position work. Good reference books on the standing position include the U.S. Army Marksmanship Unit's *International Rifle Marksmanship Guide* or *Going for the Gold* by Bill Krilling.

Get Into Position

If you're right-handed, start by facing about 90 degrees to the right of the target with your feet shoulder-width apart. Twist your upper body slightly in the direction of the target, then lean back for stability. Your left elbow should be on your left hip, or the upper arm should be on your rib cage. The rifle is supported by the left hand, either off the fist, palm or fingertips.

"When you're in the right position, the weight of the rifle is supported by bone—not muscle—and you should be able to relax your muscles," notes Foth. "That combination of bone support and relaxation produces a steady hold."

Place your cheek lightly against the cheekpiece and your right hand comfortably on the pistol grip. The buttplate should be near the bottom of its adjustment and against your right shoulder.

"Breathe a couple of times and relax. Once you've got a balanced, relaxed position you can use a very gentle touch on the trigger," said Foth. "Your focus is on sight alignment and trigger control, but you have to train your body to quickly recognize the bad stuff—any tension or movement. You need that fine muscle control to get your hold smaller and steadier, and it comes through repetition."

If you can't get to the range to practice, Foth recommends standing and holding in front of a mirror or at a dot on a wall at home. "As much as possible, you need to get in there and shoot for record," he added. "Use your score to help evaluate your

Olympian Bob Foth has a relaxed yet purposeful stance that allows him to control his breathing and muscles while aiming. Note how he rests the forend on his left hand. (Photo by Casey B. Gibson)

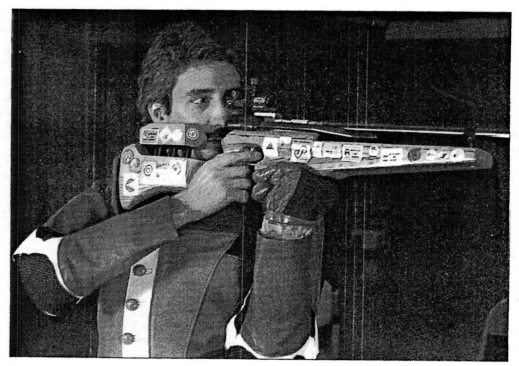

The proper equipment goes a long way toward ensuring winning scores. The rifle's forend is shaped specifically for such position shooting and the cheekpiece is adjustable for maximum comfort and repeatability of the head position. (Photo by Casey B. Gibson)

performance. It's not the only factor to use in that evaluation, but it's important. Almost every time I shoot I take sixty shots in a row without sighters. I look at the score from that string to help evaluate where I'm at and how a small change in position or things like a different aperture size, a change in equipment, or a new rear iris might help me."

Mental Preparation

"I think it's good to train every day, but for most people that doesn't mean shooting every day. If you're thinking about it, working on your equipment, doing aerobic exercise, that's training. It all adds up," said Foth. "You always want to think about building flexibility, but if you have body sway in your position, then strengthen your legs. If you have back problems, strengthen your torso. It's your responsibility to optimize your individual training program."

Foth believes shooters should start their mental training program on day one. "In the very beginning, just spend time thinking about the sport, what you like about what you did or what you want to try to do next," he said.

Eventually, your mental training should encompass visualization, relaxation techniques, and possibly other individualized programs. Top international athletes create a mental picture of what they want to see happen—whether it's as simple as a perfect sight picture or as complex as a whole string of forty or sixty shots. "Whatever it is, you have to visualize what you want to be thinking about, looking at, feeling, and doing when it's happening," said Foth.

Foth recalls once driving three hours to a match with a target taped to the steering wheel of his car. "I shot fifteen points better than I ever had in my life. Now, obviously, I had to keep my eyes on the road, but it kept my thoughts on shooting," he said. "I tell people to have a target in the back of your notebook when you go to school or in a drawer in your desk at work. It reminds you of shooting and helps you rehearse what that target should look like, what you want to see with a good sight picture. Sooner or later it'll pay off."

To build relaxation skills, practice tensing and relaxing different muscle groups. "What you're trying to do is train a relaxation response, eventually taking one deep breath and being able to relax all the muscles in your body and be aware of any areas of tension," he said. "That's the goal, and it's a progressive thing that takes years to perfect."

U.S. Olympic Committee sport psychologist Sean McCann recommends the following books for shooters seeking to improve their mental training programs: *Psyching for Sport* and *In Pursuit of Excellence* by Terry Orlick, *Athlete's Guide to Mental Training* by R.M. Nideffer, and *With Winning in Mind* by Lanny Bassham.

"Of the athletes we see here at the Olympic Training Center, shooters and archers are among the most sophisticated users of sport psychology, especially in the areas of imagery and visualization," said McCann. "It makes a difference and can speed the rise. Obviously, in the beginning, you have to practice and learn the fundamentals, but you get to a plateau at some point. That's when you need mental training to move up to the next level."

Air Pistol

In air pistol, athletes stand and shoot from a distance of 10 meters at a bullseye target with a .45-inch ten-ring. Men fire sixty shots in 105 minutes; women take forty shots in 75 minutes.

U.S. National Pistol Coach Arnie Vitarbo suggests that beginners start with the Daisy Model 747, then move up to the Daisy CO_2 import (the Model 91) when they reach an intermediate level. Men shooting between 535-550 and women shooting 350 or better should advance to the Walther CPM-1, FWB C-25 or Steyr Match. Athletes of all skill levels should train and compete with diabolo-design pellets from Crosman, H&N, RWS R-10 or Nygord Precision.

Equipment needs are minor compared to those of rifle shooters. You'll need a simple glasses frame, such as Knobloch or Champion, with a translucent blinder to block your non-shooting eye. "We don't want people squinting at the target," said Vitarbo. "It's one more muscle action that can detract from their concentration on the firing line."

Vitarbo also tells his athletes to wear concave-soled shoes cut below the ankle bone and a hat with blinders on either side to minimize distracting movement and light. Special jackets and pants are not allowed in this event.

The Proper Stance

To find your air pistol shooting stance, stand with your feet parallel and roughly 45 degrees to the target. Your finger should be placed on the trigger about half-way between the fingertip and first joint. Look through the sights, line them up with the target, close your eyes and relax.

"Then you want to open your eyes and notice the position

This 10-meter air pistol shooter makes sure that everything is properly adjusted on his Feinwerkbau CO_2 pistol before the match begins.

of the gun and how your sights are aligned on the target. If your sights are perfectly aligned underneath the bull, you're in good shape. Otherwise, you'll need to adjust your foot position. Then go through the whole routine again," he said. "I watch world-class shooters everywhere do this every time they step to the line. It's the best way to see if you're centered."

Once you've found the proper stance, focus on aligning your front and rear sights. "If the front sight is higher, you want to grip the gun a little higher. If you're aiming too much to the left, you want your hand more toward the front of the gun and the trigger," adds Vitarbo. "And if your front sight is too far to the right, you want your hand to rotate on the grip away from the trigger."

To master sight alignment and trigger control, dry and live fire at blank targets. "The better you become, the more you need blank target drills," said Vitarbo. "Bullseyes let you see the movement more readily and can distract your attention from the fundamentals. Over time, this drill builds confidence

U.S. team member Kirk Rasmussen shoots the air pistol with an unusual technique, but it allows good balance and relaxation for him. Note the shooting "glasses" with off-eye blinder. (Photo by Casey B. Gibson)

The 10-meter air pistol firing line is quite crowded at this Crosman-sponsored championship event in Canada in 1989. (Photo courtesy of Shooting Federation of Canada)

in your grip, stance, sight alignment and trigger control. And when your mind sees good things in training, it'll produce in the match."

Vitarbo tells his team to visualize the entire shot process before every squeeze of the trigger. "Whether it's training or a match, you should actually raise your gun, take a breath, align the sights, and see a perfect shot being fired. Then do it for real," he said.

To build the necessary arm and shoulder strength, hold dumbbells in both hands and rotate your arms in circles. You might also hold a dumbbell as if it's a pistol, then slowly raise your arm up and down as if you're firing a shot. Doing wrist curls in four different directions will build your wrists and forearms, and power walking is a good way to develop leg strength.

"I don't think most people know how much more shooting is than just pulling the trigger," said 1992 Olympic rifle gold medalist Launi Meili. "It's incredibly challenging—mentally

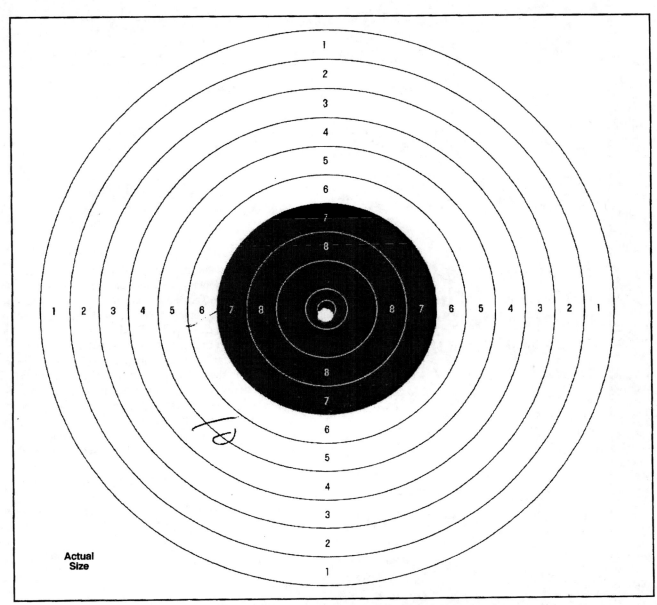

Actual Size

Although larger than the rifle target, the official 10-meter air pistol target is just as difficult when it comes to scoring a perfect shot.

and physically. Airgun is a great way to get started on the road to the Olympics."

Lones Wigger agrees. "There are now five Olympic airgun events, so it's a realistic way to get yourself to Atlanta in 1996 or Sydney in 2000."

But don't wait too long to start training. American shooters are already gearing up for the 1996 Olympics at World Cups and championships in cities like Seoul, South Korea; Munich, Germany; Cairo, Egypt; and Milan, Italy. When they aren't traveling abroad, athletes of all ages train at the U.S. Olympic Shooting Center in Colorado Springs, the largest indoor facility in the Western Hemisphere.

For more information on how you can pursue an Olympic airgun training program or attend camps at the U.S. Olympic Shooting Center, contact the U.S. Shooting Team.

Author's Note

Note: Keep in mind that dry firing a spring-piston airgun can cause serious damage to the gun in fairly short order. Pneumatic and CO_2 guns, on the other hand, can be safely fired without a pellet, as long as they have some air or gas. Extensive dry firing of pneumatic or CO_2 guns without air or gas, however, could damage their valves. Many modern world-class pneumatic and CO_2 guns incorporate trigger systems that permit dry-firing without the need to pressurize the gun.

Chapter 17

An Overview of Field Target Shooting

Field Target pioneer and world-class competitor Rodney Boyce gives us the inside story of this dynamic shooting sport.

by Rodney Boyce
Introduction by J.I. Galan

ONE OF THE most challenging and fun-filled airgun shooting disciplines is, without doubt, Field Target shooting. Although a relative late comer, Field Target has swept the airgun world like the proverbial wildfire, scooping up into its swelling ranks literally hordes of airgunners. I covered Field Target as much as possible in the Second Edition of this book, but due to space constraints, that coverage was rather limited, touching only on the key points of the sport in the chapter that covered *all* types of airgun competition. As a result, I decided this edition of AIR GUN DIGEST must have an entire chapter devoted to Field Target shooting. And in order to tap the best possible source for such a story, I asked none other than "Mr. Field Target" himself, Rodney Boyce, to give us his uniquely qualified perspective on this fascinating sport.

I first met Rodney Boyce in 1987, during the U.S. National Field Target Championship—which he won, by the way. Since then, he and I have kept in fairly frequent contact, helped by the fact that he is also based in the South Florida area. Rodney

Rodney Boyce with a prototype Daystate CR94 and a Burris 8-32x scope designed specifically for airgun use. (Harry Steiber photo.)

is one of those rare individuals who doesn't do anything halfway. When he really gets interested in something, you can bet your last shekel that he will jump in all the way and will probably come out carrying the winner's trophy. The former Duke University basketball player, race car driver and professional photographer has also had a most interesting and rewarding career in the shooting sports, and not always with guns, either.

Rodney Boyce entered competition shooting with crossbows in 1975 and went on to win the U.S. National Championships in 1979 and 1980. He then moved to Florida and took up airgun Field Target shooting, a fledgling sport at the time. In addition to winning several state championships, Rodney has won the Southern Regionals in Georgia twice, the Cajun Spring Nationals in Louisiana twice, and the U.S. National Championship in 1987, 1988 and 1991. He was a match director for the first U.S. Championship and the first World Championship. In addition, he has served on the Board of Governors of the American Airgun Field Target Association (AAFTA) since its inception; three years as chairman and currently as vice-chairman. His articles on this sport appear regularly in the British monthly *Airgun World*.

Here is his report on Field Target shooting:

• • • •

When it comes to air rifle competition shooting, Field Target has it all. It challenges the shooter and his equipment to the utmost in an atmosphere that is enjoyable. Camaraderie and gentlemanly conduct are integral parts of this activity. As a shooting sport, it is totally unlike any other airgun competition. Running target, 10-meter matches, benchrest and silhouette are well regulated as to target sizes, distances, equipment, shooting positions and even clothing. Field Target, on the other hand, is

Kevin Jackman of England, 1993 world champion, shoots his customized Air Arms 100 with a Leupold Mark 4 modified to 32x.

(Above) Bob Peiser, 1993 U.S. national champion, aims his Air Arms NJ Custom 100 with a Nightforce 8-40x scope. Note the strand of yarn below the barrel that serves as a wind indicator.

(Left) Top spring-gun shooter Cliff Smith prepares to fire his Air Arms TX-200 with Bushnell 6-18x scope.

127

Jim Smith shooting his super-radical, customized Titan Pneumatic. (Cliff Smith photo.)

George Gardner with a Marksman underlever rifle and Burris 6-24x scope.

Combat pistol instructor Will Farrugia checks out his Airmasters HW-77 before a match.

a freestyle game that takes place in woods and fields. Targets vary in size and shape and are placed at random distances from 10 to 50 yards. Shooting position and equipment are your choice. In some respects, this sport does simulate hunting conditions. However, unlike hunting, the targets are stationary and guaranteed to be there for you to shoot.

Field Target shooting is a British sport that came to our shores in the mid-1980s and has steadily grown in popularity all over the United States. The first U.S. National Championship was held in Florida in 1987. Each year since then, championship events have been held in Indiana, California, Michigan, Minnesota and three times in Louisiana. The inaugural World Championship was held in Florida in 1991, and this event put Field Target on an international level. The second World Championship was held in England and the third, in 1993, in Michigan. The British shooters so far have dominated these tournaments by taking the top honors every year. However, at Michigan, 1992 U.S. Champion Britt Harrison of Louisiana was tied for first place at the conclusion of three days of matches with British shooter Kevin Jackman of Devonshire. A shoot-off gave Jackman a one point edge, and he became the world champion. American competitors are still behind the Brits but the gap is rapidly closing. The British command of Field Target shooting is not surprising because airgunning is big business in England and each weekend thousands of shooters participate in matches. This airgunning mania is perhaps a result of the stringent firearms laws imposed on the British citizenry.

How to Play

The format of a Field Target competition is quite simple. A typical match would be thirty targets placed at varying distances in the woods—some will be on the ground, some in trees, and some scattered around the field. Among these targets, fifteen

(Left) Field Target shoots traditionally are a beehive of activity, with competitors eagerly checking their rifle/scope combos at the sight-in range.

(Below) A typical field target with the hit zone reduced to $1/2$-inch. The "paddle" must be hit to trip the sear mechanism that causes the target to fall flat.

firing points or lanes would be designated, numbering one through fifteen. Every lane would have one to three targets visible to the competitor in his or her shooting position, and each lane is separated from adjacent lanes by a minimum distance of fifteen yards. The firing positions are placed so the competitors are completely out of the line of fire of each other. Shooters are grouped into squads of three, and each squad is assigned a lane as their starting position. Therefore, fifteen lanes can accommodate up to forty-five entries. The competitors shoot one at a time at each lane, while the other two in his squad keep score and reset the targets. Scoring is simplicity itself—one point for a hit and zero for a miss. Usually, two shots are taken at each target, so for a thirty-target match, 60 points would be the possible score. When all three in the squad have completed their shots at a lane, they move on to the next lane until they have finished the course.

The heart of Field Target shooting is the target. They are silhouettes of appropriate game for air rifle hunting such as rabbit, squirrel, rat, pigeon and crow. Indigenous targets are utilized by some airgun clubs. For instance, in Louisiana, you'll see targets of various snakes, armadillo, frog, skunk and turkey. The targets are of steel construction, painted to approximate the particular critter. The front of each silhouette has a circular aperture that can vary in size from $1/2$-inch to $13/4$ inches. These are the hit zones. Behind the aperture is a steel paddle which, when hit by a pellet, trips a sear mechanism that causes the silhouette to fall backward with a satisfying "clank." When the target falls, you score one point. If you hit the front of the target, but not the hit zone, it will not fall. The dull thud of this miss tallies a zero on your scorecard. When a target has fallen, it is reset into the upright position by a cord that extends to the firing point. There is no need to go downrange to reset targets. As previously mentioned, the targets can be set at any distance from 10 to 50 yards; usually the smaller hit-zone targets are placed at closer

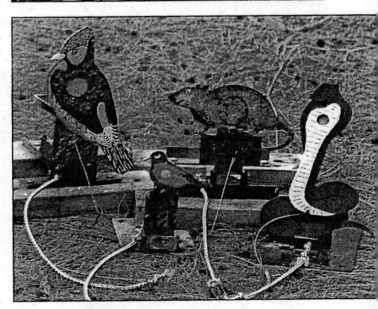

This variety of targets with different hit-zone sizes gives an idea of how the targets can be painted.

Competitors at the sight-in range prior to a match. (Ed Escue photo.)

Many shooters resort to the prone position for those really long shots.

(Left) Field Target allows basically any shooting style or position, and competitors sure make the most of it.

The J.I. Galan/Air Gun Digest "Top Gun Award" plaque was one of the honors presented for 1st Place at the second Field Target championship match in 1988.

distances with the larger ones further out. Target placement is at the discretion of the host club, but you can be assured the course will be challenging.

Because of the varying distances of the targets with their small hit zones, a Field Target shooter must know the pellet trajectory of his air rifle from 10 to 50 yards and be able to accurately judge the distances to the targets. Determining this distance is known as rangefinding. Perfecting this skill is critical for scoring a hit because pellet trajectory describes an arc that can go from 3/4-inch high at 30 yards to 2 inches low at 50 yards. Velocity and pellet weight/style are the factors that determine the trajectory arc of an air rifle, but rangefinding is another matter. There are some shooters who can estimate distances just by looking at the targets, but this is a rare skill acquired only through a lot of experience. It is the telescopic sight with adjustable objective focusing that comes to our rescue. By carefully focusing on the target, a shooter can pretty closely determine the distance by referring to the yardage index of the scope. When you know the distance and how much allowance for pellet trajectory is needed, you're ready for the shot.

The choice of shooting style is left to the competitor, but the most effective has been the sitting position, with variations usually determined by the physique of the shooter. With knees drawn up, you can support the rifle forend on one knee while grasping the knee and rifle with your hand. Another option is to cradle the gun in the crook of your arm, which in turn is supported by your knee. It takes a bit of trial and error, as well as practice, to get into a comfortable sitting position, but once mastered, it will be the most stable and steadiest of positions. It should be noted, however, that some targets may be placed so you can only shoot from a standing, kneeling or prone position. This is all a part of the variety that makes Field Target shooting unique.

Guns and Gear

The choice of equipment is also at the shooter's discretion. Any air rifle that is capable of generating about 800 fps at the muzzle can be effective in Field Target competition. By far, the caliber of choice is 177, for its inherent accuracy and flat trajectory. However, quite a number of shooters have been successful with 20 and 22 calibers. Air rifles fall into two basic categories—precharged pneumatics and piston guns—and FT matches are divided into classes along the same lines. In recent years, the pneumatics have recorded the highest scores. Being essentially recoilless and having quick lock times, they are accurate and forgiving guns. I've seen many of these rifles that are capable of 1/2-inch, ten-shot groups at 50 yards. On the downside, they are more expensive and require a scuba tank with high-pressure air, 3000 psi, for refilling the rifle every forty to seventy shots. The modern piston guns, especially those with fixed barrels, are very popular, as well as accurate. Ultimately, the difference in FT scores is not attributable to the gun, but to the skill and preparation of the shooter.

Some of the piston guns that you can expect to see at matches are the now-classic Weihrauch HW77, Air Arms TX200, RWS 48 and 52, Marksman 61 and 58, several models of Theobens, and the recoilless Whiscombe. The most popular of the pneumatics in the U.S. have been the Air Arms 100, Sportsmatch GC-2, Daystate and Titan, though two newcomers have recently come onto the scene—the Ripley AR4 and the Daystate CR94. All the pneumatics and many of the piston guns are manufactured in England. This is a direct result of the stimulus of Field Target shooting in the UK, which is the proving ground that results in better airguns for all of us.

Refilling a precharged pneumatic from a scuba tank takes but a few moments.

It could be said the most important piece of equipment for FT is the scope; without a scope, shooting at those small targets with little hit zones would be, at best, disheartening. The choice of scopes can be bewildering, but a good choice would be one with a power of at least 18x, preferably more, to allow accurate rangefinding. The higher the power, the shallower the depth of focus, which enables you to focus more critically. When referring to the yardage index of the scope, the higher power will give a more accurate reading of the distance. The most popular brands of scopes are Leupold, Tasco, Bushnell and, recently, Nightforce, Hakko and Burris. Specifically, the most competitive (but not in price) scopes are those that are 30x or more, such as the Leupold 18-40x Target ERF customized by Premier Reticles, the Tasco 8-40x, the Nightforce 8-40x, the Hakko 30x and the Burris 8-32x. The variable-power feature of a scope can be a big asset in FT shooting under some circumstances. A competitor may have to zoom down to locate a target downrange, or it may get too dark to see well at full power. Also, for standing shots, a lower power

might be the better choice. Another important feature is a target-style elevation knob. At every distance, the knob will be "clicked" up or down to compensate for the pellet's trajectory. The only alternative to clicking is holding over, and this takes lots of practice.

Preparing to Play

Getting ready for Field Target takes quite a bit of homework, and the first thing is to know your scope. Check to see that the yardage indexing is correct by focusing at various measured distances. If they are off, place adhesive tape over the existing numbers and mark your own yardages from 10 to 50 yards in 5-yard increments with a permanent ink pen. The next step is to determine the click values, and this is where the "Magic Number" comes in. The Magic Number is a system I came up with a few years ago, and it is effective in its simplicity. Scope manufacturers designate the click value in terms of minute of angle; usually they are either $1/4$- or $1/8$-minute. The $1/4$-minute would require four clicks to move the point of

Gus Guadagnoli rangefinding with his 30x Hakko.

132

impact 1 inch at 100 yards; the $\frac{1}{8}$ would require eight clicks. By multiplying the click value (for 100 yards) by 100, this gives the Magic Number—$\frac{1}{4}$-minute would be 400. Then, dividing the Magic Number by the distance of the target in yards gives the number of clicks required to move the point of impact 1 inch at that distance. For example, with a Magic Number of 400:

Yards	Clicks
50	8
40	10
30	13
20	20
10	40

The next step is to determine the trajectory of the pellet. First, select a zeroing distance, such as 35 yards, and shoot from as stable a position as you can manage at a paper target. Adjust the elevation and windage setting as necessary until you consistently hit the mark. This will be the zero. Set both knobs to this zero mark if they are adjustable; otherwise, mark them so you know where zero is. Now, you must shoot at 10, 20, 30, 40 and 50 yards and record the number of elevation clicks, either up or down, necessary to hit the mark at each of these distances. This will give you a good idea of the trajectory for that pellet and gun. Later on, it would be wise to refine the record of clicks needed for each distance by repeating the process for every 5 yards. This takes a bit of doing, but if you don't do it, hitting Field Targets at various distances would be like playing the lottery. Believe me, nothing in shooting competition is more satisfying than knocking down a steel Field Target. It is a fun challenge, but preparation is the big step to enjoying the sport.

Rules and Regulations

In 1987, at the first U.S. Championship, the American Airgun Field Target Association was formed to promote and foster the sport as well as provide a format and guidelines on how the game is played. AAFTA also publishes a monthly newsletter and in-depth Field Target Handbook that can be obtained by calling or writing the Association.

The following excerpts from the AAFTA Handbook are reproduced, courtesy of AAFTA. Hopefully, they will shed even more light on the rules governing this fascinating shooting sport.

Official AAFTA Rules

Match Terminology

Hot Line: Safe to commence firing.

Cold Line: Cease fire, unload all guns.

Shooters Meeting: A time when the match director will address all competitors and discuss rules, procedures, times, number shots and other pertinent information prior to a match.

Shooting Pad: A location from which a shot must be taken at a target in a lane.

Lane Markers: Two poles, stakes, etc., used to identify body placement on a shooter's pad.

Split: When a pellet hits the edge of a hit zone on the target and "splits" into pieces with one of the pieces striking the hit zone.

Paddle: The round disc to be hit on the target that unlatches the trigger and allows the target face to fall.

Marshall: A volunteer that administers the rules with regard to targets on the course. He also enforces the safety rules.

Range Safety Officer: Calls the line on the practice range.

Blow off a Shot: When a competitor wants to shoot a pellet into the ground because of a bad pellet or mechanical problem.

Squad or Squadding: A group of up to three shooters.

Tie Breaker Lane: A lane designated before a match to break a tie score.

Time Limit: A period of time imposed on a shooter to prepare to and shoot a target.

Lane: A designated area in which a target is placed when shooting a match.

Air Bottle: Scuba tank or equivalent.

Shooting Time: The time shooting will commence at a match.

Reset: When a string is pulled from the shooter's pad to make the target ready for the next shot.

Safety Rules

1. All Airguns shall be kept unloaded until on the firing line, with the muzzle pointed downrange and ready to fire.

2. Airgun muzzles will at all times be pointed away from all persons.

3. When on the firing line, safe Airgun procedures will be observed including:

   A. No Airgun will be cocked or loaded until a shot is ready to be fired downrange.

   B. When an Airgun is cocked or loaded on the firing line, the SAFETY will not be released until the muzzle is pointed at the target and the shooter is ready to FIRE.

   C. When cocking Spring Airguns, the Shooter must hold the cocking lever or barrel while inserting a pellet, to prevent the accidental discharge of the gun and preventing injury to himself or other shooters.

   D. Safe spacing of shooters on the firing line is both judicious and courteous.

   E. Each shooter is responsible for his or her direction of fire, and safety toward other shooters.

   F. When the Range Safety Officer or Marshall declares the line "COLD" all Shooters will break the breech, open the loading port or bolt, or unlatch the cocking lever to signify a safe "COLD" line.

   G. The Range Safety Officer should be notified when a shooter wishes to put up a new practice target. The Range Safety Officer will, at his discretion, call for a "COLD" line. At that time targets may be put up on his command. On the Field Target course the appointed marshalls will act as deputies of the Range Safety Officer (Chief Marshall).

   H. The Range Safety Officer or Marshall will have the final decision on matters of "Safety on the Range."

   I. Lead Pellets only may be used on the range.

4. Safety must be encouraged and enforced. It is therefore important that all shooters strive to practice safe Airgun handling. It is also important that shooters remind anyone of unsafe Airgun handling and, if necessary, report unsafe practices to the Range Safety Officer or Marshall.

5. NO children shall be allowed on the firing line. Junior Shooters MUST be cleared by the Range Safety Officer by being instructed on RANGE SAFETY.

6. No alcohol will be allowed on the sight-in range or Field Target course.

THESE SAFETY RULES WILL BE STRICTLY ENFORCED. ANYONE ABUSING THESE RULES MAY BE EXPELLED FROM THE SHOOTING RANGE AND MATCH PARTICIPATION.

As adopted by AAFTA on 10/30/92.

Shooting Rules

1. **Airguns:** Any safe airgun shooting a single pellet. Any airgun declared unsafe to people and/or property (including targets) by the match director will be barred from use.

2. **Sights:** Any form of sighting system may be used. No separate device designed specifically for or used for range finding may be used to view the targets.

3. **Ammunition:** Any design of pellet that is completely constructed of lead or lead alloy only.

4. **Targets:** Silhouette fall-when-hit targets resettable from the firing point will be used. Silhouettes should be of typical airgun quarry. Targets should not be closer than 10 yards, nor further than 50 yards from the firing point. The match director should assure that shooting lanes and physical limits of the firing points are clearly defined. A clear and unobstructed view of the hit zone must be afforded. Shooters shall not reset their own targets.

5. **Scoring:** Scoring shall be on the basis of one point for each "hit," and zero for each miss. A hit will be awarded when the target falls; any movement of the back plate which does not result in the target falling will be scored as a miss. Any discharge of the airgun, without first announcing one's intention to deliberately discharge the airgun into the ground shall be scored as a record shot.

6. **Shooting Position:** Any shooting position is allowed, but the range may be set up to necessitate use of a forced position on some targets. Rifle slings may be used as a means of steadying the aim, but no other form of support for the airgun or body may be used. The rifle must be supported solely by the shooter's hands and body.

7. **Seating:** The maximum height for any form of seat is 3 inches, including the backrest. The seat may not be used for gun support. *Note: Variations of Rules 6 & 7 may be applied at the discretion of the match director in recognition of shooters' desires, while ensuring that no unfair advantage is

accrued. In the event an advantage is obtained, those shooters shall compete in a separate class for awards, e.g.: a chair class.

8. **Disputed Scores:** Any challenge must be made to the marshall prior to leaving the target. Any dispute not resolved at that time will be referred to the match director, whose decision will be final.

9. **Penalties:** The penalty for unsafe practice, ungentlemanly conduct or any form of cheating is disqualification.

10. **Target Sequence:** The match director should designate a sequence for shooting targets by numbering left-to-right, nearest-to-farthest, etc. A shot at the wrong target will be scored as a miss for the correct target, with the shooter resuming at the target immediately following the correct target in sequence. The wrong target will be reset and shot in proper sequence.

11. **Time per Shot:** In the event of excessive delay at shooting lanes, the marshall and/or match director must time the shooters. In this event, shots not executed within the time limit will be scored as misses.

12. **Tied Scores:** In the event of two or more shooters tying for an award, a shoot-off, or other tie-breaking system, will take place.

13. **Match Director:** In any matters arising and not covered by these rules, the match director's decision will be final.

As adopted by AAFTA on 6/15/90.

Targets

1. **Type:** There are both commercial and "Home Made" targets that can be used in matches. Any target that is reliable and capable of withstanding 20-25 foot/pound pellet strikes can be used. Targets should be tested with both high-power and low-power airguns. The quickest way to ruin a match is to have a target that does not work properly! The target should *fall* when hit in the hit zone and not fall when *not* hit in the hit zone! Currently most targets are made in England.

2. **Hit Zone Size and Shape:** Hit zones should be round in shape! Hit zones sizes can range from $1/2$" to $1 3/4$", with the most common size being $1 1/2$" diameter. Smaller hit zones are generally used in lesser numbers.

3. **Hit Zone Size and Distance:** Target distance should be a minimum of 10 yards and a maximum of 50 yards. Care should be taken when placing a target at 10 yards, since pellets can bounce back from the target. When setting a course, shooter proficiency should be taken into consideration (i.e., good shooters can hit tougher targets than new shooters.)

The following target placement distances are for expert shooters:

Hit Zone Size	Maximum Distance
$1/2$"	25 Yds.
$3/4$"	35 Yds.
1"	45 Yds.
1+"	50 Yds.

These distances should be reduced based on the shooter's abilities and, as shooters get better, they may need to be increased.

4. **Average Target Distance:** For a Regional or National match, the average distance of all the targets should be 30-32 yards. Remember, you can put reduced hit zone targets at shorter distances to keep the average and still have a challenging course. It is not necessary to stretch all the $1 1/2$" targets to the maximum range.

5. **Target Strings and Rubber Bands:** It has been found that a good quality braided Dacron line (50-80 Lb. test) will not stretch and will last longer under ultraviolet rays than Nylon or Polypropolene. This line is

used for offshore fishing and is extremely durable, but it is rather expensive. It is recommended that Nylon not be used since it stretches and makes the target hard to reset. A simple fishing leader used through the target hole will keep the line from fraying on the metal target. Rubber bands or light bungee cords attached to the target and to the line with a little slack will curtail string snags, which prevent target knockdowns.

Note: If the braided Dacron line is too expensive, use only enough for the target placement distance (i.e., 25 Yds., 40 Yds. or 50 Yds.).

6. **Target Installation:** Targets are staked to the ground via stakes (nails) through holes in the target base. It is important that all targets be secured to the ground and leveled (a small torpedo level will do). Targets that are not secured will be loosened and pulled up with hard resettings, thereby making them unreliable. Tree targets can be secured to the tree by hose clamps or rope to prevent using nails in the tree. A base bracket should be constructed with the application in mind. In order to be reliable, tree targets must have rubber band or bungees to prevent the string from becoming too heavy to allow the target to fall when hit. Prior to installing any target on the course, it is important that the target hinges be lubricated and checked for proper movement and action.

7. **Target Painting:** Since Field Target shooting is a fun sport as well as a challenging sport, detailed painting of the targets make them more enjoyable for all competitors. Flat Black targets don't excite anyone! A little art work goes a long way in creating realism! Hit paddles should be given a base coat of white paint then dayglow orange should be applied over that. Of course, all hit paddles should be repainted between matches.

8. **Target Placement:** Placement relies on the imagination of the course designers with the following guidelines:

   A. All participants should share equal visibility of the entire hit zone.

   B. The terrain should dictate the shooting position.

   C. All competitors should have the same opportunity to shoot in the same shooting position.

   D. When placing a target in a lane, a spotter should be in a shooting position to give detailed instructions to the person setting the target. This way the spotter can make sure short and tall, as well as left and right handed shooters have the same advantage. Binoculars or a scope will allow the spotter to see if any obstructions exist. Lane markers should be adjusted to afford the shooter the ability to get a clear shot on all targets in the lane.

   E. All targets should be set from a pre-determined plan.

   F. When setting targets, the shooting sequence should be determined (i.e., shoot the nearest target then the longest target).

   G. When two targets are in one lane, care should be taken to make sure that the string from the longest target does not interfere with the other target.

   H. If the course has a tendency to have standing water or rain, make sure targets are not under water if it rains on match day.

   I. Make sure that the Marshalls can get to the targets during the match.

   J. Make sure that targets in one lane cannot be confused with targets in another lane.

   K. Look for level, firm ground when placing the targets.

Target preparation, maintenance, painting and planned target placement are essential to a successful match!

Course Preparation

1. **Course Layout:** Each course should be laid out using the available terrain. To lay out a *safe* course, remember that a "cone of fire" should be developed to direct all shooting away from competitors and in a safe direction. Things to take into consideration when laying out a course:

   A. One lane should never cross another lane...Safety.

   B. Shooting locations (i.e., "shooting pads") should be on a plane that allows safety for all.

   C. If you will be using tree targets, cut your lanes with the trees in mind for the targets.

   D. Based on the terrain, can you see the target from the "shooting pad?"

   E. Make sure that resetting strings can be run back to the firing line without tangling in briars, etc.

   F. One lane should not be too close to another lane.

   G. Will the shooter be sitting in a mud hole if it rains?

2. **Shooting Pads:** Shooting pads should be dry! When it rains, a little pea gravel helps drain water and is more acceptable to most competitors. These locations should be reasonably level, so that a competitor can safely take a shot.

3. **Lane Markers:** Lane markers are used to identify where the shooter must take the shot. Two lane markers should be used for each shooter's pad. The gun barrel should be between the markers, with the shooters body behind the markers. These markers can be made of wood, steel or other material, and should signify the lane number.

4. **Lane Trimming:** Target hit zones should be clearly visible from the shooters pad with no obstruction in the flight of the pellet. Remember both short and tall shooters when clearing the lane. When trimming the lanes, look for even the thinnest weeds, grass or vines.

A well laid out course, properly prepared, eliminates problems at match time!

Classification Rules

Open Class: Any airgun, any sight.

Standard Piston Gun Class: Any unaltered standard factory recoiling piston gun retailing for less than $600.00 (U.S.). All components must be standard factory with the exception of a sling. Scopes must be limited to 12 power or less. Variable scopes must be set at 12X or less. Elevation and/or windage settings cannot be changed while the shooter is at his shooting lane.

Unlimited Piston Gun Class: Any recoiling piston gun and/or sight that does not comply with the Standard Piston Gun Class requirements.

Additional Classes: The match director may provide additional classes if there are enough shooters to justify them.

Note: Any or all of the above classes may be divided into sub-classes, such as A & B or A, B & C. Usually this is accomplished by qualifying shooters by their scores from the first day or first round of the match. The purpose of this is to attempt to keep the number of shooters in each class fairly equal so that the percentage of prizes awarded in each class is fairly equal.

It is also customary to include a four-man state team prize at the U.S. Championship match each year.

As adopted by AAFTA on 9/30/92.

Chapter 18

Using Airguns For Self-Defense?

During the past quarter-century, there have been some very unique protection airguns.

by J.I. Galan

The Selecter was well suited for women due to its negligible recoil and relatively mild muzzle blast. Its awesome looks didn't hurt the user, either!

AIR OR GAS-POWERED weapons for personal defense have been rare exceptions, almost oddities in fact, among modern airguns. However, the concept of an air-powered defensive weapon is by no means new. Going back to other times and places, we find powerful precharged pneumatic air pistols and air canes that were quite capable of killing a man at close range.

Although air pistols of such tremendous power were apparently made in very limited numbers, unlike the more popular air canes of the late 19th century, the fact still remains that some of those surviving pneumatic pistols have been found quite up to the task of dispatching a would-be assailant. Examples of these powerful air pistols are those made in Austria during the 18th and early 19th centuries by Fruwirth, Oesterleins, Girandoni, Colnot and other less well-known airgunsmiths. Girandoni is the best known of the lot, of course, since he was the creator of the powerful pneumatic rifles used by Austrian sharpshooters with such deadly effect against Napoleon Bonaparte's troops.

The Selecter

Getting back to the latter part of the 20th century, however, the concept of the personal defense airgun has come to fruition so far in only a handful of isolated examples during the past twenty-five years or so. In most of those cases, the product in question achieved a modicum of commercial success, being useful in a limited range of applications in which lethal force was not warranted. Two of these devices were first marketed during the early 1970s. One of them, arguably the more intriguing of the lot, dubbed the Selecter, was a semi-auto CO_2 pistol that shot a variety of large-caliber plastic projectiles—impact, dye marking, CN and CS gas, and even exploding or "noise" shells meant to incapacitate an assailant without inflicting lethal or even long-lasting physical damage.

The Selecter was supposed to be a non-lethal weapon that would not kill or maim, if used properly. It could temporarily disable an attacker, or mark him for later identification if he managed to escape, something which could definitely be useful to police and security guards in some situations. The Selecter was initially manufactured and marketed by a company named SGL Industries of Rockville, Maryland. In its construction, the

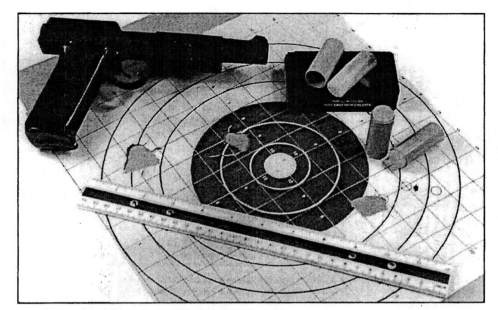

The Selecter had plenty of practical accuracy for defensive purposes, as evidenced by this three-shot group fired from 50 feet, using practice rounds.

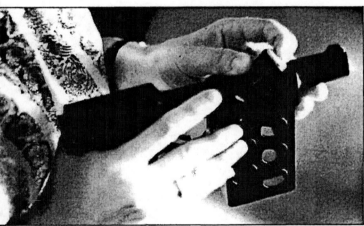

The Selecter could be easily reloaded without removing the magazine.

The Selecter pistol was a supposedly non-lethal weapon powered by CO_2, dating back to the early 1970s.

Selecter was made almost entirely of four different plastics: polycarbonate, polystyrene, nylon and polyethylene. The only major metal parts were the frame and the pressure chamber, made of zinc alloy. All exposed metal surfaces had a dull black finish, with synthetic surfaces sporting a glossy black look. Its principal moving parts were the trigger and main firing valve, made of injection-moulded nylon and polycarbonate, respectively.

The Selecter was shaped somewhat like a modern semi-automatic pistol, except its rather voluminous removable magazine was located directly in front of the trigger guard. The magazine had capacity for three cartridges, each roughly the size of a standard 12-gauge shotshell. The grip housed the CO_2 power supply, consisting of a regular 12-gram CO_2 cartridge of the type commonly used in pellet and BB guns. Each cartridge gave enough power for about ten to fifteen shots in the Selecter. The CO_2 cartridge would be placed in the grip, ready to be pierced. Since the pistol should not be kept pressurized when not in use, if the need arose, all one had to do

was to pull out the left grip panel—which pivoted at the bottom—and slap it back into place quickly. This action automatically pierced the cartridge, charging the gun and making it ready for action.

Fully loaded, the Selecter weighs approximately 19 ounces. It measures $7^3/_4$ inches overall, with a $1^3/_4$-inch smoothbore barrel in 72-caliber.

As stated earlier, the ammunition for the Selecter contained a variety of special-purpose projectiles, and these were launched at an average muzzle velocity of 160 fps from the stubby barrel. With the gun charged with CO_2 and a loaded magazine in place, the cartridge has a fairly tight fit in the open-top "chamber." Upon firing, the empty plastic casing is simply pushed out of the gun through that open top by the next round under it in the magazine. Maximum range is around 200 feet for most of the different loads available, although the maximum practical range given by the manufacturer was 50 feet, tops. It was possible to combine different types of cartridges in one magazine, since all five types were

The Selecter's light weight, ammo variety and repeater capability made it an awesome non-lethal defensive weapon.

Shown here are dramatic results from the impact of a "noise/confusion" exploding shell against a box full of newspapers. The concept of "non-lethality" appears to have been stretched to the limit with these shells!

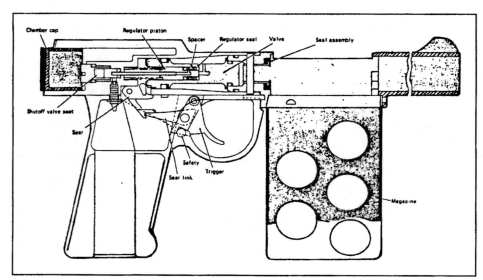

Although the Selecter pistol is fairly complex, the gun was a dependable performer.

the same size. For instance, an effective combination would have been an exploding/confusion cartridge first, in order to set off a big bang to jolt and daze the attacker, followed quickly by a CN or CS gas cartridge to further incapacitate the person. The third and final cartridge could be a dye marker, to ensure quick identification by police just in case the miscreant managed to escape the scene. The bright colored tints used in these cartridges were practically impossible to quickly remove from clothes or skin.

The non-lethality of the Selecter was based on its rather low muzzle velocity, combined with an impact area of more than ten times the frontal area of a 22-caliber bullet. Put another way, consider that the average standard-velocity 22 Long Rifle has a muzzle energy hovering around 107 foot pounds. In contrast, the average Selecter projectile carried a muzzle energy roughly ten times smaller, spread over an impact area some ten times larger than that of the 22 bullet! Thus, no pen-

etration of the body would occur with any of the various rounds available. However, the exploding/confusion rounds—which would blow up upon striking a hard object—could cause a rather nasty burn if an exposed part of the body was hit. In addition, a direct hit on the head, at short range, with any of these rounds could conceivably cause a very serious or possibly even fatal injury, despite this gun's status as "non-lethal."

The Selecter has a fairly hefty kick, despite being powered by CO_2. Another surprise is its rather loud report, which compares favorably to that of a 22 rimfire gun. If the noise/confusion rounds are used, the noise level goes up drastically, of course, particularly on the receiving end. These cute little bombs carried about $4\frac{1}{2}$ grains of flash powder and made a bang on impact roughly similar to that of a 32 ACP cartridge—perhaps a bit louder. Even if the assailant was not hit, one or more of these rounds launched in his direction would have a rather disconcerting—perhaps outright frightening—impression upon him. This could certainly buy the intended victim precious seconds to escape, assuming that the attacker was still in the mood to continue with his misdeed. In addition, a direct hit to the head could conceivably cause a rather nasty or even fatal injury.

The Selecter disappeared from the market around the mid-1970s, but was resurrected briefly some ten years later. That effort, too, seems to have been abandoned.

The Prowler-Fouler

The other CO_2-powered defense gun dating from the same time period was called the Prowler-Fouler, a device that looked like an overgrown police-style flashlight and was made by MBA Associates in San Ramon, California. This contraption actually fired a heavy beanbag projectile with sufficient force to knock down even a burly two-legged predator. I tested an original Prowler-Fouler nearly twenty-five years ago and quickly realized that this device—like the Selecter—could be quite effective in its intended role as a close-range defense weapon.

The Un-Gun

Despite its obvious practicality, however, the Prowler-Fouler was not a commercial success and, eventually, it too disappeared. Then, around 1987, a company called Trebor, based in Dublin, California, brought back the Prowler-Fouler under the name Un-Gun. It was just about identical to the old version in every way.

The gun body itself was made of Lexan, and, again, the Un-Gun looked like a fat flashlight. Overall, it measured 18 inches, 10 inches of which were taken up by the 40mm (1.6-inch) barrel. A look down the cavernous muzzle revealed the last 3 inches or so were rifled with twelve right-twist grooves.

The 8-inch-long handle contained the firing mechanism, which was quite simple in operation. A spring-loaded striker was activated by a large cocking knob, and a movable metal ring at the front end of the handle acted as a safety mechanism. Twisting the ring clockwise as far as it went would block the forward movement of the striker, preventing the latter from reaching the base of the cartridge in the breech. Pushing a button at the rear of the breech allowed the action to be opened for loading. The handle, incidentally, could be unscrewed from the barrel, making the Prowler-Fouler/Un-Gun extremely compact and convenient to transport.

The cartridge used by this unusual weapon measured $6\frac{1}{2}$ inches long and was made of plastic. The business end was $2\frac{3}{4}$ inches long and contained a plastic sealing wad at the bottom, then the beanbag (Stun-bag) projectile and a Styrofoam end wad. Behind all that went the standard 12-gram CO_2 cylinder. There was a rather wide choice of power levels offered for the Un-Gun, with low- and medium-energy CO_2 cylinders—regular 8- and 12-gram sizes, respectively—as well as nitrogen-filled medium- and high-energy cylinders in 8- and 12-gram sizes also. For the shorter 8-gram cylinder, a spacer plug was provided.

The CO_2 or nitrogen cylinder was placed in the rear section of the plastic cartridge, neck end first. Thus positioned, the narrow end of the cylinder came in contact with a fixed piercing spike or "firing pin" that was an integral part of the car-

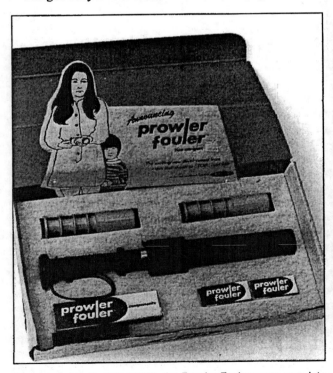

As marketed in the late 1960s, the Prowler-Fouler came complete with spare shells, beanbag projectiles, power cartridges and other necessary components.

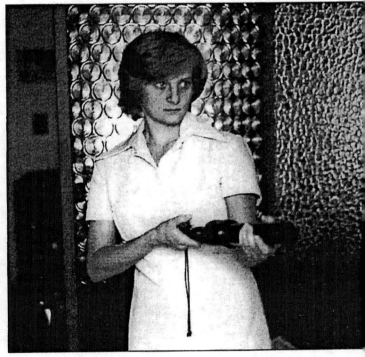

The Prowler-Fouler was an effective defensive weapon for home use, even if it was a bit unorthodox.

139

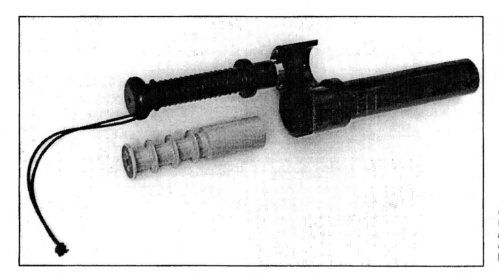

(Left) The Prowler-Fouler/Un-Gun is shown swung open in order to load a shell.

(Below) The bore of the Prowler-Fouler had rifling, but it's debatable whether this had any telling effect on the accuracy of the beanbag projectile.

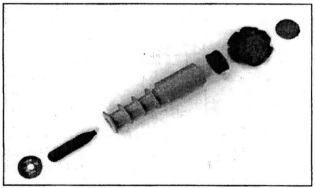

Contents of a Prowler-Fouler shell, from left to right: bottom paper seal to prevent CO_2 cartridge from falling out, CO_2 or nitrogen cartridge, plastic shell casing, plastic sealing wad, 6³/₄-ounce beanbag projectile and front cardboard wad.

Fully accessorized, the 1980s Un-Gun version of the Prowler-Fouler presents a truly intimidating sight from the business end!

tridge. When the spring-powered cocking knob was released from its cocked position, the striker slammed forward, driving the CO_2 or nitrogen cylinder against the piercing spike. This punched a large hole in the neck end of the cylinder, allowing all of its contents to be released instantaneously. This sudden burst of compressed gas pushed against the plastic sealing wad, driving it, the beanbag and the top wad out of the gun with great force.

The nitrogen-filled cylinders could drive the beanbag at about 100 fps, while the low- and medium-energy cylinders produced 70 to 80 fps. If you think these are ridiculously low muzzle velocities, think again. The 3-inch diameter beanbag—made of canvas cloth and full of small lead shot—weighed about 3010 grains, which translated into a muzzle energy of over 66 foot pounds at the high end. This kinetic energy level compares favorably with that of a standard velocity 22 Long Rifle cartridge fired in a short-barreled handgun, except the impact energy of the beanbag is spread over many times the area of the 22 bullet. For instance, the recipient of a hit to the torso would show only a bruise at the point of impact; yet the beanbag would carry enough energy to temporarily stun and even knock down the assailant.

The Prowler-Fouler/Un-Gun had substantial recoil and an intimidating muzzle blast. Despite that, a solid two-handed grip allowed enough control for practical accuracy at across-the-room range. The maximum effective range of this device was reported to be around 40 feet.

A variety of accessories were available for the later Un-Gun, including a slip-on open sight, flashlight holder, spare cartridge holder and even a detachable wooden buttstock. Most of these accessories were useful, although they tended to make the device look like some sinister sci-fi contraption. By the way, the basic Trebor Un-Gun with plastic shells, CO_2 and nitrogen cartridges, plus a couple of beanbags retailed for around $100 back in 1987. As a collector's item, the price of this device would be considerably higher now.

The Pneu-Gun

By the early 1990s, another gas-powered defense gun appeared. The Pneu-Gun was a thoroughly clever—though somewhat scaled down—version of the Prowler-Fouler/Un-Gun.

The Pneu-Gun looked like a streamlined police baton and was made of aircraft-grade aluminum with a black anodized finish. When its three sections were screwed together, the sample I evaluated measured 24 1/2 inches overall. This specific model had an 11 1/4-inch barrel extension that could be removed, leaving the gun with an overall length of just 13 inches.

The caliber of the Pneu-Gun was a respectable 710—almost identical to that of the Selecter—and the barrel had a smooth bore. Fully loaded, the three-section sample I tested weighed just over 2 pounds, although a shorter model weighing just under a pound was also produced.

The shot-bag projectile used in this device weighed 3 ounces and attained a muzzle velocity in the 175 to 225 fps range. At the low end, the shot bag carried a muzzle energy of about 89 foot pounds, which lies squarely in the energy realm of the 22 Long Rifle and 25 ACP cartridges. The big difference is, of course, the pliable shot bag spreads the kinetic energy over a much larger area on impact, causing only a temporarily stunning blow. The shot bag is propelled by one 12-gram CO_2 cartridge that is totally expended with the shot.

The CO_2 cylinder was fitted into the rear of an aluminum shell. The front section of the shell contained one plastic gas check, a black nylon shot bag and a plastic retainer disc to seal the works. Once loaded, the shell was inserted into the rear of the barrel section. Cocking was accomplished simply by pushing in a large trigger knob at the rear of the gun until a click was heard. The barrel and action sections of the Pneu-Gun were then screwed together, whereupon the device was ready to be fired. One sharp blow with the heel of the hand on the trigger knob caused the striker to push the CO_2 cartridge into the piercing pin, releasing all its pressure behind the gas check, driving out the shot bag.

The Pneu-Gun was quite a beast, despite its streamlined size. Those relatively small, sausage-like shot bags could strike with unmistakable authority out to a range of about 20 feet. Of course, the closer the assailant, the greater the impact. Once the shot bag was fired, by the way, the Pneu-Gun could still be wielded most effectively as a baton. The firing behavior of the Pneu-Gun was relatively mild, having only slight recoil. With a bit of practice, it was relatively easy to consistently hit a target the size of an average man's torso at up to 20 feet. Surprisingly, there was no sharp blast upon firing—unlike the Prowler-Fouler/Un-Gun—only a subdued whoosh followed by the "thud" of the shot bag striking the target.

The Pneu-Gun was marketed by Guardian Security Products in Phoenix, Arizona. Their basic AG-1 model retailed for just

(Above) The 911 Un-Gun is the most compact of all the baton-like stunbag shooters, measuring just 14 3/4 inches overall.

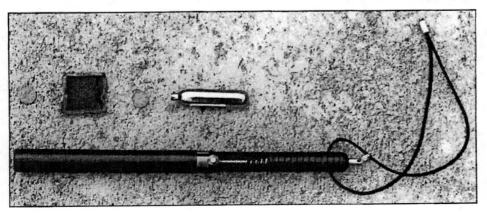

(Left) Simple, strong and delivering a staggering blow to an assailant, the 911 Un-Gun shoots a square-shaped beanbag at about 130 fps. The 12-gram CO_2 cartridge fits at the rear of the barrel, while the beanbag and wads go up front.

(Left) The Pneu-Gun was another beanbag shooter intended to temporarily stun a violent assailant without inflicting lethal damage. It was made of aircraft-grade aluminum and powered by a 12-gram CO_2 or nitrogen cartridge.

(Below) Fully disassembled for cleaning or transportation, the Pneu-Gun occupies very little room.

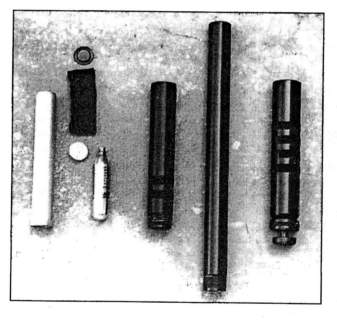

under $170 in 1992. Repeated efforts to contact the company for an update on this product, however, yielded negative results. Thus, it appears the Pneu-Gun, like its predecessors, is now history.

Instant 911 Un-Gun

Yet another gas-powered personal defense weapon that followed on the heels of the Pneu-Gun went by the rather descriptive name of Instant 911 Un-Gun. This device was produced by Protection Survival International, Inc., of Capitola, California, and it, too, appears to have gone the way of the dodo bird, as several attempts to contact the company also proved fruitless.

The Instant 911 Un-Gun is really a much scaled-down version of the old Prowler-Fouler/Un-Gun. Overall length of the 911 Un-Gun is $14^3/_4$ inches, with a $3/_4$-inch rifled bore—like the old Prowler-Fouler—that's $3^1/_4$ inches long. Its two tubular sections are made of Lexan with a dull black finish. Fully loaded, ready for action, this handy little gadget weighs just 10 ounces. The barrel and action sections are screwed together and must be separated for loading. Power is provided by one 12-gram cylinder of either CO_2 or nitrogen. The latter is the manufacturer's recommended power source, as it is claimed that CO_2 is somewhat unreliable due to temperature fluctuations. I haven't found that to be the case with any of the guns discussed in this chapter, but I concede that in a very cold environment CO_2 would not produce optimum performance.

The 911 Un-Gun shoots a 2x2-inch square-shaped stunbag weighing about 635 grains, at a muzzle velocity of 130 fps or so. This translates into a muzzle energy of roughly 23.8 foot pounds, which might seem rather anemic, especially when compared to some of the previously discussed defense guns. I can tell you from personal experience obtained during some of my tests, however, the 911 Un-Gun still delivers a distinctly stunning blow that can cause a great deal of pain and discontent to a two-legged predator, without inflicting lasting or serious physical damage in most cases.

There is no doubt that personal defense devices such as the ones discussed have a place in our increasingly violent and crime-ridden society. Although firearms are clearly the most effective and deterring weapons for personal protection, even when no shot is fired, there are simply too many variables out there which, in some cases, may dictate that something other than a firearm be employed.

Killing a violent, though unarmed assailant, for instance, even if he initiated the attack, is not generally viewed with sympathy by many segments of our criminal justice system. In addition, there are good, honest folks out there who simply can't or won't kill an attacker, preferring instead to use some non-lethal means of ending the confrontation. Beyond all that, gas-powered defense guns such as the ones we have visited here are highly interesting developments in a field where airguns had not ventured for nearly a century.

Chapter 19

The Airgun Collector

An inveterate air-gun collector, Larry Hannusch tells all about the ins and outs of a fascinating and rewarding pursuit.

by Larry Hannusch
Introduction by J.I. Galan

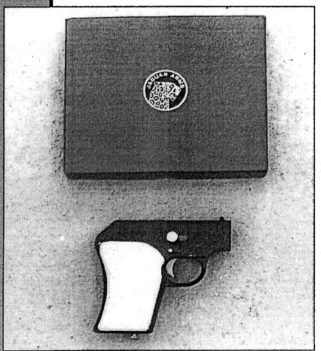

This Jaguar Arms "Cub" with its original box is a rare find indeed. It is the smallest CO_2 pistol ever made, dating back to the mid-1970s.

THIS BOOK WOULD not be complete without an in-depth look at one of the fastest growing activities currently surrounding airguns: collecting. Indeed, since I wrote the Second Edition of AIR GUN DIGEST several years ago, interest in collecting airguns has soared to new and unprecedented heights. So much so, in fact, that airgun-only shows—similar to regular firearms shows—seem to be on the upswing in the U.S. This is, in itself, a previously unknown phenomenon—something that just a few years ago would have bordered on the incredible even among seasoned airgunners.

In fact, there is now a keen and rather widespread interest in collecting all sorts of airguns. Even firearm enthusiasts are known to dabble in the previously unholy pursuit of gathering a few collectible air-powered pieces now and then. Times sure have changed, and those of us who seek old or semi-old airguns to add to our collections are, in most cases, no longer regarded as misfits in need of psychiatric counseling. Moreover, the pursuit of collecting all manner of antique and vintage airguns is now viewed by shooters and gun collectors, in general, with the same understanding as the collecting of antique firearms.

In fact, the market for collectible—as well as current, but used—airguns has grown so dramatically in recent years there is even a monthly tabloid, simply titled *Airgun Ads*, which began circulating nationwide in 1993 and appears to have met with remarkable success. Crammed full of ads for airguns of all types and vintages, as well as accessories, parts and literature, this unique publication is a must for all serious airgun collectors, since highly desirable pieces turn up in its pages on a fairly regular basis.

Having said all that, I am going to turn over this chapter to Larry Hannusch, the same fellow who earlier in this tome gave us a look at the air shotgun. As a thoroughly dedicated airgun collector, Larry Hannusch is uniquely qualified to take us through the convoluted and sometimes bizarre world of airgun collecting.

• • • •

Pouring out from the deep, dark recesses of the human psyche flows an incurable disease commonly known as collecting fever. Though the exact cause of the ailment has not been positively identified, its symptoms are unmistakably genuine and quite frightening in scope. Nowhere is this malady more seri-

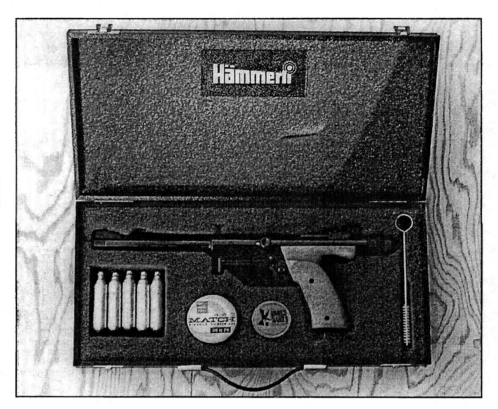

A mint-condition, cased Hammerli Master CO_2 target pistol, although of fairly recent vintage, can still be a real prize to an air pistol collector.

ously evident than in those poor, afflicted souls known as airgun collectors.

For years, the few lonely airgun collectors in society enjoyed a pseudo-cult status as a bunch of card-carrying eccentrics. They were viewed with pity as an aberrant group of wannabees who couldn't hack it as collectors of "real guns." Times change, and so do attitudes. Dealers who once scoffed at the airgun market now buy and profitably sell airguns on a regular basis.

This is not to say that airgun collecting is only a recent phenomenon. On the contrary, history tells us about an airgunner who assembled a collection more than 250 years ago, whose guns would be the envy of even the most advanced collector of today. We shall briefly look into his collection and then survey the direction of this fascinating field into the present day.

The History of Airgun Collecting

The history of the airgun from centuries past is still a rather obscure subject. Unfortunately, many of the early writings concerning airguns were rife with erroneous information. Makers often credited as inventors of airguns were usually only skillful copiers of designs witnessed on other gunsmiths' workbenches. Coupling this trend with the propensity of most writers to overlook the importance of primary research has led to records that are factually suspect in this area.

Though the lung-operated blowgun is indeed the oldest form of airgun, our area of interest concerns the mechanical airgun. By definition, this type either generates or releases compressed air to fire the projectile through some mechanical process. As such, this defined airgun can be subclassified into one of three general types: pneumatic, spring-piston or gas (usually CO_2).

These terms help us to understand and evaluate our collectable airguns, though in some cases the lines of distinction can become somewhat blurred. Airgun variations exist which could arguably be defined into more than one category. In fact, pneumatic and gas guns are so closely related that a case could be made that they should both be classified together as reservoir airguns (i.e., those using a valve). Within this viewpoint, spring-piston airguns would be the sole inhabitant of the other antithesis group known as non-reservoir airguns.

However, most airgun collectors use the familiar three-group classification to define their airguns. For the most part, the system is adequate enough to describe most available guns and will be the foundation upon which further discussion herein will be presented.

Early Pneumatics

Whereas the very earliest forms of airguns were spring-piston types or variations known as bellows guns, the invention of the valve led to a new direction in airgunning around the year 1600. After that, the air produced by a piston in a cylinder, otherwise known as a pump, could be cumulatively gathered and released upon demand. This ability to store compressed air led to exciting new possibilities in the realm of high-powered weapons in an era characterized by primitive and unreliable firearms. These powerful airguns using a compressed air reservoir are now generally referred to as pneumatics.

The early pneumatics were not toys by any stretch of the imagination. They fired large-caliber projectiles usually ranging from 30 to 75 calibers and were hunting weapons designed for use against small to full-size game. Most of the earliest pneumatics were muzzleloaders, while later speci-

144

mens display several different forms of breech-loading mechanisms.

From these early days of airgun history, we find a sinister connotation attached to these arms. The lack of smoke and noise associated with these powerful guns led many to believe the role of the airgun was simply one of ill repute. Poaching comes quickly to mind, though the high costs involved in producing these airguns would seem to severely limit their possession and use by presumably seedy customers.

The pneumatic airgun is classified by the type of reservoir employed in the gun: barrel reservoir, butt reservoir and ball reservoir. Of these types, the barrel reservoir is by far the most rare, having enjoyed only limited production in the middle of the 18th century.

As the name implies, the barrel-reservoir airgun stores its compressed air in a compartment formed between an outer barrel and the true inner barrel. Air is charged into the system via either an integral pump in the buttstock of the gun or a separate pump inserted into the buttplate. Several of the known specimens are repeaters, while most exhibit the use of a fully functional flintlock mechanism.

While the flint jaws, frizzen and pan are usually functional items, the lack of a flashhole indicates the gun's sole use was that of an airgun. While some have suggested this was to disguise the true nature of the airgun and its negative stigma, it seems more credible that this cosmetic use of the full flintlock mechanism simply imparted a proper sense of feel and familiarity to the airgun.

This latter explanation for the airgun's flintlock is further supported by such identical use in some of the ball-reservoir airguns. These arms used a large external copper, brass or steel ball placed on the top, side or bottom of the gun as the air reservoir. Such an obvious characteristic would seem to negate any thoughts of trying to further disguise the arm as anything but an airgun.

Most ball-reservoir airguns have been dated from the late 1600s to the mid-1800s. Their production ran concurrently with the third type of antique pneumatic airgun known as butt-reservoir guns. As the name implies, the tank for storing compressed air is housed within the buttstock of the gun.

Buttstock airguns are by far the most common of the three types. The early models are scarce and have the metal air tank concealed within a hollow cavity of the wooden buttstock. However, most forms encountered will have a buttstock that can be removed from the gun to allow charging from a separate pump.

Later models of British butt-reservoir guns with shark-skin-covered buttstocks have been dated well into the third quarter of the 19th century. Most of these specimens evolved to the point of having a rotating tap system to allow easy breech-loading. Extra smoothbore barrels were often supplied to give the shooter the opportunity to try his hand at air shotgunning.

The most complex manifestation of this type of airgun are the intriguing air canes. These powerful guns usually have a removable top section which contains the air reservoir in a design not unlike a modified butt-reservoir airgun. The air cane lock mechanism is a beautifully miniaturized version of the hammer-striking valve design. Many collectible examples will be found with a rifled liner inside of a smoothbore shotgun barrel. Most highly prized among airgun collectors are the superb wooden-cased sets sometimes encountered, which often include the air cane, pump and numerous other accessories.

A Royal Collection

Back to the subject of the aforementioned airgun collector of yesteryear and his marvelous collection. His name was Landgrave Ludwig VIII of Hesse (1691-1768), and he was an airgun aficionado extraordinaire. As an avid big game hunter, he

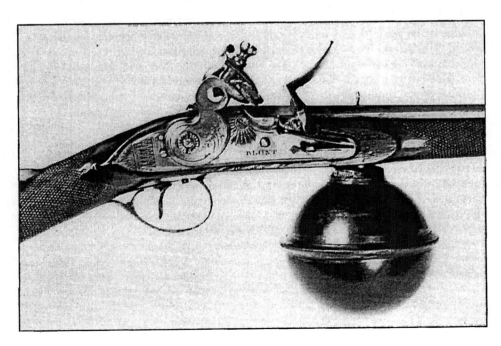

This fine ball-reservoir airgun by Blunt of London dates from the late 1700s. (Photo courtesy Larry Hannusch)

assembled an impressive collection of big bore airguns. Howard Blackmore, citing an earlier German work by E.H.K. Maleyka, records the following inventory in Ludwig VIII's airgun collection: twelve muzzle-loading, 55-caliber airguns; a handful of 38-caliber smoothbore barrel-reservoir airguns; and three convertible airgun/firearms that could be used with either power source. To say it was an impressive collection is to grossly understate the obvious.

Landgrave Ludwig was an avid airgun hunter, and a contempory royal reporter recorded the details of his hunts. One such kill dated 1747 involved the taking of a 480-pound stag with a massive rack of twenty-two points. Two years later in 1749, Ludwig reportedly took a nice-size stag at a distance of 154 paces. That same year he found the time in his busy schedule to kill more than 100 wild boar using his battery of powerful airguns.

Collecting Today

While Ludwig VIII enjoyed a marvelous working collection of big bore pneumatic airguns, things have drastically changed for today's airgun collectors some 250 years later. It would be extremely difficult to put together that kind of collection even if funds were of no concern. Many wars and numerous natural disasters have taken their toll on the number of available antique specimens.

While collectors today cherish and snap up such specimens when they occasionally do become available, most collectors focus their energies on airguns from the last 100 years or so since the Civil War. The field is unbelievably vast, and the study of the specimens and variations in existence could prove to be an exhaustive lifelong pursuit.

Airgun collecting in the past ten years has seen some tremendous changes, especially in the United States. Whereas the market in some foreign countries such as Great Britain has apparently leveled out somewhat, U.S. collecting is still growing strongly, with some areas receiving more interest than others.

A case in point is the early cast-iron-frame BB guns. These charming first guns for boys of bygone eras have always been desirable, but not overly expensive. Nowadays, if a dealer has a cast-iron BB gun, he thinks of it as gold, only worth a lot more. And even so, there are more than enough players willing to splash the cash for every one that becomes available.

Reasons for Collecting

What drives a person to participate in this sort of frenzy? What motivates even the casual collector to spend precious time and money to pursue such an unusual hobby? There are no pat answers to these questions, but several generalizations based upon years of collecting and observation come to mind.

Nostalgia plays a large role in the early development of an airgun collector, especially those interested in boys' BB guns. These airguns often sweetly remind the afflicted soul of the happier, simpler years before mortgages, cranky bosses and endless taxes.

Not to sound blatantly chauvinistic, but it is no secret most airgun collectors are men. For many, their boyhood years are filled with memories of when their fathers entrusted them with the responsibilities of a first gun—often a BB gun, even for those lads growing up in rural areas. It was a small step toward manhood and a part of the bonding process between father and son.

These memories mould and shape today's airgun collector, and he may well decide to specialize in BB guns. These guns, sometimes called tinplates for their prominent use of shiny nickel plating, offer a tremendous variety of available specimens. But because boys are notoriously rough on their possessions, it can be a real challenge to locate even the more dominant types of BB guns.

Another large segment of the airgun collecting fraternity appreciates the great variety of mechanisms and systems used in old airguns. King Solomon tells us there is nothing new under the sun, and this wisdom is never more evident than in the field of airgun design. No matter how revolutionary an airgun seems to be, its roots can usually be traced back to a previous design.

The attraction to mechanisms and their subsequent study can make for a very diverse airgun collection. In fact, the purpose of such a collection is actually to represent this great diversity. Brand names, origins, calibers, power levels and finishes are not of prime importance. Many airgun collections are built specifically around this design theme, but virtually all collectors appreciate the assortment of mechanisms found in the airguns they collect. One example of this would be the collecting of air shotguns. The large variety of specimens produced over the years can provide the interested collector with a real challenge.

Another group of collectors are those who appreciate fine quality. While it is true there are airguns from past times that display inferior workmanship, it is also true the quality of some airguns equals or surpasses that of a great number of firearms. There are plenty of airguns out there that were built to the highest levels of gunmaking standards.

Many airgunners who keep a number of guns around for plinking and hunting simply wake up one day and discover, much to their amazement, they had suddenly become a collector. In order to further validate their newfound status, they add more guns to round out their air arsenal.

There are many other reasons why people collect airguns, and often it is a combination of all these explanations.

What to Collect

Gallery Airguns

If we concentrate our discussion on post-Civil War airguns, one of the first prominent types to come to mind are the handmade American gallery guns. Evidently, the concept of these airguns came from immigrant gunsmiths who brought the designs from Europe to America.

These breech-loading airguns are all powered by a spring-piston power plant using double volute springs. These are made from flat spring steel that is wound into a two-dimensional coil, then the center of this coil is pulled upward to form a cone shape. A pair of these springs is then placed in the cylinder, smaller ends abutting each other and separated by a flat

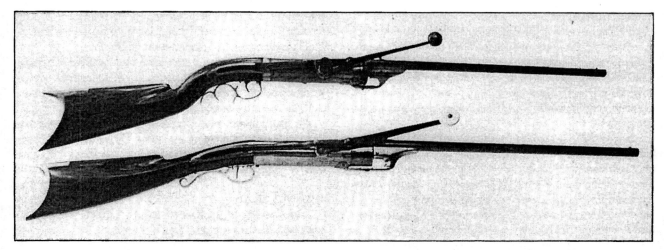

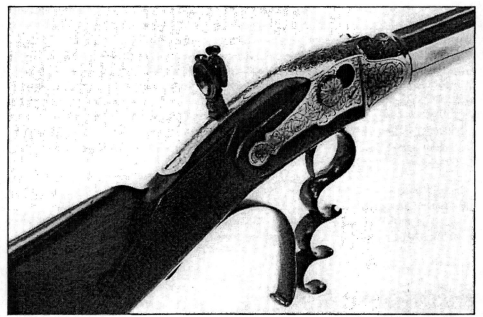

(Above) The Upstate New York gallery guns are characterized by their repeating cylinder magazines. The twelve-shot gun at the top is unmarked, while the lower fifty-five-shot specimen was made by Charles Bunge of Geneva, N.Y. Both feature all-brass construction and an attached lever-cocking system. (Photo courtesy Larry Hannusch)

(Left) Americans were not the only makers of gallery airguns, as evidenced by this fine crank specimen by Nowotny of Vienna. (Photo courtesy Larry Hannusch)

washer. The piston head is usually a flat leather disk to provide a seal.

This is a vast field that, surprisingly, has seen very limited interest among American collectors. It is possible this is due to the scarcity of specimens in relation to other types. However, these guns are much more plentiful than is sometimes acknowledged.

The quality of these airguns will range from average to awesome. Generally, as with most collectibles, the more desirable pieces are those that are signed with a maker's name. If in evidence, this is usually found on top of the barrel at the breech. However, many are found without any marks whatsoever.

Classifying American gallery airguns typically centers on the method of cocking the spring. The most common type has a long trigger guard as a lever that pivots in the butt of the gun to pull back the piston. Another, less common type uses a removable crank that acts upon an internal geared rack behind the piston to cock the action. A third type, much scarcer than the first

two, has a permanently attached lever on the right side of the receiver that pulls back on the piston to set the action. The fourth major type is a rare repeater version of the above with an attached crank and a revolving cylinder. This model is sometimes called an Upstate New York type to designate an area of known origin for several specimens. A fifth type is another rare form which has been previously unclassified. These guns cock via a top lever which is housed within the upper edge of the buttstock.

Further division of these airguns is made according to the type of breech-loading mechanism. The most common system uses a barrel that tips up to load. Another, scarcer form uses a barrel that pivots along its longitudinal axis to expose the breech, and most were designed to shoot darts. However, the Upstate New York guns, such as the fine repeaters by Charles Bunge of Geneva, New York, shot round lead balls. Other makers of single shot types, such as William Stein of Camden, New Jersey, made provision for shooting round balls by using a spring-loaded detent in the barrel to hold the projectile in place.

Pneumatic Airguns

There were a few pneumatic airguns made during the early post-Civil War era using an integral front-pump mechanism. In France, Paul Giffard made a series of pistols and rifles on this principle which are rare collectibles today. Incidentally, several decades later, Giffard was one of the first airgun makers to commercially use the power of CO_2 gas for his gas rifles and very rare gas pistols.

There were even several American makers of front-pump pneumatics during this period. Philipe Bouron and Jean Revol made similar pump rifles, while Edwin Hawley and George Snow patented and marketed an improved version of Hawley's earlier design for a front-pump pneumatic pistol. This very desirable air pistol in 25-caliber is known by collectors as the Hawley or the Kalamazoo—the Michigan hometown of Hawley.

Quackenbush's Airguns

The death knell for these pneumatics and the handmade gallery airguns came at the hands of Henry M. Quackenbush, who revolutionized the direction of airgunning by applying mass-production techniques to his guns. His airguns were actually based on a collection of patented designs from other people, including Haviland and Gunn, Augustus Carey, Albert Pope (assignee), Bedford & Walker, Johnson & Bye, and others. Each of the aforementioned names is associated with spring-piston air pistols that are quite collectible in their own right.

Most of the Quackenbush airguns are based on a push-barrel-cocking air rifle, which include his models designated #1 through #10. The exception to this is the #5, a modified break-barrel design patented earlier by Asa Pettengill and produced in limited form by Haviland & Gunn. The novel feature of the Quackenbush #5 was that it could be purchased in a version that functioned both as an airgun and as a rimfire rifle.

Another notable, unusual Quackenbush was the Lightning. This extremely rare model, patented in 1884, operated via an external moving cylinder traveling down a fixed piston and was powered by elastic rubber bands.

All Quackenbush airguns are sought by collectors. There was significant production of most models, and they have a relatively high survival rate, making them an excellent collecting category.

Daisy BB Guns

As previously mentioned, the humble BB gun is one of the most popular collectibles, especially in the U.S. While the hottest tickets continue to be the cast-iron-frame guns, there is no denying that the collectors of Daisy BB guns far outweigh all other specialty groups. No doubt this stems from such close nostalgic ties to the guns of our youth.

The great variety of Daisy airguns produced for more than 100 years makes this a field not easily exhausted. The wire-frame first model Daisy with its top lever cocking is, naturally, the focus point and a highly desirable centerpiece of any Daisy collection, but it is not the most rare. The wire-stock second model with its breakdown cocking is much more difficult to locate, as are several other early cast-iron-frame Daisy guns.

Later Daisy models from the Plymouth, Michigan, factory are no less collectible. Leading the pack is the #104 Double Barrel with its wood stocks and engraved, blued frame. However, even the recent plastic-stocked #21 Double Barrel from the Rogers, Arkansas, plant has made a strong showing.

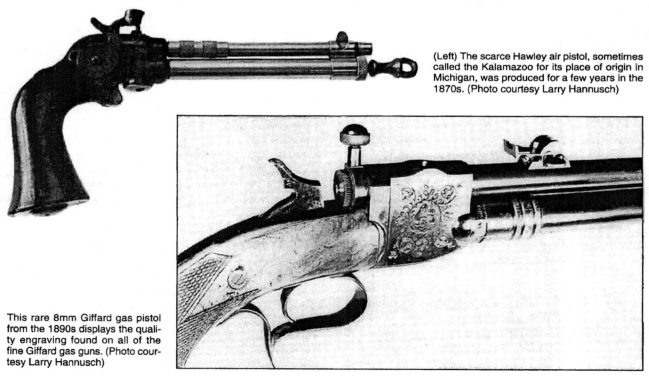

(Left) The scarce Hawley air pistol, sometimes called the Kalamazoo for its place of origin in Michigan, was produced for a few years in the 1870s. (Photo courtesy Larry Hannusch)

This rare 8mm Giffard gas pistol from the 1890s displays the quality engraving found on all of the fine Giffard gas guns. (Photo courtesy Larry Hannusch)

The military-styled Daisys are also quite popular. The WWI-era #40 Daisy is relatively common except when fitted with its original bayonet. This bayonet alone can easily double the value of the gun itself. The WWII-era #140 with its dummy bolt is also popular and seems more scarce than its Model #40 predecessor.

Another popular Daisy is the #25 trombone-pump BB gun, especially the early model with a straight walnut stock and its beautiful color case-hardened pump lever. The copper-plated Model 36 commemorated Daisy's 50th anniversary of 1936 and is desirable if complete with its rear sighting tube and copper plating intact.

The Markham King airguns, also hailing from Plymouth, have received collector interest due to the scarcity and attractiveness of many models. The appearance of the Markham guns runs the gamut from the floral scroll-engraved frames of the early lever actions to the crude all-wood Chicago that basically started the BB-gun era in the late 1880s.

Other BB Guns

This era was characterized by cast-iron-frame BB guns made by a large number of smaller companies. The names usually were cast into the grip frame, and most are quite rare today. These names include Atlas, Bijou, Crescent, Dewey, Globe, Magic and Matchless, among many others. The variations are endless.

This Bedford & Walker air pistol is shown in its original wood case with the slugs, dart tool and removable wire stock. (Photo courtesy Larry Hannusch)

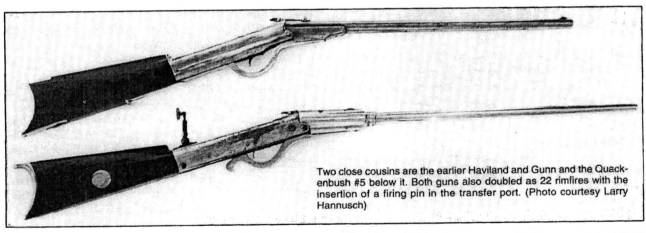

Two close cousins are the earlier Haviland and Gunn and the Quackenbush #5 below it. Both guns also doubled as 22 rimfires with the insertion of a firing pin in the transfer port. (Photo courtesy Larry Hannusch)

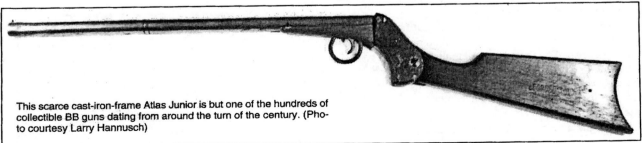

This scarce cast-iron-frame Atlas Junior is but one of the hundreds of collectible BB guns dating from around the turn of the century. (Photo courtesy Larry Hannusch)

A herd of Crosman 45 Military Auto gas pistols makes an attractive display. This pistol is sought for its realistic firing behavior and appearance. (Photo courtesy Larry Hannusch)

A popular line of these cast-iron BB guns is worth special mention because of the great profusion of models. These are the heavy and solid Heilprin BB guns. Most have the model year cast into the frame, starting in the mid-1890s and continuing well into the first decade of the 20th century. Other Heilprin models include the Columbia, Champion, Junior and several others. All are quite attractive and popular collector items.

Even Remington Arms got into the BB-gun business with their pump-action Model 26. Its production was limited to only a few short years before the Great Depression terminated the project. Today, it is sought by both airgun and Remington firearms collectors.

Crosman Airguns

Ranking closely with the Daisy BB guns are the popular guns from Crosman Arms. Starting from the unlikely origins of a seed company in 1923, Crosman has continued to develop into one of the largest airgun manufacturers in the world. One of Crosman's strong points in the industry has been their diversity of products. Consequently, this has led to a fertile hunting ground for the Crosman airgun collector.

The most desirable of the Crosman airguns are their first three pneumatic models made before full commercial production really began. The first one, commonly called the Crosman 1923 Model, used a straight front-pump system for charging. The next two models used a modified underlever pumping mechanism, the last of which evolved into the popular 100/101 series of rifles.

Among the multitude of airguns produced, there are other models that stand out as collector favorites. One is the beefy Crosman Town & Country rifle from the late 1940s, arguably their finest pneumatic ever. With dual sights and a massive receiver, it has the appearance of a very serious air arm. The 177 version, called the #107, is quite scarce compared to the 22 model, designated the #108.

But the real heart of the Crosman collector belongs to the CO_2 gas guns. Crosman's innovations in this area have been outstanding through the years. Several quickly come to mind as desirable and can still be picked up for reasonable prices.

The Crosman gas rifles, known as the CG guns, are popular because they represent a modernized version of the old ball-reservoir airguns. Developed from modified, hose-fed Model 102s in the 1930s, CG guns were made in several final variations based on calibers and tank orientation. The most desirable rifles are the 21-caliber model and the repeater.

Of the later CO_2 models, the Model 160 must be considered one of the finest Crosman sporter gas rifles ever made. Fully adult-proportioned and wonderfully blued, the late variation of this gun with its adjustable trigger and outstanding aperture sight is notorious among shooters as a tackdriver. The Model 167 is the much scarcer 177 cousin of the 160.

The Crosman bulk-fill gas pistols, series 115/116 and long-barreled series 111/112, are some of the most powerful vintage air pistols around. On a warm day with a full charge, the shooter can expect noticeable recoil as the screaming 22 pellet consistently approaches 500 fps velocities.

Probably the most popular collectible in the Crosman pistol line is the Crosman 451 Semi Auto. This six-shot, 22-caliber replica of the Colt Government 45 Auto even has a recoiling slide to recock the action upon firing. The heart of the mechanism is an ingenious, horizontally oriented cylinder which is advanced between shots by an indexing pawl inside the slide. Though it is a recent gun dating from 1969-70, limited production has made it a desirable piece in the Crosman line.

Generally speaking, the majority of Crosman airguns offered in both 177 and 22 will be much scarcer on the collector market in the smaller caliber. Original production followed demand, and American airgunners have always favored the larger caliber pellet.

Benjamin Airguns

Another major player in the American airgunning market has been the Benjamin Air Rifle Company of St. Louis, Missouri. Developed from the design work of Walter Benjamin in the late 1800s, these airguns have been going strong ever since.

The early Benjamin air rifles were derived from Mr. Benjamin's first efforts on his St. Louis air rifle. The Improved St. Louis, with its straight front-pump mechanism, became the foundation for the first forty years of Benjamin airguns. Naturally, both St. Louis models are very desirable specimens that rarely appear on the market today.

This first generation of Benjamin rifles, designated as models A-G, were all muzzle-loading front-pumpers designed to shoot round shot. It was not until Benjamin introduced their 300 series in the mid-1930s that breech-loading was introduced to allow the use of diabolo pellets. However, even at this late date, the front rod pump was still retained, being phased out in the late 1930s.

After this time, the general appearance of Benjamin air rifles remained nearly the same for decades. Because of this, collectors have largely ignored the Benjamin as a collectible. However, in recent years this has changed somewhat, as collectors began to appreciate the attractive nickel-plated brass guns with their fine walnut stocks. The repeater models especially have seen strong interest. It is worth keeping a look out for the scarce front-pump 600 Automatic as well as the similarly pumped Model 700. Even the later underlever Models 710 and 720 are making an impressive comeback with collectors.

Benjamin pistols are likewise coming around to a respectable status. The Series 250 nickel-plated gas pistols with their compact size and walnut grips are some of the most attractive air pistols of all time. The later repeater versions of the 260 gas pistols and all of the pneumatic repeaters are highly sought, especially the 22 versions.

Sheridan Airguns

Another American airgun that did not appear on the scene until the mid-1940s was the Sheridan air rifle hailing from Racine, Wisconsin. Designed as the ultimate, cost-is-no-object airgun by Bob Kraus and E.N. Wackerhagen, the Sheridan Model A was introduced in 1947 in the proprietary 5mm (20) caliber. Dubbed the Supergrade, it hit the market with a whopping retail price of $56.50. Though wonderfully constructed, the steep price forced a slightly scaled-down version called the Model B Sporter in 1948, which still carried a hefty $35 price tag.

Although hailed by contemporary writers as some of the finest air rifles to be had, price considerations were too difficult to overcome. A third version, the Model C, was offered by 1949

The Sheridan Model B Sporter was made only for a few short years and is highly sought by collectors. It is shown here with several of its accessories. (Photo courtesy Larry Hannusch)

These front-pump Benjamin BB repeaters were made in the 1930s and are desirable collectibles today. The upper gun is the Model 600 Automatic, while the lower rifle is the Model 700. (Photo courtesy Larry Hannusch)

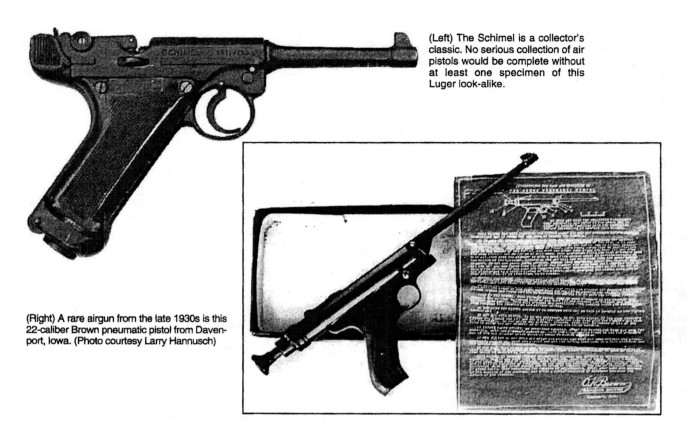

(Left) The Schimel is a collector's classic. No serious collection of air pistols would be complete without at least one specimen of this Luger look-alike.

(Right) A rare airgun from the late 1930s is this 22-caliber Brown pneumatic pistol from Davenport, Iowa. (Photo courtesy Larry Hannusch)

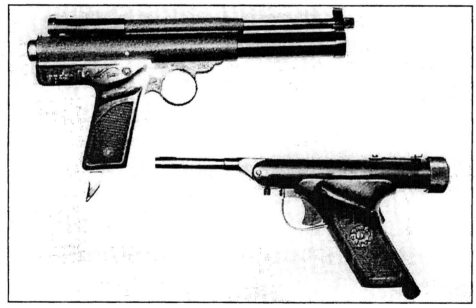

These desirable American air pistols date from the late 1940s. The gas pistol at the top is called the Winsel, while the spring-piston Targ-Aire, with its adjustable power level cocking, is shown below. (Photo courtesy Larry Hannusch)

at a competitive $19.95 and has been in continual production ever since.

A total of 2130 Supergrade A's were made between March of 1947 and September of 1953. The Sporter Model Bs are even more rare, with a total production run of only 1051 between October of 1948 and June of 1951. Both are popular collector's items, as are the early Model Cs with the hold-down safety. The Sheridan Supergrade Model A is indisputably one of the finest pump rifles ever made.

Other Collectibles

A small airgun venture that made a cameo appearance in the late 1930s was the powerful Brown pneumatic pistol from Davenport, Iowa. This beautifully made, dual-pump-action pistol is characterized by high-quality steel construction that is superbly finished throughout. Several variations, including models with different barrel lengths, were offered for a short while, but all are very rare today and highly desirable.

Two other very collectible American air pistols made brief

appearances in the early post-WWII years. One was a unique bulk-tank CO_2 gun called the Winsel, made for a short time in Rochester, New York. Another was a spring-piston air pistol featuring a backstrap-cocking system with three power levels. This pistol was called the Targ-Aire (and later Ranco) and was made in Chicago, Illinois. Both disappeared by the early 1950s and are quite scarce today.

There are some collectible American military trainers out there. These are characterized by full automatic machinegun trainers dating from around WWII. The best known is the Mac-Glashan BB machinegun from Long Beach, California. Lesser known are several models called Hot Point Trainers from Chicago, Illinois, which shot 38-caliber plastic balls.

An area of largely ignored airguns are the carnival guns, which have their roots in early-American gallery airguns. Most of these modernized types are powered by an air or gas supply hose that fed into the gun. Specimens that may be encountered are the two models of the MacGlashan Semi Auto in 24-caliber, the pump-action Drice, various full-auto models from Feltman and the numerous ABT models. Most date from the 1930s to the 1950s.

The period following WWII saw the introduction of a number of interesting airgun designs. The National Cart Co. of California offered the Apache line, which was novel because the rifles (and some pistols) were 25-caliber with a 175-inch BB barrel insert to give a dual-purpose gun. This same company also made the Plainsman line, including the collectible 28-S pump air shotgun. All of these faded from the scene by the early 1950s.

Another West Coast airgun that made an appearance in the early 1950s was the Schimel gas pistol, a faithful and powerful Luger look-alike. Though plentiful in today's market, the Schimel was soon superseded by the much rarer American Luger and Carbo Jet gas pistols. These repeaters were modified designs built around the tooling of the bankrupt Schimel company. Eventually, these two repeating pistols themselves disappeared by the late 1950s and, today, are greatly sought by collectors.

Pump rifles were popular items in postwar America, and this prompted the appearance of two short-lived ventures in upstate New York. These were the Rochester and the Kessler, both of which were gone by the early 1950s.

One of the small companies with the greatest staying power was the Hy-Score Company of Brooklyn, New York. Built around design patents by Andrew Laszlo, the concentric spring-piston Hy-Score 700 and, later, 800 series were powerful and competitively priced. The most sought-after models by collectors are the early Model 700, the later chrome variation, the repeater version, and the Sportster Model. The latter—an interesting, small version with a snub-nose appearance—allowed for interchangeable barrels and calibers in most of the variations. All were discontinued by the early 1970s.

Foreign-Made Collectibles

The field of foreign-made airguns is every bit as vast as that of U.S.-made airguns because virtually all countries have, at one time or another, made these types of arms. However, the two most prolific airgun-producing countries historically have been England and Germany.

Most collectors seeking British guns will find an abundance of products from two popular firms: Webley (and Scott) and BSA. The most well-known Webley airguns are their pistols. These fine guns are made to exacting standards and, until recent years, were all made of deeply blued, machined steel. The Mark I and Mark II Target, along with the Junior, Senior and Premier models, have all attracted a loyal following of collectors.

No less popular are the Mark I, II and III rifles. The small Mark I from the late 1920s is the most scarce, but the Mark II Service rifle of the 1930s and '40s, with its interchangeable barrel system, has always been a hot item. The Mark III underlever from the 1940s through 1970s is known as a fine piece and is especially desirable in its aperture-sighted target version, called the Supertarget.

BSA airguns are also a vast field in themselves. Most popular to collectors are the series of excellent pre-WWII underlever, tap-loading rifles made in a great variety of configurations and models. Special items to look for are the 25-caliber models, several of the small junior models and the Military Pattern version with dummy bolt and underlever cocking. Even the early postwar Airsporters with their automatic tap and sleek underlever design are quite desirable.

A great number of smaller British firms have produced airguns through the years that rank high as collector items.

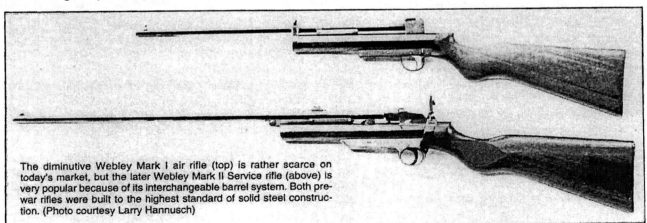

The diminutive Webley Mark I air rifle (top) is rather scarce on today's market, but the later Webley Mark II Service rifle (above) is very popular because of its interchangeable barrel system. Both pre-war rifles were built to the highest standard of solid steel construction. (Photo courtesy Larry Hannusch)

(Above) The Hubertus spring-piston air pistol is a fairly unusual German model that saw production until the mid-1930s. This specimen is in near-mint condition and, thus, is a choice collector's piece.

(Left) A comparison of prewar models from America and Germany. The Benjamin 177 front-pump pistol dwarfs the tiny spring-piston Tell 2 from Germany. Both were popular in their 1930s production years and are even more so today in current collections. (Photo courtesy Larry Hannusch)

Among the rifles possibly encountered will be the Britannia, Greener, Musketeer and Kynoch Swift, but all are quite rare today.

Rare British air pistols eagerly sought by most collectors include the Westley Richards Highest Possible, Certus, Lincoln, Parker Patent crank pistol and the Titan, all of prewar vintage. The concentric piston design seems to have been a popular British design, and many such specimens will be encountered in airgun collections. These include the prewar Anson Star, Warrior and 1921 Highest Possible, along with the early postwar models Acvoke, Abas Major and Thunderbolt Jr.

The German airguns dating from before WWII are a tremendously exciting field. Besides the popular models from the big names such as Diana and Haenel, a great many airguns sprung from this land of shooters. To simply list all of them would take countless pages. Suffice it to say, this group of prewar airguns will never be completely exhausted. Among the items likely encountered will be the Zenit, Hubertus, Tell pistols and rifles, Oscar Will guns, Eisenwerke airguns, FLZ airguns, and the Gems from several different factories.

Another area of airgun specialization receiving some collector interest is in that of military trainers and look-alikes. These have emanated from numerous countries. Among the items encountered will be the Mars 86, 100 and 115 trainers from Germany. Also from Germany, there are the rare Diana 58 bolt-action underlever trainer and the more common Haenel 33 and 33 Jr. Hailing from the Czechoslovakian factory of Ceska Zbrojovká we find the models VZ 35, VZ 36 and postwar VZ 47.

Postwar German airguns are not nearly as widely collected as their prewar counterparts. Several 1950s airguns that do come to mind are the fine products from Diana, Falke, Walther and Weihrauch.

One country of airgun origin that has been largely ignored by collectors until recently has been Japan. These guns have been

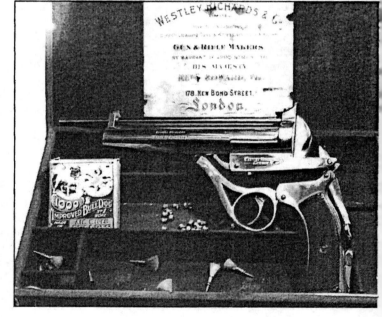

The interesting Highest Possible air pistol from Westley Richards was available from the factory in a fitted case, but such cased sets are quite rare today. (Photo courtesy Larry Hannusch)

popular in Japan since the prewar era, starting with "millita"-style copies offered by the KFC and SKB companies.

However, the postwar years, which sought to circumvent wartime reparations, saw a boom in the production of pneumatic rifles for target and field shooting. Some of the brands sold included the diverse line from the Sharp Air Rifle Co., which is still in business today. Another excellent line of pneumatic airguns was called the Heirinkan, known today as some of the finest specimens to come out of Japan. The Japanese airgun is finally getting some well-deserved recognition.

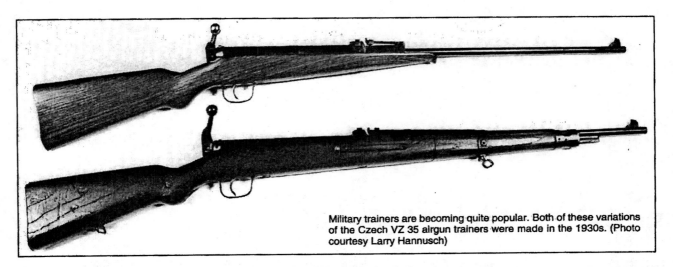

Military trainers are becoming quite popular. Both of these variations of the Czech VZ 35 airgun trainers were made in the 1930s. (Photo courtesy Larry Hannusch)

Japanese airguns are beginning to receive collector interest, such as these SKB spring-piston rifles. The top gun is a prewar break barrel, while the bottom gun is a postwar underlever with a tap-loading design. (Photo courtesy Larry Hannusch)

Other Far East countries that have made airguns considered to be collectible include Korea and the Philippines. A popular Korean airgun is the front rod-pump Yewha in 25-caliber, known for its power, though other airguns from this country are even more potent. The Filipino field of airguns is unbelievably vast and diverse, and therefore is starting to attract a lot of collector interest.

How to Find Rare Airguns

So now that we understand what kinds of airguns are considered collectible, how do we go about trying to reel in some of these rare prizes? The first is to read and study the available information, including reports of the guns in the collections of others. A collector with limited funds, but a strong desire to learn more about the vintage airgun field, will succeed where others might stagnate. Knowledge is the great financial equalizer.

The places in which to look for these older air arms are numerous. Relatives and friends who learn of your early interests can be a fruitful start. Many collectors have also had success with local newspaper ads, depending upon the locale. Antique shops, pawn shops and gun shops have all been worthwhile sources at one time or another. But the general consensus among veteran airgun collectors is that

the two most successful sources are gun shows and flea markets.

Either of these two events can, at any time, produce the most delightful of unexpected treasures. Most collectors can relate various stories (most of them true) about how some wonderfully rare airgun was bought at the tiniest of gun shows or junkiest of flea markets at a fraction of its actual value.

Another tremendous source of airguns and information that should not be overlooked are fellow collectors. No one collector is going to be exposed to every airgun in circulation without the help of other avid enthusiasts. The social benefits attained through these contacts are what moulds the direction of our mutual interests into lasting friendships beyond those goals of merely gathering iron.

We have briefly discussed only a few of the thousands of collectible airguns that are known. The marvelous diversity of these guns validates this great field as one rich in significance and opportunity. The prices on most of these collectibles have remained at reasonable levels. As time passes and their popularity increases, their values will invariably continue to escalate as well. The time to start a collection is now, while specimens still abound. There is no denying that, for the astute collector, a nice vintage airgun gives you a lot of pneumatic bang for your buck.

Chapter 20

Hunting Bushytails With Air Power

Here's what happens when John Richards, a seasoned squirrel hunter, takes up airgunning.

by John Richards
Introduction by J.I. Galan

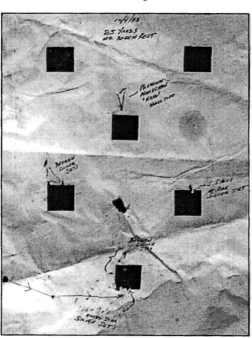

These are typical 25-yard groups obtained by John Richards with the Beeman R1 during sighting-in tests prior to his squirrel hunt.

WHEN I BEGAN to plan the topics that would be covered at some length in this book, I did not include a chapter dealing specifically with squirrel hunting. Sure, I would touch upon the subject at some point, somewhere in the book, but my original outline decidedly lacked something like this. In fact, already a few months into the actual production of the book, I still hadn't seriously considered devoting a complete chapter to the vagaries of bagging bushytails with an air rifle.

Then one day, during a telephone conversation with fellow airgun scribe Dave Wayland, he mentioned that he'd just shipped a Beeman R1 magnum air rifle on loan to a friend of his living in Kentucky. It turned out, Dave's friend was a lifelong squirrel hunter who was ready to try his hand at hunting those often elusive bushytails with a suitably potent and accurate air rifle. Dave suggested I give his friend a call, since, as luck would have it, this fellow also does a bit of outdoor writing, and perhaps he might be willing to do a story about his experiences with airgunning for squirrels. Hmm. It sure looked like I might be on to something interesting here.

From personal experience, I know that squirrels unquestionably are ideal game for the air rifle. Still, I wanted a highly skilled hunter's point of view on the matter. Besides, the fact that Dave's friend, John Richards, had always relied solely on 22 rimfires to hunt squirrels could certainly add a different perspective to the whole project, so I gave him a call.

As it turned out, John Richards couldn't wait to finish testing and sighting in the R1 rifle, in order to head out to the woods in search of them "fuzzytails," and he readily agreed to report his impressions on the gun, as well as the results obtained afield. Let's hear his story:

• • • •

My airgun experience goes back to the 1930s, when I saved $2.10 and purchased a Daisy single shot BB gun. That gun was soon confiscated by my dad, due to complaints from neighbors who saw me shooting their milk bottles. Then, some eight years ago, I acquired an "Original Will" airgun in 25-caliber. Until recently, this size pellet wasn't readily available. So, I miked the bore of my Will and found it measured .244-inch. A small

The Beeman R1 spring-piston air rifle is more than a match for elusive squirrels. A solid hit in the head or thorax area is almost certain to drop the creature instantly.

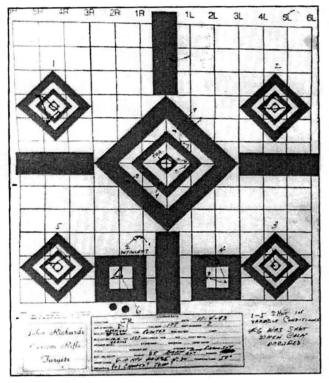

Marksman's MAKO pointed pellets produced pretty good results from the benchrested R1 at 25 yards during Richards' tests, even in windy conditions.

pack of #3 buckshot stashed in my gun room produced pellets that miked the same .244-inch and weighed 22.4 grains—a happy coincidence. However, there is also an irregularity in the diameters of the buckshot pellets that often gives a loose fit in the bore. Thus, informal plinking fun was had on occasion, but with never a thought to hunting.

The challenge began when two UPS deliveries arrived containing a Beeman Model R1 in 177-caliber, rated at 1000 fps, and six boxes of pellets. Three of the boxes contained pellets of the flat-nosed configuration, but I eliminated them from con-

sideration. The other three boxes were spire points, which I decided would deliver higher velocity and terminal energy to the animal. With all this in hand, I proceeded to check the Beeman 2-7x Blue Ribbon scope and its mountings to be sure all screws were tight.

The three boxes of pellets tested for grouping at 25 yards, off the benchrest, were Mt. Star Silver Jets, Beeman's Silver Jets and Premium Marksman #1260 MAKO pellets. I weighed all the pellets on my Ohaus Dial-O-Grain scale: Mt. Star ranged between 8.5 and 8.6 grains, Beeman pellets ran a consistent 8.1 grains, and Marksman's ran 10.4 without any variation.

I first began to sight in and go for grouping ability in early October, when the weather was in the upper 70s. I regret now that I didn't run chronograph checks. I'll get to that later.

With a target at 25 yards, using 1-inch-square black pasters for aiming points, I began with the Mt. Star pellets. By the third shot, I was on point of aim. I then switched over to the Beeman pellets. They centered 1 inch higher and ½-inch to the left from the previous group. Dispersion was diagonal, the group measuring 1.071 inches. A second sampling for this pellet was almost identical in spread, except the group was triangular. The Mt. Stars again gave me a point-of-aim group that measured .710-inch. The MAKO pellets had a vertical group measuring .671-inch, centered 1 inch above point of aim.

One month later, I again benched the rifle to check it before going out to hunt. Temperatures ranged in the middle to low 50s, and as I set up, a 20 mph wind hit the hilltops. Down in my Kentucky hollow, the wind effect was variable at an estimated 6 to 8 mph. Considering this, I opted for the heavier MAKO pellets and their grouping ability.

The first shot was 3¼ inches low and 1¼ inches left. My second shot keyholed. I adjusted the scope to center the group and proceeded to fire five groups, producing open-center patterns that ranged from ¾-inch to 1½ inches. Also, the group centers would "dance" around the point of aim, from nine o'clock to eleven o'clock and so on. The sensitivity of those 10.4-grain pellets to the wind provided an obvious answer. The

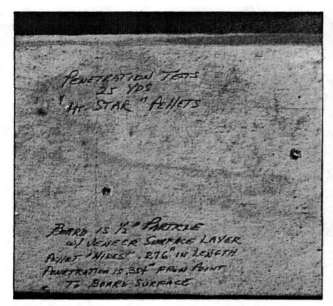

Using ½-inch-thick particle board, Richards also tested pellet penetration at 25 yards. Although obviously not strictly scientific, these tests give a good indication of the rifle/pellet combo's power.

Richards poses proudly with one of the "fuzzytails" he took using the scoped Beeman R1.

temperature differential posed another question—what effect, if any, would it have on velocity? When the wind quieted, I shot another group that centered and measured .561-inch. Penetration tests on ½-inch particle board at 25 yards measured .354-inch. Taking wind deflection and penetration into account, I decided that my maximum range for taking squirrels would be 30 yards.

Later that same week, three days before deer season opened, conditions were right—wind was calm, temperatures in the 50s. The woodlands floor had good visibility due to the heavy weed growth being killed by heavy frosts and an unusual 4-inch snow in October. White oaks had produced a particularly heavy mast, and squirrels and deer were feeding on acorns.

Below my ground deer stand, located on a south slope at the head of a drain, there is an old log about 25 yards downhill. A half-hour passed. Woodpeckers began their work, along with chickadees. Then a fox squirrel appeared to my right, coming off a bench and onto a log, where he hesitated. I slowly raised the R1, the scope set on 7x. I squeezed that delightful trigger and caught the squirrel full in the lungs. He lunged, rolled a couple of feet and was still. Some fifteen minutes later, a second fox squirrel came to that log, but from the left. He, too, paused on the end of the log, not seeing his fallen brother a short distance ahead. With the crosshairs at the base of his skull, I touched the trigger. The little fellow hunkered down on impact, then shuddered and died. I was impressed by the relative silence of the air rifle, in contrast to the sharp, disturbing crack of my high-speed 22 rounds. The sound emitted by that R1 was more like a low

thud, disturbing nothing. And at the ranges the shots were taken, the R1 and a 22 rimfire would be equal in killing power.

Almost three weeks later, after deer season, I went back up into the hills to the same deer stand. After about thirty minutes, another big fox squirrel appeared on the same log. The first shot missed. Deflected? What? No matter, the squirrel wasn't disturbed; rather, it slowly took a few steps forward and again stopped and preened. I cocked the R1 and locked it up on a point between his shoulder blades, as he was angled a bit. The pellet ranged into his head, and the fuzzy's reaction was to just slump to his left...*finis.*

So what are my conclusions with these first experiences hunting with an airgun? They are quietly lethal. Accuracy leaves nothing to be desired. If there is a shortcoming with airguns, it is only in range limitations imposed by caliber/pellet weight and wind effects. I feel that going up in caliber, say to a 22 or 25, with an increase in pellet weight, ranges can be lengthened and wind effects minimized considerably. Over a period of time and at different temperatures, I would like to fire more groups and chronograph the velocities. I would also log humidity levels into the equation to learn if there is any connection. The Beeman R1, coupled with the Beeman Blue Ribbon 2-7x scope, is a superb piece of equipment. It is a bit on the heavy side, but when it came to holding and squeezing, the weight was welcome. Another point worth noting, the little box of 500 pellets costing under $10 represents a lot of "quiet" value when compared to the comparatively costly and noisy 22.

Meanwhile, I'm hooked. And we have another month of squirrel season left. Does it get any better than this?

Chapter 21

Modern Airguns And Big Game

A pneumo-nimrod of the 1990s hunts wild boar with a large-bore airgun, just like others have been doing for centuries.

by J.I. Galan

Author tests one of the early versions of the Airrow Stealth gun with standard cam trigger. The latest models have a more conventional-appearing pneumatic trigger.

AS WE SAW in Chapter 19, the annals of the airgun feature prominent notables such as King Ludwig VIII of Hesse in Germany, an avid hunter who reportedly took a sizable number of wild boar and stag with his powerful airguns back in the 18th century. Good ol' Ludwig seems to have been quite a devotee of the airgun, and his hunting exploits remain an impressive testimonial to the capabilities of the airgun as a hunting arm against medium to large game. This was further corroborated much later, here in America, when a rather powerful pneumatic gun accompanied explorers Lewis and Clark on their legendary 1804-1806 expedition through then-uncharted wilderness. The airgun in question was, according to the chronicles of the expedition, used at least once to kill a deer.

Of course, game animals haven't been the only live targets to fall to high-power airguns in centuries past. When Napoleon Bonaparte's armies marched triumphantly across much of Europe nearly two centuries ago, the Austrians pressed the large bore airgun into military service and used it quite effectively to snipe at French soldiers. These Austrian pneumo-sharpshooters are reported to have caused such fear and consternation among Bonaparte's troops that the French High Command issued an order that any Austrian soldier caught with one of the deadly airguns was to be treated as an assassin and summarily executed. The Austrian sniper's air rifle was the creation of one Bartholomew Girandoni and had a magazine with capacity for up to twenty 51-caliber lead balls. This repeating precharged rifle had an effective killing range of roughly 150 yards. Even by today's standards, those 18th-century military air rifles would be most fearsome.

All of the preceding shows rather clearly that if the technology to produce such powerful and deadly airguns existed more than two centuries ago, it was only a matter of time before someone in this day and age decided to bring back the concept in a practical way. Given the huge popularity that airguns, in general, have enjoyed during the last twenty years or so, the appearance of airguns intended primarily for hunting game much bigger than rabbits, squirrels and such shouldn't come as a surprise.

Well, one such airgun, designed from the ground up, has been available for several years. The Airrow A-8S Stealth can

The rifled-barrel version of the Airrow Stealth is the Model A-8SRB. It normally comes in 25-caliber, but 177 and 22 are also available.

only be described as awesome, in the fullest meaning of the word. I first had the opportunity of testing one of the first production Stealth guns back in 1989, and even then it was a most extraordinary and unique airgun. The intervening years have seen this device refined to a much higher plateau of sophistication. In its original configuration, the Airrow A-8S Stealth is a truly remarkable concept, capable of launching crossbow-length bolts at about twice the speed of conventional archery equipment.

The A-8S works with both CO_2 as well as compressed air. With the latter, it is capable of shooting a broadhead-tipped hunting bolt at more than 500 fps. This decidedly high-tech gun is constructed mostly of aircraft-grade aluminum and stainless steel in modular form that permits quick and easy takedown for transport in a compact attaché-style carrying case. The complete setup would look quite at home on the set of a James Bond film or, for that matter, in a lot of real-world places where state-of-the-art shooting technology is required. And speaking of films, the Airrow A-8S was prominently featured—in a most sinister fashion—in the 1993 action-thriller *Hard Target*, starring martial arts champion Jean-Claude Van Damme.

Besides shooting hunting arrows with tremendous velocity and accuracy, the Airrow gun in its several versions can also be employed as a line-throwing gun, underwater spear gun, tranquilizer gun for wildlife management work and—last, but not least—as a fairly esoteric anti-personnel weapon for some types of paramilitary operations. In the latter version, it is widely rumored some government and military organizations have expressed a rather keen interest in this unusual gun and may, in fact, have already used it in actual operations.

The regular Airrow A-8S with standard 16-inch archery barrel measures 30 1/8 inches overall with its CAR-15 collapsible stock fully extended. Economy of weight is paramount here,

The Airrow Stealth A-8S1P with pneumatic trigger comes in a compartmentalized, waterproof attaché case, complete with bolts.

and the A-8S comes in at just under 4½ pounds with a 1.5-5x20mm factory-supplied scope mounted. The casual looker may honestly mistake the Airrow for an M-16 or AR-15 rifle, given its receiver carrying handle, black matte finish and overall military styling. In the performance area, the Airrow A-8S Stealth, with its current pneumatic trigger, is absolutely outstanding. Using CO_2 as propellant—at a pressure of approximately 850 psi—from a 7-ounce canister that screws into the front of the receiver, the Airrow can shoot a 16-inch, 320-grain bolt with field point at a muzzle velocity of 367 fps or so, which results in a muzzle energy of nearly 96 foot pounds. A 260-grain carbon arrow of the same length develops an MV of about 396 fps. The 7-ounce CO_2 canister will give somewhere between 28 and 35 shots when used in an ambient temperature of 70 degrees Fahrenheit or so.

Changing to compressed air, at an average pressure of 3000 psi, the Airrow Stealth will shoot the same 320-grain bolt at around 608 fps. The 260-grain carbon bolt, in turn, will move out at a sizzling 660 fps. Their respective muzzle energies will be 262.7 and 251.5 foot pounds. The downside of the power curve is that compressed air will allow only about twelve full-power shots, while CO_2 will yield more than twice that number.

At this point, you would think that the designers of this unique gun would be well satisfied with their creation, right? Instead, they came out with yet another version of their amazing airgun. Their latest model features a *rifled 20-inch barrel* in 25-caliber made by Lothar Walther and is available on a very limited basis, only through licensed firearms dealers.

Optional barrels in 177- and 22-caliber are also available, as is a special-order-only barrel in 38-caliber, although that one might be discontinued by the time you read this. In fact, the latest version of the Model A-8SRB (Stealth Rifled Barrel) has a clever nine-shot wheel magazine and pneumatic trigger. As you might suspect, all this magnum airgun high-tech stuff is not cheap. The bolt-shooting A-8S1P with pneumatic trigger carries a retail price tag of $1699, while the A-8SRB rifled barrel version with pneumatic trigger sells for $2599. Undoubtedly, these airguns are intended for truly dedicated enthusiasts with plenty of cash at hand. That kind of dough can sure keep Mama and the kids in groceries for some time. The Airrow, incidentally, is manufactured by Swivel Machine Works, Inc., up in Milford, Connecticut.

To give an idea of the performance capabilities of the Stealth with rifled barrel, using compressed air at 3000 psi, a 25-caliber Beeman Ram Point pellet weighing 27.1 grains develops an MV of 1275 fps. Those figures translate into a muzzle energy of 97.8 foot pounds. The accuracy obtained with the 25-caliber rifled-barrel Airrow is also reported to be quite impressive, producing dime-size groups at 50 yards.

Although I have not had the opportunity to test a rifled-barrel version of the gun, I did test one of the latest bolt-shooting models with a pneumatic trigger. Its discharge report is slightly louder than that of a magnum precharged pneumatic rifle, but still a bit less than that of a 22 Long Rifle handgun. The Stealth has already cleanly and efficiently taken quite a number of wild

(Text continued page 164)

This very nice whitetail deer was taken with the bolt-shooting Airrow Stealth.

The wily wild turkey is another prime quarry for the Airrow Stealth. An air-powered bolt dropped this Tom in its tracks.

Antique Airguns and Big Game
Dr. Robert Beeman

Visitors to the Beeman Airgun Collection in Santa Rosa, California, are often surprised at the wide array of antique airguns designed for hunting big game, including the wild boar, a potentially dangerous beast that may weigh well over 300 pounds and is notoriously hard to kill. One of the earliest reliable records of hunting wild boar with airguns comes out of the 18th century from the archives of Ludwig VIII, Landgrave of Hesse, in what is now Germany. He was so fond of airgun hunting that he had members of his court record his hunting exploits. He even had a hunt artist who drew lifelike poses of the animals killed with his airguns. Wild boar are included as a major item, but no statistics were reported. However, the killing power of his airguns is well supported by records of stags killed at distances up to 154 paces. In 1747, his highness used an air rifle to take a 480-pound stag which bore twenty-two-point antlers.

The airguns involved in such hunting are a far cry from the average American's concept of a mass-produced, youth-level airgun. The Beeman collection includes many airguns that would be capable of taking wild boar: a fascinating series of beautifully built antiques which range from an 18th-century 39-caliber carbine only 40 inches long, perhaps for use in heavy brush or on horseback, through a variety of full-sized big bore air rifles, all the way to a late-1800s air cane with an awesome 55-caliber bore.

Airguns in the big game league are all precharged pneumatics. A small pump, usually separate from the gun but rarely built-in, charges a reservoir with air pressures of 1000 psi and even more. These strong, valved reservoirs were sometimes built into the gun, but more often were screwed to the action. These metal airtanks generally were ball-shaped or shaped to serve as the rifle's buttstock. The buttstock reservoirs were often quite handsome and made warm to the touch by a covering of fine leather or an especially tough and beautiful cover made from sharkskin. Lacking plastics, the early airgun makers used cow horn as an excellent valve seat material.

The pressure of compressed air is evidently much more efficient than that of the nascent gas of burning or exploding blackpowder. One experiment compared an antique airgun containing a pressure of 750 pounds of carbon dioxide with a similar Kentucky rifle charged with 35 grains of FFG blackpowder. The Kentucky gun's bullet penetrated 2½ inches of hard pine; the air rifle's bullet went 2 inches into the test blocks despite a far lower breech pressure. How much the airgun would have beaten the Kentucky if the modern testers had the nerve

Robert Beeman displays an air pistol from his extensive collection, made by Kuchenreuter around 1750. This 30-caliber spring-piston pistol was intended to be used as a dueling trainer.

to fully charge the antique gun is indeed interesting to contemplate.

One of the reasons for the high power, versus low pressure, of the big bore airguns is the large bore size. That is, airguns are more efficient as the caliber increases. At least this is true as long as there is sufficient air to fill the barrel to peak pressure. Modern airgunners have recently rediscovered this phenomenon. With the advent of far more powerful modern airguns, shooters are discovering they can get more of the potential of their gun's energy by selecting a larger bore. Although the modern airguns are far below many of these antique airguns in power, some of them now have enough air flow that it is simply choked by some of the smaller caliber bores. The rapidly increasing popularity of the 25-caliber is a reflection of the fact this large bore simply extracts much more power out of a given airgun's power plant.

The old airguns offered numerous advantages to those early shooters who could afford them: Some could be fired many times per minute, a striking contrast to the front-feeding powder burners. Such rapid-fire was, further, more practical with airguns because they did not obscure their own line of sight with clouds of smoke. And although the oft-told tale of their complete silence is

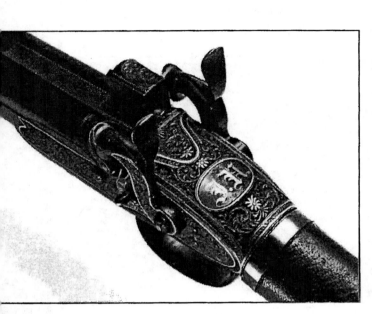

(Left and above) Double-barrel 44-caliber game rifle. The left barrel is muzzle-loading percussion; the right barrel is for air only. The breech loading block of the airgun is shown in the raised, loading position. An air power adjustment lever, just visible on the left side, has four settings, presumably from rabbit to moose level! The extremely deep engraving and extensive gold inlays indicate that this gun was made for royalty, or some other very wealthy hunter, in Austria in the early 1800s. The buttstock air reservoir is covered with fine leather. (Beeman photo)

(Right) European deer, the intended game, are engraved on the receiver of this handsome air rifle made by T. J. Mortimer in London about 1825. The upper lever is the cock; the lower one operates the tap loading breech block. This gun was built as a cased set, with 40-caliber rifled barrel and 36-gauge (about 50-caliber) shot barrel. From the Beeman Collection. (Beeman photo)

not true, their much lower report and lack of smoke and fire did help the military by making it more difficult to spot the marksman's position. An especially appealing feature was the great dependability of the airguns. Modern workers who have experimented with these old rifles have found certain problems, but misfire was certainly not among them. Other advantages, such as consistent power and lack of residual sparks, had been noted, but even a blackpowder shooter of today can well understand the delight of one of the ultimate advantages of the airgun—not having to thoroughly scrub out the bore after each day's shooting!

Charging one reservoir of these antique airguns could take from 100 to 2000 strokes of the pump. However, one of the reasons for the scarcity of old big bore airguns is that only a few very special gunsmiths could make them, and a great deal of highly skilled work was needed to make a single airgun. If you could afford one of these guns, then you could easily have afforded a servant to keep it pumped up.

For Americans, certainly the most interesting airgun of all is the large bore rifle carried by Lewis and Clark on their famous Northwest Expedition of 1804-1806. This is a rather plain looking butt-reservoir airgun with a 36-cal-

iber octagonal brass barrel bearing European-style rifling of seventeen beautifully scalloped grooves. It would have appeared, to any but a close observer, to be just a typical muzzle-loading blackpowder rifle of the period. However, its relatively quiet no-flash, no-smoke discharge must have been an amazement to observers. This gun evidently was used for big game, and Captain Clark seems to have been fond of demonstrating it to Indians encountered on the trip. Its PR value was certainly at a low the day it accidentally discharged and caused a superficial, but blood-gushing, wound on a squaw's head about 40 yards away.

The Lewis and Clark airgun was made by Isaiah Lukens, a clockmaker who is most famous as the maker of the big Independence Hall clock in Philadelphia. I confess that holding this gun in 1975, before its identity was known to the general public, and sighting down its barrel, as did Captain Clark almost 200 years ago, was one of the great thrills of my airgun-collecting career.

An airgun thrill that I look forward to is taking up *Outdoor Life* magazine's idea of sponsoring an article based on a modern wild boar hunt with one of our big bore air rifles. I probably will select a fine, cased pneumatic English air rifle made by Pritchard about 1850.

The air rifle carried by Lewis and Clark on their Northwest Expedition of 1804-06. The flintlock mechanism has no flash-pan. A separate pump was used to charge the detachable buttstock air reservoir. (Milwaukee Public Museum photo)

This gun was regularly used for deer hunting in the United States as recently as 1960. It throws a 260-grain, 44-caliber bullet at about 950 fps. At 521 foot pounds of muzzle energy, that is equivalent to several modern centerfire cartridges which have a good record on boar, provided that the shooter does his part. Another possibility would be a twenty-shot military air rifle, built in the Napoleonic period, that reportedly throws a 51-caliber lead ball about 1000 fps at a muzzle energy of about 400 foot pounds.

The advent of the firearm cartridge seems to have halted the development of airguns as powerful weapons. Modern airguns are not weapons, but, rather, have become the most accurate and efficient small game and target guns known today. Although almost unknown to Americans two decades ago, the field of *adult* airgunning is maturing, and wonderful new guns appear almost weekly. Some attempts have already been made to recreate the old big bore airguns. Unfortunately, the few to reach the market have produced less muzzle energy than the little 380 ACP pocket pistol. Hopefully, a version with power like the old-timers, feasible for production, is being developed on some modern engineer's drawing board right now.

Powerful airguns are no joke!

One of Beeman's favorites, this huge, ornate air rifle sports a flint-lock mechanism which is functional and complete except for the lack of a flashhole. A pump, built into the buttstock, charges the long air reservoir which encloses the 58-caliber bore. Made in England in the 1800s by Bate. Suitable for boar, elk, etc. This gun is in the Beeman Airgun Museum. (Beeman photo)

turkeys, deer and boar. Therefore, there is no doubt this airgun can perform very well indeed as a serious hunting arm, easily surpassing the modern crossbow in most cases as far as power, accuracy and effective range.

Another currently manufactured CO_2 gun earning well-deserved respect for its potent performance is the Farco. This brand has been available in the U.S. for several years through Air Rifle Specialists. Manufactured in the Philippines, this powerful gun was designed as a dedicated hunting arm in a nation whose government makes the lawful possession and use of firearms by most of its citizens just about impossible. Faced with such laws, many shooters and hunters in the Philippines long ago turned to airguns as the only viable alternative to firearms. The Farco was really designed as a 28-gauge single shot shotgun with a Cylinder bore barrel. As a shotgun, this interesting gun sees regular use against game such as pheasant, quail, dove and even waterfowl in its native country.

The CO_2 is charged into the gun via a standard, refillable 10-ounce canister. The gas reservoir holds about 4^1/$_2$ ounces of CO_2, which delivers an average of thirty to thirty-five shots before recharging is required. The CO_2 canister is simply screwed into the intake valve at the front of the reservoir tube located below the barrel, and the canister's spigot valve is opened for a short time until the gun is fully pressurized.

The Farco's shotshells consist of 1-inch-long brass tubes, open at both ends. Each of these can hold about 240 #8 shot, or up to twelve #4 Buck pellets, to give you an idea of the load size. After being stuffed with shot, the shells are plugged at both ends with cardboard or cork wads made with a special cookie-cutter tool supplied with the gun. A load of #8 shot throws a relatively dense pattern measuring about 14 inches across at 10 yards, at an average MV of 405 fps. This load surpasses 100 foot pounds of muzzle energy and is sufficiently powerful to kill small game at distances of up to 25 yards or so.

Although the Farco may not be the prettiest airgun, it certainly is quite practical and also lots of fun to shoot. Overall, it measures 48^1/$_2$ inches and weighs a rather comfortable 7 pounds. The barrel, receiver and CO_2 reservoir tube are all made of brass with a non-reflective finish resembling that of

Davis Schweisinger poses proudly with a wild boar he took with one shot from his scoped Farco CO_2 gun—shades of centuries gone by: hunting wild boar with an airgun!

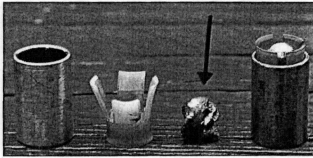

The Farco's single projectile load consists of a .433-inch lead ball in a plastic sabot loaded in the brass shell. Arrow points to deformed ball retrieved from the dead boar's neck.

Galan has always been fond of the potent Farco CO_2 gun. Even in its primary role as a shotgun, it is quite a powerhouse.

A powerful airgun intended for hunting medium game is the Hunting Master 900, a precharged pneumatic rifle in 9mm caliber. It's odd looking, but very effective.

stainless steel. This finish contrasts nicely with the light hue of its oil-finished stock. Surprisingly, the Farco still retails for its original introductory price of $395.

In order to go after prey larger than quail, pheasant and the like, the Farco, as you would suspect, must be loaded with something other than birdshot, or even buckshot, if it is to perform satisfactorily. To that effect, Davis Schweisinger, owner of Air Rifle Specialists, turned the Farco into an eminently efficient hunting arm for medium game by utilizing a single projectile of suitable caliber. He chose a .433-inch lead ball, held in a plastic sabot of the type used in some modern muzzle-loading rifles. This ball-cum-sabot combo is simply pressed into the open-ended shotshell, turning the Farco into a first-class CO_2-powered slug gun. The saboted 120-grain lead ball develops an MV of about 625 fps, which translates into a muzzle energy a tad over 104 foot pounds—a truly awesome energy figure by current airgun power levels.

In order to put the combination of the Farco with saboted ball to the acid test, Schweisinger headed south, going after wild boar in the vast expanse of the Dixie Wildlife Safaris ranch near Lake Wales, Florida. The result was the clean taking of a 79-pound boar, killed instantly with one shot to the head from a distance of about 30 yards. The only addition to the Farco during this hunt was the use of a 2-7x scope. The .433-inch diameter ball punched through the front of the boar's skull at its thickest area, according to Schweisinger, traveling through the brain and ending up some 6 inches into the neck area. Truly impressive, I must say!

Incidentally, Air Rifle Specialists also imports the awesome Hunting Master 900, a Korean-made precharged pneumatic rifle in 9mm caliber. This rifle can shoot a special 52-grain 9mm pellet at an MV of about 1100 fps, for a fantastic muzzle energy of just under 140 foot pounds. The Hunting Master 900, which retails for around $1000, was designed specifically as a hunting arm for medium-size game, and its availability is rather limited.

There is no doubt that the Airrow Stealth, the Farco and the Hunting Master 900 represent the rebirth of a type of hunting airgun the likes of which had not been seen for nearly two centuries. Interesting. Perhaps even fascinating, because it tends to confirm the old saying that there is really nothing new under the sun.

Chapter 22

Viewing the British Airgun Scene

Nigel Allen, editor of *Air Gunner* magazine, files an exclusive report from jolly ol' England on the latest British airguns and airgunning trends.

by Nigel Allen
Introduction by J.I. Galan

Nigel Allen with the Skan Mini-Bullpup Mk. 2 Deluxe (six-shot rotary magazine).

AS A LONG-TIME student and observer of the airgun world, I have witnessed quite a few changes—some subtle and slow evolving, others swift and rather radical—take place over the years. Without doubt, one of the most fascinating and even downright exciting transformations I have seen has occurred during the past decade or so in Great Britain. In fact, the changes have been so dramatic over there that today's British airguns have managed to catch up to and, in certain cases, even leave behind German airguns in a cloud of dust.

I realize that what I have just said may cause some readers to develop shortness of breath, perhaps even to faint, unable to cope with the shock of those seemingly sacrilegious words. To many dedicated airgunners, particularly here in the U.S., German-made adult airguns have traditionally been the backbone of the entire industry since at least the early 1960s. For many, they were sort of the proverbial yardstick against which all other airguns—particularly British ones—were measured. However, facts are facts; it is undeniable that the British airgun industry has taken the market by storm in the last few years, launching a huge variety of radically new models that have reached new plateaus in both workmanship as well as performance. Many airgunners here in the "Colonies," long accustomed to the basically robust, but usually rather staid products that came out of Britain for decades, can hardly believe their eyes when they discover the huge changes that have taken place over there.

Given all of the above, it would have been rather neglectful on my part not to dedicate an entire chapter of this tome to the subject of British airguns and the trends currently taking shape in that nation. Of course, my first impulse was to approach the publisher of this book and ask him to finance a fact-finding trip, during which I would travel the length and breadth of the British Isles gathering the latest information on British airguns, their airgun industry and airgunning, in general, in the old country.

Then I realized, rather wisely, I think, that my publisher could become apoplectic upon hearing of this plan. More realistically, he might have had a fit of uncontrollable laughter of such intensity to trigger either a double hernia or possibly even a massive coronary. Neither prospect, I reasoned, would bode well for the future of this book, so I had a much better idea.

Why not ask one of Britain's top airgun experts, a man who is in a strategically situated vantage point, to give us a report on the current British airgun scene? That fellow is Nigel Allen, editor of *Air Gunner*, an outstanding monthly magazine full of the latest happenings in the world of airguns in Britain and other European countries. Allen's duties at *Air Gunner* place him in a position where he is literally at the hub of the entire information network regarding British airgunning. Despite his extensive workload, he graciously agreed to give us an exclusive and extremely interesting report on what's happening on their side of the Atlantic.

• • • •

Despite being gripped in the clutches of recession, airgunning in Britain has remained as buoyant as ever. Hardly a month goes by without some sensational new model being launched. While gunmakers from all over the world are busy designing and building newer, more up-to-date air weaponry, those from Britain are acknowledged as being the ones that everyone must aim to beat. "Airgunners have never had it so good" is certainly an expression that is heard more and more in Britain these days, and compared to the choice of guns and gear available a little over a decade ago, it's easy to understand why. In fact, newcomers to the sport of airgunning are faced with a bewildering array of mouth-watering models from which to choose, and whatever branch of the sport they want to participate in, there are plenty of opportunities to satisfy both their leaning and their pocket.

The State of British Airgunning

There are a number of reasons why airgunning in Britain should have remained—if not increased—in popularity, but probably the biggest determining factor relates to the government's clamp-down on most forms of licensed shooting disciplines. Thankfully, airguns have so far escaped the ever-tightening net of restrictions so widely imposed. This, along with the huge advances in design and manufacture that have evolved since the airgun "revolution" of the mid-'80s has resulted in more and more shooters discovering that airguns are no longer the so-called "toys" they used to cut their teeth on before moving to "the bigger stuff." With the exception of Northern Ireland, airgun ownership in the U.K. does not require any form of license, providing it doesn't exceed a certain power level as stipulated by law. For air rifles, this level is 12 foot pounds of energy (fpe), while for pistols it's 6 fpe. Although it depends upon the weight of the ammo, this translates into a legal power limit for rifles of around 600 feet per second (fps) pellet velocity in 22-caliber and around 800 fps in 177. Whether the rifle is intended for use against small game, Field Target silhouettes or just general fun-gunning, that's more than enough in most instances.

Consequently, the average British airgunner is not one for lobbying Parliament for an increase in allowable power. However, in some specialized areas, where the humble airgun was once considered nothing more than a "pop-gun" suitable for no bigger challenge than tin-can work, there has been an increasing tendency to put it on a par with live-round hardware. For example, many of Britain's gamekeepers now swear by the airgun as an effective and silent way of controlling predators during the game-breeding seasons. Also, since the airguns of the '90s have been honed into finely tuned shooting machines capable of pinpoint accuracy, serious hunters are becoming interested in increasing airgun power, and thereby range as well.

Rifles which exceed the 12 fpe legal limit need police approval in much the same way as any other firearm—the owner needs to acquire a Part One Firearms Certificate (FAC). To some extent, FAC-rated airguns lose the main advantages of the off-ticket ones—like the lack of red tape—but the ever-growing band of FAC airgun shooters in Britain content to forfeit such benefits in order to use a more powerful rifle is testimony to the airgun's capabilities. Indeed, some of the regional police forces, who authorize the issuance of FACs, even recommend that high-powered airguns be used in preference to 22 rimfires.

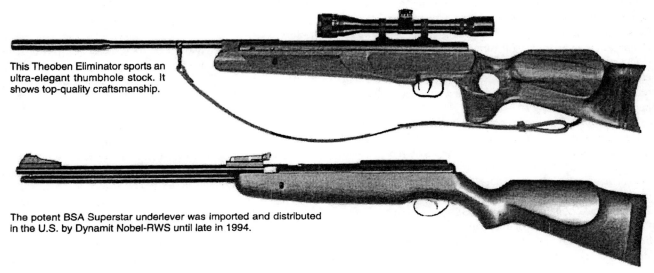

This Theoben Eliminator sports an ultra-elegant thumbhole stock. It shows top-quality craftsmanship.

The potent BSA Superstar underlever was imported and distributed in the U.S. by Dynamit Nobel-RWS until late in 1994.

Webley's FAC-rated, break-barrel Patriot. In the U.S., Beeman markets it as the Kodiak.

And for those considering an FAC-rated airgun, there's plenty of choice, too. It's not a question of buying a standard off-the-shelf model and boosting its output with a bigger and meatier spring. Plenty of gunmakers are now catering to high-power fans much more specifically.

FAC-Rated Airguns

Cambridgeshire-based Theoben, whose unique spring replacement gas-ram system has revolutionized piston-powered airguns, has for a long time been at the forefront of producing FAC-rated airguns. Their Eliminator—sold in the States as the Crow Magnum by Beeman Precision Airguns—is acknowledged as the most powerful break-barreled rifle in the world. With a monster muzzle energy of 33 foot pounds, there are few who would dare to challenge it. Despite power more than three times the average off-ticket rifle, the Eliminator is anything but a souped-up Theoben. Instead, it's a highly advanced powerhouse incorporating a stack of design features that make it a superbly efficient shooting machine. Some cocking effort is needed, but it's not unmanageable, and thanks to an ingenious spring-dampening valve inside the air chamber, the hyper-powerful Eliminator has no more recoil than a standard-rated spring gun. This, coupled with its inherent accuracy, makes the Eliminator a deadly, effective hunting tool at ranges approaching three figures when used in the right hands.

Another gunmaker who's not been slow to join the power bandwagon is Webley. Their 1993 launch of the 28 fpe, break-barrel, 25-caliber Patriot—sold in the States by Beeman as the Kodiak—has proved far more popular than even they thought. For shooters who can't justify the handbuilt luxury of an Eliminator, the Patriot makes an ideal workhorse out in the field. Other gunmakers, like Air Arms and BSA, also make "Export" versions of their rifles for the home market, usually rated between 15 and 20 fpe. But it's possible to take just about any standard air rifle and have it professionally converted into a high-performance machine via one of the highly skilled airgun workshops, known as Custom Houses, that have sprung up across Britain during the past few years.

Lower Powered Airguns

Of course, the majority of airguns in Britain fall into the sub-12 fpe category, so this is where the bread-and-butter models tend to be found. There's no disputing that rifles producing on-the-limit powers find favor amongst hunters and Field Target shooters, but since a high percentage of airgunners only shoot informally in their back-gardens, there's plenty of room for the lower-powered, budget-priced airguns, too.

While not used for any form of hunting, pistols have, therefore, become very popular with garden gunners who only have short ranges to shoot over. Handguns from Crosman, Daisy, Gamo, Record and Webley are popular choices with fun-gunners in Britain. All that's needed is a tin of ammo and some imaginative targets for a thoroughly enjoyable shooting session within the comfort of your own home.

Air-Soft Guns

Although shooting indoors with even the lowest-powered airguns is taboo—with perhaps the exception of the cork-firing, pop-out barrel Gat pistol—there's now a new craze sweeping the shores of Britain called air-soft shooting. Strictly speaking, air-soft guns are nothing more than Japanese-made plastic replicas, but they look realistic and actually shoot lightweight plastic BB ammo, making them a popular choice for youngsters and adults alike! In truth, their power is little more than $1/2$ fpe, so their accurate range is limited to between 5 and 10 yards. However, their fun-gun appeal has clearly met with approval from the British airgunning public for use both in and out of doors.

Considering the British are a fussy lot when it comes to shooting high-class, luxury airguns, it may seem a little odd that cheap and cheerful plastic replicas could become so popular,

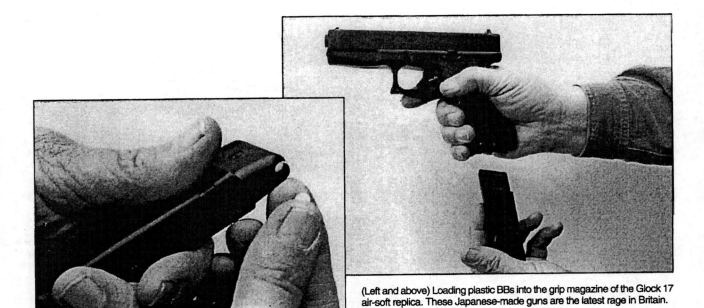

(Left and above) Loading plastic BBs into the grip magazine of the Glock 17 air-soft replica. These Japanese-made guns are the latest rage in Britain.

but it's a trend that's easier to understand after considering it in conjunction with the increasing legislative restrictions on firearms. After all, how else can you easily get to own your very own Sig/Sauer, Glock, Smith & Wesson or FAMAS for a fraction of the cost and without the hassle of all the red tape?

Airgun Trends

Despite the draw of the lifelike softies, the "proper" airguns still have their place, and gunmakers now have to keep moving on in order to satisfy the ever-increasing expectations of British airgunners. Unlike a few years ago, when an airgun was an airgun was an airgun—and was therefore usually a break-barrel sporter with fixed open sights, a beech stock and little else—today's airgunners can literally pick and choose a specific tool for the task in hand.

Break-barreled rifles are definitely still popular in Britain, with models like the BSA Supersport, Webley Excel and Weihrauch HW80 always selling well year in, year out. But since Weihrauch launched their now-legendary HW77 underlever, the British public has been swayed to the supposed accuracy advantages that fixed-barrel rifles have to offer over their break-barrel counterparts. Companies like Air Arms, BSA, Diana, Theoben and Webley have added such rifles to their line-ups, and these have since dominated the *Air Gunner* Airgun of the Year awards for the past few years, even though they're far heavier than their break-barreled equivalents.

More Weight

The trend for guns to become weightier was soon accepted as the necessary cost of improving accuracy by utilizing fixed-barrel principles. This argument was further strengthened by the fact that heavier guns absorb more recoil, making them far easier to shoot more accurately. But there came a point when British airgunners said things were getting out of hand, and gunmakers were forced to look at ways in which they could shed a few ounces to make their rifles more manageable. Webley has done their bit to combat the weight element by constructing the main cylinder of their top-of-the-line underlever Eclipse out of alloy. Still, probably the best accepted weight-saving technique has been to reduce barrel length.

Shorter Barrels

Not so long ago, airgun manufacturers took a page out of the firearms book as far as barrels were concerned—the longer the barrel, the higher the power level. With the exception of pneumatics, though, this isn't the case. As more and more resources were put into airgun research and development, it soon emerged the opposite was true—at least as far as spring guns were concerned. The acceleration of a pellet from a piston-powered rifle only occurred for the first 6 or 8 inches of barrel, after which the friction between the bore walls and pellet sides only served to slow it down. So, gunmakers concluded that lopping off 3 or 4 inches of a standard 18-inch bar-

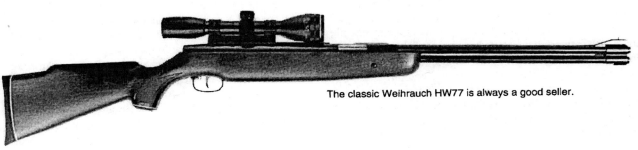

The classic Weihrauch HW77 is always a good seller.

One of the new breed of pneumatics—the budget-priced List Carbine. Notice the suppressor up front.

Top Field Target shooter Richard Beaugie with a competition-stocked Daystate precharged pneumatic.

rel should make no difference to the power level—and so the Carbine, or "K," derivative was born. In fact, sizing down barrels to around 15 inches long had a lot more advantages than just saving weight, and it didn't take long for the carbine gravy train to take hold throughout Britain. As a start, carbines brought the weight of the rifle closer to the shooter, making them balance and handle much better. Also, since the recoil from a piston-powered spring or gas-ram airgun takes place while the pellet is still traveling up the bore, shorter barreled rifles were an ideal way of speeding up the lock time—the time between the trigger being pulled and the pellet leaving the barrel. By allowing the pellet to exit the muzzle earlier in the rifle's firing cycle, the accuracy was therefore greatly improved. Such downrange benefits soon established the shorter-barreled carbine models as the most popular in the eyes of the British airgunning public. It's now not uncommon to find rifles sporting barrels of minute proportions, say just 7 or 8 inches long.

Pneumatic Power Plants

Ironically, in their constant quest to speed up and smooth out the firing cycle, gunmakers have eventually come to look on the pneumatic gun as being the wave of the future as far as British airgunners are concerned. Multi-pump pneumatics—like those from Crosman, Daisy and Sharp—have been around for years, but for some reason, they've never enjoyed the sort of popularity with British airgunners that spring-powered rifles have.

In the early '80s, an enterprising Staffordshire company called Daystate took the precharged pneumatic principles used in their tranquilizer guns and applied them to the airgun. The first Daystates were extremely powerful, provided a high number of shots per charge without calling for any effort by the shooter, and delivered the pellet to the target with pinpoint accuracy, thanks to their totally recoilless action. Although they weren't sold in large quantities in the early years, Daystates had, in fact, laid the foundation for the "pneumania" epidemic that ripped through Britain toward the back end of the last decade when shooters demanded the ultimate in accurate air weaponry. Almost simultaneously, airgunners were presented with two brand-new pneumatics, the Air Arms Shamal and Sportsmatch GC2. Both of these immediately found favor with the precise requirements of Field Target shooters—a band of competitive-minded airgunners who wouldn't be happy until they found perfection.

Field Target Shooting

The new British sport of Field Target shooting—where airgunners shoot a course of metal, fall-when-hit, animal silhouette targets—was demanding for both shooter and equipment, so it was only natural that manufacturers of precharged pneumatics, the majority of whom were British, specifically aimed their goods toward this activity. When compared to the number of airguns reportedly in circulation in Britain (about four to five million), the Field Target sector certainly couldn't be considered as a mass market, but gunmakers saw the very real needs of this sport as the ideal medium to promote their wares. For the airgunner, it was good news—since only the best survived in the cut-throat competitive world of FT, gunmakers were ploughing more time and resources into their rifles. The end result was that match-winning developments associated with top-flight Field Target equipment began filtering into the "standard" airgun market. Pretty soon, the pneumatic airgun became as much a part of the hunter's armory as any other traditional sporter.

As the sport of Field Target matured—enough for Britain and America to hold annual World Championships—so, too, did the equipment. Thumbhole stocks with multi-adjustable cheekpieces and forends are now commonplace on the British FT circuit. So, too, are rifles with a regulator—a valve device fitted to precharged pneumatics that regulates a precise amount of air for each shot. This has two big advantages to the precharged user: first, it ensures a very consistent shot-to-shot variation; second, its efficient use of air contained within the chamber allows a higher number of shots before the rifle needs to be refilled. Topping up is done via a diver's aqualung, which is easy to obtain in Britain and is relatively easy to have refilled with air. No special certificates are needed to own or use a diver's bottle, although they do need to undergo an official safety check every couple of years.

As newer gunmakers like List, Ripley and Titan have entered the scene, pneumatics have become more fashionable—especially because their recoilless actions make accurate

shooting so much easier and they offer a large number of shots with hardly any cocking effort. Whereas you once expected to see a pneumatic only dressed in competition livery, rifles like the Titan MPT and Theoben Rapid Seven were soon developed with the serious pest controller in mind. The downside of this advancement in technology, though, is pneumatics tend to cost more and need to be fueled from relatively expensive and cumbersome diving gear. This often means the shooter has to make an unscheduled journey for refilling. Unlike other types of airguns, they don't have a self-contained power source, either. Run out of air with a pneumatic, and unless you have your bottle handy, you just won't be able to shoot. Gunmakers haven't been slow to recognize this, and one or two of the more forward thinking of them have looked at ways to combine all the advantages of the pneumatic with the simplicity of the spring gun.

The South Coast gunmakers at Air Arms approached the problem in two steps. Even though their then-current 100 Series line-up of precharged pneumatics was favored by Field Target champions like Nick Jenkinson, Air Arms took the bold move to cater for the grass-roots shooter by designing the TX200 fixed-barrel, spring-driven, underlever rifle. In the face of stiff competition from both the spring and pneumatic markets, the recoiling TX200 was voted the overall Airgun of the Year in 1992—but by then Air Arms was already working on making it recoilless. The Airgun of the Year for 1993 was the TX200 SR—the slight recoil version

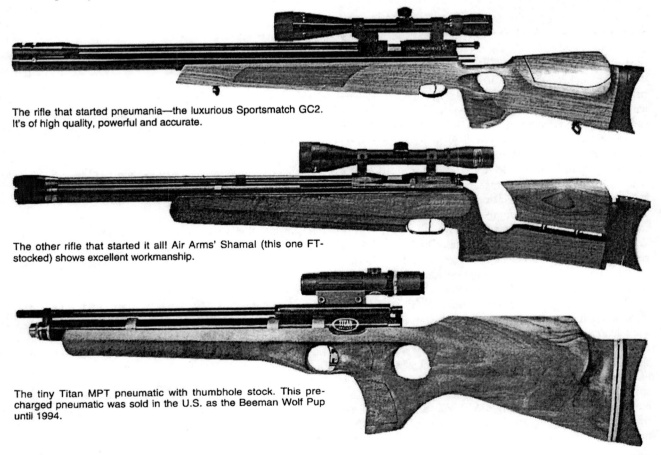

The rifle that started pneumania—the luxurious Sportsmatch GC2. It's of high quality, powerful and accurate.

The other rifle that started it all! Air Arms' Shamal (this one FT-stocked) shows excellent workmanship.

The tiny Titan MPT pneumatic with thumbhole stock. This precharged pneumatic was sold in the U.S. as the Beeman Wolf Pup until 1994.

The luxurious Theoben Rapid Seven—a pneumatic that uses a detachable "buddy" bottle as its power source.

British airgun writer Jack Stanton with Parker-Hale's Dragon.

Jack Stanton with 1993 "Airgun of the Year"—Air Arms' TX200 SR (walnut version). It's an effective hunting tool.

of the TX200 incorporating a sliding action (scope and all) within the stock. So although the rifle *did* move backward on firing, the shooter didn't feel anything, as all the movement happened within the stock and wasn't transferred to the shoulder. This system has become highly popular with British airgunners, not because they're patriotic toward homemade gunmakers of distinction, but because the TX200 SR has the traditional feel, look and action of a spring rifle without the need for any extras. Although Air Arms didn't aim their new rifle at the precision-minded followers of Field Target, the fact that many competitors switched to it is proof that Air Arms hit the mark dead center.

Another rifle that caused a real stir upon its launch and has since become a popular choice in Britain is the Dragon from Parker-Hale, the first air rifle to leave the factory of one of the world's most renowned manufacturers of firearms. For such a famous name to turn its attention to airpower, this further confirms the credibility of the airgun, and this historic entry is quite a revolutionary piece. Its pneumatic action is charged via a single stroke of the sidelever cocking arm, fairly typical of the spring-powered stalwarts like Air Arms' Khamsin and Webley's Tracker. Thanks to an ingenious sliding pivot system, this sidelever generates the very high air pressure needed for a full-power shot with no more effort than cocking a spring-powered rifle. But since it's a pneumatic, the Dragon is totally recoil-free to shoot.

For hunters, rifles like the Dragon and TX200 SR are just the ticket—their recoilless actions allow the rifle to be shot from all angles and stances without any loss of zero, a feat which can't be said of typical recoiling rifles. This brings match performance into the field and is one of the many reasons why more huntsmen are leaning toward recoilless airguns.

Smaller gunmakers, of which Britain has many, are also going down the pneumatic route. List Engineering, Ripley Rifles and Skan AR all produce precharged models in limited numbers which can easily compete with the offerings from larger gunmakers like Air Arms, Daystate and Theoben.

The "buddy bottle," a small back-up air container that divers use in an emergency, has been incorporated into some gunmakers' designs in an effort to keep cost and weight to a minimum and make charging much easier. It works like this: Once the rifle's main air chamber is exhausted, it's just a simple matter of unscrewing the empty cylinder (which can then be recharged at the user's convenience) and replacing it with a full one. Daystate, List and Theoben all use a buddy bottle as part of the forend, while Skan uses a thin screw-in cylinder hidden within the military-styled stock of their pump-action Bullpup. This design allows instant charging for each shot, which is just as well, because it is entirely possible to let rip with the entire ninety-six-shot magazine in less than two minutes.

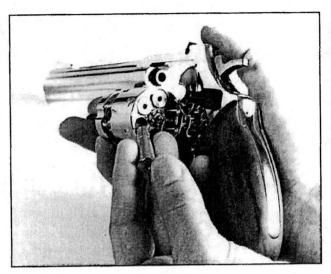

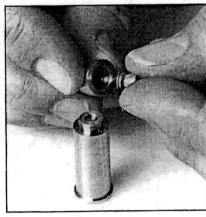

Wasp's Crown air cartridge is the latest advancement in airgunning. Here a pellet is being loaded.

(Left) An air cartridge is slipped into the chamber of this mean-looking PDS Classic Cobra Six handgun.

Air Cartridge

But there's one type of airgun power source that is quietly gaining a large following of fans, not just because it offers the recoilless advantages of the pneumatic system, but because it takes airgunning into a new direction. Some shooters don't want anything to do with guns that aren't "gun-like," so the air cartridge system that Midlands-based Brocock has perfected for their revolvers is for them. Loading up with their air cartridge "ammo" gives you the same sort of buzz as when chambering 38-caliber live rounds. The cartridges, which can be used over and over again, are effectively regulated miniature air chambers that can either be filled directly from a diver's bottle or, more arduously, from a hand pump which requires several pumps to give full power.

British airgunners can choose from two types of air cartridge: the Tandem version (TAC) from Brocock or the Crown air cartridge system from Wasp. Although they're slightly different from each other, and non-compatible, they work on the same principle—a release valve is situated at the center of the cartridge base and the pellet is placed into a screw cap at the front. Once placed into the breech of an air cartridge gun, all that's required is for the hammer to strike the valve that releases the air, thus projecting the pellet forward up the barrel. In operation, air cartridges are much the same as live rounds except there's no primer, just high-pressure air. The benefits of this system are numerous, and Brocock's Orion, Python and Cobra revolvers have long been favorites with British airgunners who want to experience the thrills of fast-fire shooting with the feel of cold steel for that final touch of realism. Pick up an air cartridge revolver, and you, too, will be bitten by this bug.

The Crown air cartridge system is a more recent arrival onto the airgun scene, but in conjunction with Wasp (Weapons and Shooting Products), it brings the opportunity to own a firing replica of a real firearm without having to worry about any form of licensing. Already the British airgunning public has been treated to a 410 folding shotgun look-alike airgun, and gun-slinging enthusiasts can now get a selection of Wild West single-action revolvers and the famous Winchester Yellowboy

Nigel Allen prepares to fire the Brocock Python six-shot air cartridge revolver.

rifle, made by Italian replica specialists Uberti for use exclusively with airgun ammunition. Judging by the enthusiasm of both the gunmakers and shooters, there's plenty of scope to develop the air-cartridge principle. Who knows? Maybe Smith & Wesson's great magnum models—along with other famous makes—will one day be available in air cartridge format. And providing there's a healthy release of air cartridge-firing guns in the next few years, it's also a safe bet that a new airgun sport is likely to evolve within Britain—a sort of airgunning equivalent of practical pistol shooting.

Whatever the future may hold for British airgunning, it certainly looks rosy. Since the beginning of the century, when the airgun played such an important role in the training of the British armed forces, things seem to have gone in a full circle. Between the wars, airgunning's niche was somehow relegated to the bottom of the firearm hierarchy, but since then it's gradually regained respect. In Britain, at least, the airgun is once more a force to be reckoned with!

Airgun Test Reports

Models from the entire spectrum are put to the test by our experts.

THIS AIRGUN TEST report chapter is certainly one of the key chapters—perhaps the most important one—in this book. In this section we put a wide variety of modern airguns, spanning the entire airgun scene, under close scrutiny, trying to extract every bit of information possible about how they perform, often under various conditions and in various roles.

The final outcome of each test, however, is based upon the performance of that *individual sample* airgun. Thus, there is always the possibility that the sample being tested may be the one in a thousand that performs slightly below par vis-a-vis other guns of the same make and model. An example of this would be a gun that shoots below the manufacturer's advertised muzzle velocity or one that doesn't produce the tight groups we are told it's capable of, even when carefully benchrested using pellets of superior quality. Conversely, someone may rush out and buy a given airgun after reading a glowing test report, only to be disappointed and irate because his gun fails to perform *exactly* as the one in the test report. As in everything else, there are always variations involved and a test report is meant as a general guideline regarding an airgun's window of performance.

Keep in mind that some guns have individual tastes as far as ammo preference is concerned. Over the years I have tested countless airguns of the same make and model that sometimes produced widely different results with the same brand and type of pellet.

After the above comments, I must also add that an airgun "lemon" is a fairly rare occurrence these days. Quality control has been tightened to a very high degree throughout the airgun industry during the last two decades, both here as well as abroad. Still, the occasional lemon squeaks through once in a long while. When it does, it really stands out.

No series of test reports on airguns can be complete without including at least two or three guns that are considered classics. The ones I have selected were interesting, cleverly designed guns made about a quarter-century ago. They all shared a more or less brief moment of glory and then faded away to become prized collectors' pieces as the years passed. It sure is intriguing to put some of these vintage guns through their paces. In all probability, no serious test report on these classics was ever published because back then all airguns were largely regarded as toys.

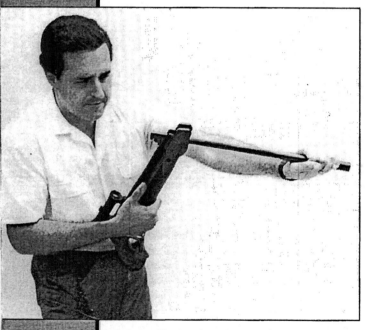

Galan, and a number of others, put each specimen through a bettery of tests.

ARS Farco Shotgun

THE AIR OR gas-powered shotgun, as we have seen elsewhere in this tome, is a rather uncommon design that has seen fairly limited acceptance in this country, despite the fact that some models have been truly outstanding in design and performance. One example of this is the Crosman Model 1100, marketed back in 1968. Powered by two 12-gram CO_2 cartridges, the gun was a creditable performer in a variety of limited-area recreational and training applications. Unfortunately, the shooting public at that time did not recognize the potential of this gun, and it was quietly dropped from the Crosman lineup less than two years after its introduction. No other CO_2-powered shotgun had been available in the domestic market until the Farco was introduced in the late 1980s.

The Farco is made in the Philippines, a nation with extremely restrictive gun control laws that amount to the virtual prohibition of firearms for the civilian population. As a result, airguns have filled some of the gaps in the areas of recreational shooting, such as target practice and small game hunting. In fact, the Farco was specifically designed to serve in the latter category and is used in that part of the world to hunt quail, dove and pheasant.

At a glance, the Farco looks fairly ugly, sort of a cross between an over/under shotgun and a bolt-action rifle. The stock is made from a light-colored Oriental hardwood, and is decidedly rifle-like, complete with massive stippled pistol grip and Monte Carlo comb. There are three longitudinal recesses

ARS FARCO SHOTGUN SPECIFICATIONS

Power:	CO_2; 10-oz. tank
Caliber:	28-gauge
Barrel:	30 ins.
Weight:	7 lbs.
Overall Length:	48½ ins.
Sights:	Fixed notch rear, blade front
Trigger:	Two-stage; non-adjustable
Muzzle Velocity:	About 400 fps
Cocking Effort:	NA
Source:	Air Rifle Specialists

on each side of the forend that further enhance the rifle-like design of the entire stock.

The single shot bolt action further adds to the unusual appearance of the gun. The top tube is the 28-gauge barrel, a rather longish 30 inches in length. Below that and extending all the way up to the muzzle lies the tube that contains the CO_2 reservoir, as well as the valve and other key components of the gun. Both of these tubes are made of brass and have a non-reflective, pewter finish. The trigger guard is also made of brass.

The Farco is supplied with a 10-ounce CO_2 tank for filling the gun's gas reservoir. The gun's reservoir holds about 4½ ounces of CO_2, giving 30 to 35 shots before refilling is needed.

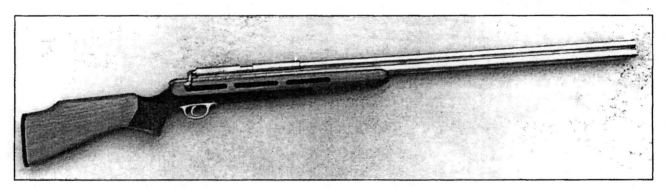

The ARS Farco CO_2-powered shotgun is made in the Philippines, where strict gun laws severely affect the private ownership and use of firearms for sport.

The Farco is a man-sized shotgun and packs a hefty punch, despite its hybrid looks.

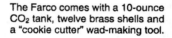

The Farco comes with a 10-ounce CO_2 tank, twelve brass shells and a "cookie cutter" wad-making tool.

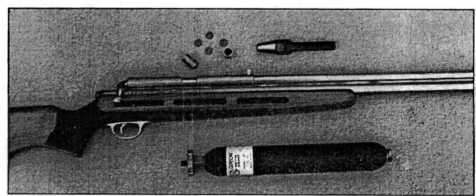

In order to charge the gun with CO_2, the tank is simply screwed into the intake valve at the front of the reservoir tube and the spigot on the tank opened for about 30 seconds until the reservoir is full. Also supplied with the gun are a dozen 1-inch-long brass shells. These are simply small tubes open at both ends. A special "cookie cutter" tool is also supplied that enables the shooter to make his own cork or cardboard wads for closing the ends of the shells. A bunch of wads can be easily cut in just a few minutes with this tool.

By modern airgun standards, the Farco is extremely powerful, fully capable of putting out over 100 foot pounds of muzzle energy with each shot. Handloaders in particular can readily appreciate the many possibilities offered by the shotshells of this gun. During my tests, I tried a variety of shot sizes, like a load of about 240 #8 shot, and one of twelve #4 Buck pellets. The smaller shot gave far superior results, averaging 405 fps at the muzzle and producing a rather dense pattern about 14 inches in diameter at 20 yards. This load exceeds 100 foot pounds of muzzle energy and is quite capa-

That big 28-gauge bore of the Farco makes this the largest caliber airgun of modern times.

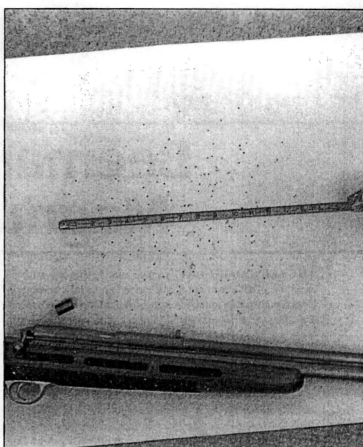

Using a load of about 240 #8 shot, the Farco throws a pattern measuring about 14 inches across at 20 yards.

(Left) Although a bit stiff at first, the action of the Farco became increasingly smoother with use. Galan found that this strange-looking shotgun tends to grow on you.

Davis Schweisinger, president of Air Rifle Specialists, proudly displays one of his star imports, the Farco CO_2 shotgun, at the SHOT Show.

ble of bringing down a variety of small game animals cleanly and humanely at up to 30 yards or so. The loads using smaller shot are ideal for aerial targets and birds, while the aforementioned load of #4 Buck pellets can be quite effective on rabbits and squirrels. The Farco obviously must be treated and used with the same respect and care accorded any powder-burning scattergun. The Farco incorporates a manual trigger safety, but as with all guns, the best safety is always in the shooter's own head. The discharge report is quite loud, easily surpassing that of most multi-pump pneumatic and CO_2 rifles on the market. The noise factor, coupled with the gun's high power, tend to rule out using the Farco around most suburban settings, further affirming that this gun was intended primarily as a hunting arm.

The Farco is clearly a most unique airgun. Powerful, sturdy and affordable, its arguably unconventional looks tend to fade given its impressive performance. No collection of contemporary airguns would be complete without one of these gas-powered scatterguns.

J.I. Galan

Beeman Kodiak Magnum Rifle

THE BEEMAN KODIAK is a pure hunting rifle any way you look at it. That statement is almost certain to raise some eyebrows, particularly among those who still group all airguns into the category of low-powered plinkers. The fact is, however, there is a class of airguns that we now call "magnums," and for the past dozen years or so, we have witnessed a rapidly growing number of air rifles—and a few air pistols, as well—joining this exclusive high-power group.

Generally speaking, an air rifle qualifies as a magnum if it is capable of producing a muzzle energy in excess of 11 foot pounds. Most magnum air rifles, in fact, fall roughly in the 12- to 19-foot pound bracket, with some rather pricey models—mostly precharged pneumatics and gas-ram types—reaching even higher levels of energy. Obviously, a vast number of magnum air rifles are extremely well suited to serious hunting applications.

When the first modern magnum air rifles began to appear back in the late 1970s, most of them were of European manufacture, which meant they utilized the spring-piston power plant. Over the years, the spring-piston system was developed to such a degree that top power could be achieved without ruining the gun's firing behavior and accuracy, not to mention requiring a cocking effort that only a muscle-bound individual could muster. Thus, just when we were almost resigned to accept the precharged pneumatic system as the rising king among magnum airguns, a magnum spring-piston rifle of unheard-of power shattered all previous records.

The Beeman Kodiak is even more remarkable because it is of fairly conventional appearance and utilizes the break-barrel cocking system. It has an overall length of 45.6 inches, 18 inch-

BEEMAN KODIAK SPECIFICATIONS

Power:	Spring-piston; barrel cocking
Caliber:	25, 22
Barrel:	18 ins.
Weight:	9 lbs.
Overall Length:	45.6 ins.
Sights:	Open adjustable rear, blade front
Trigger:	Adjustable
Muzzle Velocity:	775 fps in 25, 865 fps in 22
Cocking Effort:	48 lbs.
Source:	Beeman Precision Airguns

es of which belong to the nicely rifled 22- or 25-caliber barrel. The Kodiak is a big rifle, and its hefty 9 pounds further indicate that it is intended for full-sized folks. This becomes even more apparent when one realizes that the Kodiak requires a cocking effort of about 48 pounds.

All steel surfaces of the Kodiak show an impeccably blued finish that rivals that of some of the ritziest hunting rifles around. The generous sporting-style stock is made of beech and has a walnut stain finish. There is a well-shaped pistol grip with impressed checkering and a black plastic cap with white line spacer. The buttstock has an attractive and rather pronounced cheekpiece, and the whole thing ends with a curved rubber buttpad having another white line spacer. The stock is nice looking and functional, but I still would have preferred either checkering or finger grooves along the forend to help afford a firm grasp with sweaty hands.

In the sight department, the Kodiak is also very well

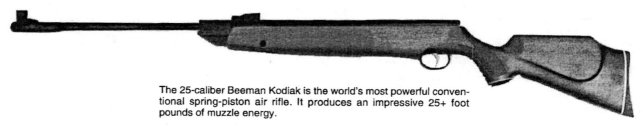

The 25-caliber Beeman Kodiak is the world's most powerful conventional spring-piston air rifle. It produces an impressive 25+ foot pounds of muzzle energy.

There is an automatic trigger safety catch that pops out from the rear of the cylinder whenever the gun is cocked.

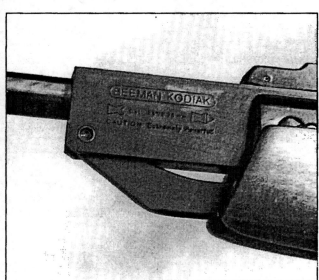

The shooter is clearly cautioned about the Kodiak's tremendous power.

There's no doubt the Kodiak is a man-sized air rifle all the way. Cocking it requires approximately 48 pounds of effort.

equipped. The open rear sight is fully adjustable for windage and elevation via slotted screws. In fact, the elevation screw employs a click system, although for some reason the windage screw does not. All the same, I found the sight to be eminently practical. The front sight consists of a stout blade on a ramp surrounded by a sturdy hood. However, current production guns apparently no longer come with the hood. The whole unit is mounted on the muzzle weight piece and can be easily removed via a single Allen screw. At any rate, many Kodiak owners are certain to mount a telescopic sight on this powerhouse anyway. To that effect, the rear of the cylinder is grooved for tip-off scope mounts.

The adjustable two-stage trigger was sweet and smooth, with a crisp let-off. This is a noteworthy feature in light of the fact

that the sear must hold back the tremendous pressure exerted by the oversized mainspring when it is compressed. There is an automatic trigger safety catch that pops out of the rear of the cylinder whenever the Kodiak is cocked. To disengage, the safety catch is simply pushed in until a red warning ring can be seen on either side. By the way, the safety catch can be manually reset.

There are very good reasons why the Beeman Kodiak is currently the world's most powerful air rifle of conventional spring-piston design. The $1/4$-inch bore is one major factor in this rifle's awesome energy output. In addition, the gun's air-compression stroke exceeds by more than 1 inch the compression stroke of the highly popular—and also extremely powerful—Beeman R1 Magnum air rifle. This is a crucial

Galan found the Kodiak surprisingly smooth and quiet, despite its awesome power.

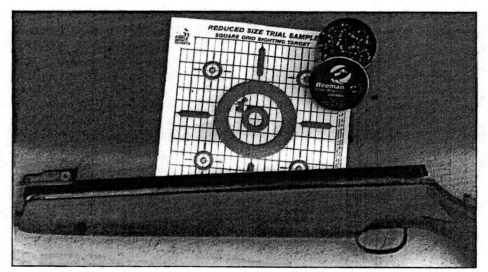

This is a typical five-shot group fired from 25 yards, using 25-caliber Beeman Crow Magnum pellets. This rifle is hard-hitting and highly accurate.

element in determining the Kodiak's tremendous power, because the resulting swept volume is about 25 percent higher than that of the R1. In addition, the Kodiak uses a longer mainspring than just about any other magnum spring-piston rifle.

Tests carried out with the Kodiak soon revealed that this rifle not only packs quite a punch, but delivers creditable accuracy as well. A selection of 25-caliber pellets were tried with excellent results. Incidentally, Beeman now carries twelve different pellet types in 25-caliber. The Kodiak on test was partial to Beeman Crow Magnum pellets (26.2 grains), printing five-shot groups at 25 yards averaging 1/4-inch center-to-center. These tests were fired from a sandbag rest, using only the rifle's open sights. A scope tightened up those groups even further as testing progressed.

The early production 25-caliber Kodiak tested was given an average muzzle velocity rating of 820 fps by Beeman. Using Beeman's own Silver Jet 21.5-grain pellets, that Kodiak averaged 822 fps, for a muzzle energy of 32.2 foot pounds. Switching over to the heavier Crow Magnum pellets, the ener-

gy jumped to 33.4 foot pounds, even though the velocity decreased somewhat. Crow Magnum pellets, with their gaping hollowpoint head, also produced impressive results on a variety of targets. Make no mistake about it, the Kodiak is intended first and foremost for hunting small game. Even out to 50 or 60 yards, the 1/4-inch pellet still carries more kinetic energy than smaller-caliber pellets from most other magnum air rifles. Despite all that power, the firing characteristics are surprisingly mild, with practically no vibration thanks to a well-designed spring damper that really works. The firing noise is also rather subdued, comparable to that of a medium-power spring-piston rifle. Beeman currently rates the 25-caliber model at 775 fps.

The Kodiak is also available in 22-caliber. Smaller calibers cannot handle the tremendous air flow generated by this rifle with the same efficiency as the 25-caliber version. Therefore, this is really the caliber of choice for optimum performance. Without any doubt, the Kodiak lives up to its name, which is synonymous with a big, rugged beast of awesome power.

J.I. Galan

Beeman R10 Deluxe Rifle

SINCE ITS INTRODUCTION in 1986, the Beeman R10 has been portrayed as capable of producing a muzzle velocity of close to 1000 fps in 177-caliber right out of the box. In those days, few regular production spring-piston rifles were able to live up to that kind of performance straight off without special lubrication and/or special tuning. In light of the above, the R10 had a substantial claim to live up to when it made its debut.

The first thing one notices about the rifle is its strong resemblance to the superb Beeman R1 Magnum rifle, a top-selling spring-piston powerhouse since the early 1980s that is still pretty much in production. Of course, both the R1 and the newer R10 are barrel cockers made by Weihrauch in Germany, so the family resemblance is to be expected.

The R10 Deluxe measures 46 inches overall and has a 19.8-inch barrel. The mirror-bright bore of the R10 comes rifled with twelve grooves in a right-hand twist. This gun is also available in 20-caliber (5mm). Gun weight, incidentally, is a comparatively light 8.2 pounds, something quite welcome in a rifle intended mostly for field use. One of the principal reasons for the relatively light weight of the R10 vis-a-vis its potent power plant stems from the fact that its receiver (compression cylinder) wall is thinner than that of its heavier relative, the R1. Because of that, the R10 cannot have the customary scope mount grooves cut into its receiver. A separate scope base has been screwed to the receiver instead. I like this setup better anyway, because it mounts the scope higher, permitting a more natural head-up position relative to the stock.

The R10 Deluxe has a nicely styled, but entirely practical, walnut-stained beech stock with genuine cut checkering on the pistol grip, a rubber buttpad with white line spacer, grip cap and

BEEMAN R10 DELUXE SPECIFICATIONS	
Power:	Spring-piston; barrel cocking
Caliber:	177, 20
Barrel:	19.8 ins.; 12-groove rifling (16.1 ins. carbine)
Weight:	8.2 lbs. (7.8 lbs. carbine)
Overall Length:	46 ins. (42.4 ins. carbine)
Sights:	Fully adjustable open rear, tunnel front
Trigger:	Adjustable; two stage
Muzzle Velocity:	950 fps (177)
	850 fps (20)
Cocking Effort:	34 lbs.
Source:	Beeman Precision Airguns

Monte Carlo-style comb. The extended forend gives a slim profile to the R10 Deluxe. The R10 Standard, in contrast, lacks the graceful teardrop cheekpiece, checkering, white line spacers and long forend. The Standard, however, can be used by both lefties and right-handers.

The all-steel sights of the R10 are the traditionally sturdy Weihrauch open type that we have admired over many years. The rear sight is fully adjustable via micrometer click discs. Up front, there is a tunnel that allows different inserts to be used, and the test gun came with a variety of these. The iron sights can be removed easily, should the owner wish to mount a telescopic sight, but don't expect to utilize the full accuracy potential of the R10 using only its open sights. A good scope is a virtual must for that, particularly when shooting at longer distances. The rifle on test was accompanied by one of the excellent Beeman SS-2 short scopes, and the results obtained with this combo were quite impressive.

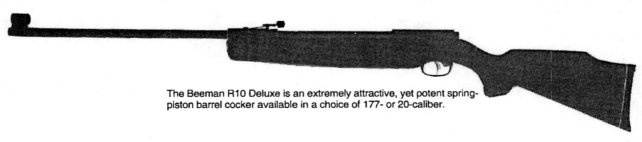

The Beeman R10 Deluxe is an extremely attractive, yet potent spring-piston barrel cocker available in a choice of 177- or 20-caliber.

Galan puts the adult-size Beeman R10 Deluxe through its paces using a Beeman SS-2 scope.

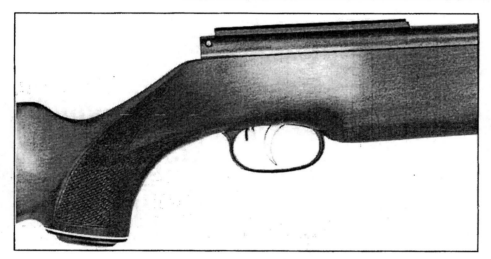

The Beeman R10 Deluxe has a hand-checkered pistol grip. The trigger adjustment screw is behind the trigger. The gun comes with the scope base.

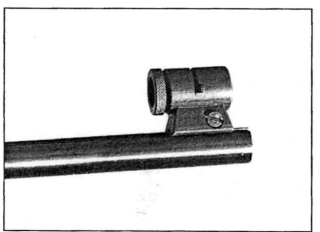

The removable front sight of the R10 accepts a variety of inserts to suit different tastes.

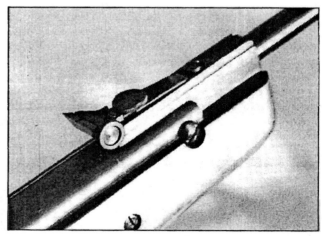

The all-steel rear sight is fully adjustable via micrometer knobs. Both sights are removable for scope mounting.

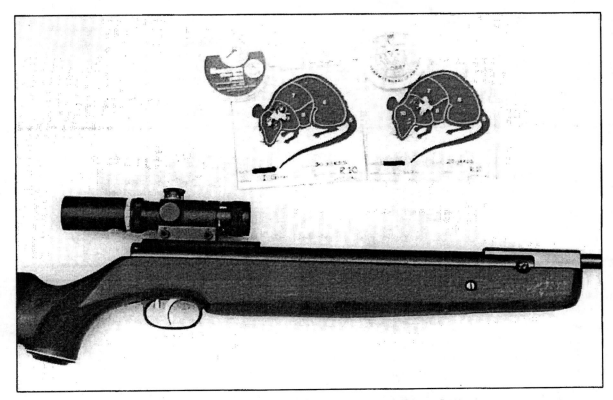

These two rat targets, shot at 30 and 20 yards attest to the R10's inherent precision. The left target (30 yards) has a ten-shot group; right target (20 yards) shows a five-shot group.

Another area in which the Weihrauch stamp comes through clearly is in the R10's trigger. The well-known Weihrauch Rekord trigger unit used in many of their air rifles is also in the R10. This two-stage, adjustable unit is so sweet that it practically falls in the match category. It comes from the factory set at approximately 2^1/$_2$ pounds of pressure. Completing the works is a trigger safety that engages automatically upon cocking the rifle and must be manually disengaged in order to shoot. As with *all* mechanical safeties, it must be kept in mind that none of these devices can ever replace safe gun handling practices.

My first set of tests with the 177-caliber R10 involved the electronic chronograph, in order to verify Beeman's initial claim that the rifle could reach (and even surpass) the 1000 fps mark right out of the box. Using both Beeman Laser and RWS Hobby pellets—6.5 grains and 7.0 grains, respectively—the R10 consistently broke the 1000 fps boundary. RWS Hobby gave average velocities in the 1000 to 1003 fps range, while the lighter Beeman Lasers averaged 1011 fps, with several shot strings averaging as high as 1027 fps.

Of course, I expected those figures to decrease as soon as heavier pellets were used and, sure enough, it happened. A variety of popular field pellets, weighing between 7.5 and 8.6 grains, gave velocities between 912 and 980 fps. Beeman's original claim, however, had passed the chronograph test with flying colors. Occasional dieseling shots were experienced during the first hundred rounds, but it soon disappeared. Despite its considerable power, however, the R10 manages to have a surprisingly

smooth firing behavior. The latest version of the 177 R10, however, is rated at an MV of 950 fps, which is still quite hot.

Velocity really is meaningless without accuracy. The R10 also showed it can send those pellets straight to the target, provided the shooter does his part. Most of the various pellet types used gave great accuracy, although Beeman Silver Bear hollowpoints seemed to group a bit better than the rest. Most accuracy tests were carried out using Beeman's SS-2 telescopic sight. This ultra-compact 4x scope has razor-sharp optics and was designed to withstand the pronounced "double recoil" typical of magnum-class spring-piston rifles. At 30 yards, with the gun rested solidly atop sandbags, the groups were impressively small. Moving out to 50 yards, the R10 still performed with sufficient accuracy and power to nail rabbit-sized game or knock down metallic silhouettes. This air rifle really inspires confidence, which is one very important aspect of any successful shooting endeavor.

Beeman gives muzzle velocities of 950 fps and 850 fps for the 177- and 20-caliber R10s, respectively. Those are pretty hot figures by current magnum air rifle standards, which translate into muzzle energies in the 12- to 15-foot pound range, depending upon caliber and pellet weight used. Another plus for the Beeman R10 is its competitive price, which compares quite well with several other popular magnum-class airsporters. Considering the high quality, impressive performance and pedigree of the R10, the price tag is really of secondary importance for those who can appreciate a truly superb sporting air rifle.

J.I. Galan

183

Beeman/Webley Tempest Pistol

BACK IN 1979, the famous, old British firm of Webley & Scott, Ltd., introduced an air pistol that almost immediately gained wide popularity in America. Dubbed the Tempest, that monicker followed Webley's 1970s penchant for naming its air pistols after some of nature's powerful forces. The Webley Hurricane, for instance, is also quite popular and a fine example of British air pistol technology. It preceded the Tempest by just a couple of years.

However, the Tempest filled the gap left by the phasing out of Webley's classic Senior and Premier air pistols, which were in production for decades. Following in the tradition of those earlier models, the Tempest retained the compactness and robust design that has endeared Webley air pistols to generations of shooters around the world.

There has always been a real need for a powerful, yet compact air pistol with plenty of practical accuracy. Hikers, fishermen and other outdoorsmen often like to pack just such an air pistol in their kit for a variety of reasons, including inexpensive recreational shooting, dispatching small pests, etc. I bought my first Tempest shortly after Beeman began distributing them in

BEEMAN/WEBLEY TEMPEST SPECIFICATIONS

Power:	Spring-piston
Caliber:	177, 22
Barrel:	6⅞ ins; rifled steel
Weight:	2 lbs.
Overall Length:	8.9 ins.
Sights:	Adjustable notch rear, blade front
Trigger:	Single stage; adjustable
Muzzle Velocity:	500 fps (177)
	400 fps (22)
Cocking Effort:	25 lbs.
Source:	Beeman Precision Airguns

the U.S. about 1980. That 177-caliber Tempest has performed very well over the years as a plinking gun both at home and afield. A few years ago, I acquired a second Tempest, this time in 22-caliber, and it, too, has earned its keep by dispatching pests from time to time.

Without question, the Tempest is a chopped-down Webley

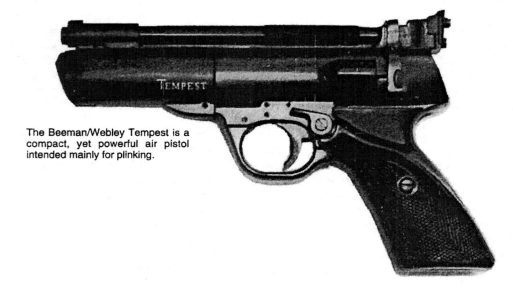

The Beeman/Webley Tempest is a compact, yet powerful air pistol intended mainly for plinking.

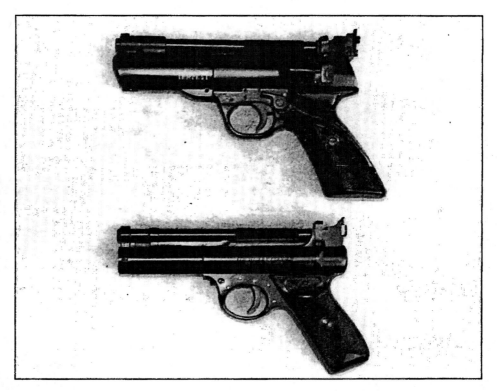

The Tempest follows in the long tradition of other Webley classics, such as the Premier model at bottom.

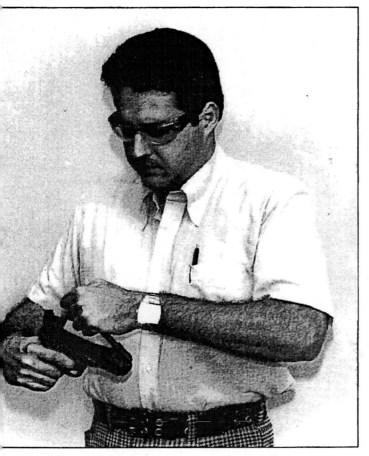

The Tempest can be safely uncocked by opening the barrel, pulling the trigger and slowly allowing the barrel to swing closed.

Hurricane. There is more to it than that, of course, and I must say this little pistol really has a character all its own. With an overall length of just under 9 inches and a weight of 2 pounds, the Tempest is about 2¹/₄ inches shorter and about 6 ounces lighter than the Hurricane. All of that gives the Tempest nearly the same size and weight as the old Webley Senior and Premier classics.

The traditional Webley system of having the barrel located above the compression chamber, pivoting forward in order to cock and load, is also used in the Tempest. Webley's classic stirrup-shaped barrel latch is also incorporated. The steel barrel is 6⁷/₈ inches long, nicely rifled with twelve right-twist grooves. A knurled section near the breech gives a non-slip surface for cocking the action. It requires an effort of about 25 pounds, but this can be reduced slightly by the careful application of moly lubricant.

The high-tensile aircraft aluminum alloy frame Tempest has a hard-wearing, baked-on black epoxy finish. The adult-sized grip has a comfortable angle and sports checkered plastic sideplates, with the one on the left side having a narrow thumbrest.

As for sights, the Tempest is really quite down to earth. Up front is a stubby blade, with the rear sight consisting of a steel plate with a square notch that is adjustable for windage and elevation via two screws. The upper screw controls elevation, while the one below regulates windage. Nothing fancy, just a simple and sturdy setup.

As triggers in sporting air pistols go, that of the Tempest rates fairly high. It is a single-stage, adjustable with the Allen wrench provided, from about 5 to 8 pounds. The trigger adjustment screw can be reached through a hole at the rear of the trigger guard. A manual trigger safety is incorporated on the left side

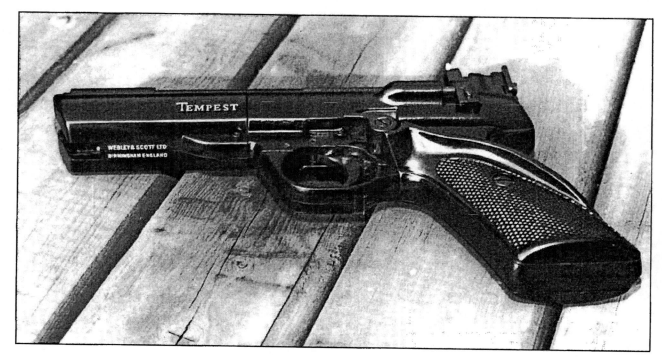

The trigger of the Tempest can be adjusted via a small screw accessible with an Allen wrench through the trigger guard.

just above the trigger. The Tempest, incidentally, can be easily uncocked if the shooter decides not to shoot, thereby enhancing any real or imagined advantage the manual safety might offer. The best safety, it must be remembered, is always common-sense behavior on the part of the shooter.

The current Beeman catalog lists a muzzle velocity of about 500 fps for the 177-caliber Tempest and 400 fps for the 22-caliber version. Tempests sold on the British market are reportedly less powerful as a result of Britain's tight regulations on airgun power.

Firing my 177 Tempest from a rest at 15 yards, using a two-hand hold and match pellets, produces groups averaging 1 to 1 1/4 inches across. Although that kind of accuracy may be considered rather pedestrian by some precision buffs, I find it quite acceptable in a knockabout plinking gun that can take lots of rough use and keep on shooting reliably. Yes, the firing behavior takes some getting used to compared to that of more traditional spring-piston pistols, but it is still pleasant enough. The recoil of Webley air pistols has always resembled that of cartridge hand-guns and the Tempest is no exception. This is because the piston moves to the rear during the firing sequence. Of course, this feature turns the gun into a superb firearm trainer.

The Tempest comes with a spare breech washer, trigger adjustment Allen wrench, and a comprehensive set of factory instructions that cover everything from basic operation to complete stripping should any internal components ever need replacing.

The Tempest is definitely not a target air pistol; however, it will provide a virtual lifetime of trouble-free plinking pleasure in a handy and rugged package that truly lives up to its name when it comes to making old tin cans bounce around.

J.I. Galan

As a general-purpose plinking pistol or firearm trainer, the Tempest definitely earns its keep. This pistol is rugged and hard-hitting.

Benjamin Sheridan Model E22 Pistol

ALTHOUGH IT'S BEEN a couple of years now, we still remember the scene quite vividly. It was during the opening minutes of the 1992 SHOT Show in New Orleans, Louisiana, where, from high atop the Crosman trade exhibit, a purchase agreement had just been concluded that would give the New York-based firm total ownership and control over its long-time rival, Benjamin Sheridan. And what a shocker that was!

Though word of this impending acquisition had actually been circulating for several months, it nevertheless surprised a good many in the trade. Of course, immediately after the deal was announced came the usual flood of questions: Would the company retain its present management and trade name? Would the company relocate and, if so, where? New York perhaps? Even more importantly, how would the sale affect the current Benjamin Sheridan product line—particularly as it pertains to the firm's longstanding tradition of quality. Very compelling questions, indeed.

True professionals that they are, the Crosman team patiently answered each question. Their responses were always pretty

BENJAMIN SHERIDAN MODEL E22
SPECIFICATIONS
Power:	CO$_2$; one 12-gram cartridge
Caliber:	22
Barrel:	6.3 ins.
Weight:	1.13 lbs.
Overall Length:	9.8 ins.
Sights:	Fully adjustable open rear, blade front
Trigger:	4^1/$_2$ lbs., non-adjustable
Muzzle Velocity:	430 fps, with standard-weight pellets
Cocking Effort:	NA
Source:	Benjamin Sheridan

straightforward, too, letting concerned customers know that things would be left alone for the time being. As one Crosman spokesman confidently put it, "We realize that Benjamin Sheridan occupies a unique niche in the upper-end domestic airgun marketplace. As a consequence, any future design or material

A classic design that has been made in one form or another for the past four decades, the Model E22 (center) is flanked by the venerable Benjamin 250 (left) and the later Benjamin 267 Rocket (right).

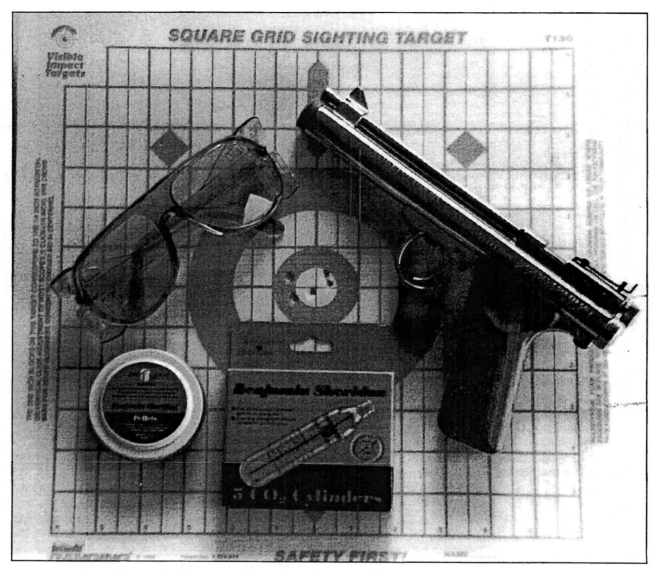

Well made, reliable and potent, the compact Benjamin Sheridan E22 also delivers the goods on the target range. The pistol's basic design format has been around since the early 1950s.

revisions will be made solely to further enhance product quality and performance. Moreover, Benjamin Sheridan products have long been regarded as the best offered by a U.S. firm, and as far as Crosman is concerned, they will continue to be the very best available. Simple as that."

With the company now entering into its fourth year under Crosman management, we believe the time has finally come to bring everyone up to speed by examining a current Benjamin Sheridan product. For this purpose, we've selected the venerable Model E series CO_2-powered pistol, which is not only a personal favorite, but is also a gun that truly represents a blending of both Benjamin and Sheridan design philosophies.

The gun was introduced under the Sheridan banner in 1977, and its design roots can actually be traced back to the early 1950s. The basic construction, in fact, closely follows the classic Benjamin 250 series, although the gun's actual proportions favor the later Benjamin 260 Rocket series gas pistols. However, unlike the 260 series (which was offered in several calibers and in repeating versions), the Model E would be available only as a single shooter and in one chambering—Sheridan's traditional 20-caliber.

Colorful lineage notwithstanding, the Model E's remaining production history is also quite noteworthy. Though enjoying moderate success during the late '70s and early '80s, the stage wasn't really set for things to come until the advent of paintball sports.

Almost overnight, the potent and robust Model E became the basis for literally dozens of paintgun designs. At the forefront were airgun professionals like author Tim "MAC-1" McMurray, who used the Sheridan pistol's lower frame and tube assembly as a development platform for his custom accessories. The original slide-action pump and autotrigger were exclusive McMurray creations, which made Sheridan-based paintguns "the weapon of choice" for many of the sport's top professional players. In fact, by the middle '80s, demand was so great for Model E components that the company quietly dropped the 5mm pellet version from its line.

After a hiatus of several years, the much-lamented Model E would reappear in 1990. This time around, though, the pistol sported metalwork plated in gleaming nickel and hardwood grip plates carved from American walnut. Just one year later, the entire Benjamin Sheridan line (including the E series) was substantially revised. Besides receiving a major facelift, the Model E would now be offered for the first time in three bore sizes: 177, 20 and 22, plus two metal finishes—matte black or bright nickel.

As for current production guns, Crosman engineers have influenced design, albeit very subtly. On this account, the latest E series CO_2 pistol has a revised grip frame that appears to mimic the style used on the original Model E. In addition, the filler cap assembly now sports a coin slot to make things a little easier during the charging operation. All in all, the pistol's lines are certainly cleaner, and the slotted filler cap ain't a bad idea either—especially for weak-wristed types.

Aside from a few miscellaneous internal modifications that you can't see, but can still appreciate nonetheless, the E series remains faithful to its original specifications. Known for its compact design, the pistol measures a scant 9.8 inches long and weighs only 1.13 pounds. Barrel length is just over 6 inches, while the sight radius is a useful 7¾ inches.

Still offered in the aforementioned calibers and metal treatments, the E series is constructed from the usual combination of premium-grade brass and steel. Like its other pistol and rifle stablemates, all exposed metal surfaces receive either matte black or nickel plating—with the exception of the breech bolt assembly, which is fashioned from stainless steel.

Well known for our jaded attitudes, we somehow managed to convince the nice folks at Benjamin Sheridan into sending us one of the pretty nickeled versions. Chambered in 22-caliber (hence the E22 monicker), the sample gun sports ambidextrous grip plates carved from American walnut. The gun shares several common components and features now standard on both H series pump-up and E series CO_2 pistols. These include the Sheridan-pattern high-blade front sight, screwdriver-adjustable square notch rear sight, grip frame assembly and breechbolt assembly.

The sample gun's non-adjustable single-stage trigger is acceptable at the 4½-pound pull and will be rather creepy until it's broken in. The trigger blade is something of a design compromise, being well curved, but a bit on the narrow side. A trigger shoe is highly recommended here.

With ease of use being the main attraction of most CO_2-powered arms, the E22's operational format is about as simple as they come, thanks to its compact design. To charge, first retract the breechbolt to its rear position and engage the safety. The filler cap assembly is then removed from the valve tube and a single 12-gram CO_2 cartridge is inserted neck first. The filler

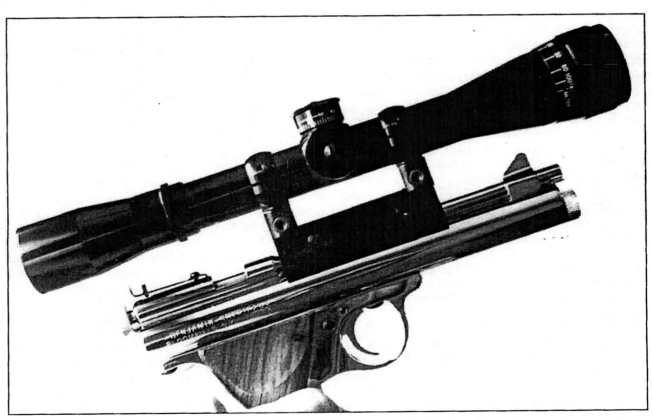

The Model E22 has the power and accuracy for metallic silhouette and small vermin out to 20 yards or so. A decent scope is a must, though.

Like the old Benjamin 250 series, the new Model E22 sports a coin slot on its filler cap. Weak-wristed shooters rejoice!

cap assembly is then replaced (threaded hand tight only, please) and the pistol testfired to confirm that gas has entered the valve. From this point on, the pistol can be fired to the extent of its gas supply. We did just that, of course, and soon discovered the sample gun would yield some forty to fifty usable shots before requiring a fresh cartridge. Of these three dozen or so shots, the first twenty-five are consistent enough for casual target work or close-range vermin control.

The E22 is quite potent for its relative small size and gave just under 6 foot pounds (or 357 fps) using the extra-heavy 21.1-grain Beeman Kodiak pellets. It's surprisingly efficient as well, as even after the twenty-fifth shot, the average velocity dropped only slightly, to 340 fps or nearly $5\frac{1}{2}$ foot pounds. Although heavy 22-caliber pellets are certainly more energy efficient when fired from CO_2-powered arms, lighter types have the advantage of higher velocity (meaning shorter barrel or lock time) and flatter trajectory. Most of the better dome-style pellets, such as the Marksman FTS, RWS Superdome, Crosman Premier and Eley Wasp, were also good all-round performers, returning velocities that averaged 375-425 fps, respectively, over the course of twenty-five shots.

Projectile weight, shape and ballistic efficiency aside, determining the most accurate pellet for a particular gun is another matter entirely. On this occasion, the authors had to put a good many pellets through the test gun before finally settling on the best four or five. Mind you, the E22 proved its worth on the target range, but we did cheat just a bit by mounting a 4x32 scope sight.

At the compulsory 10 meters, best accuracy was achieved with 14.6-grain Marksman FTS pellets, printing five-shot groups averaging $\frac{5}{8}$-inch. Coming in a close second was the fine 14.3-grain Crosman Premier at $\frac{3}{4}$-inch, followed by the big 21.1-grain Beeman Kodiak with 1-inch spreads and the 14.4-grain Superdome, averaging $1\frac{1}{4}$ inches. Easily capable of respectable field accuracy at ranges of 15 to 20 yards, the E22's open sights are simply not fine enough for precise aiming. Not deterred in the least, we bolted on the Sheridan Intermount base and a suitable air rifle scope sight.

Back on the target range, the superb Marksman FTS once again proved to be the pellet of choice, recording five-shot spreads of just $1\frac{1}{2}$ inches at 18 yards—the exact distance of the ram target used in official air pistol silhouette competition. As a matter of fact, from a padded rest it was possible to hit virtually all the ram targets without fail. Of course, shooting from the traditional standing position is a great deal tougher.

Potent, accurate and rugged, the Benjamin Sheridan E series can be managed by anyone competent enough to safely (and legally) handle an airgun. The pistol's firing behavior is also quite tame, but muzzle blast is somewhat excessive due to its short barrel. (Backyard plinkers beware.) Additionally, operation is about as routine as it gets for a gun of this genre.

And there you have it. Having spent a couple of weekends putting the E22 through its paces, we can now state with total confidence that all is well at Benjamin Sheridan. Their products have been America's best for more than a century and, indeed, they remain among the very best this country has to offer. Simple as that.

Tim McMurray and Stephen R. Gibbons

Benjamin Sheridan VM-68 and VM-68 Magnum Pistols

HUNDREDS OF PAINTBALLS, shot as fast as you can pull the trigger! That's Benjamin Sheridan magic from the rugged semi-automatic VM-68. In winter's cold or summer's desert heat, these open-bolt, blow-back semi-autos are a proven first choice of players worldwide.

The black and silver camo-pattern VM-68 and its upscale version, the all-black VM-68 Magnum, offer competitive power and reliability. Players regularly turn their opponents into spectators with either the VM-68's 10-inch brass barrel or the 14.5-inch aluminum barrel standard with the Magnum. These removable barrels, and all internal parts, are interchangeable between the two models.

The Magnum provides extra advanced features for pro-level players. It adapts for either left- or right-handed shooting, and in about a minute's time, a player can move the direct feed and cocking bar to the desired side of the paintgun. When seconds count, fast field-stripping matters, so quick takedown thumbscrews on the Magnum replace certain Allen-head screws on the VM-68. It's less than two minutes for takedown and fast cleaning. The Magnum also lets a player add either a $^3/_8$-inch dovetail or a Weaver-mount sight for that extra competitive edge.

Through 1993, the VM-68 came with a 7-ounce, refillable CO_2 constant-air bottle, and the Magnum with a refillable 3.5-ounce bottle, that screwed into the paintgun's constant-air port. The VM-68's single port is under the barrel, so the bottle extends forward parallel to the barrel. The VM-68 Magnum has the same front port, as well as an additional rear port, so a player may take extra CO_2 onto the playing field. A bottle attached to the rear port can be used in a shoulder stock configuration.

The VM-68 Magnum shooter can cap one port and use the other, or go into a game with two bottles for extra air. When the primary bottle is empty, it must be turned off using the On-Off knob on the valve before the secondary air source is turned on. This keeps the CO_2 pressure from equalizing between the bottles. Benjamin Sheridan stopped supplying bottles with these paintguns after 1993, but players can con-

BENJAMIN SHERIDAN VM-68 SPECIFICATIONS

Power:	CO_2
Caliber:	68
Barrel:	10 ins., brass
Weight:	4 lbs. w/o cylinder
Overall Length:	18.6 ins.
Sights:	None furnished
Muzzle Velocity:	261-295 fps
Cocking Effort:	NA
Source:	Benjamin Sheridan

BENJAMIN SHERIDAN VM-68 MAGNUM SPECIFICATIONS

Power:	CO_2
Caliber:	68
Barrel:	14.5 ins., aluminum
Weight:	4 lbs., 14 oz. w/o cylinder
Overall Length:	24.9 ins.
Sights:	None furnished; comes with sight rail and Weaver base
Muzzle Velocity:	270-292 fps
Cocking Effort:	NA
Source:	Benjamin Sheridan

tinue purchasing them separately. Different size constant-air bottles are readily available through the company.

To ready a new-in-the-box VM-68 paintgun for shooting is simple: Screw on the barrel and attach the cocking bar to the bolt. The cocking bar rides forward and back as the bolt moves back and forth while shooting. With the ambidextrous VM-68 Magnum, the shooter can attach the cocking bar and feed port to either side. Toward the rear of the slot is an upward cut-out notch. Before adding CO_2 power, pull the cocking knob back and latch it securely upward in the notch so the gun does not shoot when CO_2 enters the paintgun.

Attach a filled constant-air CO_2 bottle. With the Magnum,

Dual CO_2 ports and a 14.5-inch aluminum barrel on the gleaming black Benjamin Sheridan VM-68 Magnum semi-auto are nice features.

Benjamin Sheridan VM-68 semi-auto paintgun, with 10-inch brass barrel, camo pattern finish.

The VM-68 Magnum's direct feed (seen between thumb and forefinger of left hand) attaches to either side of the paintgun, as does the cocking handle. Note quick take-down screws, featured on the Magnum.

cap the unused port before attaching the bottle. Nearly all paintball stores and playsites refill constant-air bottles, so we had our bottles filled before going out to shoot. If the air bottle being used has an On-Off knob, turn it on to power up.

With the bottle attached, add the bulk loader and fill it with paintballs. Since the cocking knob is latched back, gravity will pull a paintball down into position to be shot. Gently push the cocking bar down so it can ride back and forth in the long slot. Now it's time for fast semi-auto shooting.

We did a test shoot with both models at a Los Angeles target

From box to shooting line in minutes, the VM-68 Magnum is a player's dream.

New for 1994 is Benjamin Sheridan's EXC-68, the newest in the VM-68 line. It has many advanced features from the VM-68 Magnum, plus a new CO_2 expansion chamber for greater gas efficiency—meaning more shots per bottle.

A CO_2 bottle power source screws into the lower front of both the VM-68 and the VM-68 Magnum. Behind the screw-in barrel, and accessible from the front, is a 12-position velocity adjuster. The VM-68 Magnum here has large take-down screws for easy field-stripping.

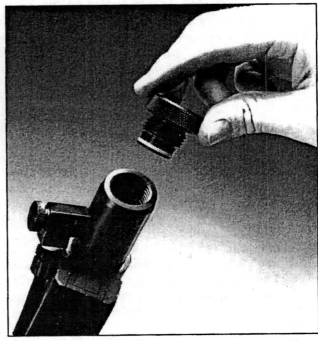

Either CO_2 port on the VM-68 Magnum can be capped when a player only wants to use one bottle. Here, the rear bottle port is being capped.

range. The temperature was in the mid-70s, with low humidity, clear skies and virtually no wind. We shot orange Nelson paintballs over a Pro Chrono chronograph.

Mark Thompson powered up both a VM-68 and a Magnum, and easily tuned them to shoot in the 285-290 fps range. The key to adjusting velocity is to remember the adjuster in the bolt has twelve positive-click positions. The shooter must put the adjuster positively in one of the positions, not between them. Larger velocity adjustments (40 fps or more) may require partial disassembly and use of a special tool to adjust an internal four-position air chamber valve.

Thompson used a benchrest to shoot test groups at an 8-inch round target set 50 feet downrange. He attached an ADCO Mirage 30mm red dot sight to the VM-68 Magnum's sight rail. A ten-ball group held less than 4 inches off center horizontally, and less than 3 inches off center vertically. One stray paintball splatted 11 inches off center (a fluke). The velocity stayed, respectably, between 270 and 292 fps. The VM-68, which has no sight rail, shot within 5 inches of center horizontally and vertically. Velocity ranged a little wider, from 261 to 295 fps, with two fluke shots (one 13 and one 15 inches off center). Importantly, neither gun's velocity soared above the industry's maximum speed limit of 300 fps.

Both semi-auto paintguns can rain paint at a good six paintballs per second. The guns are a bit on the heavy side, but the weight provides rugged construction that keeps them running smoothly for thousands of shots. Any first-time player can pick up these semi-autos, add paint and have a good time. Make these a must-see, must-shoot on your shopping list.

Jessica J. Sparks

Component Concepts Phantom Paintball Gun

FROM BELGIUM TO Boston and points west, paintballers respect the Phantom pump. Simplicity and pure performance, nothing less, are the gun's trademark.

Component Concepts' closed-bolt Phantom pumpgun comes in two internally identical models, the Phantom Stockgun and the "modified" class Phantom with direct feed. Both are available with a choice of 9-, 11- or 14-inch aluminum screw-in barrel. Standard with the direct-feed Phantom is a bulk loader by Viewloader that holds ninety paintballs, a velocity adjusting rod, power seal, O-ring kit and a special Phantom shoulder patch. The Stockgun comes with all those items and a 12-gram twist-changer, but without the Viewloader because stockguns do not use bulk loaders.

For players who want to compete both in stockgun and modified events, the company offers the Pro Stock Kit 2000. The kit lets a player easily convert a modified-class Phantom into a limited-feature stockgun—no need to buy another paintgun.

Easy takedown for cleaning or changing parts makes owning the Phantom a pleasure. I took a direct-feed Phantom out of the box, removed two thumbscrews and the barrel, and had all the major moving parts out in less than a minute, no tools required. A few seconds later, the valve retainer was gently unscrewed from the constant-air back bottle adapter to remove the power tube assembly, cup, seal and valve spring.

A single bolt cocking rod runs in a positive channel under the breech, which means almost no fouling dirt or rain gets into the gun. The non-scratching ribbed pump is made of self-lubricating Delrin. Internal parts are machined, not cast. Not only are the bolt, hammer, trigger and sear heat-treated and case-hardened to reduce metal wear, but all except the trigger are also electroless nickel-plated to prevent corrosion. The trigger and all other metal parts are black-oxided for long life.

The hammer's extended length covers the entire mainspring when the sear locks to the bolt. This design prevents the bolt and hammer from kinking and dragging along the breech side

PHANTOM STOCK PAINTBALL SPECIFICATIONS

Power:	CO$_2$; closed bolt pump
Caliber:	68
Barrel:	11 ins. (9-in., 14-in. optional)
Weight:	2 lbs. (w/o power source)
Overall Length:	22^1/$_2$ ins. (w/11 in. barrel and 12-gram adapter)
Sights:	NA
Muzzle Velocity:	Approx. 280 fps
Cocking Effort:	NA
Source:	Component Concepts

PHANTOM PUMP PAINTBALL CONSTANT-AIR DIRECT FEED SPECIFICATIONS

Power:	CO$_2$; closed bolt pump
Caliber:	68
Barrel:	11 ins. (9-in., 14-in. optional)
Weight:	1.8 lbs. (w/o power source)
Overall Length:	21 ins. (11 in. barrel)
Sights:	NA
Muzzle Velocity:	Approx. 290 fps
Cocking Effort:	NA
Source:	Component Concepts

walls, particularly critical when the sear releases. The parts move smoothly, stabilizing velocity from shot to shot.

The Phantom's aluminum screw-in barrel is machined and then roller-burnished for accurate sizing and temper. A bore micrometer from Brownell's confirmed the inside barrel diameter as .691-inch throughout. Standard barrels are black, with other colors available from the maker. The three barrel lengths available are the Shadow 9-inch (pistol length), the Tournament 11-inch (carbine length) and the Express 14-inch (rifle length). The different lengths and colors respond to market demand in the U.S. and to airgun laws in other countries.

To see how easy the conversion would be with the Pro Stock

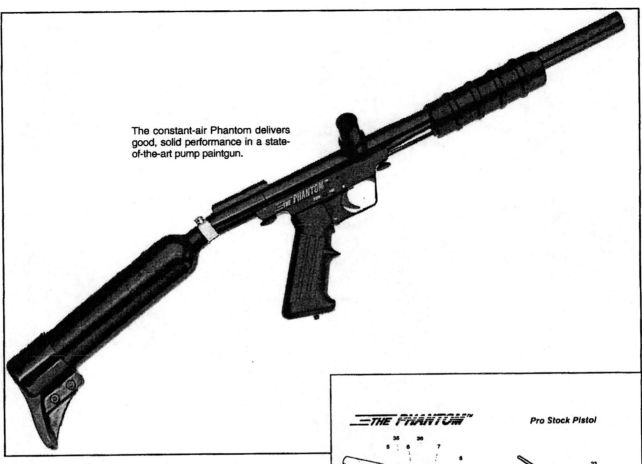

The constant-air Phantom delivers good, solid performance in a state-of-the-art pump paintgun.

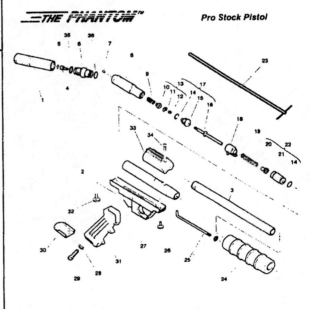

THE PHANTOM™   *Pro Stock Pistol*

Kit 2000, I re-assembled a direct-feed Phantom as a stockgun. Replacing the gravity-feed breech assembly on the direct-feed model is the stockgun's top feeding breech assembly. A stockgun feed must run parallel to the barrel so a player has to rock-and-cock the gun to load a paintball.

All the internal parts are the same. I simply reattached the bolt cocking rod to the bolt, set the parts in place, replaced the barrel and added the 12-gram twist changer to the constant-air adapter. From direct feed to stockgun took less than five minutes—earning the Phantom an A+ for its uncomplicated design.

At the Los Angeles target range, Mark Thompson conducted velocity and accuracy tests. The temperature stayed in the mid-70s, with less than 10 percent humidity and no wind. Velocity measurements were taken using a Pro Chrono chronograph, starting by setting the paintguns at 290 fps. He shot orange Nelson paint for all testing and used a benchrest for consistency. Test groups were chronographed while being shot at an 8-inch round target set 50 feet downrange.

The direct-feed Phantom powered by a constant-air bottle put ten paintballs tightly on the target. No shot fell more than $1\frac{1}{2}$ inches off center horizontally, with none off center more than 2 inches vertically. Velocities held remarkably consistent, between 285 and 291 fps.

The Phantom stockgun, powered by 12-gram CO_2, shot a nearly identical pattern. This time, there was no more than a 2-inch variance horizontally. Vertically, the pattern ran 1 inch above center and 3 inches below. Velocity ranged from 277 to 289 fps.

Adjusting velocity is very simple: Insert the dialing rod (included) down the barrel and into the adjuster, which is inside the bolt; to increase velocity, turn the dialing rod clockwise (looking down the muzzle—with goggles on, of course). To decrease velocity, turn the rod counter-clockwise. The spring compensator changes the rate of speed by compressing the mainspring's length.

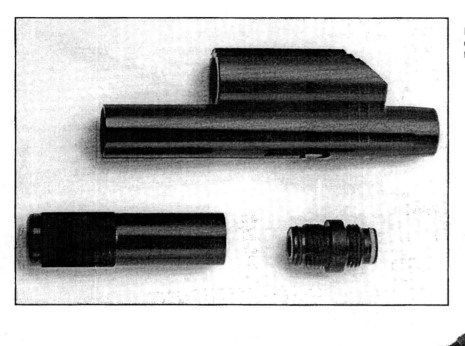

Phantom's own Pro Stock Kit 2000 allows quick conversion of the constant-air model to the stockgun version.

The Phantom stock model is powered by one standard 12-gram CO_2 cylinder housed in the short adapter at the rear.

On another Los Angeles testing day, we checked a stock Phantom's velocity every hour one morning. Conditions: temperature in the mid- to upper-70s, low humidity, clear skies and almost no wind. We began at 8 a.m. by setting the gun to shoot in the 280 fps range. The sun came out, the temperature rose about 15 degrees, and by 10 a.m. we found the velocity had dropped to about 265 fps. We easily dialed the Phantom back up to 280 fps. It stayed between 270 and 283 fps through the final velocity check at noon. That's good, solid performance.

Another few moments at the range went for testing the Phantom's auto-trigger. To use it, the shooter simply squeezes and holds the trigger, and keeps pumping the gun. Every pump sends a paintball toward the target at full speed, with no need to release and squeeze the trigger for each shot. We watched closely and found the bolt is timed to close just as the sear trips, for full-power auto-triggering. Yes, the Phantom auto-trigger works, and very well.

Both stock and modified Phantom models earn top marks for straight shots and consistency, two things every player demands from a paintgun.

Component Concepts of Portland, Oregon, was founded fifteen years ago, principally designing controls for dental hand pieces. In 1987, company president Mike Casady discovered the fun of paintball. He researched the market before designing the first Phantom in early 1988. Early models sold in 1988 for $475 with a 12-gram twist changer. Over time, Casady shifted to the Ram Line M-16-style grip frame and re-designed the Phantom for it. He replaced the original one-piece barrel with a screw-in barrel and improved performance by changing to the anti-kink bolt-hammer assembly.

Worldwide, Phantoms sell exceedingly well, even in the face of competition from semi-autos. The recent industry move back to stockguns places the Phantom in prime position for that worldwide market, too.

Jessica J. Sparks

Crosman
Auto Air II Pistol

SOMETIMES I ENJOY testing general-purpose airguns far more than the expensive and highly specialized adult airguns. You can't, after all, expect an inexpensive plinking/training gun to shoot one-hole groups, so the atmosphere during tests is more relaxed, leading to greater fun and enjoyment of the entire process. Such was exactly the case when I decided to give the Crosman Auto Air II pistol a workout that included lots of good ol' fashioned plinking.

My first tests with the Auto Air II were conducted some years ago, when I was sent an early pre-production sample for a two-day evaluation. Due to a busy schedule, I could manage only a couple of short plinking sessions back then, but my initial impression was highly positive. After the pistol went into full production, I received another sample and was able to do a more thorough job.

Those familiar with current self-loading pistols will instantly recognize the likeness of this Crosman to the AMT Auto Mag II pistol. The latter is, of course, a potent 22 WMR handgun, while its spittin' image from Crosman is powered by CO_2 and

CROSMAN AUTO AIR II SPECIFICATIONS	
Power:	CO_2; 12-gram Powerlet
Caliber:	177
Barrel:	6⅝ ins.; steel; smoothbore
Weight:	13 oz.
Overall Length:	10¾ ins.
Sights:	Blade front, fully adjustable rear
Muzzle Velocity:	480 fps (BBs)
	430 fps (pellets)
Cocking Effort:	NA
Source:	Crosman Corp.

comes in 177-caliber. Even the stainless steel color of the AMT model has been rather faithfully reproduced in the high-impact plastic body of the Auto Air II.

Weighing 13 ounces and with an overall length of 10¾ inches, the Auto Air II is just about right for both adults and younger shooters. The smoothbore steel barrel is 6⅝ inches long and tips up for manually loading pellets one at a time. For quick-

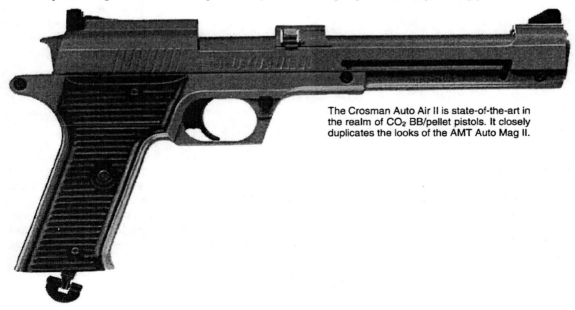

The Crosman Auto Air II is state-of-the-art in the realm of CO_2 BB/pellet pistols. It closely duplicates the looks of the AMT Auto Mag II.

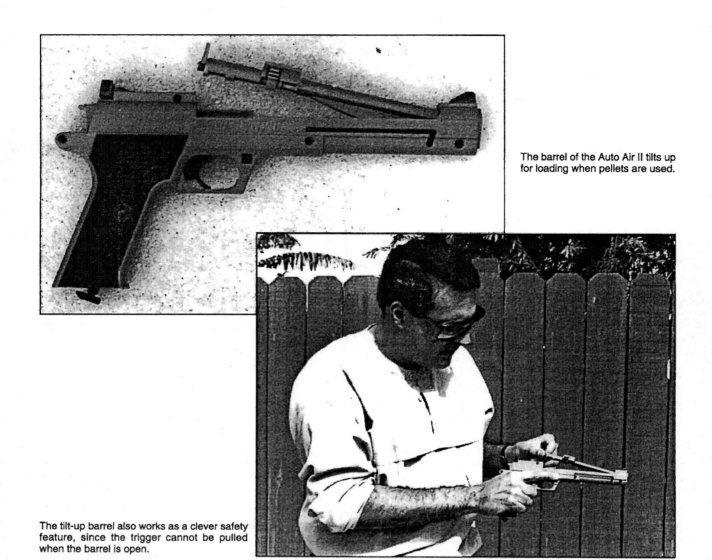

The barrel of the Auto Air II tilts up for loading when pellets are used.

The tilt-up barrel also works as a clever safety feature, since the trigger cannot be pulled when the barrel is open.

shooting fun, however, the Auto Air II is also a semi-auto BB repeater with capacity for seventeen BBs in its force-fed horizontal magazine.

Firing more than 500 BBs during tests with the Auto Air II, I did not experience one single snag; it spit those BBs out with alacrity and respectable accuracy. Some individuals dismiss smoothbore BB guns as intrinsically inaccurate, but nothing could be further from the truth and the Auto Air II certainly proves my point. The sample gun could put a magazine-full of BBs inside a 1½-inch circle at 25 feet, which is darned good plinking accuracy for a smoothbore pistol. Lead pellets perform even better with the added advantage of delivering a slightly greater punch to the target due to their heavier mass. Small rodents could be easily dispatched with pellets out of the Auto Air II at up to 20 feet or so.

The Auto Air II produces a muzzle velocity of about 480 fps with BBs and 430 fps with pellets. Each 12-gram CO_2 Crosman Powerlet will yield an average of eighty shots with BBs and fifty shots with pellets. That's lots of shots per Powerlet, which offsets somewhat the added cost of shooting a CO_2-powered gun. Keep in mind also that if a CO_2 gun is used in hot weather,

the number of usable shots usually increases by roughly 10 percent.

Somewhat surprisingly for a smooth-bored plinking pistol, the Auto Air II comes with a fully adjustable rear sight. The sight also has two white dots that, when lined up with the red dot on the front sight, permit fast target acquisition and are a definite asset during those lively plinking sessions.

The Auto Air II has a stout, manually operated cross-bolt trigger safety. Additionally, the trigger cannot be pulled the moment the barrel is opened, which is a good commonsense feature that adds safety to the gun without unnecessarily complicating a simple, yet sound design.

After spending hours testing the new Crosman Auto Air II, I have to say this pistol is addicting. In fact, I liked it so much I have used it in several training sessions involving young shooters.

If you are looking for an easily affordable, high-performance BB/pellet pistol for plinking and possibly even for firearms training, the Crosman Auto Air II should rank on your list of candidates.

J.I. Galan

Crosman Model 357-8 Pistol

THE CROSMAN CORPORATION has enjoyed a mile-long record of successful CO_2-powered guns to its credit since they began producing CO_2 guns—as Crosman Air Guns—back in the 1940s. In the realm of CO_2-powered revolvers, Crosman has been a solid world leader, with such popular models as the 38T, 38C, 44 and, more recently, the Model 357. The latter was introduced some 13 years ago, following the demise of the Model 38T.

From the start, the Model 357 was highly popular with shooters looking for a cartridge handgun look-alike that could be used safely even in the tight confines of a house or apartment. The 357 was at first available with a choice of two barrel lengths—4- and 6-inch. An 8-inch barrel version was added a bit later, along with a pistol scope and mount to fit it. This gave tremendous versatility to a handgun that was already quite useful in a variety of recreational and training activities, enabling the shooter to take advantage of the gun's inherent accuracy. The longer barrel also extended the practical range by a few more yards.

There is no doubt that the looks of the Crosman 357 have

CROSMAN SILVER SERIES 357-8 SPECIFICATIONS

Power:	CO_2; 12-gram Powerlet
Caliber:	177
Barrel:	8 ins.; rifled brass
Weight:	37 oz.
Overall Length:	13³/₈ ins.
Sights:	Fully adjustable rear, blade front
Muzzle Velocity:	About 475 fps
Cocking Effort:	NA
Source:	Crosman Corp.

had a lot to do with the gun's widespread acceptance. By closely duplicating the distinctive styling of the justly famous Colt Python, the Crosman became an almost instant best-seller. Few shooters would argue that the Python is quite possibly the most elegant of all modern revolvers and, let's face it, where else could you buy an almost exact replica of it for relatively inexpensive pellet practice for well under a hundred

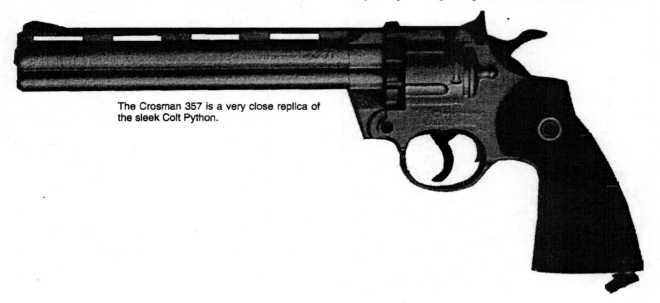

The Crosman 357 is a very close replica of the sleek Colt Python.

(Right) One 12-gram CO_2 Powerlet yields about sixty shots in the Crosman gun. It's easy to reload both "cylinder" and Powerlet.

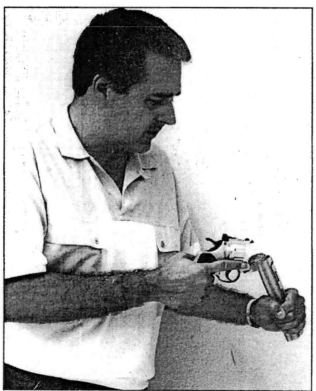

(Below) Reloading is a cinch—just break open the action and replace the empty clip with a loaded one.

bucks? With such a successful model, you'd think that the designers at Crosman would just let matters remain as they were. However, a new pellet clip with ten chambers—instead of the original six—was introduced late in 1987. It works in all Crosman 357s, old and new, and really enhances the appeal of this wheelgun. Ten quick shots between reloads sure beats six anytime!

At the same time, Crosman designers also gave the Model 357-8 a face-lift by jazzing up its finish. While all versions of the 357 came in basic black, the current edition of the 357-8 comes with a sharp-looking satin gray finish that simulates stainless steel quite closely. This baked-on finish seems to be quite durable. After several weeks of frequent use during tests, the test gun still looked as if it had just come out of the box. By the way, the 4- and 6-inch barrel versions are still offered in black only.

Another update was the addition of black plastic grip panels—instead of the older brown ones—which contrast beautifully with the stainless-like finish. The hammer, trigger blade, rear sight and safety bar all retain their original black finish for accent, while the front sight blade now comes with a blaze orange sticker.

To my eyes, one thing that spoils the otherwise great looks of the Crosman 357-8 is the hammer-block safety. Yet, in order to fall in line with the realities of today's consumer market, the 357 must have just such a device.

The Crosman 357 Shooter's Kit includes a 357-4 revolver with interchangeable 8-inch barrel, plus everything else needed to start shooting right away.

The Crosman 357-8, with its long rifled barrel, was always a good performer and this stainless-like model is no exception. Various 177-caliber pellets, from wadcutter to pointed heads, were tried with good results, both in the single- and double-action modes. The revolver on test, however, seemed to prefer Crosman's own Copperhead match-style pellets, producing impressive groups at 25 feet in slow, deliberate fire. Remember, this gun is *not* intended for formal paper-punching matches, although it could certainly hold its ground against several general-purpose, European spring-piston air pistols. At 15 yards or so, this CO_2 revolver would be quite capable of dispatching rats and mice. One 12-gram CO_2 Crosman Powerlet gives enough gas for up to sixty shots or so in this gun.

The muzzle velocity, due to the long barrel, is in the 475 fps range, which is sufficient to get the job done at normal air pistol distances. Like all CO_2 guns, the 357 is affected by ambient temperature to some degree; shooting it below 70 degrees Fahrenheit will decrease the number of useful shots from each Powerlet, while the opposite holds true in temperatures higher than 70 degrees.

Even six-gun purists must admit that a ten-shot revolver is a terrific idea, whether the gun is powered by powder or by carbon dioxide. The Crosman 357-8 certainly embodies a host of features that make it a top choice in the world of domestic air pistols.

J.I. Galan

The Crosman revolver incorporates a manual hammer-block safety located just under the rear sight. In the "off" position there is a blaze orange dot clearly visible to alert the shooter.

Crosman Model 451 Pistol

DON'T KID YOURSELVES, my friends...don't say it could never happen to you. The time *will* come when you find yourself having to defend your hobby against a barrage of disparaging remarks from some poor, misguided firearms collector who thinks that airguns are merely toys for little boys. Do yourself a favor and whip out a 3-pound package of respectability, otherwise known as the Crosman 451.

The Crosman 451 is a six-shot, repeating CO_2 air pistol designed to look, feel and shoot like the Colt 1911 Government 45 Auto. As you can see, the 451 strongly resembles its powder-burning cousin. Only the protrusion of the CO_2 cartridge holder at the base of the grip frame gives away its true identity.

The 451 was made for a short time in 1969-70 and was available in 22-caliber only. The pistols were sold under the designation "Military 45 Auto," but the factory name used by most collectors is the Crosman 451. Though not a rare pistol, the total production is reported to be only about 10,000 pieces. It is

CROSMAN MODEL 451 PISTOL SPECIFICATIONS	
Power:	CO_2; 12-gram cartridge
Caliber:	22
Barrel:	$4^1/_2$ ins., rifled
Weight:	2.8 lbs.
Overall Length:	$10^1/_2$ ins.
Sights:	Fully adjustable rear, blade front
Trigger:	Single stage; 5 lbs.
Muzzle Velocity:	300-350 fps
Cocking Effort:	NA
Source:	No longer made, collector's item

thought that high production costs, coupled with servicing problems from the rather complex design, led to its early demise. But the 451 is sought by collectors, because of its appealing shooting design.

As a collectible, the 451 is in a league of its own. It repli-

Sold as the (Military) 45 Auto, Crosman was anything but subtle about the military appeal of the gun.

cates the handsome appearance of a classic sidearm in an air pistol suitable for city plinking. But the gun was engineered even beyond the cosmetics and was made to simulate the firing sequence of the 45 ACP. At the heart of this accomplishment is the patented "Roto-Mag" mechanism that makes it all possible.

This unique design involves a revolving cylinder that rotates around a hollow vertical axis. Around the peripheral face of this cylinder are six equally spaced chambers which house the pellets when the pistol is loaded. At the top of this cylinder are six small pins which are acted upon by the indexing pawl during the firing sequence. These pins serve not only to help advance the cylinder to the next round, but to also securely lock in the alignment between the chambered pellet and the barrel.

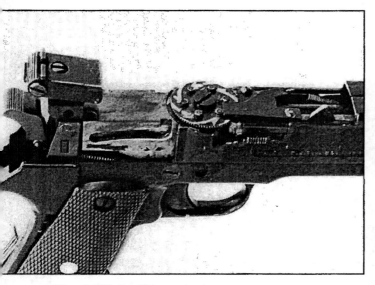

(Above) With the slide removed, the "Roto-Mag" and indexing pawl which acts upon it can be clearly seen. It's a complicated design!

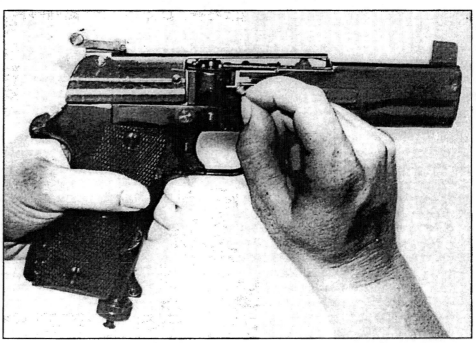

Loading the 45 Auto involves the "skirt first" insertion of six pellets into the magazine through a trap door on the right side of the receiver.

In keeping with the Colt 45 Auto replica theme, the 451 has a "slide" that flies backward upon firing to simulate recoil-activated loading. This slide is actually only a sheet metal shell, permitting weight reduction and, therefore, proper functioning of the mechanism. The genius in the design is that when all of these components function properly together, it provides a realism in firing not often encountered among airguns.

The Crosman 451 has an unloaded weight of 2.8 pounds and an overall length of $10\frac{1}{2}$ inches. The button-rifled 22-caliber barrel is $4\frac{1}{2}$ inches long. The alloy frame has a tough blue-painted finish, and the slide is blued steel. The rear sight is adjustable for windage and elevation. The checkered reddish-brown plastic grips are attractive and functional, giving a secure feel in the hand. The nonadjustable, single-stage trigger breaks cleanly at 5 pounds of pull. There is no safety except for the presence of the external hammer.

To fire the Crosman 451, the shooter must remove the right grip (a simple snap fit) and insert a 12-gram CO_2 cartridge, neck upright, into the hollow of the grip. The grip is then replaced and the knurled nut at the base of the grip is tightened to puncture the cartridge, allowing the gas to fill the reservoir behind the valve. The pistol is now ready to be loaded.

The small loading gate on the upper right side of the frame is slid forward to expose an empty chamber in the cylinder magazine. In doing so, the gate lifts the slide free of the indexing pins to facilitate loading. A pellet is then inserted, skirt first, into the exposed chamber. The cylinder is then advanced one click position until the next empty chamber appears. This procedure is repeated until all six rounds are loaded. The gate is then slid back, locking in the pellets and lowering the slide to its normal static position.

The oversized external hammer is drawn back until the sear

Except for the presence of the gas cartridge screw at the base of the grip, the 451 (bottom) closely follows the appearance of the real McCoy (top).

engages. Pulling the trigger will now set off an instantaneous chain of events which constitutes the firing sequence. As the hammer falls, it strikes the exposed valve stem from the exhaust valve. The escaping CO_2 gas rushes up the hollow central axis of the cylinder and forces the pellet out of the chamber and out through the barrel.

In the meantime, some of this gas is vented into a secondary chamber behind the cylinder which contains a nylon sealed piston with a steel stem. The gas forces this piston backwards and causes the stem to sharply strike an intermediate member at the back of the slide. This, in turn, causes the slide to fly backward and recock the hammer. The slide is now automatically pulled forward to the rest position by a return spring. While moving forward, a small notch on the slide catches one of the cylinder's indexing pins and advances it one click, in turn bringing a fresh pellet into the ready position at the breech.

The entire complex cycle takes place in an instant, of course, with the slide movement and re-indexing being almost too quick to see. In this manner, all six rounds may be fired in under two seconds. True to proper semi-auto form, the trigger must be fully released between shots to allow the next round to be fired.

The firing action of the Crosman 451 produces recoil similar to that of a 22 rimfire semi-automatic. Because of this, it can be an excellent training tool for shooting firearm handguns. However, it seems that most shooters flock to the 451 for the simple pleasure of firing it and enjoying its function.

With its blowback-operated slide and exposed hammer, the 451 went to great lengths to authenticate the feel of the 45 ACP powder burner.

Because of the manner in which the pellets are chambered, this repeating air pistol can fire a number of different pellets flawlessly. Most pellet pistol repeaters depend upon the manner in which the pellets stack in the linear magazine to ensure proper feeding. The 451 does not face this same design limitation.

This design bonus allows for the testing of a variety of pellets, including 22-caliber round balls, which feed perfectly. Not many semi-autos can claim full functionality while changing from diabolo pellets to round balls without any modification. The only real restriction is that of pellet length, which must be under .265-inch. This allows the use of different types of ammo, with the noted possible exceptions of RWS Superpoints, Superdomes and other longer pellets.

As "pepper-can" Crosman Super Pells were contemporary with the era of the 451, they were the control standard for the firing tests. All accuracy tests were six-shot groups benchrested at a distance of 30 feet. Because the recoil is pronounced, benchresting the pistol on a hard surface will yield the same

problems that one faces with a recoiling spring-piston airgun. In other words, the recoil action transmitted off of the hard rest will cause accuracy problems because the pellet is still in the barrel while the gun is jumping from the recoil. Therefore, all accuracy tests were conducted over a cushioned rest.

To be painfully blunt, the Crosman 451 is a gas hog. Most gas cartridges yielded only about eighteen to twenty shots before the pressure dropped to the point when the hammer was not automatically recocked. This translates to about three clips of shooting before gas reloading becomes necessary. But considering all of the action taking place with the pistol's semi-auto function, this is actually quite reasonable.

Because the gas pressure curve seems to drop rather dramatically with each shot, all velocity figures were averaged from only the first six shots of a fresh cartridge. The velocity will obviously continue to drop until the gas supply is depleted.

I've had a number of 451s over the years and have experienced both good times and bad with them. Most will fly through ammo with nary a hiccup, while with others it seems more like a case of terminal whooping cough. The problems usually center on a hammer that fails to reset, but this often can be attributed to a faulty seal in the secondary gas piston chamber. This is a relatively easy repair for a competent airgunsmith.

Overall, most airgunners would agree the Crosman 451 is a special gem. From a designer's viewpoint, it is a marvel of functional beauty. For the shooter, the realistic sensation of the cyclic firing imparts a rush of adrenaline sure to win the heart of even the most hardened anti-airgun cynic.

Larry Hannusch

CROSMAN 451 PISTOL
Performance Data

Pellet	Weight (grs.)	Velocity (fps)	Energy (foot pounds)	Group Avg. (ins.)	Best Group (ins.)
Crosman Pell	14.5	344	3.8	1.21	1.0
Hobby	12.1	368	3.6	1.04	.75
Wasp	14.4	331	3.5	1.21	1.125
Roundball	15.3	305	3.2	1.17	.875

Crosman Model 1077 Repeat Air Rifle

THE FIRST TIME I saw a Crosman 1077 was at the 1993 SHOT Show. As a traffic builder, the folks at Crosman set up a plexiglass booth with an airgun range inside to find the fastest 1077 shooter and raise money for shooter education. They handed me this air rifle that looked a lot like a Ruger 10/22, and a salesman then loaded the gun for me with twelve excellent Crosman Premiers. He told me to shoot at will, my first shot would start the electronic timer. I stopped and looked around the booth at all the name tags to find the guy named Will. I shot so slow that Ed McGivern rolled in his grave. Crosman could not donate any money to shooter education because my performance was so painfully slow.

My first impression when this new airgun was thrust into my hands was abject terror with a bit of concern. Where would it shoot? Did it have a trigger? Could I use it? Most of my fears were moot points. This was fun. Now, I hate to call the 1077 a fun gun because that seems like an oxymoron (especially if you are a rabbit or a squirrel). Let's call the 1077 a fun gun to shoot. It is every kid's dream, but it is best suited to kids over the age of sixteen, unless an adult is in control of the CO_2.

I've been spoiled over the years by shooting a lot of high-ticket airguns. I tend to ignore airguns like the 1077. That's a shame, because this Crosman is just fun to shoot no matter your age or size—just bring some CO_2 cartridges, a bunch of pellets, some tin cans and let's shoot.

The 1077 comes in a cardboard box with moulded cardboard spacers to protect the gun from the ravages of shipping. Cros-

CROSMAN 1077 REPEAT AIR SPECIFICATIONS	
Power:	CO_2; 12-gram cartridge
Caliber:	177
Barrel:	20.3 ins.
Weight:	3 lbs., 11 oz.
Overall Length:	38.8 ins.
Sights:	Adjustable open rear, blade front
Muzzle Velocity:	625 fps
Cocking Effort:	NA
Source:	Crosman Airguns

man uses paper rather than foam/plastic packing in this endeavor. I applaud Crosman for making the effort to cut down on waste/pollution, but I have to chuckle because most of the gun is made of dead dinosaurs.

The 1077's instruction book is so complete and clear that it would make any product liability attorney proud. Spanish- and English-speaking customers are covered by this tome. Flip the manual one way and it's in English, turn it over and the instructions are in Spanish. One thing I especially liked in the manual was the offer by Crosman to unjam your 1077 during the warranty period. This may sound silly to you old salts, but think back to when you were a tyro and wondered what was right or wrong to do to your airgun.

The sights consist of a ramp front and adjustable rear that moves for the customary windage and elevation. The top of the

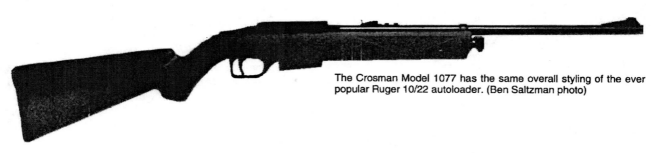

The Crosman Model 1077 has the same overall styling of the ever popular Ruger 10/22 autoloader. (Ben Saltzman photo)

The 1077 also doubles as a superb training rifle for younger shooters, under adult supervision, of course.

receiver is moulded for standard scope mounts. A scope is highly suggested by this old foggy with duff eyes.

There is no magic to the way the 1077 shoots so fast. It is a twelve-shot revolver. Pull the double-action trigger and it shoots. Loading and charging are simple, and clearly explained in the manual. The techno-babble, for those so inclined, is printed on the side of the box: velocity 625 fps, with the average number of shots being forty-eight out of a 12-gram CO_2 cartridge.

Some people would call the 1077 a kid's airgun, but I see it as too powerful and too easy to shoot the second shot. It would be a ball for kids of any age to shoot provided there was close adult supervision.

So go out and buy one and then go perforate some tin cans or punch some paper in the backyard. And bring some kids; you won't have to wait long to see some smiles.

Ben Saltzman

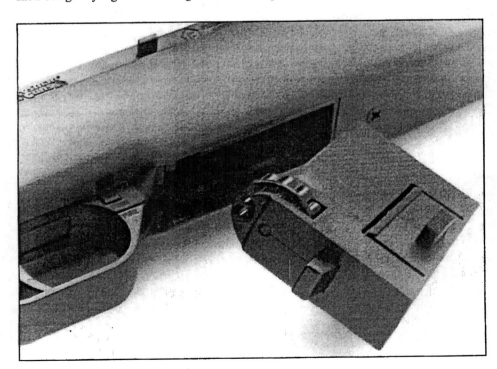

Crosman's patented twelve-shot rotary pellet magazine fits neatly in the 1077's dummy magazine. (Ben Saltzman photo)

Crosman Model SSP 250 Pistol

THE CROSMAN CORPORATION has produced a wide variety of outstanding gas-powered pellet pistols over several decades, from single shot models to repeaters. In the latter category, Crosman has had huge successes, such as the Model 600, a true semi-auto that could shoot a bunch of 22-caliber pellets in a hurry, along with wheelguns such as the Models 38C and 357. These last two are copies of the Smith & Wesson Combat Magnum and Colt Python, respectively, but only the Model 357 remains in production at this time. In the area of single shot CO_2 handguns, Crosman has also excelled. Such classics as the compact, yet hard-hitting Model 150 as well as the Mark I and II models come immediately to mind. The Mark I and II models, however, went out of production in

CROSMAN MODEL SSP 250 SPECIFICATIONS

Power:	CO_2, one 12-gram cartridge
Caliber:	177, 20, 22
Barrel:	$9^7/_8$ ins., rifled
Weight:	3 lbs., 1 oz.
Overall length:	14 ins.
Sights:	Open/aperture adjustable rear, hooded post front
Muzzle Velocity:	Variable high/low:560/525 fps (177) 490/434 fps (20) 500/424 fps (22)
Cocking Effort:	NA
Source:	Crosman Corp.

The Crosman SSP 250 bears the overall profile of a target-style pistol.

The forestock comes in handy for a bit of extra support when shooting from a number of positions.

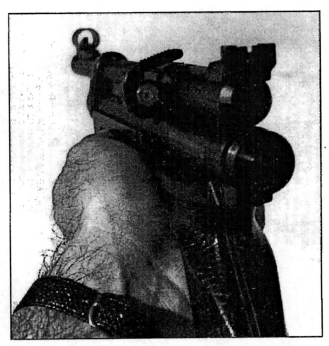

The loading chamber pivots open to allow insertion of a pellet.

the early 1980s, without any other single shot pistol to replace them. Then, in 1989, realizing there was a real demand for a powerful, yet accurate single shot CO_2 pellet pistol, Crosman launched the Model SSP 250.

The SSP 250—the letters stand for Silhouette Sport Pistol—is really a handful, well in keeping with its intended purpose as a metallic silhouette gun. Overall, it measures 14 inches, tipping the scales at a hefty 3 pounds, 1 ounce. With a decidedly target pistol profile, the gun uses the same grip/frame assembly of the long-popular Crosman 1377 and 1322 pneumatic pistols. However, since the SSP 250 is powered by CO_2, there is no pumping lever up front. The

fixed forestock and target-style grip panels are made of moulded black plastic with a woodgrain texture and are big enough for just about any adult hands. I must add that the pistol has excellent balance, well-suited for its role as a target gun.

In the sight department, the SSP 250 comes with a rear unit that has a reversible element with a square notch on one end, an aperture on the other. The aperture is there in case the owner decides to mount Crosman's #1399 shoulder stock—which is easily done by removing the pistol's grip panels—and turn the SSP 250 into a nifty mini-carbine. A word of caution: Shoulder stocks made before 1989 need a bit of alteration prior

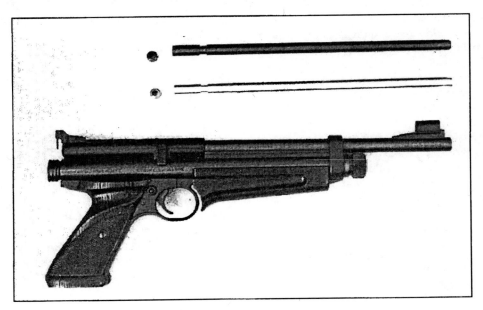

Additional barrels in 22- (top) and 20-caliber are available from Crosman for the SSP 250.

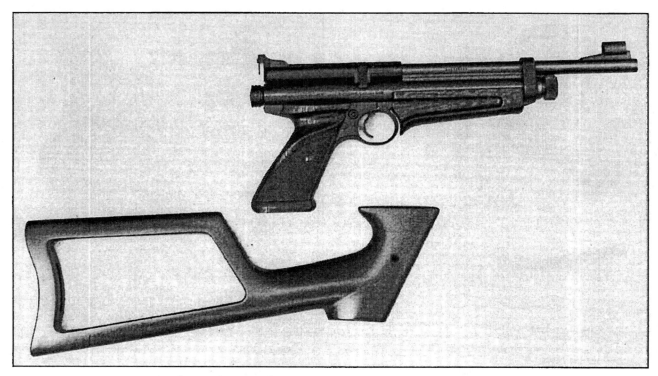

Crosman's #1399 shoulder stock is a useful accessory, turning the
SSP 250 into a neat mini-carbine.

to installation due to small projections in the pistol's frame, but that has been corrected and current stocks fit perfectly. Elevation and windage adjustments are carried out by loosening slotted screws, moving the sight as necessary and retightening the screws. Target pistol purists may laugh at this method, but it is uncomplicated, and after all, this is not an Olympic gun. The front sight is a thick blade atop a ramp, surrounded by a removable tunnel. The rear of the receiver is grooved for scope use, a virtual must in a pistol of this type when metallic silhouettes are the intended targets. A scope is also useful against pests.

The SSP 250 has a loading chamber that pivots to the left, allowing a pellet to be manually inserted. Once seated flush in the chamber, it is simply returned to the closed position, bringing the pellet in line with the bore. This plastic chamber forms a tight seal when closed, preventing the escape of CO_2 during the firing sequence. Should a leak develop in this critical area, the synthetic ring insert that forms the heart of the chamber can be easily replaced.

The trigger of the SSP 250 is not adjustable in any way. However, I can't really criticize its performance after putting the gun through various tests. Following a rather short and light take-up, the trigger of my test sample broke cleanly at around 4 pounds of pressure. The wide face of the trigger blade certainly makes the pressure feel lighter than it really is, though. A manual cross-bolt trigger safety completes the works in this area.

The most remarkable feature of the SSP 250 is its capability to interchange barrels of different calibers. The pistol comes with a $9^7/_8$-inch rifled steel barrel in 177-caliber. Additional bar-

rels in 20- and 22-calibers—made of brass and steel, respectively—are available from Crosman at extra cost. These barrels are easily changed by means of Allen screws, making the pistol highly versatile for a variety of uses.

The SSP 250 also has two distinct power settings, depending upon how far back the cocking knob is pulled. When pulled all the way to the rear for high power in 177-caliber, a Crosman 12-gram CO_2 Powerlet yields about forty shots at an average muzzle velocity of 560 fps. In the low power setting—pulling the knob only to the first click position—nearly twice as many shots can be had, at an average velocity of 525 fps. With the 20-caliber barrel, velocity for high power runs around 490 fps, with 434 fps for low power. In 22-caliber, the figures run about 500 fps and 424 fps. Interestingly, the 22-caliber barrel produces a slightly higher velocity than the 20 at the maximum power setting, given pellets of nearly the same weight. The test pistol confirmed the manufacturer's claims, staying quite close to the above figures and in some instances surpassing them. Even in the low power setting, the SSP 250 is nothing to sneeze at. Those low-end muzzle velocities are more than adequate for plinking and punching paper targets, while cranking up the power will do nicely for metallic silhouettes, as well as drilling mice and rats at up to 20 yards.

The test gun printed some creditable groups at ranges out to 20 yards, using iron sights only. While definitely not in the category of a world-class match air pistol—what more can you honestly expect from a pistol retailing for around $50?—the Crosman Model SSP 250 is a real sizzler in the realm of sporting air pistols.

J.I. Galan

Crosman Trapmaster 1100 Shotgun

WHILE THE DECADE of the '60s brought us peace signs and love beads, Crosman was ironically bringing us a highly successful line of handgun-replica airguns. The field of replica long guns, however, was still a marketing uncertainty. Their first such offering was the M-1 Carbine in the mid '60s, which proved to be quite popular. Based on this success, Crosman soon ventured into the uncharted waters of a replica CO_2-powered shotgun which they officially christened the Trapmaster 1100.

The gun was designed as a look-alike to Remington's Model 1100 autoloading shotgun. In case the public missed the visual connection, Crosman used the same numerical designation to link the two. The Trapmaster 1100 was made from about 1968 to 1973, with a total production run of approximately 30,000 pieces. Though well made, the 1100 had a relatively high retail price of $49.95 for the gun alone, while the complete Skeet shooting kit sold for $89.95. Although uniquely different, this price seemed steep when compared to the other domestic airguns of the day.

The Crosman 1100 is an adult-size, single-shot CO_2 shotgun

CROSMAN TRAPMASTER 1100 SHOTGUN SPECIFICATIONS

Power:	CO_2; two 12-gram cartridges
Caliber:	.380-in.
Barrel:	28 ins.
Weight:	6¼ lbs.
Overall length:	46½ ins.
Sights:	Bead front
Trigger:	Single stage; 4 lbs.
Muzzle Velocity:	386-442 (low-high power)
Cocking effort:	NA
Source:	No longer made, collector's item

with a bore of .380-inch. The gun measures 46½ inches in overall length and weighs 6¼ pounds. The 28-inch matte-finish barrel is Cylinder bore and has a full-length solid rib with a simple sighting bead at the muzzle. The two-piece hardwood stock is fitted with a plastic buttplate that hides the single stock bolt. The length of pull of the stock is a full 14¼ inches. Earlier guns

The Crosman Trapmaster 1100 shotgun was not only built to resemble a powder-burning scattergun, but the complete shooting kit was designed around the sport of Skeet.

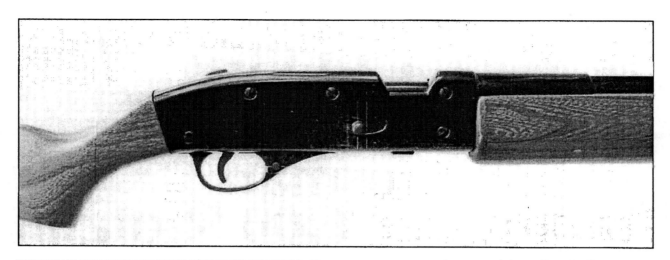

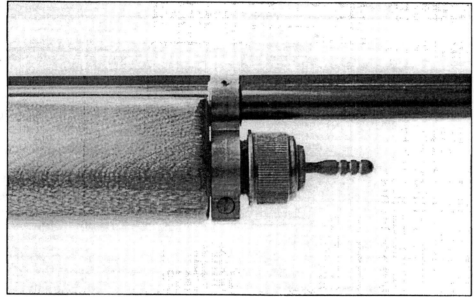

(Above) The knob on the right side of the receiver is pushed forward to cock the action. The barrel release button used to load the gun is just visible on the bottom, directly below the breech opening.

The toggle gas cap that punctures one of the two CO_2 cartridges is unique to the Crosman 1100.

sport an attractive glossy black finish on the alloy receiver, while later guns are matte finished.

In order to push the heavy shot loads through the Trapmaster, Crosman produced several design innovations. One was a high-gas-volume valve body to move the required amount of CO_2 behind the shot; another was the impact hammer device capable of delivering more strike energy to the exhaust valve stem than on any other previous model. Because this design necessarily consumed enormous amounts of CO_2, a dual power device was fitted to the back of the receiver to allow more economical shooting via reduced hammer spring tension.

The 1100 borrowed its CO_2 system from the earlier Crosman 160 where two cartridges were used back-to-back and then punctured simultaneously. However, unlike the 160, the Trapmaster used a different piecing cap. This toggle-operated cap was unique to the 1100 and produced more consistent results than the earlier design.

To shoot the Crosman 1100, a sequence of actions must be performed. After verifying the gun is empty of a shell and any residual gas, the toggle cap may be unscrewed and removed.

Next, the cocking knob on the right side of the receiver is pushed forward until the sear engages. The cross-bolt safety at the rear of the trigger guard is then pushed to the Safe position. One 12-gram CO_2 cartridge is inserted neck first; the second cartridge then must be loaded with the neck pointed toward the muzzle. It is usually advisable at this point to push the power selector switch to the forward, low-power position.

After replacing the toggle gas cap, the safety is moved to the Fire mode and the trigger is pulled to pierce the rear cartridge. The toggle lever on the piercing cap should then be rocked several times to puncture the front cartridge. Reapply the safety to Safe.

The 1100 is now ready to be loaded with a proprietary plastic shotshell known as the Crosman #70 shotshell. To do so, the square barrel release button underneath the receiver is depressed to allow the sliding barrel to spring forward. This exposes the breech, allowing a shotshell to be inserted. Once loaded, the barrel is manually returned back until it clicks into the closed position. The power selector may be pushed back to the high-power mode, if desired, and the safety taken off.

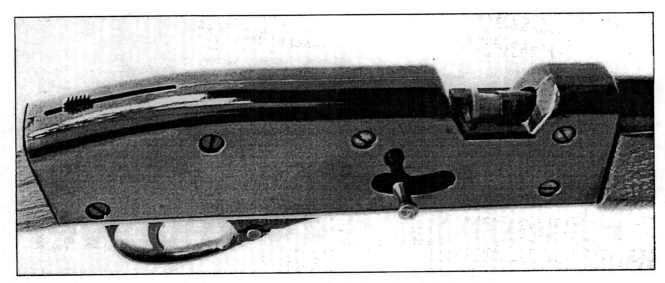

The breech is shown in the open position with a plastic shotshell about to be ejected. The power selector switch is in a slot on top of the receiver and is shown in the high-power mode.

With the muzzle now pointed safely downrange, the 4-pound, single-stage trigger is pulled to release the goods. The report is modest, while recoil is nonexistent. To reload, simply depress the barrel release again to allow the barrel to fly forward and automatically kick out the spent shell. Insert another loaded round into the breech and repeat the above firing sequence. When the CO_2 pressure drops too low, the 1100 will automatically vent the remaining gas. The gun averages about twenty shots on high power and about thirty on low.

The factory-loaded #70 shotshell is a red plastic shell filled with about fifty-five pellets of #8 shot. In addition, Crosman offered empty plastic hulls that were made in both yellow and green variations. This color coding was designed to allow reloading by the shooter with either #4 or #6 size shot, respectively. This was easily accomplished using the plastic wads and measuring/reloading tool available from Crosman. All tests herein, however, were conducted using the red factory-loaded #8 shells to ensure consistency of data.

The Crosman 1100 is a popular guinea pig among shooters who like to experiment with power modifications and large-cal-iber slug loads. Properly tweaked, the 1100 will produce some impressive energy figures. But in its factory-stock form, the gun will yield more moderate, albeit still respectable, numbers.

The power of the Crosman 1100 is well suited to its intended purpose, that being a training tool for Skeet shooting. The gun was offered as part of a Skeet shooting kit which included the gun, special break-apart plastic aerial clay birds and a thrower to launch these targets.

These ingenious, reusable Crosman targets are made of two yellow plastic components, an inner disk surrounded by a removable ring. A solid hit on the target is indicated by the separation of the two parts. Though not exactly giving the same giddy sensation as when smoking a clay bird, a hit is actually quite satisfying nonetheless. It is particularly enjoyable if local ordinances and space permit one to shoot the Crosman Skeet in areas that would otherwise be prohibited for powder-burners.

Effective range for this Skeet shooting should be considered 50 feet or less, at which distance controlled tests showed an average group size of 14 inches. Beyond this, power fall-off and increased group sizes make hits more infrequent. One small quirk of the Trapmaster Skeet system is that, because shot velocity is so much less than with a firearm, lead times need to be increased to compensate. However, this is quickly overcome with minimal practice, and the novice can soon be busting 'em with the best of them.

Because the Crosman 1100 is a full length and weight replica shotgun, it not only has recreational value but possesses true training potential as well. For the young, aspiring shotgunner, a father could do no better than to use the gun as a training tool with his child. But be forewarned, the thrill of shooting the 1100 is such that when it comes time for the shooter to give up his turn, there are likely to be some ugly temper tantrums with a lot of kicking and screaming. So please, be understanding, act your age, and let your kid try out the Trapmaster, too.

Larry Hannusch

CROSMAN TRAPMASTER 1100 TEST RESULTS

Performance Data	Low	High
	Power Setting	
Number of shots	31	20
Velocity, fps (80°F)	386	442
Energy, foot pounds	19.7	25.8

Distance (feet)	Pattern Size (ins.)
10	2½
20	6
40	12
50	14

All tests were conducted with factory-loaded #8 shot red shells using 59.4 grains of shot each.

Daisy
Power Line 44 Revolver

BACK IN 1987, Daisy introduced the Power Line 44, a CO_2-powered 177-caliber six-shot pellet revolver that, unless you look at it closely, will fool you into believing it is a product of S&W. This is a superb replica of the 44 Magnum S&W Model 29, also popularly known as the "Dirty Harry" gun. Besides its impressive looks, this CO_2 revolver closely duplicates the heft and "feel" of the real hand-cannon.

The Daisy 44 even has a swing-out pellet cylinder—the first CO_2-powered revolver ever to boast such a realistic feature. However, the cylinder release latch is located on the crane, as in Dan Wesson revolvers, rather than behind the recoil shield, like on Smith & Wesson wheelguns. This is a minor point, but one dictated by the necessities of mating a rather narrow pellet cylinder to a CO_2 power system. The bottom line is that it works, and extremely well at that.

Another minor discrepancy which may annoy purists is the manually operated hammer-block safety, located just below the rear sight. It consists of a cross bolt with detent action, pushed in

DAISY POWER LINE 44 SPECIFICATIONS

Power:	CO_2; 12-gram cylinder
Caliber:	177
Barrel:	6 ins. (4-in., 8-in. optional)
Weight:	2.4 lbs.
Overall Length:	13.1 ins.
Sights:	Blade front, fully adjustable rear
Muzzle Velocity:	Up to 400 fps
Cocking Effort:	NA
Source:	Daisy Mfg. Co.

from the left to activate. When in the "Off" position, a red warning indicator is clearly visible on the cross bolt. This manual safety may appear ridiculous on a revolver, but American airgun manufacturers are extremely safety-conscious and their products reflect that fact.

Most CO_2-powered handguns traditionally have the CO_2

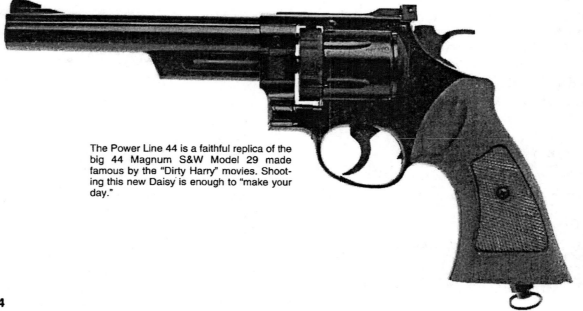

The Power Line 44 is a faithful replica of the big 44 Magnum S&W Model 29 made famous by the "Dirty Harry" movies. Shooting this new Daisy is enough to "make your day."

One 12-gram CO_2 cartridge provides enough power for about seventy-five shots in the Power Line 44. The left grip panel is easily removed for changing cartridges.

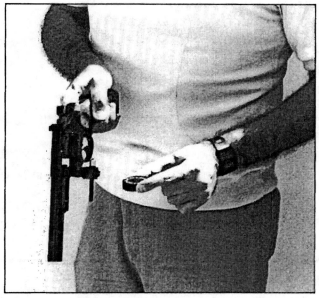

The swing-out plastic pellet cylinder is easily removed/replaced when one runs dry. It's easy to burn through a lot of pellets and CO_2 with this gun.

cartridge housed in the grip, and the Power Line 44 is no exception. Each 12-gram cartridge will provide somewhere around seventy-five shots before it runs out of gas, at a muzzle velocity of up to 400 fps with a variety of 177-caliber lead pellets. Accuracy tests with Daisy Quick Silver match-style pellets soon disclosed that the Model 44 can shoot impressively, too, producing really tight groups at 10 meters, both offhand as well as from a sandbag rest. The 6-inch rifled barrel and fully adjustable rear sight share in the credits on this one. Mice and rats are dead meat anywhere within 15 yards of the 44, if the shooter does his part. By the way, the plastic six-shot pellet cylinders are easily removable for loading. This also allows the shooter to carry a number of pre-loaded cylinders that can be quickly installed when the previous one runs dry.

Another important feature of the 44 is that its standard 6-

inch barrel can be easily replaced with optional 4- or 8-inch barrels to fit a variety of plinking and training applications. There is a special barrel nut wrench plus a barrel spacer gauge supplied with each gun for just such a purpose. The shroud provided with all the barrels, incidentally, is made of a die-cast zinc alloy, as is the frame, rather than plastic. However, plastic is used to make the realistic-looking checkered wood-grain grips.

As a firearms trainer, the Power Line 44 certainly looks like an ideal tool in almost every respect. Simple plinking and informal paper punching, however, are what this gun is all about. Even shooters who own the real McCoy should find plinking with the mild-mannered Daisy 44 a most pleasant experience after the jarring recoil and blast of the 44 Magnum.

J.I. Galan

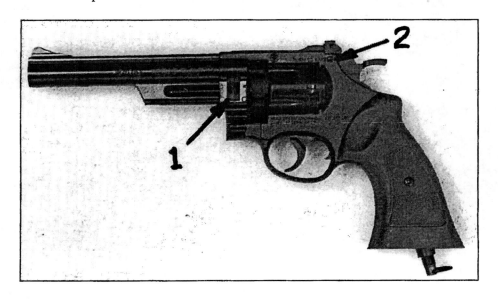

The cylinder release latch (1) is "a la Dan Wesson" rather than S&W style. Notice the cross-bolt hammer-block safety (2) below the rear sight.

Daisy
Power Line 93 Pistol

IT IS ONLY fair to warn you that the Daisy 93 is highly addicting. Although most airguns are intended for recreational shooting of one kind or another, it is no secret that some can have a higher "fun index" than others. Take high-capacity CO_2 repeaters, for example. Few of us are immune to the fun that these guns can generate in limited-area plinking. Furthermore, when the guns in question happen to be almost identical replicas of well-known firearms, the fun factor seems to increase radically, and this certainly seems to be the case with the Daisy Power Line 93.

Most shooters will find it hard to put this BB spitter down

DAISY POWER LINE 93 SPECIFICATIONS

Power:	CO_2; 12-gram cartridge
Caliber:	BB (4.5mm)
Barrel:	4³/₈ ins.; steel; smoothbore
Weight:	1.1 lbs.
Overall Length:	7⁷/₈ ins.
Sights:	Fixed
Muzzle Velocity:	Approx. 400 fps
Cocking Effort:	NA
Source:	Daisy Mfg. Co., Inc.

The Daisy Power Line 93 is an almost exact replica of the Smith & Wesson Model 5904 combat autoloader.

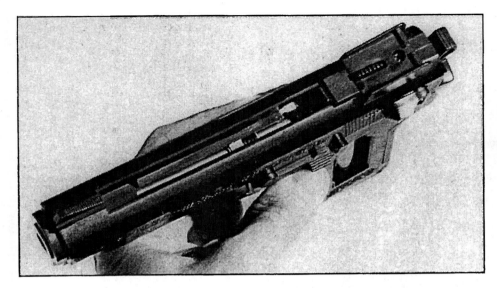

This shows the top of the dummy slide with BB magazine removed.

after squeezing off a few dozen shots from it. Fans of high-capacity autoloaders, in particular, would appreciate the incredibly realistic "feel" and look of the Daisy 93, which, as can be readily seen, is a close replica of the Smith & Wesson Model 5904 "wondernine." In fact, this pistol looks so much like the real thing that it should never be displayed in public or left lying about where casual observers might see it.

The moulded plastic construction and black finish of the 93 will fool most people, except on close inspection. A two-tone—matte-silver and black—version of this pistol, dubbed the 693 Custom, is also available. However, despite the tremendous realism of the gun, neither the dummy hammer nor the slide move at all. Being a CO_2-powered BB repeater, this pistol has a truly clever firing mechanism that relies upon a removable, spring-loaded magazine that mounts horizontally atop the smoothbored barrel. The magazine snaps almost flush into a longitudinal recess in the dummy slide and can be easily removed by means of a catch located in the rear sight base. Up to fifteen BBs can be loaded into each magazine, so it is possible to do quite a bit of plinking by simply having a pocketful of loaded magazines.

The trigger of the Daisy 93 also replicates the long double-

Magazine removal for loading is a snap.

The BB magazine of the 93 fits nearly flush atop the non-moving "slide." With a pocketful of loaded mags, lots of quick shooting is possible. Notice the safety-lever in the "On" position.

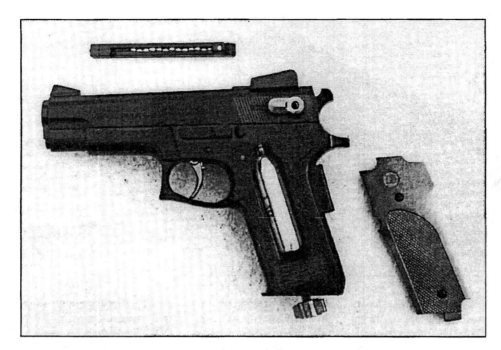

One 12-gram CO_2 cylinder housed in the grip provides power for well over 100 shots in the Daisy 93.

action pull of the S&W autoloader, except that in the Daisy all shots must be fired DA only. But that's OK; all fifteen BBs in the magazine can still be squeezed out rather quickly. There is a manual trigger-block safety catch on the left rear of the "slide," just like in the real S&W pistol. Flicking this catch down all the way prevents the trigger from being pulled. The words *Fire* and *Safe* are moulded in relief at either end of the safety catch travel and are clearly visible. In addition to the manual safety, the Power Line 93 incorporates a Colt-style "lemon-squeezer" grip safety that must be depressed when the pistol is grasped, or no CO_2 will be released, even if the trigger is pulled. This is an interesting idea that, if nothing else, will ensure that the shooter adopts a proper and consistent grip on the pistol.

The Daisy 93 has a sophisticated valving system that can yield up to 150 shots from each 12-gram CO_2 cylinder. That is truly amazing firepower for a gun of this type and is something that any dedicated plinker can appreciate right away. Add to that the aforementioned high-capacity, easy-to-change mags and you have what is probably the closest thing yet to the ideal fun-gun.

Because of the smoothbored barrel and BB ammunition used in this pistol, the sights are non-adjustable. That, however, did not keep my test gun from giving surprising accuracy at all normal BB pistol distances, which usually means anywhere between 15 and 50 feet. With regard to power, the Daisy is certainly no weakling, producing an average muzzle velocity of 400 fps. Because of that velocity and the fact that those steel BBs have a tendency to ricochet off hard surfaces, the wearing of shooting glasses is basically a must. Eye protection, in fact, should always be worn whenever BB guns are used—just in case.

Despite its BB-gun classification, the Daisy 93 is intended for shooters aged sixteen years or older, and the manufacturer indicates so clearly, not only in the owner's manual, but even in a warning note moulded right into the dummy slide. After spending quite a bit of time popping away in my backyard with the gun, I must say that in sheer recreational value this pistol ranks way up there.

J.I. Galan

Galan puts the Daisy 93 through its paces during a shoot-ing session. He quickly found that this puny plinker is addicting.

Daisy
Power Line 500 Pistol

DAISY HAS ESTABLISHED a hugely successful trend producing a stunningly realistic line of cartridge handgun replicas for recreational shooting. Their growing list of spittin'-image handguns began back around 1986 with the introduction of the Power Line 92, a 177-caliber pellet repeater that could be easily mistaken for the famous Beretta 92F autoloader. Unfortunately, the design had some problems with its pellet feeding system, and it was quietly dropped a few years after its introduction.

Then came some real hot performers like the Models 93 and 45, shooting BBs and 177 pellets, respectively, as fast-firing repeaters that duplicate the looks of two other classics among

DAISY POWER LINE 500 PISTOL SPECIFICATIONS	
Power:	CO$_2$; 12-gram cylinder
Caliber:	177
Barrel:	5^3/$_8$ ins., rifled steel
Weight:	1.4 lbs.
Overall Length:	8^1/$_2$ ins.
Sights:	Fixed; open rear, blade front
Trigger:	4^1/$_4$ lbs., non-adjustable
Muzzle Velocity:	480 fps
Cocking Effort:	NA
Source:	Daisy Mfg. Co., Inc.

The Daisy Power Line 500 is a single shot pellet pistol that's a spittin' image of the famous Beretta 92F.

Keeping the barrel open acts as a safety feature in the Daisy 500. There is also a simple, yet positive hammer-block manual safety.

self-loading combat pistols. The designers at Daisy had obviously gotten it just right by then, and those two fun guns remain top sellers to this day. Still, the folks who make the big decisions up at Daisy surmised—quite correctly, in my opinion—that they should try to bring back another CO_2-powered,

177-caliber look-alike of the big Beretta 92F, albeit with a much simpler pellet-feeding system and a more powerful punch than any other handgun in their line.

The resulting pistol is, in a nutshell, a real winner all the way. The Daisy Power Line 500 Raven, as this model has

The barrel of the Power Line 500 tilts up to facilitate the loading of pellets.

Galan found the Daisy 500 a real joy to shoot. Its performance was most impressive.

been officially dubbed, is also a faithful replica of the prized Beretta wondernine, right down to its non-reflective black finish.

As far as a simplified pellet-feeding mechanism goes, the Daisy 500 certainly has the simplest of them all: It is a single shot and must be manually loaded for each shot. The 5³/₈-inch barrel pivots at the front of the dummy, non-moving "slide." Grasping the rear section of the barrel—which forms part of the dummy slide at that point—between thumb and index finger, the barrel can be easily tilted upward through about 30 degrees, exposing the breech in order to load a pellet. The barrel liner, incidentally, is made of rifled steel.

The hammer of the 500 must be manually cocked for each shot. Thus, the gun works in single-action mode only. I must tell you, though, this pistol has one of the sweetest trigger actions I have ever experienced in any handgun. Taking up the initial slack, the trigger travels about ¹/₄-inch until resistance is met. Pulling through an additional ¹/₈-inch or so discharges the gun. The trigger pull weight of the test sample was glass-smooth, breaking cleanly and consistently at 4¹/₄ pounds.

This pistol has a manual, ambidextrous hammer-block safety located in exactly the same place as it is on the Beretta 92. The lever is rocked downward with the thumb in order to activate. This still allows the hammer to be cocked and dropped, except the valve stem—the "firing pin" in this type of CO_2 gun—is now rotated safely out of the way of the hammer, preventing discharge of the pistol. Most definitely, this is a simple, yet highly effective safety. There is one additional built-in safety feature in the 500: As long as the barrel is kept open, no pellet can be fired, even if the trigger is pulled with the manual safety off.

In keeping with its simple, yet eminently state-of-the-art design, the Daisy 500 comes with fixed sights—blade up front and square notch at the rear. My test sample, I soon discovered, was shooting dead-on at between 10 and 15 yards with most of the pellets tried. My only suggestion to Daisy would be to add a three-dot system in order to even more closely duplicate the real McCoy.

Daisy's own Quick Silver pellets performed quite well here, as did RWS Hobby and RWS Superpoint pellets. Using the Superpoints, the Model 500 even accounted for a couple of backyard pests one evening. Although by no means a target pistol, the 500 can print nickel-sized groups at 30 feet all day with a variety of popular pellets, if the shooter does his part. By the way, the muzzle velocity of the gun on test hovered around 492 fps with a fresh CO_2 cartridge. After the first ten rounds or so, it settled back to an average of 480 fps for quite a while. I was able to get about seventy shots from each CO_2 cartridge—in an ambient temperature of 92° F—before power dropped off severely. As is the norm with most CO_2 pistols of this type, the 12-gram cartridge is housed in the grip.

The Daisy 500 has mostly ABS and zinc alloy construction with matte black finish. Another version sporting a sharp-looking stainless-like finish on the frame, dubbed the Model 501, is also available. The balance and heft of the 500 are also relatively close to that of the Beretta, another decided plus for those who already own the real thing and would consider buying this pistol as an inexpensive duplicate for home practice. In fact, the Model 500 is just ideal for such a role, as well as for teaching new shooters the basics of handgun safety and handling.

If I sound like I am extremely enthusiastic about the Daisy Model 500, it's because this pistol deserves it.

J.I. Galan

221

Howa
Model 55G Rifle

"AS A MATTER of fact, Steve, I've been aware of the gun's existence for some time, but have never personally handled or even seen an actual specimen. If you can get ahold of a clean example, a piece on the Howa 55G would be a welcome addition to the new AIR GUN DIGEST."

With the green light given by Jess Galan, work began in an effort to document one of the most intriguing airguns manufactured in the past half-century. So what exactly is the Howa Model 55G anyway? Would you believe it is an absolutely stunning CO_2-powered replica of a famous Weatherby firearm from yesteryear!

As its moniker indicates, the Model 55G was produced by Japan's premier arms company, Howa Machinery Ltd. For many years, Howa was the chief sub-contractor for Weatherby, Inc. (and others), and this internationally respected firm has also produced fine sporting rifles under its own trade name, as well as various types of unrelated precision equipment.

The company's rendering of an airgun in the image of a

HOWA MODEL 55G SPECIFICATIONS

Power:	CO_2; two 12-gram cartridges
Caliber:	177, 22
Barrel:	20½ ins., rifled
Weight:	6 lbs.
Overall Length:	38.9 ins.
Sights:	Adjustable notch rear, blade front; scope optional
Trigger:	Two stage, non-adjustable
Muzzle Velocity:	600 fps
Cocking Effort:	NA
Source:	Howa Machinery Ltd.

Howa-made firearm is therefore not all that unusual. In fact, over the years, a number of firearm makers, both foreign and domestic, have also produced airguns. However, the Model 55G isn't modeled after one of the firm's own rifles.

If you go back far enough in years (I'm pushing forty myself), then you might recall a certain famous Weatherby

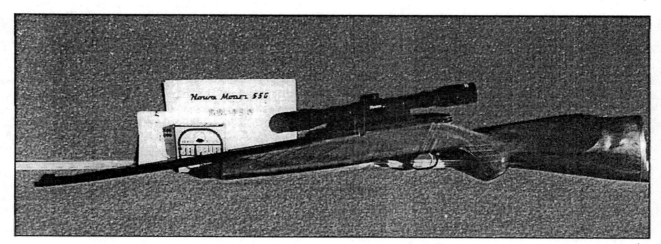

Shown is one of only two sample guns imported by Weatherby in the late 1970s. This particular specimen, serial number HO3001G, is in like-new condition and includes its original factory literature, shipping box and original Weatherby hanging sales tag.

import that was first marketed in 1964. Any takers? The gun in question is the now-discontinued Weatherby Mark XXII, an Italian-made autoloading rimfire rifle of extreme quality and elegance. One of the very finest 22 autos ever made, the Mark XXII was in the Weatherby line for well over twenty years and must have seemed a natural for cloning into airgun form.

As it happened, Howa did exactly that in 1976, taking the basic outline of the Mark XXII and translating the classic styling into an equally well-made and elegant CO_2-powered, bolt-action pellet repeater. The end result is an airgun so meticulously constructed that its manufacture is virtually as time-consuming as the firm's firearm line, meaning production would also be just as limited.

Given its relatively low production rate (about 100-200 guns are produced annually), very few examples have made it to North America. Most are sold in Asia and places such as Australia, with a handful managing to find their way into Europe on occasion. Howa even sent a couple of sample guns to Weatherby back in 1978 for test marketing, but with an asking price of $220, the rifles failed to attract any interest whatsoever. Incidentally, the only known original Howa/Weatherby 55G is featured (for the first time anywhere) on these pages. Enjoy.

Despite its lackluster commercial success, the Howa 55G is nonetheless a gunmaker's work of art. Machining and metal finish are literally without flaw. The rifle's fine ordnance steel barrel, compression tube and alloy receiver are all lavishly polished and chemically blackened to the highest custom-grade standard. Even the trigger guard (typically plastic or cast metal on lesser guns) is machined from alloy and meticulously hand-finished.

The Model 55G's one-piece hardwood stock is also flawlessly executed, every bit the equal of its metalwork. Like the classic Weatherby, styling is traditional Monte Carlo, with raised cheekpiece and comb complementing the gracefully tapered forend. Panels of intricate hand-cut checkering (basket weave or skip-line pattern) adorn both the pistol grip and

forend, while the butt is finished off with a ribbed hard rubber pad. Stocking wood on the current deluxe model is usually grade-three Claro walnut, though a special synthetic stock (i.e. Weatherby Weatherguard) can be ordered.

Dimensionally, the 55G is just shy of the Mark XXII, measuring a tad under 39 inches overall and weighing in at 6 pounds. Pull length seems on the short side at $13\frac{1}{2}$ inches, but handling is quick and precise nevertheless. The $20\frac{1}{2}$-inch precision crowned and rifled barrel (eight grooves, right-hand twist) also contributes greatly to the rifle's good pointing manners, as does its 11-inch forend.

Over its nineteen-year production span, the 55G has been offered in both scoped and open-sight versions. Surprisingly, the standard notch rear sight is nothing more than a simple bent sheet-metal affair, obviously not appropriate on a rifle of such high quality. Consequently, the gun is most often seen with a

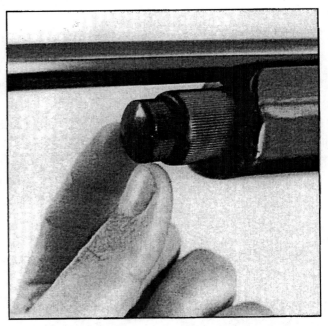

(Above) The two-stage piercing cap has a secondary knob to puncture the forward CO_2 cartridge. Turning the knob counterclockwise will safely vent all gas from rifle.

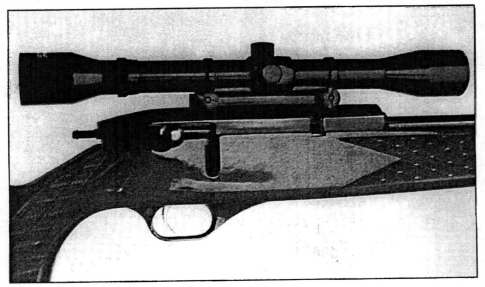

To cock the rifle, the bolt handle is lifted up and pulled fully to the rear. Returning the handle transfers a pellet from the magazine to the bore.

4x scope sight. The Hakko-made glass has a duplex reticle, coated lenses, separate one-piece mount, and parallax correction for airgun use. The receiver is dovetailed and will accommodate many other standard mount combinations.

The Howa's two-stage trigger is excellent, but has no provision for adjustment. Factory-set at exactly 3 pounds, a lightly sprung first stage is then followed by a clean-breaking final release. A manual cross-bolt safety is also housed within the trigger guard.

The Howa is powered by two 12-gram CO_2 cartridges. Insertion and piercing are quite similar to Crosman's long-discontinued Model 160 rifle. To charge, the rifle's breech bolt is pulled back to its rear position and the cross-bolt safety engaged. The first cartridge is then inserted neck down into the exposed compression tube, followed by the second CO_2 cartridge, which is inserted neck up. This, in turn, is followed by a two-stage piercing cap, which is threaded by hand until finger-tight. The piercing cap's secondary knob is then hand-tightened to pierce the forward cartridge. After closing the breech bolt and disengaging the safety, the rifle is dry fired to pierce the rear cartridge.

Also reminiscent of a long-past Crosman rifle (notably, the venerable 102/104 series multi-pump pneumatic repeaters), the Howa 55G employs a laterally moving breech lock to transfer pellets from an internal five-shot magazine to the bore. Manually actuated via a traditional bolt handle, both cocking and loading are accomplished on the bolt's opening and closing motions, and operation is smooth and positive.

Although the gun uses conventional technology, the repeating system is still quite a slick piece of engineering. For example, pellets are loaded into the rifle's magazine through a small hinged gate that reminds me of the scalloped cartridge port used

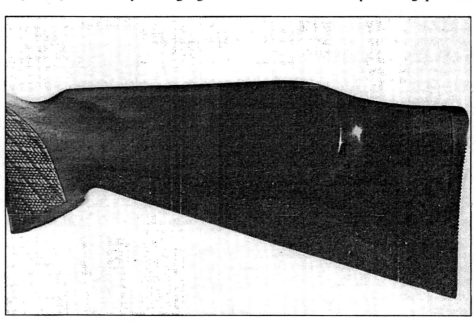

Like the classic Weatherby Mark XXII, the Howa 55G sports traditional Monte Carlo-styled timber. Stocking wood on this specimen is grade-three Claro walnut.

The follower release button is located at the rear of the rifle's action. The beautifully machined and finished trigger guard is a nice touch.

Although somewhat ammo sensitive due to its repeating system, the Howa is capable of very fine target accuracy.

on the Winchester 1894. Once all five pellets have been inserted, a separate spring-backed follower is snapped into place. Withdrawing the follower for reloading is as easy as pushing the knurled release button at the end of the action. The number of remaining pellets is also easily checked via a milled slot on the left side of the rifle's receiver.

As expected, the Howa's ballistic prowess is comparable to the old Crosman 160. Although somewhat limited by its special ammo requirements in repeating mode (semi-round head pellets), the rifle is fully capable of pushing along the heavy 15-plus-grain Jet pellet at just under 600 fps, generating around $11\frac{1}{2}$-12 foot pounds. The rifle can also be loaded single shot style with other round or wadcutter pellets of standard length. Most will produce muzzle energies in the 10 to 12 foot pound range. (The 177-caliber version will produce slightly higher velocities and correspondingly lower energy figures.)

Thanks to its quality optics and precision barrel, the Model 55G's target accuracy is predictably outstanding. Once again, given its exclusive pellet diet, the rifle can place a magazine full of 22-caliber Jets in a $\frac{3}{4}$-inch center-to-center circle at 30 yards. When single-loaded, pellets such as the popular Crosman Dome and Marksman FTS were particular standouts, cutting group sizes by almost half at the same distance. The 177-caliber version is marginally more accurate.

Besides its magnificent aesthetics and creditable performance in the field, the Howa 55G is an absolute delight to shoot. Firing behavior is naturally recoilless, without the slightest hint of perceived movement or action vibration. Upon discharge, there is the usual CO_2 gun "crack," of course, though it's no more pronounced than other gas or precharged pneumatic models.

Testing completed, the time has now come to return the rifle to its (very anxious) owner. Which brings me to the final point regarding this exquisite airgun. With an extremely limited production rate and an equally extreme price tag, the Howa 55G will never be a "common" gun. And perhaps it's just as well, because the world's finest CO_2-powered sporting rifle is anything but.

Stephen R. Gibbons

Note to the Collector

According to a factory source, only a few thousand rifles have been produced since the gun's introduction. Approximately sixty percent are 177-caliber versions and the remaining guns are in 22-caliber. Standard and Deluxe have been offered in both calibers, though only the Deluxe model is now being made.

Marksman
Model 45 Rifle

CURRENT ECONOMIC TIMES notwithstanding, it would seem that most every manner of goods and services costs a great deal more these days. Not unlike death and taxes, inflation affects virtually everyone, driving up prices in what is a never-ending spiral.

Naturally, airgun enthusiasts are by no means immune. Like many other precision-manufactured products, adult airguns have taken a tremendous leap in pricing over the past decade or so. This is especially true for entry-level, spring-piston "sporter" rifles, which traditionally have been the most active in terms of volume sales. As for Marksman Products, affordability has always been the key to its marketing strategy. Since 1985, the firm's International collection of adult airguns has effectively held the line on rising costs, while at the same time offering high-quality products to the discriminating airgunner.

Marksman's latest spring-piston import is a magnum-class sporter designated the Model 45. Precision-crafted in Spain by

MARKSMAN MODEL 45 SPECIFICATIONS	
Power:	Spring-piston, barrel cocking
Caliber:	177
Barrel:	19 ins.
Weight:	7 lbs., 3 oz.
Overall Length:	46³/₄ ins.
Sights:	Fully adjustable square notch rear, tunnel front
Trigger:	Adjustable; two-stage
Muzzle Velocity:	900 fps
Cocking Effort:	27 lbs.
Source:	Marksman Products

Norica, the new rifle made its trade debut at the 1993 SHOT Show.

A conventional barrel-cocking design, the Marksman 45 is every bit an adult-proportioned air rifle. In fact, with an overall

Whether used for hunting, competition, target practice or just plain fun plinking, the Marksman Model 45 is one of the best economy-priced sporting air rifles available today.

The Marksman 45's two-stage trigger is adjustable for weight. The small tab just forward is an auto safety.

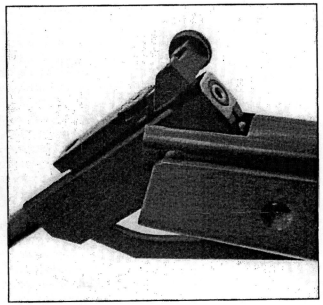

The Model 45 is of traditional break-barrel design. An O-ring is used to seal the breech when closed.

length of 46 inches and a pull length of 14½ inches, its size actually exceeds most other models in its class. On the other hand, this is by no means a fat sporter. Outward dimensions aside, the gun weighs in at just over 7 pounds with its factory open sights. Even when a good scope and mount are added, the rifle is still an easily managed package in the field.

Made mostly of steel and hardwood, the action (including the barrel and compression tube) is traditionally hot-blued, while the walnut-stained beechwood furniture has been given the usual semi-gloss urethane finish. Both surface treatments are executed to acceptable standards, as is the rifle's wood-to-metal fit. As it happens, the Model 45's stock design is somewhat of a departure from the typical Spanish pattern. The stock has classic American styling with Monte Carlo comb, raised cheekpiece, semi-pistol grip and squared forend gracefully tapered along its length. Devoid of checkering or stippling (in order to hold the price line), the stock does have a nicely curved plastic buttplate, though this, oddly enough, also lacks some form of gripping surface.

Factory-issue sights are Norica's standard-pattern, micro-click, square notch rear and tunnel front sight. Made from high-impact plastic, the rear sight unit is adjustable for windage and elevation via two small control wheels. The front tunnel sight is also moulded from tough synthetic material and accepts a variety of inserts. In addition, the rifle's compression tube is dovetailed and fitted with a separate arrester block to allow easy mounting of most scope sights.

One feature that surprised me was the Model 45's adjustable two-stage trigger. Although the first stage is a little on the long side, the final release is clean and predictable. Adjustments for weight are made via a standard screwdriver. Access is through a small hole in the trigger guard, which also houses the automatic safety tab located just forward of the trigger blade. Additionally, the unit's plastic blade is well curved and textured on its face.

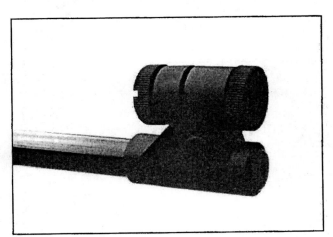

Made from a durable synthetic, the tunnel front sight will accept various inserts.

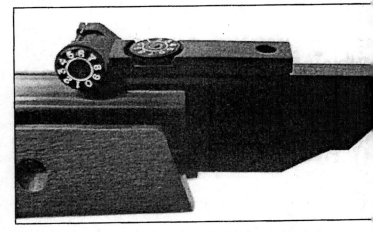

Also moulded from plastic, the rear sight unit is micro-click adjustable via two small control wheels.

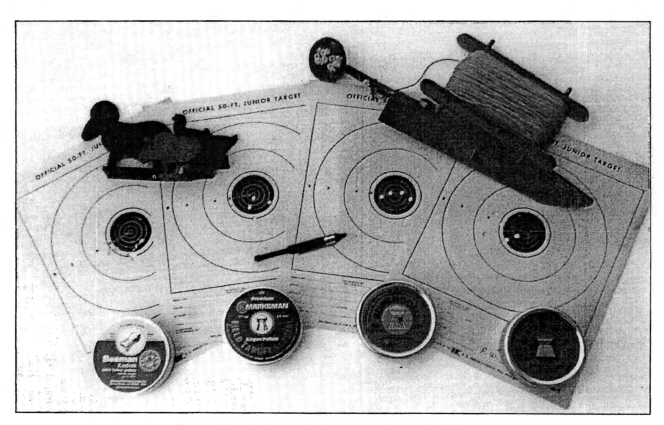

Fired at 35 yards, it's clear by these groups that the Model 45 performs well above its entry-level price tag.

As barrel-cockers go, operating the Marksman 45 is fairly routine for its genre. Once cocked and loaded, the auto safety must be pushed forward to disengage before firing. The safety can also be reset, of course, and the rifle can be uncocked as well.

Considering this is a magnum-class sporter, the firing behavior is relatively mild. After the customary 250-500 break-in shots, the sample rifle exhibited nothing more than the normal amount of moderate spring-piston gun recoil and discharge noise. Also, the cocking effort was not excessive at 27 pounds and was surprisingly smooth right from the start.

One of the most powerful air rifles in its class, the Model 45 can readily push along very light 6- to 7-grain 177-caliber pellets in excess of 900 fps. However, in more practical ballistic terms, the sample rifle was most efficient (and accurate) with heavier pellets in the 8- to 10½-grain range. Round or dome-head styles—such as 7.9-grain Crosman Dome, 8.4-grain RWS Superdome, 8.8-grain Marksman FTS and 10.5-grain Beeman Kodiak—were the pellets of choice here, tallying muzzle energies that ranged from 11 to 13½ foot pounds.

While not a super tackdriver by match gun standards, the Marksman 45 can nevertheless hold its own on the target range. At 30 feet, the rifle would routinely group five shots into .25- to .35-inch center-to-center using factory open sights and match pellets. Best results were obtained with pellets seated well into the rifle's breech and a barrel that was cleaned every fifty to one hundred shots.

Moving out to actual field distances of 25 to 50 yards, the accuracy story was very much the same. This time topped with a Marksman 4-12x40 scope sight, the gun regularly printed five-shot groups of ³/₄- to 1 inch center-to-center at 25 yards, and 2 to 3 inches at 50 yards. Once again, best results were achieved with a clean bore and well-seated dome-head pellets. Marksman's 8.8-grain FTS and the 8.4-grain RWS Superdome were especially outstanding performers.

Having proved itself worthy on the target range, the test gun and a tuned Beeman R1 were entered in a local air rifle silhouette competition. Fired side-by-side for purposes of comparison, the author managed a 26x40 with the tricked-out R1, while the Marksman 45 recorded a very respectable 21x40. No question about it, folks, this is one of the best entry-level magnum spring rifles on the market today.

So what *didn't* yours truly like? The rifle's slippery buttplate and stock finish do leave something to be desired in the gripping department. And the plastic trigger and sights are also a bit disconcerting on a rifle that will undoubtedly see hard use. Then again, production costs must be kept within reasonable limits.

Of course, in the final analysis, affordability is still the key to marketing this or any other entry-level adult airgun. As an additional bonus, the Marksman 45 is also a great performer. And with a retail price of just under $200, it's easily one of the best airgun bargains around.

Stephen R. Gibbons

Marksman Models 56-FTS and 58-S Rifles

IN RESPONSE TO increasing demand from American Field Target shooters for an out-of-the-box rifle suitable for that sport, Marksman Products introduced the Model 56-FTS (Field Target Special) a few years ago. This thoroughly purpose-built rifle meets head-on the unique requirements of Field Target competition. Along with the 56-FTS, Marksman also introduced the Model 58-S (Silhouette) air rifle, realizing that the sport of metallic silhouette shooting with airguns was also generating an impressive following.

The two guns are basically the same as far as power plant and method of operation are concerned. They are both traditional barrel cockers, capable of producing muzzle velocities in the 910 to 940 fps range with a variety of pointed and round-head 177-caliber pellets. Both models are manufactured by none other than Weihrauch.

During the mid-1980s, Weihrauch purchased the remaining assets of BSF (Bayerische Sportwaffen Fabrik), itself a former

giant in airgun production, adding the latter company's know-how to an already highly respected product line. These two Marksman models certainly incorporate some of the best features found in Weihrauch and former BSF guns.

MARKSMAN MODELS 56-FTS AND 58-S SPECIFICATIONS	
Power:	Spring-piston; barrel cocking
Caliber:	177
Barrel:	19⅝ ins. (56-FTS); 16 ins. (58-S)
Weight:	8.8 lbs (56-FTS); 8.5 lbs. (58-S)
Overall Length:	47 ins. (56-FTS); 42 ins. (58-S)
Sights:	None furnished; scope base only
Trigger:	2 lbs.; adjustable
Muzzle Velocity:	910-940 fps
Cocking Effort:	22-24 lbs. (56-FTS); 24 lbs. (58-S)
Source:	Marksman Products

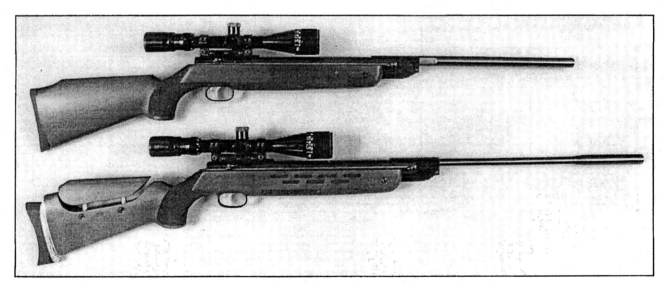

The Marksman Models 58-S (top) and 56-FTS are prime examples of state-of-the-art spring-piston air rifle technology from Germany.

(Above) The Model 56-FTS is a man-sized rifle with a surprisingly mild cocking effort, despite its creditable power. That long barrel certainly helps, though.

One of the most salient features common to both models is the well-known Rekord trigger. This Weihrauch design is one of the best trigger units ever used in an adult air rifle, coming very close to the performance and smoothness of triggers usually found only in Olympic-grade air rifles. Both of these Marksman rifles have their triggers set at 2 pounds of pressure by the factory; however, they can be easily adjusted down to just a few ounces. I did not change the adjustment on either model during my tests, given their sharp performance throughout.

The trigger safety is automatically activated when the barrel is broken open for cocking and must be manually disengaged in order to shoot. Conveniently located at the right rear of the receiver, the safety-lever is large enough to permit easy manipulation.

Because these two rifles are intended for competitive shooting at often relatively long distances—up to 50 yards or so—both of these guns are meant to be used with telescopic sights only and are, therefore, supplied without iron sights. Marksman's own #6941 scope, mated to the #6007 compensating mount, is a superb choice for either rifle. This scope is a 4-12x

(Right) Both the thick buttplate and the ample cheekpiece are adjustable in the 56-FTS. The 4-12x scope and adjustable mount are also distributed by Marksman.

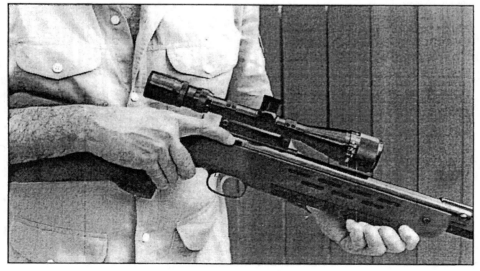

Both the Model 56-FTS and Model 58-S have conveniently located trigger safeties that go on automatically when the guns are cocked.

glass with a 40mm focus-adjustable objective, duplex reticle and razor-sharp optics. Shooters have the option of mounting the scope of their choice or purchasing either rifle already outfitted with the Marksman mount/scope combo. The receiver cylinders of both rifles have raised dovetail scope bases of the type formerly used on some BSF models.

The most visible differences between the two are the barrel lengths and stock styles. The 56-FTS sports a decidedly match-style stock with adjustable buttplate and cheekpiece. There is a large area of stippling on the pistol grip, as well as along the bottom of the forend. The forend also has several cutouts for those shooters who like a firmer grip up front. In sharp contrast, the Model 58-S lacks the adjustable cheekpiece and buttplate—but still incorporates a substantial rubber buttpad—and has no forend cutouts either, although there is plenty of stippling in key areas. Both stocks, by the way, are ambidextrous, a definite plus for southpaws considering either model. The Model 58-S has a bull barrel that is almost 4 inches shorter than that of the 56-FTS. The full-length barrel sleeve weight is removable, as is the silencer-like muzzle weight of the 56-FTS. Both barrel weights enhance in their own way the outstanding balance and solid "feel" of these rifles.

Extensive testing of these Marksman air rifles yielded few surprises. As expected, they were both capable of consistently hitting a wide variety of targets to 60 yards or so. Considering that the "kill zone" of most targets used in field competition is about 1½ inches in diameter, and the airgun-style metallic silhouettes are equally small, it is easy to see just how accurate these two rifles really are. In addition, their precision and magnum-class power are also well suited to small game hunting, an activity in which I definitely prefer the 58-S due to its slightly shorter length and reduced weight. The chronograph showed that both guns were generating muzzle velocities that surpassed Marksman's own listed figures by about 20 fps with Eley Wasp round-head pellets, which are also distributed by Marksman.

Marksman definitely has two field rifles here. They can certainly take on some of the far more costly air rifles in the outdoor target circuit and come out winners.

J.I. Galan

With its short bull barrel and rather plain stock, the Model 58-S is an outstanding rifle capable of pinpoint precision.

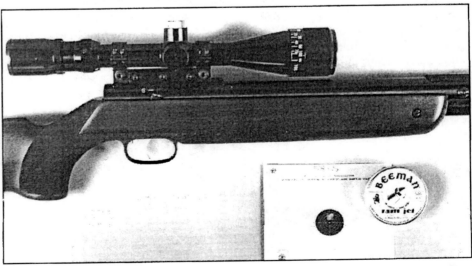

There is no doubt that the Model 58-S is capable of outstanding precision. Beeman Ram Jet pellets performed very well indeed in this model.

Marksman Model 1790 Biathlon Trainer Rifle

IN THE WORLD of airguns, there is an unwritten dogma of sorts which says no spring-piston air rifle retailing for less than $70 or so in today's economy should be taken too seriously. Indeed, it seems as if any bona fide spring-piston rifle worthy of consideration by adults—or even for dedicated training by younger shooters—has to carry a price tag of well above one C-note in order to be regarded a reliable prospect.

Well, I am here to tell you one of the most enjoyable spring-piston rifles I have tested in recent years carries a suggested retail price of just $66.95 (as of late 1994) and is every bit as spunky as many air rifles costing far more.

Despite a monicker linking it directly with the popular biathlon cross-country skiing and shooting event of the Winter Olympics, this 177-caliber air rifle is really meant for basic marksmanship training and plinking all year round. The Marksman Model 1790 Biathlon Trainer has decidedly eye-catching styling. Its skeletonized stock is moulded from high-impact synthetic and finished in a charcoal-gray tone that enhances the racy match lines of the gun. The stock has a length of pull of 12½ inches, which I found surprisingly comfortable despite my long arms. I am particularly fond of the simple, contoured pistol grip and hooked butt, too. The three stippled cutouts on either side of the forend are helpful in the correct and consistent placement of the supporting hand. Naturally, the stock design closely follows that of the rifles used in world-class biathlon rifles, where extreme economy of weight and simplicity are of crucial importance.

MARKSMAN MODEL 1790 BIATHLON TRAINER SPECIFICATIONS	
Power:	Spring-piston; barrel cocking
Caliber:	177
Barrel:	15 ins.; rifled steel
Weight:	4.9 lbs.
Overall Length:	39½ ins.
Sights:	Match diopter rear, tunnel front
Trigger:	4 lbs.; non-adjustable
Muzzle Velocity:	450 fps
Cocking Effort:	16 lbs.
Source:	Marksman Products

Overall, the Marksman Model 1790 measures 39½ inches, which, thanks to its unusually light stock, translates into just 4.9 pounds at the scale. The 15-inch rifled steel barrel requires a mild cocking effort of just 16 pounds, something that practically anyone over the age of ten years can handle with ease.

Although the gun does not have an adjustable trigger, I can't criticize it. Two samples tested early on revealed trigger pull weights hovering around 4 pounds, both smooth enough to allow some serious target practice. I have seen my share of imported air rifles—most costing considerably more than the 1790—whose triggers were not nearly as smooth. One interesting feature of this rifle's trigger system is its automatic safety, which is activated whenever the rifle is cocked and must be manually disengaged in order to shoot. Even if the

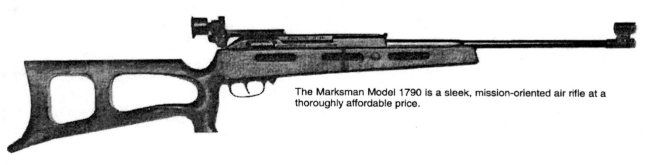

The Marksman Model 1790 is a sleek, mission-oriented air rifle at a thoroughly affordable price.

The Marksman Biathlon Trainer comes with a full-fledged diopter match rear sight.

rifle is not cocked, pulling the trigger will flick the safety catch to the On position, preventing any further pulling of the trigger.

One slick feature of the Marksman Model 1790 is its set of match-style sights. The rear is a full-fledged diopter unit, complete with removable eyeshade. Elevation adjustments are easily carried out by turning the large red knob on top of the sight. For windage adjustments, a second knob at the rear of the unit must be loosened and the diopter moved manually to left or right. Both adjustments have their corresponding graduated

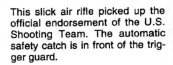

This slick air rifle picked up the official endorsement of the U.S. Shooting Team. The automatic safety catch is in front of the trigger guard.

Galan truly enjoyed testing the Marksman Biathlon Trainer. This rifle is really hard to put down.

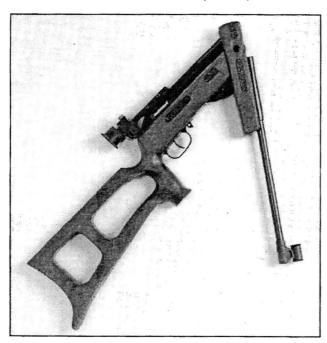

The spring-piston-powered Model 1790 requires a cocking effort of just 16 pounds and produces a muzzle velocity of about 450 fps.

scales. The rear sight is mounted on the receiver dovetail and can be easily removed if the shooter wishes to use a telescopic sight instead. The tunnel front sight has a slightly tapered post. Both front and rear sights are also made of a durable moulded synthetic material.

The 1790 is not an exceedingly powerful air rifle. It has a factory-listed muzzle velocity of 450 fps. My own chronograph tests showed muzzle velocities averaging between 453 and 475 fps with a selection of match and pointed pellets of various weights. Although quite moderate by air rifle standards, those velocities are still quite acceptable for backyard plinking and target practice. In fact, even some small pests, such as mice, can be quickly and quietly dispatched with this rifle, as long as shots are kept to no more than 15 yards or so. Precise shot placement is no problem, as my accuracy tests amply demonstrated. This rifle is plenty accurate for its intended role as a trainer.

Since its introduction back in 1989, the Marksman Model 1790 Biathlon Trainer has picked up the official endorsement of the U.S. Shooting Team. With its low retail price, there is no doubt this gun will continue to be a good choice for those seeking a thoroughly affordable spring-piston barrel cocker with world-class styling and creditable performance.

J.I. Galan

RWS/Diana Model 36 Rifle

THERE IS NO doubt that traditional barrel-cocking spring-piston air rifles will always remain popular with many shooters. Despite the growing number of sidelever and underlever rifles, the barrel-cocker has maintained its appeal with shooters who like its rugged simplicity and straightforward operation.

Some ten years ago, Dynamit Nobel-RWS introduced a barrel-cocking air rifle that was soon to become a top contender among magnum air rifles, the RWS Model 36. This was followed shortly after by a no-frills version dubbed the RWS 34 and, later, by a carbine version of the Model 36 called the Model 36C. All of them are made by Dianawerk, the world-renown German airgun giant.

The RWS Models 36 and 34 are basically alike, except for the Model 36's fancier hardwood stock with checkering in the pistol grip area, a sleek Monte Carlo cheekpiece and a rubber recoil pad. Both models, however, utilize the same power plant and their length and weight specifications are very close.

The hardwood stock of the Model 36 has a slim, graceful profile and sports a nice oil finish. There is a rubber recoil pad set off by a white-line spacer. The Monte Carlo cheekpiece is not as pronounced as that found on other magnum airsporters, but is certainly elegant and every bit as practical. As far as the stock goes, I give the Model 36 top marks. Metal finish is top-notch with all surfaces exhibiting rich, deep bluing and no evidence of toolmarks.

The RWS Model 36 has an overall length of 45 inches, barrel length of 19 inches, and tips the scales at around 8 pounds. No doubt about it; this is a full-sized adult air rifle. The rear open sight is all metal with micrometer click knobs for windage and elevation adjustments. The front sight consists of a tunnel that accepts various inserts, although the test rifle

RWS/DIANA MODEL 36 SPECIFICATIONS	
Power:	Spring-piston, barrel cocking
Caliber:	177, 22
Barrel:	19 ins.
Weight:	8 lbs.
Overall Length:	45 ins.
Sights:	Fully adjustable rear; tunnel front with removable element
Trigger:	3.3 lbs., adjustable
Muzzle Velocity:	1000 fps (177)
	800 fps (22)
Cocking Effort:	33 lbs.
Source:	Dynamit Nobel-RWS, Inc.

came with only one straight post element. A standard dovetail base sits atop the compression tube for scope use; however, the RWS micrometer peep sight unit could also be used on this model.

This air rifle (along with Models 34 and 36C) has several important improvements over older RWS models. The trigger mechanism is now a one-piece unit which can be easily slipped out from the rear of the compression tube should it ever be required. The trigger, incidentally, is two-stage and can be adjusted for let-off. It comes with a factory-adjusted weight of 3.3 pounds. The trigger safety automatically engages when the rifle is cocked and consists of a small tab protruding from the rear of the cylinder. The tab must be pushed forward in order to shoot. Another improvement is the addition of a nylon mainspring guide for a quieter cocking sequence. Also, there is a nylon piston seal that can now be replaced in a matter of minutes, unlike some of the older types which required highly specialized tools.

The RWS Model 36 is a traditional barrel-cocking spring-piston air rifle of magnum-class power.

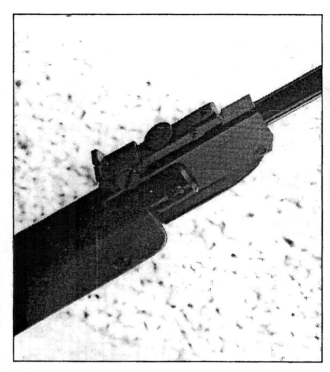

The rear sight is all steel, adjustable for windage and elevation via click knobs. The shooter also can choose from among four different notches.

The trigger safety engages automatically when the rifle is cocked. It is shown in the "On" position. The pistol grip has small checkered panels.

Author found the RWS Model 36 capable of delivering a powerful, accurate punch. The open rear sight/tunnel front is a great combination for general practice and short-range hunting.

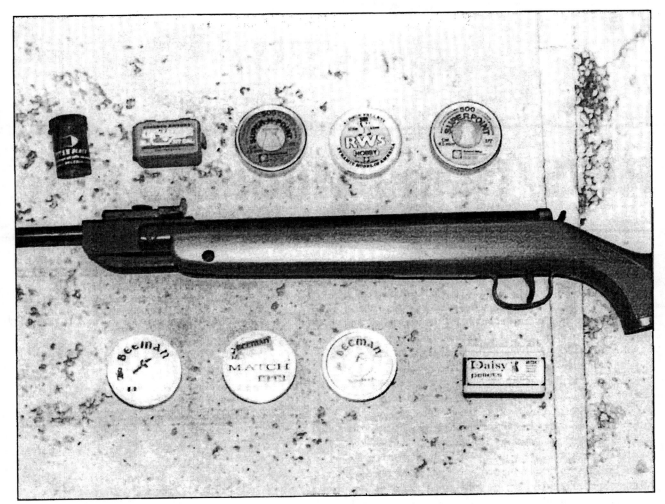

A wide variety of pellets were tried in this early RWS Model 36. Most gave excellent results.

Shooting the RWS Model 36 is a truly pleasant experience. It has no harsh recoil or vibration despite its rugged looks and heavy-duty power plant. An early test sample was in 177-caliber, although it is also available in 22-caliber. (The Model 36C carbine is available in 177-caliber only.) The trigger was clean-breaking, without any roughness or backlash.

The Dynamit Nobel-RWS catalog lists the Model 36 as producing a muzzle velocity of about 1000 fps in 177-caliber and 800 fps in 22-caliber. The test rifle chronographed an average of 897 fps using RWS Hobby pellets. Why the slight discrepancy? A number of variables may enter into play here. First of all, not all spring-piston airguns, even of the same model, ever perform exactly alike. Internal lubrication and "wearing in" of parts certainly affect performance, particularly when the gun is new. The lubricants placed in the power plant at the factory must be given a chance to dissipate and the action to "wear in" before the rifle settles into its true performance figures. Because of time constraints, I was able to fire only about 200 rounds before I began chronographing. I would expect at least a 5 percent increase in muzzle velocity after 1000 rounds or so. RWS Superpoint pellets averaged 952 fps.

As far as accuracy is concerned, the RWS Model 36 has more than enough for all practical purposes short of serious competitive shooting. Benchrest tests indicated good match potential with five-round groups averaging .18-inch center-to-center, at 10 meters, using RWS Meisterkugeln match pellets. Most benchrest groups could be covered by a dime. RWS Superpoints opened up the groups slightly, while RWS Super H Point pellets gave good plinking accuracy out to about 30 yards. Several other brands and types of pellets were also tried in this gun, with varying degrees of success. As expected, most German-made pellets shot very well, although Crosman Premier domed pellets also performed most impressively.

I didn't have time to take the RWS 36 afield, but I have no doubt it would perform admirably out in the woods. With a good scope it should prove deadly on small game out to 40 or 50 yards in either caliber. All in all, I give an overall rating of excellent to the RWS Model 36. It merits serious consideration by those looking for a moderately priced spring-piston magnum airsporter of traditional German quality.

J.I. Galan

RWS/Diana Model 45 Rifle

ONE UNDENIABLE MODERN classic in the already crowded world of high-power air rifles is the RWS/Diana Model 45. This rifle was introduced to the U.S. by Beeman in the late 1970s and was marketed initially as the Beeman Model 250. Beeman sold the gun for about three years, while Dynamit Nobel-RWS continued to make this Dianawerk rifle one of the top offerings in their RWS line of precision adult airguns. Until the introduction of the RWS 45, the relatively limited field of magnum air rifles had been dominated by the Feinwerkbau 124/127. That has changed drastically in the intervening years and, currently, magnum air rifles appear with staggering frequency due to the demand—especially here in America—for powerful and accurate air rifles for hunting and Field Target use. It is a telling measure of the RWS 45's quality and performance that, after more than sixteen years since its introduction, this model is still one of the best-selling magnum airsporters around. Let's see why.

This is undoubtedly a big air rifle. It measures 45 inches

RWS/DIANA MODEL 45 SPECIFICATIONS

Power:	Spring-piston; barrel cocking
Caliber:	177 (22, discontinued)
Barrel:	19 ins.; rifled steel
Weight:	8 lbs.
Overall Length:	45 ins.
Sights:	Tunnel front, fully adjustable rear
Trigger:	3.3 lbs.
Muzzle Velocity:	1000 fps
Cocking Effort:	33 lbs.
Source:	Dynamit Nobel-RWS, Inc.

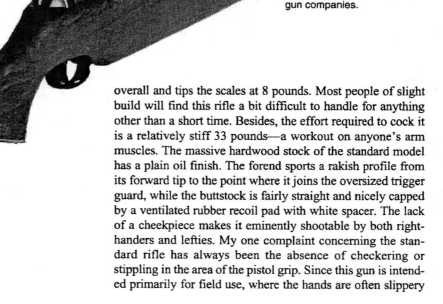

The RWS Model 45 is a robust, hand-hitting air rifle made by one of Germany's oldest and most respected airgun companies.

overall and tips the scales at 8 pounds. Most people of slight build will find this rifle a bit difficult to handle for anything other than a short time. Besides, the effort required to cock it is a relatively stiff 33 pounds—a workout on anyone's arm muscles. The massive hardwood stock of the standard model has a plain oil finish. The forend sports a rakish profile from its forward tip to the point where it joins the oversized trigger guard, while the buttstock is fairly straight and nicely capped by a ventilated rubber recoil pad with white spacer. The lack of a cheekpiece makes it eminently shootable by both right-handers and lefties. My one complaint concerning the standard rifle has always been the absence of checkering or stippling in the area of the pistol grip. Since this gun is intended primarily for field use, where the hands are often slippery

Galan has always been partial to his RWS 45. Extensive testing of several versions of this rifle over the years has confirmed its accuracy and magnum-class power.

with sweat, it would be nice to have a secure surface to provide a better grasp.

All metal surfaces of the RWS 45 have a deep blued finish. One of the characteristics of this gun is that it utilizes steel for most of its main components, including the safety catch. The front sight tunnel is also made of steel and accepts interchangeable inserts. It comes with one straight post insert, but additional elements are available at extra cost. The all-steel open rear sight is fully adjustable via micrometer click knobs. There are four different notches available, which can be changed simply by rotating a spring-loaded plate.

The RWS 45 comes into its own when a telescopic sight is mounted on it and taken afield. A dovetailed scope base is attached at the rear of the receiver. Dynamit Nobel-RWS currently offers eight scopes specially designed for use on spring-piston air rifles. These can take the awkward "double snap" that these types of rifles, particularly high-powered ones, are capable of dishing out. Regular firearm scopes have been known to fall apart after only a couple of hundred rounds when mounted on one of these magnum air rifles. The RWS 45 is capable of delivering all of its built-in accuracy only when it is equipped with a good scope. I highly recommend using an RWS Scope Stop block if a scope is used to avoid slippage.

The two-stage trigger of the RWS 45 is also massive, a feature I like. Its let-off weight of 3.3 pounds is ideal for field use. It breaks cleanly without creepiness or backlash. Although fairly complicated in design, this is one area where Dianawerk did a superb job after abandoning their long-favored ball-type sear.

The trigger safety goes on automatically upon cocking the rifle and is a steel tab that slides rearward from the end of the receiver. It must be manually disengaged prior to shooting by pushing it back into the receiver tube.

The current Dynamit Nobel-RWS catalog lists a muzzle velocity of 1000 fps in 177-caliber. My older 177-caliber RWS

RWS Superpoint pellets penetrate deeply and are very accurate in author's RWS 45.

45 still chronographs at an average of 1017 fps with Hobby pellets. The heavier RWS Superpoint pellets, at around 7.7 grains, average 973 fps.

Benchrest tests reveal groups of just under 3/16-inch center-to-center at 10 meters, the norm when top-quality wadcutter pellets such as RWS Meisterkugeln and H&N Match are used. Switching over to pointed and round-head pellets slightly opens up the groups with average center-to-center spreads of around 1/4-inch. This translates into the kind of long-range accuracy necessary to drop rabbits and other small quarry, consistently and humanely.

The firing behavior of the RWS 45, while authoritative, is nevertheless remarkably free of vibration. This solid "feel" is carried over to the firing sequence, and part of that is undoubtedly due to the generous stock and overall good balance of the rifle.

J.I. Galan

239

RWS/Diana Model 52 Rifle

ONE OF THE most overused—if not abused—terms in the field of high-performance air rifles is the word "magnum." Although I am the first to confess that I'm guilty of using that word countless times, the fact remains there are literally dozens of really potent air rifles out there that deserve to be labeled magnums. At the risk of sounding repetitious, however, I find that I must employ that term once more in order to talk about the RWS/Diana Model 52.

The Model 52, along with the less frilly Model 48, has been available for a number of years, imported by Dynamit Nobel-RWS, Inc. By all current standards, both of these guns represent state-of-the-art design in the field of magnum-class spring-piston air rifles. The two models differ only in the degree of stock refinement and are the direct heirs of the long and distinguished tradition established by the old classic Diana Model 50. That gun, introduced by Dianawerk over four decades ago, was arguably the most elegant underlever air rifle produced since the end of World War II.

The Model 50 underwent a number of improvements over the years, culminating in the superb RWS 50T.01, a relatively powerful and accurate rifle with a classic profile. Dianawerk sure had their work cut out for them when they chose to discon-

RWS/DIANA MODEL 52 SPECIFICATIONS

Power:	Spring-piston; sidelever cocking
Caliber:	177, 22, 25
Barrel:	17 ins.
Weight:	8¼ lbs.
Overall Length:	43 ins.
Sights:	Fully adjustable open rear, movable post on ramp front
Trigger:	3.3 lbs.; adjustable
Muzzle velocity:	1100 fps (177)
	900 fps (22)
	630 fps (25)
Cocking Effort:	39 lbs.
Source:	Dynamit Nobel-RWS, Inc.

tinue the big Model 50 in favor of a brand-new rifle—a sidelever, no less!

I obtained an RWS Model 52 shortly after it was introduced, and it has always performed impressively indeed. The first thing I noticed about this rifle is that it appears to be much lighter than its hefty 8¼ pounds. Shooting it, however, one quickly realizes every ounce of that weight is useful in maintaining a steady hold during the firing sequence in such a pow-

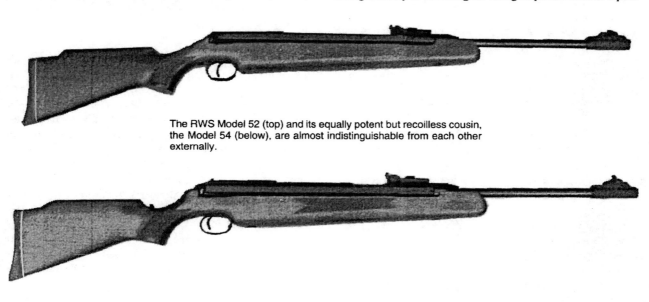

The RWS Model 52 (top) and its equally potent but recoilless cousin, the Model 54 (below), are almost indistinguishable from each other externally.

Galan cocks the RWS Model 52 during tests. The sidelever mechanism requires about 39 pounds of force.

(Below) The sidelever release latch engages automatically during cocking and must be depressed before the lever can be closed.

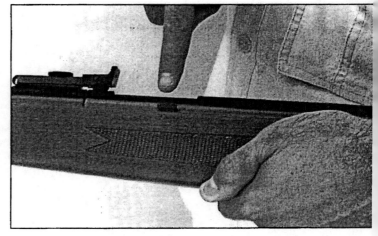

erful rifle. The gun measures 43 inches overall and has a 17-inch precision-rifled steel barrel.

One of the most salient features of the Model 52 is its sidelever cocking action. This was a radical departure for magnum-class air rifles produced by Dianawerk. The only models in the Dynamit Nobel-RWS lineup prior to the 52 and 48 that used a sidelever action were the superb world-class recoilless match models in their 75 series. The sidelever of the Model 52, at 15³/₄ inches, is certainly long enough to make cocking quite manageable by most adults. Dynamit Nobel-RWS lists a cocking effort of 39 pounds for this rifle.

There is a well-designed safety system that prevents the breechblock and the cocking lever from slamming shut during loading, even if the trigger is pulled. In addition, once the cocking lever is fully open for loading, a small catch on the left side of the receiver must be pushed down in order to close the action.

The RWS 52 (as well as the 48) has a sturdy, fully adjustable rear sight. Besides a micrometer disc to take care of elevation and a click screw for windage, this sight also gives a choice of four different notches. The front sight is also strongly built and quite practical. It consists of a tapered blade that can be placed anywhere along a 2⁵/₈-inch ramp, offering even more choices of elevation adjustments. The sight radius spans about 16 inches, but that doesn't seem to affect accuracy in a negative manner. By the way, the receiver has a mount base that allows the use of a scope on this rifle, and Dynamit Nobel-RWS carries a line of scopes especially designed for high-performance spring-piston rifles.

As expected in an airgun made by Diana in Germany and sold under the prestigious RWS label, the Model 52 is very nicely finished. Its stock sports a Monte Carlo comb with raised cheekpiece, checkered pistol grip and forend, and rubber buttpad with white-line spacer. In contrast, the more economically priced Model 48 has a fairly plain stock with straight comb, no cheekpiece and no checkering. It does, however, come with the rubber buttpad and white spacer. There is also a Model 52 Deluxe being offered with a custom-made walnut stock. This neat gun, available only in 177-caliber, retails for a little over $200 more than the standard Model 52. Both models have the heft and feel of big-game hunting rifles, due to their stock designs and rigid barrel configuration. Interestingly, the Model 48 is listed by the importer as being a quarter-pound heavier and 1 inch shorter than the Model 52. The suggested retail prices of these two air rifles reflect the differences in their stocks.

Galan found the RWS Model 52 to be a man-sized, powerful and accurate air rifle. The 25-caliber version in particular makes an ideal field rifle.

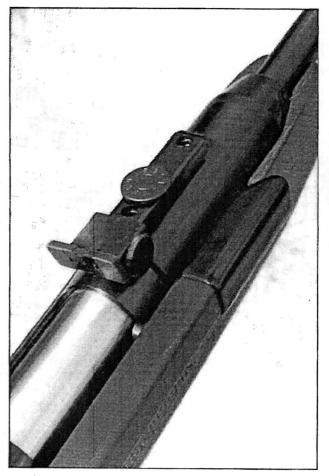

The front sight has a movable post on a ramp that works quite well.

The RWS Models 48, 52 and 54 all come with first-class open sights. They are fully adjustable via click knobs.

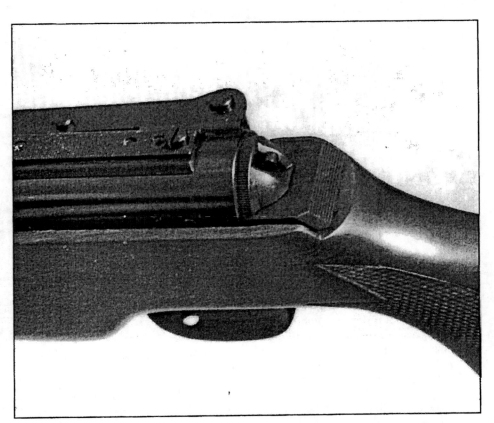

The entire action of the RWS Model 54 slides rearward within the stock during the firing sequence to cancel recoil.

Incidentally, both models come with crisp, adjustable triggers. The factory sets them at around 3.3 pounds, which is quite adequate for magnum-class air rifles. There is a safety catch that goes on automatically when the rifle is cocked. To disengage, the small tab protruding from the receiver end cap is simply pushed in with the thumb.

Although both the 52 and 48 behave quite nicely upon discharge, they still have enough recoil to remind you they are sizzlers. Periodic chronographing of my Model 52 in 177 has shown muzzle velocities averaging 1083 fps with RWS Club pellets weighing around 7.1 grains. Heavier pellets drop the velocity down closer to the 1000 fps mark and even below, which still makes this air rifle a hot performer indeed. In 177-caliber, both the 52 and the 48 can produce up to 1100 fps according to Dynamit Nobel-RWS, while the 22-caliber versions of the same models can give a hard-hitting 900 fps. As if all of this power was not enough, in 1994 Dynamit Nobel-RWS introduced both models in 25-caliber for even more punch at the receiving end, something that small game and varmint hunters will really appreciate.

As for accuracy, the Model 52 is also quite impressive, producing dime-sized groups at up to 35 yards or so with a variety of top-class pellets. However, best performance is generally obtained with heavy field pellets such as RWS Super Mags (9.5 grains in 177) and Marksman MAKO (10.5 grains in 177).

With such a pair of top guns on their roster, you'd think that Dynamit Nobel-RWS would take it easy for a while, but that's not the case.

In 1992, they unveiled their Model 54, which can be rightly regarded as the quintessential refinement in a magnum spring-piston rifle. The Model 54 delivers the same awesome power of the Models 52 and 48, albeit in a rifle that has a totally *recoilless* action. Outwardly, there is little, if anything, to distinguish the 54 from the Model 52. Their crucial difference is that the 54's action slides rearward in the stock, sledge fashion, for about 3/4-inch during the firing sequence, in order to cancel out recoil. The net result is an incredibly well-behaved rifle that feels a lot like a world-class match rifle, except the pellet strikes with the kind of oomph that a traditional 10-meter match air rifle would never muster.

The 177-caliber RWS Model 54 that I tested—so far, the Model 54 is available in 177 and 22 only—also generated velocities very similar to those of its older, recoiling Model 52 cousin. However, a slightly bigger difference between their respective performances was found in the area of accuracy, where the 54 has a distinct edge due to its lack of recoil. At the prescribed 10-meter match distance, the 54 performed almost like a full-fledged match air rifle. Of course, this recoilless technology costs a bit more than a regular recoiling rifle, carrying a suggested retail price of around $680 as of early 1995. For the money, the Model 54's awesome power and recoilless operation bring to mind the old saying about having your cake and eating it, too.

To be absolutely fair, though, I must close by saying that any one of these models—48, 52 or 54—would make a fine choice as a field rifle. Although the recoil of the 52 and 48 is certainly not going to shake loose any fillings, many shooters—myself included—enjoy the quiet manners of a recoilless rifle. As they say, "You pays your money and you makes your choice."

J.I. Galan

RWS/Diana Model 100 Rifle

AS WITH ALL dedicated world-class air rifles, the RWS/Diana Model 100 was designed from the ground up to deliver hair-splitting accuracy at the official 10-meter distance used in formal international competition. This is obvious the moment you pick up the rifle. Despite its hefty weight of nearly 11 pounds, the gun is so well balanced that it feels considerably lighter.

The oil-finished European walnut stock is a delight to behold, managing to retain a trim profile in spite of its massiveness. I particularly liked the adjustable cheekpiece, which permits a wide range of positions, both horizontally as well as vertically, to suit basically anyone's preference. The thick, hard rubber buttpad is also adjustable. The large pistol grip area is stippled over its entire lower half, permitting a secure grasp even with a sweaty hand. An accessory rail in the bottom of the forend allows the use of a palm rest or sling for shooters wishing to use the rifle as a practice companion to the formerly available Diana 820L 22-caliber rimfire Olympic rifle.

The Model 100 was a very important step for Diana because it was the first airgun produced by that long-established firm to utilize the single-stroke pneumatic power plant. Up to that point, all existing airguns in the Diana line, including the superb Series 75 match rifles, used the spring-piston power plant. Diana has the distinction of being a true pioneer in the field of spring-piston match airguns, having incorporated the famous Giss contra-piston system of suppressing recoil more than thirty years ago. Incidentally, the aforementioned Series

RWS/DIANA MODEL 100 SPECIFICATIONS	
Power:	Single-stroke pneumatic
Caliber:	177
Barrel:	19 ins.
Weight:	10.8 lbs.
Overall Length:	43 ins.
Sights:	Match peep rear, tunnel front
Trigger:	Match; fully adjustable
Muzzle Velocity:	580 fps
Cocking Effort:	16 lbs.
Source:	Dynamit Nobel-RWS, Inc.

75 match air rifles still use the Giss contra-piston system. One of the major advantages of a pneumatic power plant is the absence of any vibration whatsoever during the firing cycle. This is a definite plus because even a minimal amount of vibration could negatively affect the accuracy of a 177-caliber pellet.

The single-stroke pneumatic system also generally produces a shorter lock time than most spring-piston systems, minimizing any shooter movement during the firing sequence. This is especially the case in match airguns, which have muzzle velocities that are comparatively low, seldom surpassing 630 fps, and the Model 100 certainly falls in that category. Interestingly, most of the power plant's components are made of stainless steel, to avoid problems with rust in that important area.

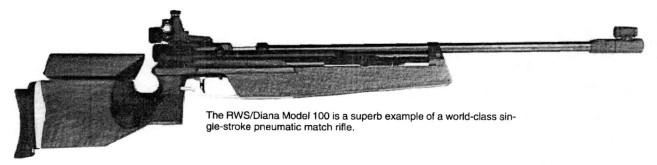

The RWS/Diana Model 100 is a superb example of a world-class single-stroke pneumatic match rifle.

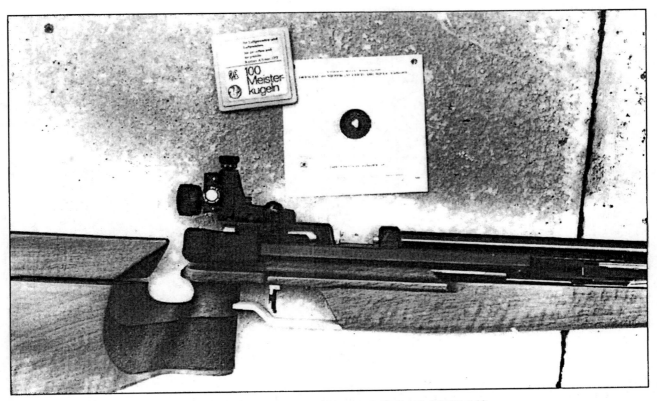

This typical five-round group fired from a rest with the Model 100 at 10 meters illustrates the tremendous accuracy delivered by this air rifle.

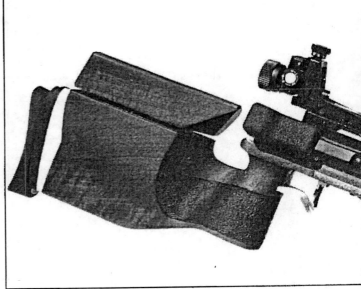

The ample walnut stock of the Model 100 is match-style all the way, incorporating a fully adjustable cheekpiece and rubber buttpad. Diana's latest diopter match sight is standard equipment here.

The Model 100's single-stroke pneumatic system is cocked and pumped via a stout sidelever. The cocking effort can be easily managed by most adults.

Shooting the RWS/Diana Model 100 proved very enjoyable. The rifle balances beautifully and delivers hair-splitting precision.

As befits a rifle intended for the highest levels of 10-meter competition, the Model 100 comes equipped with a full-fledged match trigger and the latest diopter sight system from Dianawerk. The trigger blade is adjustable for a wide range of positions, while other adjustments take care of length of trigger travel and let-off weight. Pull weight is adjustable from a mere 50 grams (1.7 ounces) up to a still ultra-light 250 grams (8.8 ounces).

As can be readily gathered from the photographs, the Model 100 could be mistaken for a 22 rimfire rifle due to its bolt-action mechanism. This is, once again, of great value to those who would use the 100 as a training companion to a 22 rimfire match rifle—a well thought out feature.

Cocking and pumping are done with the massive lever on the right side. The single pump stroke requires a bit of effort, but this is typical of single-pump pneumatics and is easily manageable by most adults. From a safety standpoint, one interesting feature of the pumping mechanism is the addition of a sliding lock that prevents the pump lever from snapping open.

Extensive testing of the Model 100 merely affirmed that the rifle is as accurate as it looks, which is to say it can hit a pinhead at 10 meters, shot after shot. The excellent match sights supplied are easy to adjust and can be used for longer-range shooting as well. Since I am not a habitual 10-meter paper puncher, I eventually replaced the diopter sight with a big 4-12x parallax-adjustable airgun scope and began scoring seemingly impossible hits on all sorts of small targets way out to 35 yards. Most of the shooting was done with RWS Meisterkugeln match pellets, but excellent results were also obtained with H&N and other world-class brands. The Model 100 can certainly place those pellets with razor-sharp accuracy at all ranges up to around 50 yards.

The RWS/Diana Model 100 is a superb example of the long and proud tradition of Dianawerk as one of the true giants in the field of world-class match airguns.

J.I. Galan

Herr Peter Mayer, owner of the world-famous Dianawerk in Rastatt, Germany, proudly displays a Model 100 at the SHOT Show.

Skan Bullpup Rifle

ABOUT SIX YEARS ago, I saw a small article written about a double-barreled airgun. I was intrigued, so I called everyone I knew in England to find out about this rifle, but no one knew anything about it. After awhile, I gave up on it. A few years later, I was talking to a friend in the U.K. who makes chronographs and repeating air rifles about this mystery gun. I asked him if he could put me in touch with the maker, and he told me I was talking to him! Mike Childs, the builder of the Skan Bullpup, was the same guy who masterminded the Double Express air rifle and all of those Skan chronographs.

Now we go from a guy building a classic-looking double air rifle to a military-look, slide-actuated, precharged pneumatic repeating air rifle that can hold about eighty rounds of ammo in its magazine and shoot accurately. Childs' reason for producing this gun was twofold. The idea of his Double Express was to have the quickest second shot in airgundom, but the problem was the third shot. You needed to stop and pump the darn thing up to resume shooting. This prompted him to come up with a way to get that third shot, and a fourth and a fifth. He felt the precharged path was the way to go and designed a repeater based on compressed air. Secondly, the

SKAN BULLPUP SPECIFICATIONS

Power:	Precharged pneumatic
Caliber:	177, 22
Barrel:	17 ins.; Lothar Walther
Weight:	8 lbs.
Overall Length:	34 ins.
Sights:	None furnished
Trigger:	2 lbs.; single stage
Muzzle Velocity:	700 fps (22)
Cocking Effort:	NA

Double Express took him so long to build that he only made about 50 pence per hour. He earned so little he was getting faint from the lack of food (this made the building of the Double Express even slower).

The Skan Bullpup was not meant to be a military look-alike; it just ended up that way because of Childs' desire to make the gun functional. The Skan Bullpup is all business. There are no illusions of style and grace, just rough and tumble function. Black anodized aluminum, cap-head screws, extrusions, springs,

The full-size Skan Bullpup is available in a choice of either practical plastic furniture (above) or with walnut grip, butt and forend, for those who prefer a more traditional rifle.

247

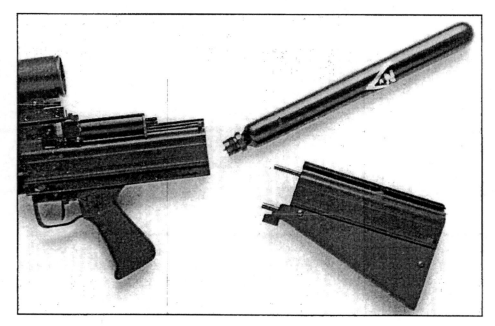

The Skan's air bottle can be easily accessed by removing the buttstock.

mil-spec plastic parts and heavy steel are all muckled into a creation that looks like a air-soft gun on steroids—but the thing can shoot accurately and fast.

The first time I shot a Skan Bullpup in my basement, standing 15 yards from the target box, it surprised me. My expectations were low as I placed the red dot of the unmagnified sight on the 10-meter pistol target and shot as fast as I could pump the forend to load new pellets. Eight pellets went downrange lickety-split. Afterward, I walked toward the target to see how much damage was done to the basement wall. To my delight, I found a 50mm eight-shot group smack in the middle of the black area of the target and no fliers on the wall. This Skan was more than just an ugly face, it was shootable and fast. I ran up the basement stairs, waving this

target in front of my wife, who said, "Very nice," patted me on the head and told me to wash the dishes. I said, "After I see how many shots I get out of the air bottle," and bolted down the stairs. Thirty-two plus the previous eight equals forty. Forty shots in 22-caliber at about 700 fps. This is cool—I can get sixty-four Z-2 pellets in the rotary magazine and around forty shots per 2700 psi air bottle. I then went upstairs and washed the dishes.

The Skan Bullpup is not a target airgun; it is a hand-built repeater made for hunting, vermin control and rough service. It is accurate, but if you are wishing for little ragged one-hole groups at 50 yards, look elsewhere. Don't look for a better-made airgun, but for better pellets. Mike claims sub-$\frac{1}{2}$-inch groups with Bisley Magnums at 50 yards in 22-caliber are pos-

The Skan has a unique high-capacity pellet magazine and interesting follower.

This Mini Bullpup sports a shorter barrel, which adds less overall weight. This specimen has walnut furniture.

sible. One of the two Skans I shot is set up for Barracudas (Bisley Magnums/Kodiaks) and the other for Paragon Z-2s. Both are 22s. Mike prefers this caliber, because, just like any other precharged airgun, it is more efficient in its use of bottled air than 177.

The Skan Bullpup is set up like a military rifle with a pistol grip and most of the weight between your shoulder and trigger hand. The Skan is heavy—around 9 pounds—but the balance is so good you forget about the weight. Most of its mass comes from the steel air bottle hidden within the stock. It is so well balanced that you can hold it out at arm's length like an overgrown pistol and shoot. The valve assembly is attached to the air bottle, so when you unscrew and remove the bottle from the airgun, the gun cannot fire, regardless of whether there are pellets in the magazine or not. This is a boon for households with curious children. The other good part is the whole valve assembly can be rebuilt without dismantling the gun. Additionally, if you have an air bottle valve go south when you're up north hunting, all you have to do is swap bottles and go shooting, then replace or clean the simple O-rings later.

The astute reader will notice a similarity between the Skan and the Crosman 600, but the similarity is only skin-deep. The Skan has many differences not noticeable at first blush. The cam that picks up the pellet is of the double-action variety. It not only moves left to right to pick up and load the pellet, but it slides fore and aft, too, to keep the mechanism from jamming. The cam on the Skan is adaptable/adjustable to a variety of pellet lengths. One of the Skans I have can shoot Paragon Z-2s, Magnums and Bisley Pest Control pellets interspersed in the magazine without adjustment.

I keep talking about the magazine and have explained nothing about it yet. The magazine is indexed with a ball bearing detent. Pump the forend and slap the trigger until the slot is out of pellets, and then draw back the spring-loaded follower, turn the magazine one click around, release the follower and resume shooting. The first time I loaded sixty-four Z-2s into the Skan I

SKAN MINI SPECIFICATIONS

Power:	Precharged pneumatic
Caliber:	22
Barrel:	11 ins.; Lothar Walther
Weight:	7 1/2 lbs.
Overall Length:	28 ins.
Sights:	None furnished
Trigger:	2 lbs.; single stage
Muzzle Velocity:	Approx. 700 fps
Cocking Effort:	NA

said, "Geez, this takes a while to load," not to mention it left only a few pellets in the box. But then I remembered it takes just as much time to load my single shot airguns; I just do it one pellet at a time. After you load sixty-four pellets into the Skan (your results may vary depending on pellet length), the only times you need to pause from shooting are when you use the sight, advance (rotate) the magazine and change air bottles after about forty 18 to 20 foot pound shots.

How can I wrap up such a glowing review? With caution. The Skan is a fun airgun. It is also a sort of complicated device; not overwhelmingly so, but there are lots of things to consider to use it safely. I don't mean to scare anyone, but you have to pay attention to what you are doing. Any gun/airgun that loads itself bears watching. Once you understand how the Skan functions and know what can go wrong, that is the time to watch out. A single shot airgun is either loaded or unloaded, and this can be determined rather easily. The Skan, with its ability to hold sixty-four pellets and the precharged airpower to fire at least forty of them, can confuse. My advice is to read and reread the instructions right off. Discharge the gun in a safe direction and remove the air bottle if in doubt. Err on the side of safety.

Ben Saltzman

249

Sportsman
Model QB22 Rifle

I RECALL IT was miserably humid and hot that particular morning. Very hot, in fact. The year was 1969, and it was another typical mid-summer day in southeast Michigan. I had been making my way slowly along a favorite creek bed, its banks eroded almost vertically by decades of spring flooding, rising some 15-20 feet in many places. Exposed tree roots hung menacingly down to the water's edge, and a recent heavy rain had so thoroughly saturated the bank walls that foot travel was difficult at best, if not downright treacherous. And then, of course, there was the water itself. Years of industrial pollution from several nearby automotive plants had taken their toll as well. Add a dash of raw sewage for good measure, and what wildlife had managed to survive did so in an extremely precarious environment. Still, this was my creek.

I had been harassing the local grackle population, using the creek bank for cover while maneuvering into shooting position. Just beyond the effective range of my pet Crosman 160

SPORTMAN MODEL QB22 SPECIFICATIONS	
Power:	CO$_2$; two 12-gram cartridges or bulk-fill
Caliber:	22
Barrel:	20^1/$_2$ ins.
Weight:	5^3/$_4$ lbs.
Overall Length:	40 ins.
Sights:	Fully adjustable square notch rear, blade front
Trigger:	Single stage; adjustable
Muzzle Velocity:	Approx. 635 fps
Cocking Effort:	NA
Source:	Air Rifle Specialists, Inc.

(a late SP version with adjustable trigger, match peep sight and leather sling), there remained another 30 yards or so to negotiate before reaching the next firing point. Edging my way the last few yards, I had only to round a slight bend when the rain-soaked earth beneath me started to fall away.

The QB22 was found to be quite accurate and very ammo tolerant.

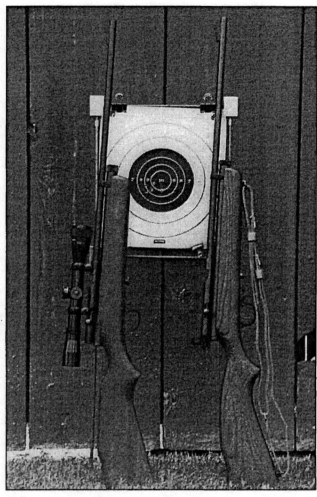

Back with us once more, the new Sportsman QB22 (left) is a line-for-line copy of the classic late-model Crosman 160 bolt-action, CO$_2$-powered rifle (right). Best of all, it's a 22! Both guns are equally well made, though the QB22 has the edge on performance.

Not especially alarmed at first, I quickly back-pedaled to regain my footing, while simultaneously grabbing for a handful of the aforementioned exposed tree roots. Lucky me, those particular roots were rotten to the core. Mistake number one. Now realizing that, in all probability, I would indeed be taking an unscheduled dip, saving the rifle from a similar fate received top priority. With just seconds to react, I seized upon the idea of tossing the unloaded gun to either side of me (allowing it to land reasonably unscathed in the soft mud below) or across the creek itself, which was only about 15 feet wide at that point. For some unknown reason that eludes me to this day, I chose the latter option. Mistake number two. Like an Olympic high diver, the rifle arced picturesquely out over the stream, but instead of landing on the opposite bank, it met up with yet another clump of exposed tree roots. Not the least bit rotten this time, the gun rebounded back toward open water. It landed smack dab center, and in the deepest part, too. Figures.

After forty-five minutes of probing the muddy creek bottom with a stick, the rifle was finally located and retrieved. It was then immediately taken home to be completely stripped and cleaned, but the gun never seemed to shoot as well afterward. Sometime later, the almost-new rifle was traded in for a popular pneumatic model, the excuse being that it cost too much to operate. Mistake number three.

As the years passed, I would come to deeply regret that decision. With Crosman discontinuing the Model 160 in 1970, the supply of new guns quickly dried up, leaving only second-hand examples available. Then again, I didn't want someone else's basket-case rifle—I yearned for a *new* gun. Fat chance of that happening, right?

Well, it did happen. Unveiled for the first time at the 1992 SHOT Show, the Sportsman QB77 was virtually a line-for-line reproduction of the classic late-model Crosman 167. The 177-caliber, CO$_2$-powered, bolt-action rifle would also be offered in both Standard and Deluxe versions, with the latter

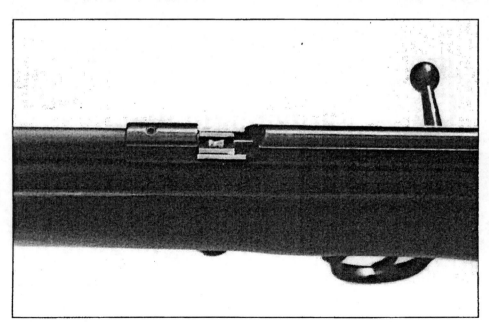

Pellets are loaded in conventional single shot fashion. Operation is quick and effortless.

type featuring a high-performance valve and bulk-fill CO_2 adapter.

The real surprise, though, was the fact that the gun was made in China. Not your typical crude Chinese model, the QB77 was every bit the equal of the much-lamented Crosman. This wasn't simply by chance either, as the idea for the reproduction project came from old Crosman pro Tim McMurray of Southern California. Together with his collaborator, Henry Harn—a Chinese engineer also living in the L.A. area—they conceived a plan to reverse-engineer the venerable American rifle, using one of McMurray's custom guns as a design platform. It was a little less than a year later when the first production rifles hit the streets. Beautifully made, inexpensive and a terrific shooter to boot, the QB77 was well received by gas gun fans. Still, for me anyway, this was a 177-caliber version, and although a good performer, it just wasn't the classic 22-caliber model of my youth.

There would indeed be a 22 rifle, albeit it took another year to arrive. Well worth the wait, the new Sportsman QB22 is now here, and like the earlier 177 model, it's available in both Standard and Deluxe versions, with the latter featuring the aforementioned tuned valve and bulk-fill CO_2 adapter.

A precise reproduction in almost every detail, the QB22 naturally mirrors Crosman 160 series specs. Overall length is

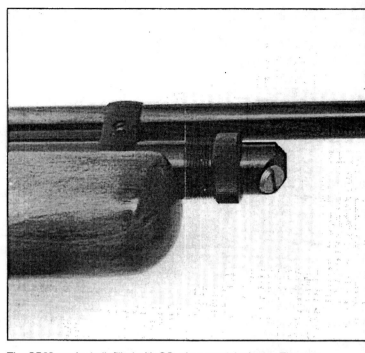

The QB22 can be bulk-filled with CO_2 via a special adapter. The unit is a clone of Crosman's original adapter.

Offhand, the QB22 handles remarkably well. Weighing just under 6 pounds, field carry is no problem either.

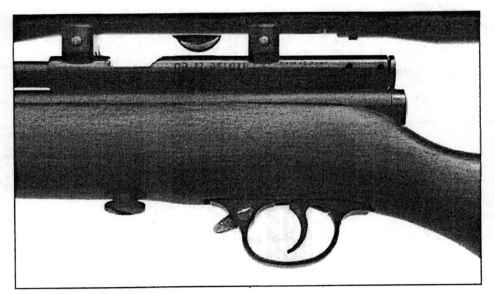

Acknowledged as one of its best features, the QB22 sports a three-way adjustable, single-stage trigger. The manual lever-bar safety is housed in the trigger guard and can be reversed to suit right- or left-handers. The receiver is grooved for easy scope mounting and is also drilled and tapped for a Crosman-pattern match peep sight.

exactly 40 inches, and unloaded weight hovers around 5 3/4 pounds. Pull and forend length also follow suit, measuring 14 1/4 inches and 11 inches, respectively, while the twelve-groove button-rifled barrel comes in at 20 1/2 inches. Factory-issue sights are the traditional Crosman-pattern ramped blade up front and the usual square notch at the rear. The latter unit adjusts for elevation via a stepped elevator, while windage is handled by loosening two Phillips-head screws and drifting the sight blade as required. The new gun's breech is also grooved for scope use, and drilled and tapped to accommodate a Crosman-pattern match peep sight.

Acknowledged as one of the 160 series' key features, the QB22's single-stage trigger is the same three-way adjustable unit. Precisely tunable for sear engagement, weight and overtravel, the stock must be removed to gain access to the unit's controls. The unitized trigger block assembly/guard also houses a manual lever-bar safety, which is located just forward of the blade. The trigger is nicely curved and sports a grooved face, allowing more positive finger contact when triggering the shot.

The rifle is powered by two 12-gram CO_2 cartridges (or bulk-filled via a special adapter), and the charging format is basic for its genre. First, the breech bolt is retracted fully to the rear and the safety engaged. The piercing cap is then removed and two 12-gram CO_2 cartridges are inserted back-to-back into the compression tube. (Crosman Powerlets are recommended.) After replacing the piercing cap (hand-tighten only, please), the cap is given a quick quarter-turn counterclockwise to pierce the front cartridge. Closing the action and dry firing the rifle in a safe direction pierces the rear cartridge.

Bulk charging follows the same aforementioned procedures, although the standard piercing cap is replaced with an adapter. Easily threaded to the gun's compression tube, the unit will accept the older 10-ounce Crosman fill tank or any modern equivalent with 1/4-inch threads. Charging takes roughly 6 to 8 seconds to complete, by the way.

Whether charged via CO_2 cartridges or bulk-filled, the test gun (a Deluxe version) delivered forty to fifty usable shots,

which is virtually identical to the 177-caliber model. However, due primarily to its larger (and thus more efficient) bore size, the QB22's ballistic performance was superior by 3 to 4 foot pounds. As predicted, standard-weight 22-caliber pellets in the 14- to 15-grain range produced energy levels averaging 11 1/2 to 12 1/2 foot pounds, respectively, over the course of twenty-five shots. The highest muzzle energy was obtained with 21-plus-grain Beeman Kodiak, averaging 13 1/4 foot pounds for the first twenty-five shots.

The Model 160 was originally developed for the NRA's 25-foot marksmanship training program, and knowledgeable shooters soon discovered the gun was capable of respectable field accuracy. The QB22 also proved to be extremely ammo tolerant, grouping remarkably well with a wide range of pellet brands. As a matter of fact, so much so that determining a real standout was difficult at best. At 10 meters, the 13.9-grain RWS Diabolo held a slight edge over several other popular 22-caliber wadcutters, averaging .40-inch center-to-center for five shots. This pellet also performed quite well out to 30 yards, printing five-shot groups that averaged just over 1 inch center-to-center. Dominating the long-range accuracy race were a mixed bag of popular round-head pellets. Despite rather windy conditions at the test range, most brands would routinely group around 1 to 1 1/2 inches center-to-center at 30 yards. Again, there were few obvious standouts, although I recommend Crosman Dome (or Benjamin Sheridan Dome), Marksman FTS, RWS Superdome, Eley Wasp and Beeman Kodiak as prime candidates for most field sport applications.

A classic single shot American CO_2 rifle is back with us once more, thanks to the Sportsman QB22. Covered by a limited 90-day warranty, the QB22 is fully supported by its North American distributor, with reliable factory authorized service available right here in the U.S. The rifle is also accompanied by the most comprehensive and easily understood owner's manual you'll find anywhere. It's been a long time coming, but an old friend and I are going for a walk along a favorite creek.

Stephen R. Gibbons

253

Sterling Model HR83 Rifle

FOR THOSE NOT familiar with the history of the Sterling air rifle, allow me to give you a short update. The Sterling Model HR81 was introduced in England about fifteen years ago. Its manufacturer, Sterling Armament Co., Ltd., is one of the U.K.'s leading producers of military small arms, perhaps best known for their famous Sterling submachine gun, which has been in widespread use throughout the U.K. and many other countries for decades.

Sterling decided to take a crack at an expanding airgun market and the Model HR81 became their initial offering, followed a short time later by the more elegant Model HR83. From the beginning, the Sterling air rifle was well received in its native country. The British airgun press gave it mostly good reviews, and the rifle was even briefly imported into the U.S. by a small entrepreneur, although it was never available in any significant numbers.

By late 1983, it was announced, much to everyone's surprise, that Sterling had sold their entire airgun operation to the Benjamin Sheridan Company of Racine, Wisconsin. Apparently, Sterling decided to stick to the manufacture of military hardware, despite their initial success with the HR81. All of this meant that America's oldest maker of *pneumatic* guns was now going to be the first company in this country to manufacture an adult spring-piston air rifle.

Then came a rather extensive wait. First, there were technical problems regarding the machinery shipped over here from England. Rumors were rife in American airgun circles as the months turned into years and still no Sterlings were forthcoming from Benjamin Sheridan. I even remember hearing at one point that

STERLING MODEL HR83 SPECIFICATIONS

Power:	Spring-piston; underlever cocking
Caliber:	177, 20, 22
Barrel:	18 1/2 ins.; rifled steel
Weight:	9 lbs.
Overall Length:	42 ins.
Sights:	Williams peep rear with click knobs, tunnel front with interchangeable elements
Trigger:	3 1/2 lbs.; single stage
Muzzle Velocity:	740 fps (177)
	640 fps (20,22)
Cocking Effort:	NA
Source:	Benjamin Sheridan (discontinued 1994)

the entire project had been scrubbed. Benjamin Sheridan was decidedly aloof during all of this, saying only that the Sterling would come out in due course—presumably after all the "bugs" had been worked out of the rifle. At last, however, by late 1985 the Sterlings began rolling off the assembly line up in Racine. So much for history.

The first thing that draws attention to the Sterling is its somewhat unique bolt-action loading system. The design has been common in pneumatic and CO_2 rifles for years, but it is definitely unusual in a spring-piston air rifle. In the Sterling, the bolt-action mechanism is housed in a tube that sits atop the compression cylinder, directly behind the barrel. This arrangement makes the Sterling look rather like a pneumatic or CO_2 rifle, which, of course, it isn't. In fact, at first glance

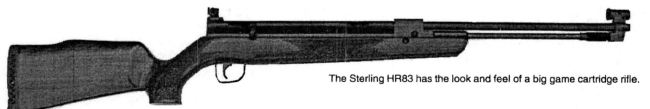

The Sterling HR83 has the look and feel of a big game cartridge rifle.

it does resemble the old and venerable Crosman 160 CO_2 bolt-action rifle.

The Sterling's spring-piston power plant is cocked by means of a sturdy lever located under the barrel. The front end of the lever has a spring-loaded latch that engages firmly in a receptacle at the bottom of the front sight assembly.

The Model HR83 Deluxe has a genuine American walnut stock with a medium glossy finish. There is exquisite hand-cut checkering (not impressed, mind you) on both sides of the forend and on the large pistol grip. The stock also sports a Monte Carlo-style cheekpiece and a thick, ventilated rubber recoil pad. The plain Model HR81 also has a walnut stock, but it has no checkering or cheekpiece. I found out quickly that the stock of the HR83 fit me almost perfectly, coming up to the shoulder with ease, despite the rifle's hefty weight of 9 pounds. The overall length is 42 inches, by the way.

Another difference between the HR81 and the HR83 is the rear sight. The HR81 came with an adjustable open rear sight. In contrast, the HR83 has a Williams peep sight unit, fully adjustable by means of micrometer click knobs. Both models have tunnel front sights that accept different inserts. My original test rifle came with three of these. In addition, the top of the receiver on both models is grooved for scopes with 3/8-inch dovetail bases.

The British-made Sterlings had single-stage adjustable triggers. It was tricky at best to carry out any adjustments, though. The American-made Sterlings also have single-stage triggers, but there is no provision for adjustment. At least, I didn't find any, and the instruction manual that came with the rifle didn't mention it. Some shooters undoubtedly will object to the lack of adjustment in this critical area. At any rate, the test rifle had a decent enough trigger pull weight of about 3 1/2 pounds. The

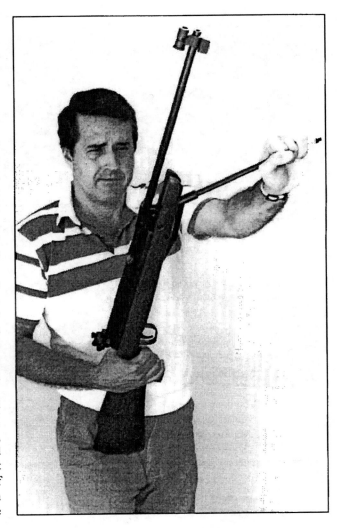

(Above) Cocking the HR83 does not require Herculean effort.

The bolt-action loading mechanism of the Sterling is unique among spring-piston air rifles.

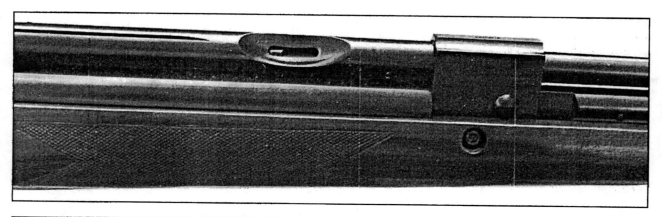

Opening the bolt allows the shooter to place a pellet on the loading trough.

(Left) The HR83 comes with a neat Williams rear peep sight. The trigger safety-lever was added to the design by Benjamin Sheridan.

The pistol grip and forend areas of the HR83 stock are checkered to allow a non-slip hold.

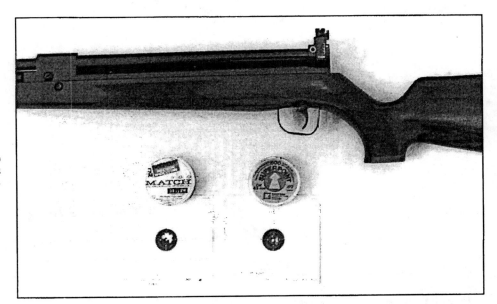

At 10 meters, the Sterling gave near-match accuracy with a variety of pellets.

single-stage pull was consistently crisp, with no wobbliness whatsoever.

A manual safety mechanism was added to the trigger by Benjamin Sheridan. It consists of a lever on the left side of the trigger and positively locks it when pulled all the way down and to the rear.

One of the things that stands out right away about this rifle is its solid steel construction throughout. The Sterling feels like it's built to last a lifetime and more. I did not detect any plastic parts anywhere. Even the trigger guard, which nowadays is nearly always made of plastic or alloy, is made of steel.

Having an underlever cocking mechanism means, of course, the gun has a rigid barrel. There have been many arguments over the years regarding the supposed advantage of a rigid-barrel air rifle over a barrel-cocking gun. Some pundits insist that a fixed barrel gun is more accurate than a barrel-cocker in the same class. They allege that there are minute discrepancies in barrel lock-up from shot to shot in the barrel-cocker which obviously can't exist in a fixed-barrel gun. While I am not about to step into this controversy here, I can tell you that the 177-caliber Sterling on test was capable of razor-sharp accuracy with a variety of match and sporting pellets.

The impressive accuracy of the Sterling can probably be traced directly to the fact that the barrels for these rifles came from Lothar Walther in Germany, long known as one of the best makers of precision barrels in the world. Most groups fired at 10 meters, from the sitting position, could be easily covered by a dime. At 30 yards, I had no difficulty keeping all shots inside a 3/4-inch circle. As one of the nearby photos shows, the groups obtained speak for themselves. All tests were conducted using the rifle's peep sight.

The Sterling's solid construction and cartridge rifle looks probably will lead some folks to the conclusion that this is a magnum-class rifle. Well, not really. If you're looking for a magnum blaster, then the Sterling is not for you.

Don't get me wrong, though. I wouldn't laugh at average

muzzle velocities in the 740 fps range (in 177), even with lightweight pellets, such as RWS Hobby and Beeman Laser. Those muzzle velocities are not enough to earn the Sterling a place among the magnums, but they're certainly more than good enough to do just about anything that an air rifle can be expected to do, including pest control. Rabbits and squirrels can be quickly and efficiently nailed at up to 30 yards or so with this rifle, especially in view of its respectable precision.

Heavier pellets of various configurations brought the average muzzle velocities down to around 720 fps. The firing behavior was surprisingly mild, due in great part to the sheer massiveness of the rifle. The sedate power accounts for an extremely low report on firing, consistent with that normally found in youth-oriented BB-guns. I also found that you don't have to be a weightlifter to cock this gun, even for long shooting periods. The cocking effort is well within the capabilities of most able-bodied people past the age of twelve.

The Sterling deserves top marks for overall workmanship and performance, particularly in the area of accuracy. It is perhaps a tad too heavy and mild to be considered an out-and-out field rifle, although it could nicely fill that bill if required, as long as the distances are kept reasonable. The Model HR83 is definitely more at home on the target range. Both the HR81 and HR83 were made in 20 and 22 calibers as well, with muzzle velocities of about 640 fps in both calibers. The Sterling air rifle, in either configuration, was truly an outstanding example of spring-piston technology that crossed the Atlantic and benefitted from good ol' Yankee know-how.

In mid-1994, the folks at Benjamin Sheridan decided to remove the Sterling from their lineup, apparently due to slow sales. That's too bad, because the gun is a solid, reliable performer. I really deplore its demise, but the realities of the current airgun market apparently dictate such a course of action. This is, after all, the age of the magnum air rifle, and not too many folks are willing to pay serious money for a sporting-class air rifle— no matter how well made—of medium power.

J.I.Galan

Steyr
CO₂ Match 91 Rifle

THE STEYR CO₂ Match rifle carries all of the features that any serious 10-meter shooter could want, and then some. The rifle measures 44¹/₂ inches overall and weighs 10¹/₂ pounds. Additional barrel weights can be purchased as accessories, available in 50- and 100-gram units that fit between the two barrel sleeve weights that come with the gun. These weights can, incidentally, be positioned along the barrel to suit the shooter's preference regarding the rifle's balance.

As befits a world-class match rifle, the Steyr CO₂ comes with a massive laminated stock that is a sheer pleasure to look at. The beauty of the stock, however, belies the fact that it has been carefully designed to meet the most rigorous practical demands of international-style 10-meter events. The thick rubber buttplate can be adjusted for length, height and lateral angle. The cheekpiece is adjustable for height and cant. One clever feature is that the sights can be moved around the bore axis, up to a maximum of 15 degrees to either side of their normal position. This, combined with the stock adjustments, allows quite a range of changes to adapt the rifle fully to the shooter's individual stance and style.

The trigger system is also top-notch with a choice of adjustments that include height of the trigger blade, length of first-stage travel, rotation and lateral displacement. The let-off weight can be increased from an ultra-light 30 grams (1.05 ounces) all the way up to 200 grams (7 ounces). Each rifle, however, leaves the factory with its trigger set at 80 grams (2.8 ounces). Dedicated match shooters who like to engage in dry-fire practice will find that the Steyr is also equipped with

STEYR CO₂ MATCH 91 SPECIFICATIONS	
Power:	CO₂ reservoir
Caliber:	177
Barrel:	23³/₄ ins. (13³/₄ ins. rifled)
Weight:	10¹/₂ lbs.
Overall Length:	44¹/₂ ins.
Sights:	Match; peep rear, tunnel front; sight radius 32 ins.
Trigger:	Adjustable
Muzzle Velocity:	577 fps
Cocking Effort:	NA
Source:	Nygord Precision Products

a mechanism that permits dry-firing without damaging the rifle.

The 177-caliber cold-hammer-forged barrel is one reason for the superb precision of this rifle. Although the barrel measures approximately 24 inches overall, the actual rifled part is only 13³/₄ inches long. Many of the newest world-class air rifles sport similarly short rifling as it has been shown that more length is not really needed to ensure top precision. At any rate, the Steyr's pinpoint accuracy is ample proof that the short rifled bore works.

One of the principal advantages of CO₂ operation in a match rifle is the lack of effort required to cock the gun. Unlike spring-piston and pneumatic rifles, CO₂ guns do not have a long and sometimes bothersome cocking or pumping lever. Therefore, the shooter is less fatigued by the shot-to-shot operation of the

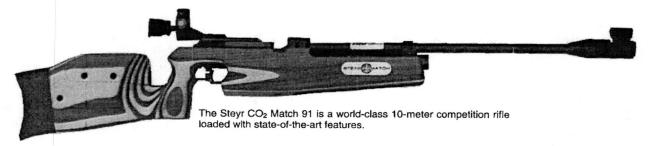

The Steyr CO₂ Match 91 is a world-class 10-meter competition rifle loaded with state-of-the-art features.

The Steyr's match trigger incorporates a wide range of adjustments to suit the individual shooter. Galan found the rifle a delight to shoot.

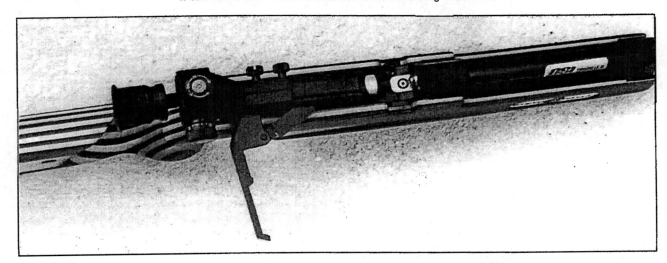

The short-throw cocking lever requires little effort to operate.

The laminated stock of the Steyr CO_2 Match 91 rifle is beautiful yet practical. Both the buttpad and cheekpiece are adjustable in various ways.

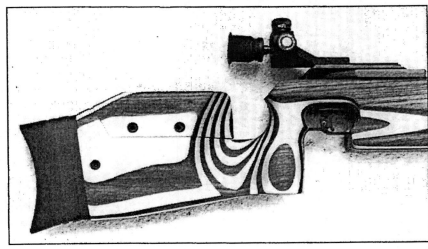

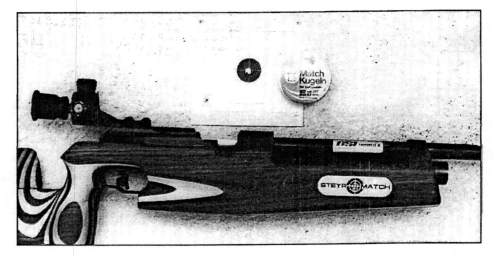

There is no question that the Steyr is capable of world-class precision at 10 meters, as this target shows.

(Right) Cocking the rifle simultaneously exposes the breech for direct pellet insertion.

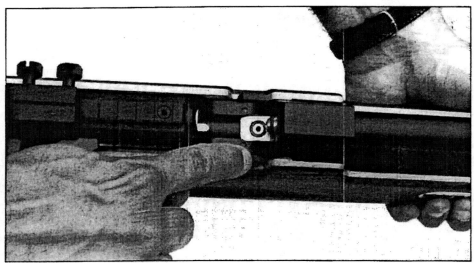

(Below) The Steyr CO_2 Match 91 comes with two muzzle weights. The front and rear sights can be canted 15 degrees to right or left. The barrel sleeve extends some 11 inches beyond the rifled portion of the barrel.

gun and can concentrate more on aiming and firing. The Steyr's short cocking lever requires only minimal effort to operate. Pulling it back also exposes the breech end of the barrel for easy manual pellet insertion. As for CO_2 capacity, each of the two slender cylinders supplied with the Steyr will give about 250 shots when fully pressurized. They can be easily filled from a medium-size CO_2 tank by means of a threaded adapter supplied with the gun.

I always find it a pleasure to test a super-accurate match rifle, and the Steyr was no exception. Single-hole accuracy was the rule when firing from the bench at 10 meters. The muzzle velocity was a sedate 577 fps, which is average for most of the top world-class match air rifles. The Steyr is so precise, even off-hand, that one soon gets the impression that any target the shooter can see, even out to 35 or 40 yards, can be hit without fail.

Although it carries a hefty price tag of over $1400, the many refinements and razor-sharp accuracy make it an excellent example of a rifle that would be right at home in the Olympics, or simply in the hands of those who can appreciate state-of-the-art technology combined with old-world craftsmanship.

J.I. Galan

Swivel Machine Works Airrow Model A-6 Pistol

ONE OF THE most unusual airguns produced during the past half-dozen years shoots neither BBs nor pellets. As a matter of fact, the gun is so far removed from the ordinary that its legal status might be a bit fuzzy in some states as far as hunting applications are concerned. Consider, for example, having a handgun-sized airgun capable of shooting special hunting arrows at a muzzle velocity of up to 375 fps, or a rifle-sized model that can launch arrows tipped with razor-sharp broadheads at nearly 600 fps using compressed air.

Those velocities are produced by the Airrow airguns made by Swivel Machine Works, Inc. Initially, there were three basic Airrow models: the Series 10, Series 8 and Series 6. The first two were marketed in 1989, while the Series 6 made its debut a year or so later. The Series 10 is a harpoon- and line-throwing gun intended mainly for marine rescue and spear fishing applications. The Series 8—which is the mainstay of the whole Airrow line—is a high-power hunting/target gun that can shoot Easton aluminum arrows at about twice the velocity generated by the most powerful crossbows currently available. A newer version of the Series 8 can be had with

AIRROW MODEL A-6 SPECIFICATIONS	
Power:	CO_2 or compressed air to 1800 psi
Caliber:	Arrows
Barrel:	10¾ ins.
Weight:	1.2 lbs.
Overall Length:	16½ ins.
Sights:	Fully adjustable peep rear; bead front
Trigger:	Adjustable
Muzzle Velocity:	357 fps (#2512 arrow)
	450 fps (#1608 arrow)
Cocking Effort:	NA
Source:	Swivel Machine Works, Inc.

rifled barrels in 25 and other calibers in order to shoot bullet-shaped projectiles.

I had the opportunity to test an early Series 8 model at some length several years ago and found it to be nothing short of awesome. The quality of workmanship was of the highest order, rivaling that of many top-notch firearms and airguns. Its performance was also most impressive, delivering terrific accuracy

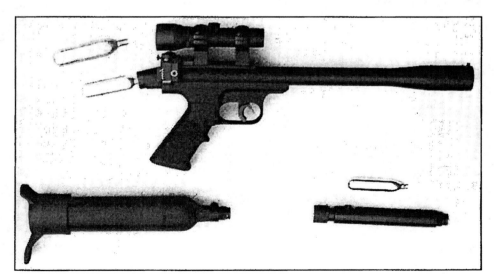

The Airrow Series 6 accepts a wide range of CO_2 sources, as well as compressed air.

Galan puts the Airrow Series 6 through its paces in its mini-carbine configuration. The 7-ounce CO_2 bottle/shoulder stock yields around forty shots in this gun.

out to about 25 yards, with a practical range of about three times that distance. Of course, all that quality and performance are reflected in a retail price of about $1700 for the current Model A-8S1P Stealth.

In an effort to make the Airrow concept more affordable, the maker developed the more compact and somewhat less power-

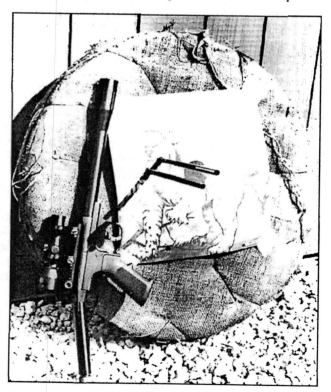

This gun is capable of superior accuracy, as shown by these two arrows fired at 30 yards.

ful Model A-6, which retails for about $600. Although initially only 125 Model A-6 guns were made, the maker reportedly still has some available. In addition, they haven't ruled out continued production of this gun, depending upon future demand. In any event, this is an intriguing airgun that definitely deserves a closer look.

In its basic configuration, the Airrow Model A-6 is a pistol that, due to its modular design, can be turned into a nifty mini-carbine. This is easily accomplished by using a standard 7-ounce CO_2 bottle that doubles as a shoulder stock. The A-6 comes with a 10³/₄-inch barrel, but 16- and 20-inch barrels to shoot longer arrows are also available.

Besides the 7-ounce CO_2 bottle, the A-6 can be powered by standard 12-gram CO_2 cartridges of the type used in most CO_2 guns. In addition, larger CO_2 cartridges of 16 and 25 grams—available at marine supply outlets—can be used with a special adapter. The regular 12-gram cartridges can deliver three to four shots each, while the 16- and 25-gram cartridges can give up to six and eight shots, respectively. In contrast, a fully charged 7-ounce bottle packs sufficient oomph for up to forty shots.

It's amazing how light this gun really is. In its mini-carbine configuration with 7-ounce CO_2 bottle, RWS CS-10 scope and 10³/₄-inch barrel loaded with a broadhead-tipped arrow, the A-6 tips the scales at just 3¹/₄ pounds. The low weight is due to the aircraft-grade aluminum and stainless steel used in the construction of the gun, which also means it can be subjected to heavy use and keep on shooting reliably. Standard equipment for the A-6 includes a fully adjustable Williams peep sight. The front is a shotgun-style bead mounted on the removable muzzle guard. The rear sight rests on a dovetail base that permits use of a scope with tip-off rings. I mounted the RWS CS-10 compact scope with see-through rings, permitting an instant switch to iron sights, if required.

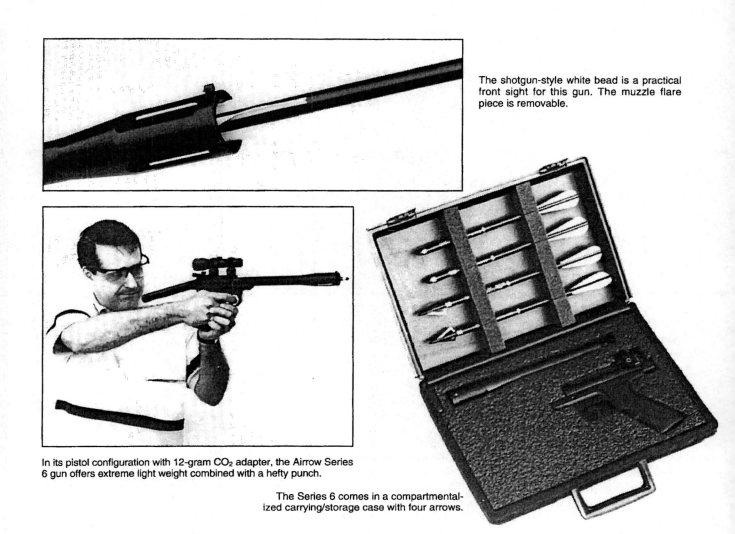

The shotgun-style white bead is a practical front sight for this gun. The muzzle flare piece is removable.

In its pistol configuration with 12-gram CO_2 adapter, the Airrow Series 6 gun offers extreme light weight combined with a hefty punch.

The Series 6 comes in a compartmentalized carrying/storage case with four arrows.

Another unique feature of the Airrow A-6 is its adjustable trigger. Although conventional in appearance, it must be snapped rather than squeezed slowly in order to fire reliably. This takes a bit of getting used to, as far as keeping the gun on target is concerned, but can be mastered without too much difficulty. The reason for this unusual design is that the trigger acts directly upon the main valve. Thus, the number of shots and the velocity of the arrows can actually be regulated through trigger adjustment.

The aluminum arrows used in Airrow guns are open at the base. The arrow is placed over the thin self-aligning inner barrel—protected by the solid shroud—and pushed all the way down until fully seated. A rotating motion is used to twist the plastic vanes into a spiral that will act as "rifling" when the shot is fired, spinning and thus stabilizing the arrow along its flight trajectory. Unlike conventional crossbows, which push their bolts from the base with a string, the Airrow releases a jet of CO_2 or compressed air inside the arrow, blasting it out of the gun with tremendous speed and accuracy. Incidentally, compressed air will produce about 100 fps more than CO_2 in these guns, but CO_2 does yield more shot-to-shot consistency in velocity. The A-6 is so accurate that, firing from 15 yards, I had to deliberately change the point of aim on the target in order to avoid splitting the previously fired arrow. Now that's accuracy!

One quickly realizes the tremendous hunting potential of this super-compact gun after firing a few shots. I can also discern a variety of uses in the hands of anti-terrorist operatives and other special hush-hush units needing a quiet, yet powerful and accurate weapon for certain special jobs. The noise level of the A-6, by the way, is comparable to that of a regular CO_2 pistol, while the recoil—yes, there is some—is akin to that of a 22 rimfire.

Undoubtedly, the Airrow Model A-6 qualifies as a magnum airgun in every respect. A $10^3/_4$-inch arrow weighing 89 grains and leaving the gun at, say, 350 fps, has a kinetic energy a tad over 24 foot pounds, which is nothing to laugh at. This is particularly true if the arrow carries one of those shaving-grade broadhead tips. In addition to regular arrows, the A-6 can also shoot special tranquilizer syringe bolts for capturing larger animals.

The Airrow A-6 is one heck of an interesting piece. Hopefully, it will remain in production. In any case, the A-6 is sure to become a highly prized collector's item in the foreseeable future.

J.I. Galan

263

Whiscombe
JW-60 Fixed-Barrel Rifle

JOHN WHISCOMBE HAS been building airguns ever since he took a look at a BSA Meteor about twelve years ago. John realized that if he could use two pistons moving toward each other, he could have an airgun with no recoil and more power. The tricky part was getting the two pistons to move in sync. In his tiny garage/workshop in England, John worked out the details on how to make a practical air rifle with two opposing pistons. The solution was to gear the two pistons together. With this direct mechanical link, the two pistons moved as one. The first production Whiscombe air rifles had a flip-up barrel for direct loading of a pellet into the breech and an underlever for cocking, plus an excellent trigger.

The development of the Whiscombe air rifle has been one of constant evolution. Whenever John has an inspiration, he puts it to the test in one of his personal guns. If he thinks it is a real improvement, he puts the change into the production product. John had been happily building his break-barrel air rifle until one day about two years ago, when he saw the Steyr Mannlicher 10-meter CO_2 target rifle. A huge, brightly lit light bulb appeared over his head, a gong was heard for miles, and he cried: "Eureka, that's it!"

What interested him was the articulated bolt the Steyr boys used in their 6-foot pound paper puncher. John realized this was

WHISCOMBE JW-60FB SPECIFICATIONS	
Power:	Spring-piston; underlever cocking
Caliber:	177, 20, 22, 25
Barrel:	16 ins.; Lothar Walther
Weight:	10 lbs.
Overall length:	44 ins.
Sights:	None furnished
Trigger:	Adjustable
Muzzle velocity:	940 fps (177)
Cocking Effort:	NA
Source:	Pelaire Products

the way for him to make a fixed-barrel (breech) air rifle. Using this bolt system, he could have a direct-loading breech, barrel interchangeability, a direct transfer port behind the pellet the way he likes, and a more rigid barrel attachment to the receiver (a plus for the accuracy addicts). John is not afraid to admit that other people have brilliant ideas, too. If he sees something good elsewhere, his ego has little trouble using that information to improve his airgun. John will still make you a flip-up barrel rifle, but I would suggest you look at the FB.

The Whiscombe FB comes in three delicious flavors, depending on how much power you crave. For the normal light

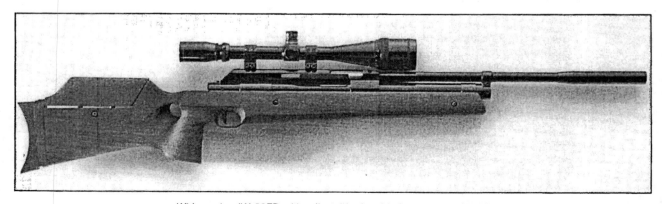

Whiscombe JW-60FB with adjustable thumbhole target stock and Burris 6-24x44 scope.

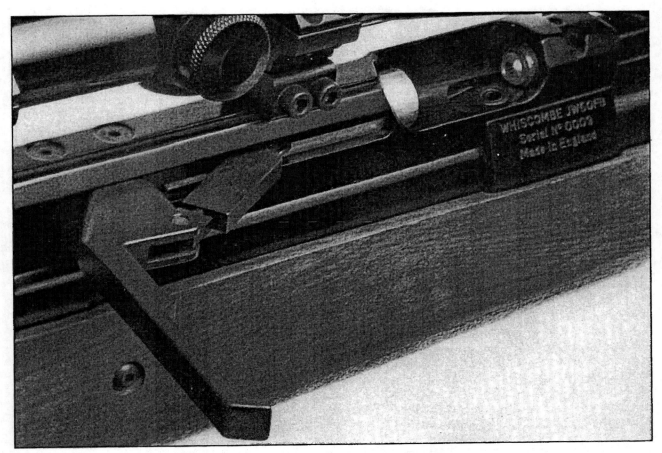

Detail of the bolt and loading port of the Whiscombe JW-60FB. The craftsmanship is superb.

British appetite, the JW-50 is *the* air rifle. Americans on a low-cholesterol diet will love the smooth taste of the JW-60. If you have a craving for red meat, the JW-75 is your dish. The number attached to the various models indicates the stroke of each piston in millimeters (times two for the total). The bigger the number, the higher the power. Once you decide how much you want, you then have to decide what kind of timber you want to wrap it in. The stock choices are sporting, thumbhole target and adjustable cheek thumbhole target. The standard wood is two-star walnut with sharp checkering on the sporting stock and stippling on the two thumbhole units. If you want a better tree wrapped around your metal, anything up to five- or six-star is available (just bring more cash). I am a fan of the adjustable cheek thumbhole stock because it shifts the weight bias a bit rearward and allows me to get my face in just the right spot behind any scope.

The Whiscombe Fixed-Barrel air rifle, contrary to its name, still has the ability to interchange barrels. Bore sizes from 177 up to 25 are available. The JW-50 is not recommended for 22- or 25-caliber duty because John thinks the power is a little light, but you can have it your way. The JW-50 is best suited to 177, as it puts out about 12½ foot pounds without the restrictor on the bolt face installed, which then knocks the power down to the British sub-12 foot pound limit. The JW-60 is my favorite at around 16 foot pounds (de-

pending on caliber). The JW-75 pounds out about 24, making it the ultimo hunting airgun.

The Whiscombe family are all underlevers. The JW-75 takes three strokes to cock; the JWs 50 and 60 take two. Now you are thinking, "Can I cock these only once and get half the power?" No! That's not how they work. The stroke of the cocking lever is short and ratcheted—you partially cock the springs with each stroke. It only takes two strokes on the 50 and 60 because the swept area is less than the 75, which needs three to fully compress the springs. The last of the final cocking stroke sets the trigger.

Ah, the trigger. John builds two triggers, standard and match. Frankly, the standard trigger is so good that I couldn't understand why anyone would order the match model, but after living with the match trigger, I know why. Not that it's better than the standard trigger; it is not. The match trigger is just safely adjustable to a hair's breadth. I now call the match unit the "subconscious" trigger. You *will* the airgun to go off—you don't squeeze the trigger.

All Whiscombes have an automatic safety with a release on the back of the receiver. I shoot Field Target with a JW-60FB and hate the *!&%$** automatic safety because it works so well. I forget to take it off and try to squeeze off a shot to no avail.

I've shot all of the various models of the Whiscombe air rifle and my favorite is the JW-60. "But the JW-75 is more power-

Galan is a fan of the Whiscombe Fixed-Barrel air rifle. Here he's shooting a JW-75FB with a high-mounted scope.

ful," you muse. You are correct; it is more powerful and would be a great choice if you ran with a big caliber. You could push 177-caliber pellets out the barrel of a JW-75 into the supersonic range, but it is a pointless exercise because those poor little pellets would feel naked without their skirts completely on. I bet they would reward you with sub-par accuracy and a leaded barrel! However, stick a 20-caliber barrel on a JW-75FB and put some Crosman Premiers through it—14.3 grains of 20-caliber alloy moving down the barrel at around 900 fps is a treat. The JW-60 on test shoots 7.9-grain 177 Premiers out its spout at 940 fps. Accurately.

All of the Whiscombe air rifles are recoilless. The only difference is the way they feel when you shoot them. The JW-75 is smooth, but you have a strong feeling that something happened after you release the trigger. The JW-60 is smoother, giving you only a small sense of mechanical movement after the trigger does its job. The JW-50 is the smoothest. Hardly a trace of movement is felt; you just watch the pellet move toward the target through the scope. This all makes sense when you know that all three use the same mainsprings. The difference is how much the springs are compressed. The JW-75 squishes them more to get a longer stroke and more power. The JW-50 less.

I just got off the phone with John Whiscombe. As you might have guessed, he has made another improvement to his rifle.

The latest innovation has further isolated the mounting of the action to the stock in the forend area. This will help minimize point-of-impact shifts due to varying temperature and humidity effects on the stock. He has always used elastinomer isolators (O-rings) on the front stock screws, but the more-is-better bunch would tighten the screws down so much that it would negate the effects. He hopes this new system of isolators and pillow blocks will eliminate the woes.

Recently, I shot the 177-caliber JW-60FB in the World Field Target Championship in Michigan. I was one of about six Whiscombe shooters at the match. What I liked was the fact that I had a self-contained airgun; no need for scuba air in a strange town. My Whiscombe and 6-24x Burris scope shot consistently over the three-day event. I had minimal impact shift from day to day even though the weather changed from shorts to longjohns. In the morning, when I would sight-in the gun, it would shoot dead on but 1 1/2 inches low at 40 yards. If you look at the stats, you will find my score to be lacking at the Worlds, but I assure you, all of the blame is between my ears and not with the gun or scope.

Innovation, attention to detail and an eye for aesthetics are all elements that make the Whiscombe FB the apex of spring-powered airguns. If you have an aversion to scuba tanks, look into a Whiscombe FB.

Ben Saltzman

Airgun Catalog 268

Airgun and Equipment Manufacturers' Directory 286

Airgun Associations and Publications 288

Airguns–Handguns

AIRROW MODEL A-6 AIR PISTOL
Caliber: #2512 10.75″ arrow.
Barrel: 10.75″.
Weight: 1.75 lbs. **Length:** 16.5″ overall.
Power: CO_2 or compressed air.
Stocks: Checkered composition.
Sights: Bead front, fully adjustable Williams rear.
Features: Velocity to 375 fps. Pneumatic air trigger. Floating barrel. All aircraft aluminum and stainless steel construction; Mil-spec materials and finishes. Announced 1993. From Swivel Machine Works, Inc.

BEEMAN P1 MAGNUM AIR PISTOL
Caliber: 177, 5mm, single shot.
Barrel: 8.4″.
Weight: 2.5 lbs. **Length:** 11″ overall.
Power: Top lever cocking; spring piston.
Stocks: Checkered walnut.
Sights: Blade front, square notch rear with click micrometer adjustments for windage and elevation. Grooved for scope mounting.
Features: Dual power for 177 and 20-cal.—low setting gives 350-400 fps; high setting 500-600 fps. Rearward expanding mainspring simulates firearm recoil. All Colt 45 auto grips fit gun. Dry-firing feature for practice. Optional wooden shoulder stock. Introduced 1985. Imported by Beeman.

Beeman P2 Match Air Pistol
Similar to the Beeman P1 Magnum except shoots only 177 pellets; completely recoilless single-stroke pnuematic action. Weighs 2.2 lbs. Choice of thumbrest match grips or standard style. Introduced 1990.

BEEMAN/FEINWERKBAU C20 CO_2 PISTOL
Caliber: 177, single shot.
Barrel: 10.1″, 12-groove rifling.
Weight: 2.5 lbs. **Length:** 16″ overall.
Power: Special CO_2 cylinder.
Stock: Stippled walnut with adjustable palm shelf.
Sights: Blade front, open rear adjustable for windage and elevation. Notch size adjustable for width. Interchangeable front blades.
Features: Fully adjustable trigger; can be set for dry firing. Separate gas chamber for uniform power. Cylinders interchangeable even when full. Short-barrel model also available. Introduced 1988. Imported by Beeman.

BEEMAN/FEINWERKBAU C25 CO_2 PISTOL
Caliber: 177, single shot.
Barrel: 10.1″; 12-groove rifling.
Weight: 2.5 lbs. **Length:** 16.5″ overall.
Power: Vertical, interchangeable CO_2 bottles.
Stocks: Stippled walnut with adjustable palm shelf.
Sights: Blade front, rear micrometer adjustable. Notch size adjustable for width; interchangeable front blades.
Features: Fully adjustable trigger; can be set for dry firing. Has special vertical CO_2 cylinder and weight rail for balance. Short-barrel model (C25 Mini) also available. Introduced 1992. Imported by Beeman.

Airrow Model A-6

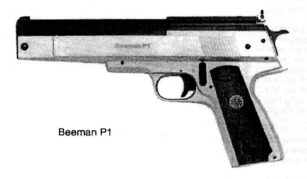
Beeman P1

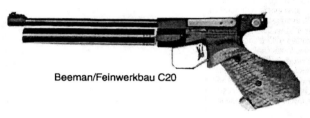
Beeman/Feinwerkbau C20

Beeman/Feinwerkbau C55

Beeman/Feinwerkbau 102

BEEMAN/FEINWERKBAU C55 CO_2 RAPID FIRE PISTOL
Caliber: 177, single shot or 5-shot magazines.
Barrel: 7.3″.
Weight: 2.5 lbs. **Length:** 15″ overall.
Power: Special CO_2 cylinder.
Stocks: Anatomical, adjustable.
Sights: Interchangeable front, fully adjustable open micro-click rear with adjustable notch size.
Features: Velocity 510 fps. Has 11.75″ sight radius. Built-in muzzle brake. Introduced 1993. Imported by Beeman Precision Airguns.

BEEMAN/FEINWERKBAU 65 MKII AIR PISTOL
Caliber: 177, single shot.
Barrel: 6.1″ or 7.5″, removable bbl. wgt. available.
Weight: 42 oz. **Length:** 13.3″ or 14.1″ overall.
Power: Spring, sidelever cocking.
Stocks: Walnut, stippled thumbrest; adjustable or fixed.
Sights: Front, interchangeable post element system, open rear, click adjustable for windage and elevation and for sighting notch width. Scope mount available.
Features: New shorter barrel for better balance and control. Cocking effort 9 lbs. Two-stage trigger, four adjustments. Quiet firing, 525 fps. Programs instantly for recoil or recoilless operation. Permanently lubricated. Steel piston ring. Special switch converts trigger from 17.6-oz. pull to 42-oz. let-off. Imported by Beeman.

BEEMAN/FEINWERKBAU 102 PISTOL
Caliber: 177, single shot.
Barrel: 10.1″, 12-groove rifling.
Weight: 2.5 lbs. **Length:** 16.5″ overall.
Power: Single-stroke pneumatic, underlever cocking.
Stocks: Stippled walnut with adjustable palm shelf.
Sights: Blade front, open rear adjustable for windage and elevation. Notch size adjustable for width. Interchangeable front blades.
Features: Velocity 460 fps. Fully adjustable trigger. Cocking effort 12 lbs. Introduced 1988. Imported by Beeman.

Airguns–Handguns

BEEMAN HW70A AIR PISTOL
Caliber: 177, single shot.
Barrel: 6¼", rifled.
Weight: 38 oz. **Length:** 12¾" overall.
Power: Spring, barrel cocking.
Stocks: Plastic, with thumbrest.
Sights: Hooded post front, square notch rear adjustable for windage and elevation. Comes with scope base.
Features: Adjustable trigger, 31-lb. cocking effort, 440 fps MV; automatic barrel safety. Imported by Beeman.

Beeman HW70A

Benjamin Sheridan CO₂

BENJAMIN SHERIDAN CO₂ PELLET PISTOLS
Caliber: 177, 20, 22, single shot.
Barrel: 6⅜", rifled brass.
Weight: 29 oz. **Length:** 9.8" overall.
Power: 12-gram CO_2 cylinder.
Stocks: Walnut.
Sights: High ramp front, fully adjustable notch rear.
Features: Velocity to 500 fps. Turn-bolt action with cross-bolt safety. Gives about 40 shots per CO_2 cylinder. Black or nickel finish. Made in U.S. by Benjamin Sheridan Co.

BENJAMIN SHERIDAN PNEUMATIC PELLET PISTOLS
Caliber: 177, 20, 22, single shot.
Barrel: 9⅜", rifled brass.
Weight: 38 oz. **Length:** 13⅛" overall.
Power: Multi-pump pneumatic.
Stocks: Walnut stocks and pump handle.
Sights: High ramp front, fully adjustable notch rear.
Features: Velocity to 525 fps (variable). Bolt action with cross-bolt safety. Choice of black or nickel finish. Made in U.S. by Benjamin Sheridan Co.

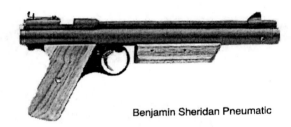
Benjamin Sheridan Pneumatic

BRNO AERON-TAU CO₂ PISTOL
Caliber: 177.
Barrel: 10".
Weight: 37 oz. **Length:** 12.5" overall.
Power: 12.5-gram CO_2 cartridges.
Stocks: Stippled hardwood with palm rest.
Sights: Blade front, open fully adjustable rear.
Features: Comes with extra seals and counterweight. Blue finish. Imported by Century International Arms.

CROSMAN AUTO AIR II PISTOL
Caliber: BB, 17-shot magazine, 177 pellet, single shot.
Barrel: 8⅝" steel, smoothbore.
Weight: 13 oz. **Length:** 10¾ overall.
Power: CO_2 Powerlet.
Stocks: Grooved plastic.
Sights: Blade front, adjustable rear; highlighted system.
Features: Velocity to 480 fps (BBs), 430 fps (pellets). Semi-automatic action with BBs, single shot with pellets. Silvered finish. Introduced 1991. From Crosman.

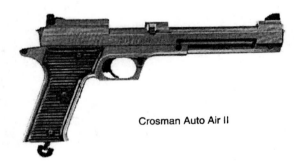
Crosman Auto Air II

CROSMAN MODEL 357 AIR PISTOL
Caliber: 177, 6- and 10-shot pellet clips.
Barrel: 4" (Model 357-4), 6" (Model 357-6), rifled steel; 8" (Model 357-8), rifled brass.
Weight: 32 oz. (6"). **Length:** 11⅜" overall (357-6).
Power: CO_2 Powerlet.
Stocks: Checkered wood-grain plastic.
Sights: Ramp front, fully adjustable rear.
Features: Average 435 fps (Model 357-6). Break-open barrel for easy loading. Single or double action. Vent. rib barrel. Wide, smooth trigger. Two cylinders come with each gun. Model 357-8 has matte gray finish, black grips. From Crosman.

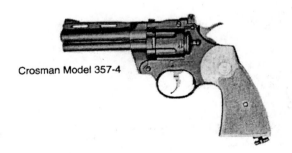
Crosman Model 357-4

Airguns–Handguns

Crosman Model 1008

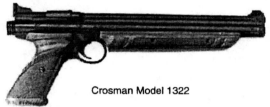

Crosman Model 1322

Crosman Model SSP 250

CROSMAN MODEL 1008 REPEAT AIR
Caliber: 177, 8-shot pellet clip
Barrel: 4.25", rifled steel.
Weight: 17 oz. **Length:** 8.625" overall.
Power: CO_2 Powerlet.
Stocks: Checkered plastic.
Sights: Post front, adjustable rear.
Features: Velocity about 430 fps. Break-open barrel for easy loading; single or double semi-automatic action; two 8-shot clips included. Optional carrying case available. Introduced 1992. From Crosman.

CROSMAN MODEL 1322, 1377 AIR PISTOLS
Caliber: 177 (M1377), 22 (M1322), single shot.
Barrel: 8", rifled steel.
Weight: 39 oz. **Length:** 13⅝".
Power: Multi-pump pneumatic.
Sights: Blade front, rear adjustable for windage and elevation.
Features: Moulded plastic grip, hand size pump forearm. Cross-bolt safety. Model 1377 also shoots BBs. From Crosman.

CROSMAN MODEL SSP 250 PISTOL
Caliber: 177, 20, 22, single shot.
Barrel: 9⅞", rifled steel.
Weight: 3 lbs., 1 oz. **Length:** 14" overall.
Power: CO_2 Powerlet.
Stocks: Composition; black, with checkering.
Sights: Hooded front, fully adjustable rear.
Features: Velocity about 560 fps. Interchangeable accessory barrels. Two-stage trigger. High/low power settings. From Crosman.

CZ MODEL 3 AIR PISTOL
Caliber: 177, single shot.
Barrel: 7.25".
Weight: 44 oz. **Length:** 13.75" overall.
Power: Spring piston, barrel cocking.
Stocks: High-impact plastic; ambidextrous, with thumbrest.
Sights: Hooded front, fully adjustable rear.
Features: Velocity about 420 fps. Externally adjustable trigger; removable screwdriver threaded into receiver. Imported from the Czech Republic by Action Arms.

DAISY MODEL 91 MATCH PISTOL
Caliber: 177, single shot.
Barrel: 10.25", rifled steel.
Weight: 2.5 lbs. **Length:** 16.5" overall.
Power: CO_2, 12-gram cylinder.
Stocks: Stippled hardwood; anatomically shaped and adjustable.
Sights: Blade and ramp front, changeable-width rear notch with full micrometer adjustments.
Features: Velocity to 476 fps. Gives 55 shots per cylinder. Fully adjustable trigger. Imported by Daisy Mfg. Co.

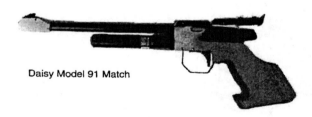

Daisy Model 91 Match

Daisy Model 288

DAISY MODEL 288 AIR PISTOL
Caliber: BBs, 24-shot.
Barrel: Smoothbore steel.
Weight: .8 lb. **Length:** 12.1" overall.
Power: Single stroke spring air.
Stocks: Moulded resin with checkering and thumbrest.
Sights: Blade and ramp front, open fixed rear.
Features: Velocity to 215 fps. Cross-bolt trigger block safety. Black finish. From Daisy Mfg. Co.

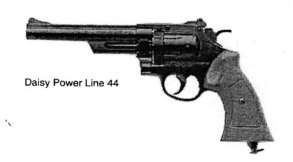

Daisy Power Line 44

DAISY POWER LINE 44 REVOLVER
Caliber: 177 pellets, 6-shot.
Barrel: 6", rifled steel; interchangeable 4" and 8".
Weight: 2.7 lbs.
Power: CO_2.
Stocks: Moulded plastic with checkering.
Sights: Blade on ramp front, fully adjustable notch rear.
Features: Velocity up to 400 fps. Replica of 44 Magnum revolver. Has swingout cylinder and interchangeable barrels. Introduced 1987. From Daisy Mfg. Co.

Airguns—Handguns

Daisy Power Line 45

Daisy Power Line 93

Daisy Power Line 400

Daisy Power Line 500

DAISY POWER LINE 45 PISTOL
Caliber: 177 pellets, 13-shot clip.
Barrel: 5", rifled steel.
Weight: 1.25 lbs. **Length:** 8.5" overall.
Power: CO_2.
Stocks: Checkered plastic.
Sights: Fixed.
Features: Velocity 400 fps. Semi-automatic repeater with double-action trigger. Manually operated lever-type trigger block safety; magazine safety. Introduced 1990. From Daisy Mfg. Co.

DAISY POWER LINE 93 PISTOL
Caliber: BB, 15-shot clip.
Barrel: 5", steel.
Weight: 17 oz. **Length:** NA.
Power: CO_2.
Stocks: Checkered plastic.
Sights: Fixed.
Features: Velocity to 400 fps. Semi-automatic repeater. Manual lever-type trigger-block safety. Introduced 1991. From Daisy Mfg. Co.

DAISY POWER LINE 400 BB PISTOL
Caliber: BB, 20-shot magazine.
Barrel: Smoothbore steel.
Weight: 1.4 lbs. **Length:** 10.7" overall.
Power: 12-gram CO_2.
Stocks: Moulded black checkered plastic.
Sights: Blade front, fixed open rear.
Features: Velocity to 420 fps. Blowback slide cycles automatically on firing. Rotary trigger block safety. Introduced 1994. From Daisy Mfg. Co.

DAISY POWER LINE 500 RAVEN PISTOL
Caliber: 177 pellets, single shot.
Barrel: Rifled steel.
Weight: 36 oz. **Length:** 8.5" overall.
Power: CO_2.
Stocks: Moulded plastic with checkering.
Sights: Blade front, fixed rear.
Features: Velocity up to 500 fps. Hammer-block safety. Resembles semi-auto centerfire pistol. Barrel tips up for loading. Introduced 1993. From Daisy Mfg. Co.

DAISY POWER LINE 717 PELLET PISTOL
Caliber: 177, single shot.
Barrel: 9.61".
Weight: 2.8 lbs. **Length:** 13 1/2" overall.
Power: Single-pump pneumatic.
Stocks: Moulded wood-grain plastic, with thumbrest.
Sights: Blade and ramp front, micro-adjustable notch rear.
Features: Single pump pneumatic pistol. Rifled steel barrel. Cross-bolt trigger block. Muzzle velocity 385 fps. From Daisy Mfg. Co. Introduced 1979.

Daisy Power Line 747 Pistol
Similar to the 717 pistol except has a 12-groove rifled steel barrel by Lothar Walther and adjustable trigger pull weight. Velocity of 360 fps. Manual cross-bolt safety.

DAISY POWER LINE MATCH 777 PELLET PISTOL
Caliber: 177, single shot.
Barrel: 9.61" rifled steel by Lothar Walther.
Weight: 32 oz. **Length:** 13 1/2" overall.
Power: Sidelever, single pump pneumatic.
Stocks: Smooth hardwood, fully contoured with palm and thumbrest.
Sights: Blade and ramp front, match-grade open rear with adjustable width notch, micro. click adjustments.
Features: Adjustable trigger; manual cross-bolt safety. MV of 385 fps. Comes with cleaning kit, adjustment tool and pellets. From Daisy Mfg. Co.

Daisy Power Line 777

Daisy Power Line 1200

Daisy Power Line 1700

GAT Pistol

HAMMERLI MODEL 480 COMPETITION AIR PISTOL
Caliber: 177, single shot.
Barrel: 9.8″.
Weight: 37 oz. **Length:** 16.5″ overall.
Power: Air or CO_2.
Stocks: Walnut with 7-degree rake adjustment. Stippled grip area.
Sights: Undercut blade front, fully adjustable open match rear.
Features: Under-barrel cannister charges with air or CO_2 for power supply; gives 320 shots per filling. Trigger adjustable for position. Introduced 1994. Imported from Switzerland by Hammerli Pistols USA.

MARKSMAN MODEL 1010 REPEATER PISTOL
Caliber: 177, 18-shot BB repeater.
Barrel: $2^{1}/2″$, smoothbore.
Weight: 24 oz. **Length:** $8^{1}/4″$ overall.
Power: Spring-piston.
Stocks: Cast checkered metal.
Sights: Fixed.
Features: Velocity to 200 fps. Thumb safety. Black finish. Uses BBs, darts or pellets. Repeats with BBs only. From Marksman Products.

MARKSMAN MODEL 1015 SPECIAL EDITION AIR PISTOL
Caliber: 177, 24-shot repeater.
Barrel: 3.8″, rifled.
Weight: 22 oz. **Length:** 10.3″ overall.
Power: Spring-piston.
Stocks: Checkered brown composition.
Sights: Fixed.
Features: Velocity about 230 fps. Skeletonized trigger, extended barrel with "ported compensator." Shoots BBs, pellets or bolts. From Marksman Products.

DAISY POWER LINE 1200 CO_2 PISTOL
Caliber: BB.
Barrel: $10^{1}/2″$, smooth.
Weight: 1.6 lbs. **Length:** 11.1″ overall.
Power: Daisy CO_2 cylinder.
Stocks: Contoured, checkered moulded wood-grain plastic.
Sights: Blade ramp front, fully adjustable square notch rear.
Features: 60-shot BB reservoir, gravity feed. Cross-bolt safety. Velocity of 420-450 fps for more than 100 shots. From Daisy Mfg. Co.

DAISY POWER LINE 1700 CO_2 PISTOL
Caliber: BB, 60-shot magazine.
Barrel: Smoothbore steel.
Weight: 1.4 lbs. **Length:** 11.2″ overall.
Power: CO_2
Stocks: Moulded checkered plastic.
Sights: Blade front, adjustable rear.
Features: Velocity to 420 fps. Cross-bolt trigger block safety; matte finish. Has $^{3}/_{8}″$ dovetail mount for scope or point sight. Introduced 1994. From Daisy Mfg. Co.

"GAT" AIR PISTOL
Caliber: 177, single shot.
Barrel: $7^{1}/2″$ cocked, $9^{1}/2″$ extended.
Weight: 22 oz.
Power: Spring piston.
Stocks: Cast checkered metal.
Sights: Fixed.
Features: Shoots pellets, corks or darts. Matte black finish. Imported from England by Stone Enterprises, Inc.

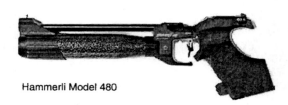

Hammerli Model 480

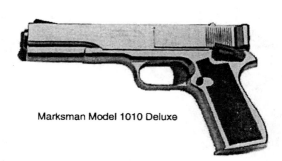

Marksman Model 1010 Deluxe

Marksman Model 1015

Airguns–Handguns

RECORD JUMBO DELUXE AIR PISTOL
Caliber: 177, single shot.
Barrel: 6", rifled.
Weight: 1.9 lbs. **Length:** 7.25" overall.
Power: Spring-air, forward-swinging cocking system.
Stocks: Smooth walnut.
Sights: Blade front, fully adjustable open rear.
Features: Velocity to 322 fps. Thumb safety. Grip magazine compartment for extra pellet storage. Introduced 1983. Imported from Germany by Great Lakes Airguns.

RWS/DIANA MODEL 5G AIR PISTOL
Caliber: 177, single shot.
Barrel: 7".
Weight: 2³/₄ lbs. **Length:** 16" overall.
Power: Spring-air, barrel cocking.
Stocks: Plastic, thumbrest design.
Sights: Tunnel front, micro-click open rear.
Features: Velocity of 450 fps. Two-stage trigger with automatic safety. Imported from Germany by Dynamit Nobel-RWS, Inc.

Record Jumbo

RWS/Diana Model 5G

RWS/Diana Model 6M Match

RWS/DIANA MODEL 6M MATCH AIR PISTOL
Caliber: 177, single shot.
Barrel: 7".
Weight: 3 lbs. **Length:** 16" overall.
Power: Spring-air, barrel cocking.
Stocks: Walnut-finished hardwood with thumbrest.
Sights: Adjustable front, micro. click open rear.
Features: Velocity of 450 fps. Recoilless double piston system, movable barrel shroud to protect from sight during cocking. Imported from Germany by Dynamit Nobel-RWS, Inc.

RWS/Diana Model 6G Air Pistols
Similar to the Model 6M except does not have the movable barrel shroud. Has click micrometer rear sight, two-stage adjustable trigger, interchangeable tunnel front sight. Available in right- or left-hand models.

RWS/Diana Model 6G

RWS GAMO PR-45 AIR PISTOL
Caliber: 177, single shot.
Barrel: 8.3".
Weight: 25 oz. **Length:** 11" overall.
Power: Single-stroke pneumatic.
Stocks: Composition.
Sights: Blade front, adjustable rear.
Features: Velocity to 430 fps. Recoilless and vibration free. Manual safety. Previously imported from Spain by Dynamit Nobel-RWS, Inc.

SHARP MODEL U-FP CO₂ PISTOL
Caliber: 177, single shot.
Barrel: 8", rifled steel.
Weight: 2.4 lbs. **Length:** 11.6" overall.
Power: 12-gram CO_2 cylinder.
Stocks: Smooth hardwood. Walnut target stocks available.
Sights: Post front, fully adjustable target rear.
Features: Variable power adjustment up to 545 fps. Adjustable trigger. Also available with adjustable field sight. Imported from Japan by Great Lakes Airguns.

STEYR CO₂ LP1 MATCH PISTOL
Caliber: 177, single shot.
Barrel: 9".
Weight: 38.7 oz. **Length:** 15.3" overall.
Power: Rechargeable CO_2 cylinders.
Stocks: Fully adjustable Morini match with palm shelf; stippled walnut.
Sights: Interchangeable blade in 4mm, 4.5mm or 5mm widths, fully adjustable open rear with interchangeable 3.5mm or 4mm leaves.
Features: Velocity about 500 fps. Adjustable trigger, adjustable sight radius from 12.4" to 13.2". Imported from Austria by Nygord Precision Products.

Sharp Model U-FP

STEYR LP5 MATCH PISTOL
Caliber: 177, 5-shot magazine.
Barrel: NA.
Weight: 40.2 oz. **Length:** 13.39" overall.
Power: Rechargeable CO_2 cylinders.
Stocks: Adjustable Morini match with palm shelf; stippled walnut.
Sights: Movable 2.5mm blade front; 2-3mm interchangeable in .2mm increments; fully adjustable open match rear.
Features: Velocity about 500 fps. Fully adjustable trigger; has dry-fire feature. Barrel and grip weights available. Introduced 1993. Imported from Austria by Nygord Precision Products.

Airguns–Long Guns

AIRROW MODEL A-8S1P STEALTH AIR GUN
Caliber: #2512 16" arrow.
Barrel: 16".
Weight: 3.5 lbs. **Length:** 30.12" overall.

Power: CO_2 or compressed air.
Stocks: Checkered composition.
Sights: Bead front, fully adjustable Williams rear.
Features: Velocity to 600 fps. Pneumatic air trigger. Floating barrel. All aircraft aluminum and stainless steel construction; Mil-spec materials and finishes. Announced 1993. From Swivel Machine Works, Inc.

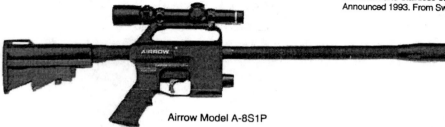

Airrow Model A-8S1P

AIRROW MODEL A-8SRB STEALTH AIR GUN
Caliber: 177, 22, 25, 38, 9-shot.
Barrel: 19.7"; rifled.
Weight: 6 lbs. **Length:** 34" overall.
Power: CO_2 or compressed air; variable power.
Stock: Telescoping CAR-15-type.
Sights: 3.5-10x A.O. variable power scope.
Features: Velocity 1100 fps in all calibers. Pneumatic air trigger. All aircraft aluminum and stainless steel construction. Mil-spec materials and finishes. Introduced 1992. From Swivel Machine Works, Inc.

ARS SPORTSMAN QB77, QB22 DELUXE AIR RIFLES
Caliber: 177, 22, single shot.
Barrel: 21 1/2".
Weight: 5 1/2 lbs. **Length:** 40" overall.
Power: Two 12-oz. CO_2 cylinders.
Stock: Walnut-stained hardwood.
Sights: Blade front, adjustable rear.
Features: Velocity to 625 fps (22), 725 fps (177). Receiver grooved for scope mounting. Imported by Air Rifle Specialists.

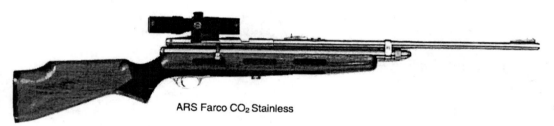

ARS Farco CO_2 Stainless

ARS Farco CO_2 Stainless Steel Air Rifle
Similar to the ARS Farco CO_2 shotgun except in 22- or 25-caliber with 21 1/2" barrel; weighs 6 3/4 lbs, 42 1/2" overall; Philippine hardwood stock with stippled grip and forend; blade front sight, adjustable rear, grooved for scope mount. Uses 10-oz. refillable CO_2 cylinder. Made of stainless steel. Imported from the Philippines by Air Rifle Specialists.

ARS FARCO FP SURVIVAL AIR RIFLE
Caliber: 22, 25, single shot.
Barrel: 22 3/4".
Weight: 5 3/4 lbs. **Length:** 42 3/4" overall.
Power: Multi-pump foot pump.
Stock: Philippine hardwood.
Sights: Blade front, fixed rear.
Features: Velocity to 850 fps (22 or 25). Receiver grooved for scope mounting. Imported from the Philippines by Air Rifle Specialists.

ARS AR6 AIR RIFLE
Caliber: 22, 6-shot repeater.
Barrel: 25 1/2".
Weight: 7 lbs. **Length:** 41 1/4" overall.
Power: Precharged air from 3000 psi diving tank.
Stock: Indonesian walnut with checkered grip; rubber buttpad.
Sights: Blade front, adjustable peep rear.
Features: Velocity over 1000 fps with 32-grain pellet. Receiver grooved for scope mounting. Has 6-shot rotary magazine. Imported by Air Rifle Specialists.

ARS FARCO CO_2 AIR SHOTGUN
Caliber: 51 (28-gauge).
Barrel: 30".
Weight: 7 lbs. **Length:** 48 1/2" overall.
Power: 10-oz. refillable CO_2 tank.
Stock: Hardwood.
Sights: Blade front, fixed rear.
Features: Gives over 100 ft. lbs. energy for taking small game. Imported from the Philippines by Air Rifle Specialists.

ARS Magnum 6 Air Rifle
Similar to the King Hunting Master except is 6-shot repeater with 23 3/4" barrel, weighs 8 1/4 lbs. Stock is walnut-stained hardwood with checkered grip and forend; rubber buttpad. Velocity of 1000+ fps with 32-grain pellet. Imported from Korea by Air Rifle Specialists.

ARS AR6

Airguns–Long Guns

ARS King Hunting Master

ARS KING HUNTING MASTER AIR RIFLE
Caliber: 22, 5-shot repeater.
Barrel: 22³/₄".
Weight: 7³/₄ lbs. **Length:** 42" overall.
Power: Precharged air from 3000 psi diving tank.
Stock: Indonesian walnut with checkered grip and forend; rubber buttpad.
Sights: Blade front, fully adjustable open rear. Receiver grooved for scope mounting.
Features: Velocity over 1000 fps with 32-grain pellet. High and low power switch for hunting or target velocities. Side lever cocks action and inserts pellet. Rotary magazine. Imported from Korea by Air rifle Specialists.

ANSCHUTZ 2002 MATCH AIR RIFLE
Caliber: 177, single shot.
Barrel: 26".
Weight: 10¹/₂ lbs. **Length:** 44¹/₂" overall.
Stock: European walnut; stippled grip and forend.
Sights: Globe front, #6824 Micro Peep rear.
Features: Balance, weight match the 1907 ISU smallbore rifle. Uses #5019 match trigger. Recoil and vibration free. Fully adjustable cheekpiece and buttplate. Introduced 1988. Imported from Germany by Precision Sales International.

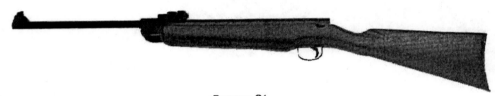

Beeman C1

BEEMAN C1 CARBINE
Caliber: 177, single shot.
Barrel: 14", 12-groove rifling.
Weight: 6¹/₄ lbs. **Length:** 38" overall.
Power: Spring-piston, barrel cocking.
Stock: Walnut-stained beechwood with rubber buttpad.
Sights: Blade front, rear click-adjustable for windage and elevation.
Features: Velocity 830 fps. Adjustable trigger. Receiver grooved for scope mounting. Imported by Beeman.

Beeman Crow Magnum II

BEEMAN CROW MAGNUM II AIR RIFLE
Caliber: 20, 22, 25, single shot.
Barrel: 16"; 10-groove rifling.
Weight: 8.6 lbs. **Length:** 46" overall.
Power: Gas-spring; adjustable power to 32 foot pounds muzzle energy. Barrel cocking.
Stock: Classic-style walnut; hand checkered.
Sights: For scope use only; built-in base and 1" rings included.
Features: Adjustable two-stage trigger. Automatic safety. Introduced 1992. Imported by Beeman.

BEEMAN KODIAK AIR RIFLE
Caliber: 22, 25, single shot.
Barrel: 17.6".
Weight: 9 lbs. **Length:** 45.6" overall.
Power: Barrel cocking.
Stock: Stained hardwood.
Sights: Blade front, open fully adjustable rear.
Features: Velocity to 865 fps in 22. Up to 30 foot pounds muzzle energy. Introduced 1993. Imported by Beeman.

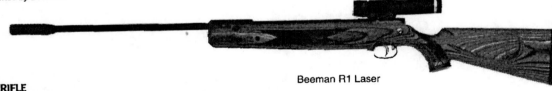

Beeman R1 Laser

BEEMAN R1 AIR RIFLE
Caliber: 177, 20, 22, single shot.
Barrel: 19.6", 12-groove rifling.
Weight: 8.5 lbs. **Length:** 45.2" overall.
Power: Spring-piston, barrel cocking.
Stock: Walnut-stained beech; cut-checkered pistol grip; Monte Carlo comb and cheekpiece; rubber buttpad.
Sights: Tunnel front with interchangeable inserts, open rear click-adjustable for windage and elevation. Grooved for scope mounting.
Features: Velocity of 940-1050 fps (177), 860 fps (20), 765 fps (22). Non-drying nylon piston and breech seals. Adjustable metal trigger. Milled steel safety. Right- or left-hand stock. Available with adjustable cheekpiece and buttplate at extra cost. Custom and Super Laser versions available. Imported by Beeman.

BEEMAN R1 LASER AIR RIFLE
Caliber: 177, 20, 22, 25, single shot.
Barrel: 16.1" or 19.6".
Weight: 8.4 lbs. **Length:** 41.7" overall (16.1" barrel).
Power: Spring-piston, barrel cocking.
Stock: Laminated wood with Monte Carlo comb and cheekpiece; checkered p.g. and forend; rubber buttpad.
Sights: Tunnel front with interchangeable inserts, open adjustable rear.
Features: Velocity up to 1150 fps (177). Special powerplant components. Built from the Beeman R1 rifle by Beeman.

Airguns–Long Guns

BEEMAN R1 CARBINE
Caliber: 177, 20, 25, single shot.
Barrel: 16.1".
Weight: 8.6 lbs. **Length:** 41.7" overall.
Power: Spring-piston, barrel cocking.
Stock: Stained beech; Monte Carlo comb and checkpiece; cut checkered p.g.; rubber buttpad.
Sights: Tunnel front with interchangeable inserts, open adjustable rear; receiver grooved for scope mounting.
Features: Velocity up to 950 fps (177). Non-drying nylon piston and breech seals. Adjustable metal trigger. Machined steel receiver end cap and safety. Right- or left-hand stock. Imported by Beeman.

BEEMAN R8 AIR RIFLE
Caliber: 177, single shot.
Barrel: 18.3".
Weight: 7.2 lbs. **Length:** 43.1" overall.
Power: Barrel cocking, spring-piston.
Stock: Walnut with Monte Carlo cheekpiece; checkered pistol grip.
Sights: Globe front, fully adjustable rear; interchangeable inserts.
Features: Velocity of 720 fps. Similar to the R1. Nylon piston and breech seals. Adjustable match-grade, two-stage, grooved metal trigger. Milled steel safety. Rubber buttpad. Imported by Beeman.

Beeman R7 Air Rifle
Similar to the R8 model except has lighter ambidextrous stock, match-grade trigger block; velocity of 680-700 fps; barrel length 17"; weight 5.8 lbs. Milled steel safety. Imported by Beeman.

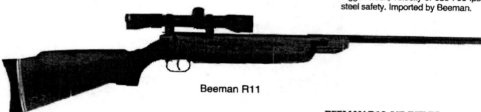

Beeman R11

BEEMAN R11 AIR RIFLE
Caliber: 177, single shot.
Barrel: 19.6".
Weight: 8.8 lbs. **Length:** 47" overall.
Power: Spring-piston, barrel cocking.
Stock: Walnut-stained beech; adjustable buttplate and cheekpiece.
Sights: None furnished. Has dovetail for scope mounting.
Features: Velocity 875 fps. All-steel barrel sleeve. Imported by Beeman.

BEEMAN R10 AIR RIFLES
Caliber: 177, 20, single shot.
Barrel: 16.1"; 12-groove rifling.
Weight: 8.2 lbs. **Length:** 46" overall.
Power: Spring-piston, barrel cocking.
Stock: Standard is walnut-finished hardwood with Monte Carlo comb, rubber buttplate; Deluxe has white spacers at grip cap, buttplate, checkered grip, cheekpiece, rubber buttplate.
Sights: Tunnel front with interchangeable inserts, open rear click adjustable for windage and elevation. Receiver grooved for scope mounting.
Features: Over 950 fps in 177-cal. only; 34-lb. cocking effort; milled steel safety and body tube. Right- and left-hand models. Similar in appearance to the Beeman R8. Introduced 1986. Imported by Beeman.

BEEMAN RX-1 GAS-SPRING MAGNUM AIR RIFLE
Caliber: 177, 20, 22, 25, single shot.
Barrel: 19.6"; 12-groove rifling.
Weight: 8.8 lbs.
Power: Gas-spring piston air; single stroke barrel cocking.
Stock: Walnut-finished hardwood, hand checkered, with cheekpiece. Adjustable cheekpiece and buttplate.
Sights: Tunnel front, click-adjustable rear.
Features: Velocity adjustable to about 1125 fps. Uses special sealed chamber of air as a mainspring. Gas-spring cannot take a set. Introduced 1990. Imported by Beeman.

Beeman RX-1 Magnum

BEEMAN SUPER 7 AIR RIFLE
Caliber: 22, 7-shot repeater.
Barrel: 19"; 12-groove rifling.
Weight: 7.2 lbs. **Length:** 41" overall.
Power: Precharged pneumatic, external air reservoir.
Stock: Walnut; high cheekpiece; rubber buttpad.
Sights: None furnished; drilled and tapped; 1" ring scope mounts included.
Features: Two-stage adjustable trigger; 7-shot rotary magazine. Receiver of anodized aircraft aluminum. All working parts either hardened or stainless steel. Imported by Beeman.

Beeman Super 7

Airguns–Long Guns

Beeman/Feinwerkbau C60

BEEMAN/FEINWERKBAU C60 CO₂ RIFLE
Caliber: 177.
Barrel: 16.9″. With barrel sleeve, 25.4″.
Weight: 10 lbs. **Length:** 42.6″ overall.
Stock: Laminated hardwood and hard rubber.
Sights: Tunnel front with interchangeable inserts, quick release micro. click match aperture rear.
Features: Similar features, performance as Beeman/FWB 601. Virtually no cocking effort. Right- or left-hand. Running target version available. Introduced 1987. Imported from Germany by Beeman.

Beeman/Feinwerkbau 300-S

BEEMAN/FEINWERKBAU MODEL 601 AIR RIFLE
Caliber: 177, single shot.
Barrel: 16.6″.
Weight: 10.8 lbs. **Length:** 43″ overall.
Power: Single stroke pneumatic.
Stock: Special laminated hardwoods and hard rubber for stability.
Sights: Tunnel front with interchangeable inserts, click micrometer match apperture rear.
Features: Recoilless action; double supported barrel; special, short rifled area frees pellet from barrel faster so shooter's motion has minimum effect on accuracy. Fully adjustable match trigger. Trigger and sights blocked when loading latch is open. Imported by Beeman. Introduced 1984.

Beeman/Feinwerkbau 601 Running Target
Similar to the standard Model 601. Has 16.9″ barrel (33.7″ with barrel sleeve); special match trigger, short loading gate which allows scope mounting. No sights—built for scope use only. Introduced 1987.

BEEMAN/FEINWERKBAU 300-S SERIES MATCH RIFLE
Caliber: 177, single shot.
Barrel: 19.9″, fixed solid with receiver.
Weight: Approx. 10 lbs. with optional bbl. sleeve. **Length:** 42.8″ overall.
Power: Single stroke sidelever, spring piston.
Stock: Match model—walnut, deep forend, adjustable buttplate.
Sights: Globe front with interchangeable inserts. Click micro. adjustable match aperture rear. Front and rear sights move as a single unit.
Features: Recoilless, vibration free. Five-way adjustable match trigger. Grooved for scope mounts. Permanent lubrication, steel piston ring. Cocking effort 9 lbs. Optional 10-oz. barrel sleeve. Available from Beeman.

BEEMAN/FEINWERKBAU 300-S MINI-MATCH
Caliber: 177, single shot.
Barrel: 17⅛″.
Weight: 8.8 lbs. **Length:** 40″ overall.
Power: Spring piston, single stroke sidelever cocking.
Stock: Walnut. Stippled grip, adjustable buttplate. Scaled-down for youthful or slightly built shooters.
Sights: Globe front with interchangeable inserts, micro. adjustable rear. Front and rear sights move as a single unit.
Features: Recoilless, vibration free. Grooved for scope mounts. Steel piston ring. Cocking effort about 9½ lbs. Barrel sleeve optional. Left-hand model available. Introduced 1978. Imported by Beeman.

Beeman HW97

BEEMAN HW30 AIR RIFLE
Caliber: 177, single shot.
Barrel: 17″ (177), 12-groove rifling.
Weight: 5.5 lbs.
Power: Spring piston; single-stroke barrel cocking.
Stock: Walnut-finished hardwood.
Sights: Blade front, adjustable rear.
Features: Velocity about 600 fps (177). Double-jointed cocking lever. Cast trigger guard. Synthetic non-drying breech and piston seals. Introduced 1990. Imported by Beeman.

BEEMAN HW97 AIR RIFLE
Caliber: 177, 20, single shot.
Barrel: 17.75″.
Weight: 9.2 lbs. **Length:** 44.1″ overall.
Power: Spring-piston, underlever cocking.
Stock: Walnut-stained beech; rubber buttpad.
Sights: None. Receiver grooved for scope mounting.
Features: Velocity 830 fps (177). Fixed barrel with fully opening, direct loading breech. Adjustable trigger. Imported by Beeman Precision Airguns.

Airguns–Long Guns

Benjamin Sheridan CO₂

BENJAMIN SHERIDAN PNEUMATIC (PUMP-UP) AIR RIFLES
Caliber: 177 or 22, single shot.
Barrel: 19³/₈″, rifled brass.
Weight: 5¹/₂ lbs. **Length:** 36¹/₄″ overall.
Power: Multi-pump pneumatic.
Stock: American walnut stock and forend.
Sights: High ramp front, fully adjustable notch rear.
Features: Variable velocity to 800 fps. Bolt action with ambidextrous push-pull safety. Black or nickel finish. Introduced 1991. Made in the U.S. by Benjamin Sheridan Co.

BENJAMIN SHERIDAN CO₂ AIR RIFLES
Caliber: 177, 20 or 22, single shot.
Barrel: 19³/₈″, rifled brass.
Weight: 5 lbs. **Length:** 36¹/₂″ overall.
Power: 12-gram CO₂ cylinder.
Stock: American walnut with buttplate.
Sights: High ramp front, fully adjustable notch rear.
Features: Velocity to 680 fps (177). Bolt action with ambidextrous push-pull safety. Gives about 40 shots per cylinder. Black or nickel finish. Introduced 1991. Made in the U.S. by Benjamin Sheridan Co.

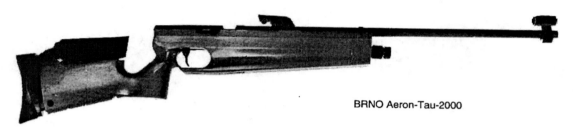

BRNO Aeron-Tau-2000

BRNO AERON-TAU-2000 AIR RIFLE
Caliber: 177, single shot
Barrel: 23″.
Weight: 6 lbs., 8 oz. **Length:** 40″ overall.
Power: 12-gram CO₂ cartridges.
Stock: Synthetic match style with adjustable comb and buttplate.
Sights: Globe front with interchangeable inserts, fully adjustable open rear.
Features: Adjustable trigger. Rear sight converts to aperture on receiver. Comes with sling, extra seals, CO₂ cartridges, large CO₂ bottle, counterweight. Introduced 1993. Imported by Century International Arms.

BRNO 630 SERIES AIR RIFLES
Caliber: 177 single shot.
Barrel: 20.75″.
Weight: 6 lbs., 15 oz. **Length:** 45.75″ overall.
Power: Spring piston, barrel cocking.
Stock: Beechwood (Model 630); checkered, walnut stained (Model 631).
Sights: Hooded front, fully adjustable rear; grooved for scope mount.
Features: Velocity about 600 fps. Automatic safety; externally adjustable trigger; sling swivels. Imported from the Czech Republic by Action Arms, Ltd.

Crosman Model 664X

CROSMAN MODEL 66 POWERMASTER
Caliber: 177 (single shot pellet) or BB, 200-shot reservoir.
Barrel: 20″, rifled steel.
Weight: 3 lbs. **Length:** 38¹/₂″ overall.
Power: Multi-pump pneumatic.
Stock: Wood-grained ABS plastic; checkered p.g. and forend.
Sights: Ramp front, fully adjustable open rear.
Features: Velocity about 645 fps. Bolt action, cross-bolt safety. Introduced 1983. From Crosman.

CROSMAN MODEL 781 SINGLE PUMP
Caliber: 177 pellets (5-shot pellet clip) or BB (195-shot BB reservoir).
Barrel: 19¹/₂″; steel.
Weight: 2 lbs., 14 oz. **Length:** 35.8″ overall.
Power: Pneumatic, single pump.
Stock: Wood-grained ABS plastic; checkered pistol grip and forend.
Sights: Blade front, open adjustable rear.
Features: Velocity of 405 fps (pellets). Uses only one pump. Hidden BB reservoir holds 195 shots; pellets loaded via 5-shot clip. Introduced 1984. From Crosman.

CROSMAN MODEL 760 PUMPMASTER
Caliber: 177 pellets (single shot) or BB (200-shot reservoir).
Barrel: 19¹/₂″, rifled steel.
Weight: 2 lbs., 12 oz. **Length:** 33.5″ overall.
Power: Pneumatic, hand pumped.
Stock: Walnut-finished ABS plastic stock and forend
Features: Velocity to 590 fps (BBs, 10 pumps). Short stroke, power determined by number of strokes. Post front sight and adjustable rear sight. Cross-bolt safety. Introduced 1966. From Crosman.

CROSMAN MODEL 782 BLACK DIAMOND AIR RIFLE
Caliber: 177 pellets (5-shot clip) or BB (195-shot reservoir).
Barrel: 18″, rifled steel.
Weight: 3 lbs.
Power: CO₂ Powerlet.
Stock: Wood-grained ABS plastic; checkered grip and forend.
Sights: Blade front, open adjustable rear.
Features: Velocity up to 595 fps (pellets), 650 fps (BB). Black finish with white diamonds. Introduced 1990. From Crosman.

Airguns–Long Guns

CROSMAN MODEL 788 BB SCOUT RIFLE
Caliber: BB only, 20-shot magazine.
Barrel: 14", steel.
Weight: 2 lbs. 7 oz. **Length:** 31½" overall.
Power: Pneumatic; hand pumped.
Stock: Wood-grained ABS plastic, checkered p.g. and forend.
Sights: Blade front, open adjustable rear.
Features: Variable pump power—three pumps give MV of 330 fps, six pumps 437 fps, 10 pumps 465 fps (BBs, average). Steel barrel, cross-bolt safety. Introduced 1978. From Crosman.

CROSMAN MODEL 1077 REPEATAIR RIFLE
Caliber: 177 pellets, 12-shot clip
Barrel: 20.3", rifled steel.
Weight: 3 lbs., 11 oz. **Length:** 38.8" overall.
Power: CO_2 Powerlet.
Stock: Textured synthetic.
Sights: Blade front, fully adjustable rear.
Features: Velocity 590 fps. Removable 12-shot clip. True semi-automatic action. Introduced 1993. From Crosman.

Crosman Model 2200

CROSMAN MODEL 1389 BACKPACKER RIFLE
Caliber: 177, single shot.
Barrel: 14", rifled steel.
Weight: 3 lbs. 3 oz. **Length:** 31" overall.
Power: Hand pumped, pneumatic.
Stock: Composition, skeletal type.
Sights: Blade front, rear adjustable for windage and elevation.
Features: Velocity to 560 fps. Detachable stock. Receiver grooved for scope mounting. Metal parts blued. From Crosman.

CROSMAN MODEL 2100 CLASSIC AIR RIFLE
Caliber: 177 pellets (single shot), or BB (200-shot BB reservoir).
Barrel: 21", rifled.
Weight: 4 lbs., 13 oz. **Length:** 39¾" overall.
Power: Pump-up, pneumatic.
Stock: Wood-grained checkered ABS plastic.
Features: Three pumps give about 450 fps, 10 pumps about 755 fps (BBs). Cross-bolt safety; concealed reservoir holds over 200 BBs. From Crosman.

CROSMAN MODEL 2200 MAGNUM AIR RIFLE
Caliber: 22, single shot.
Barrel: 19", rifled steel.
Weight: 4 lbs., 12 oz. **Length:** 39" overall.
Power: Pump-up, pneumatic.
Stock: Full-size, wood-grained ABS plastic with checkered grip and forend.
Sights: Ramp front, open step-adjustable rear.
Features: Variable pump power—three pumps give 395 fps, six pumps 530 fps, 10 pumps 595 fps (average). Full-size adult air rifle. Has white line spacers at pistol grip and buttplate. Introduced 1978. From Crosman.

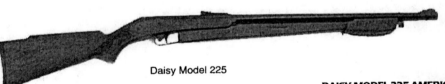

Daisy Model 225

DAISY MODEL 225 AMERICAN LEGEND
Caliber: BB, 650-shot magazine.
Barrel: Smoothbore steel.
Weight: 2.8 lbs. **Length:** 37.2" overall.
Power: Single-pump spring air.
Stock: Moulded woodgrain plastic.
Sights: Blade and ramp front, adjustable open rear,
Features: Velocity to 330 fps. Grooved pump handle; Monte Carlo-style stock with cheekpiece and checkered grip. Cross-bolt trigger block safety. Introduced 1994. From Daisy.

Daisy Model 840

DAISY MODEL 840
Caliber: 177 pellet single shot; or BB 350-shot.
Barrel: 19", smoothbore, steel.
Weight: 2.7 lbs. **Length:** 36.8" overall.
Stock: Moulded wood-grain stock and forend.
Sights: Ramp front, open, adjustable rear.
Features: Single pump pneumatic rifle. Muzzle velocity 335 fps (BB), 300 fps (pellet). Steel buttplate; straight pull bolt action; cross-bolt safety. Forend forms pump lever. Introduced 1978. From Daisy Mfg. Co.

DAISY MODEL 990 DUAL-POWER AIR RIFLE
Caliber: 177 pellets (single shot) or BB (100-shot magazine).
Barrel: Rifled steel.
Weight: 4.1 lbs. **Length:** 37.4" overall.
Power: Pneumatic pump-up and 12-gram CO_2.
Stock: Moulded woodgrain.
Sights: Ramp and blade front, adjustable open rear.
Features: Velocity to 650 fps (BB), 630 fps (pellet). Choice of pump or CO_2 power. Shoots BBs or pellets. Heavy die-cast receiver dovetailed for scope mount. Cross-bolt trigger block safety. Introduced 1993. From Daisy Mfg. Co.

Airguns–Long Guns

Daisy Model 1894 Commemorative

DAISY MODEL 1894 COMMEMORATIVE
Caliber: BB, 40-shot magazine.
Barrel: 17.5″. Octagon shroud.
Weight: 2.2 lbs. **Length:** 39.5″ overall.
Power: Spring air.
Stock: Moulded woodgrain plastic.
Sights: Blade on ramp front, adjustable open rear.
Features: Velocity 300 fps. Side loading port; sliding sear-block safety; silk screened die-cast receiver. Has commemorative foil medallion in the stock. Made in U.S. From Daisy Mfg. Co.

DAISY MODEL 1938 RED RYDER CLASSIC
Caliber: BB, 650-shot repeating action.
Barrel: Smoothbore steel with shroud.
Weight: 2.2 lbs. **Length:** 35.4″ overall.
Power: Spring air; lever cocking.
Stock: Walnut stock burned with Red Ryder lariat signature.
Sights: Post front, adjustable V-slot rear.
Features: Walnut forend. Saddle ring with leather thong. Lever cocking. Gravity feed. Controlled velocity. One of Daisy's most popular guns. From Daisy Mfg. Co.

Daisy Model 1938 Red Ryder

DAISY POWER LINE 753 TARGET RIFLE
Caliber: 177, single shot.
Barrel: 20.9″, Lothar Walther.
Weight: 6.4 lbs. **Length:** 39.75″ overall.
Power: Recoilless pneumatic, single pump.
Stock: Walnut with adjustable cheekpiece and buttplate.
Sights: Globe front with interchangeable inserts, diopter rear with micro. click adjustments.
Features: Includes front sight reticle assortment, web shooting sling. From Daisy Mfg. Co.

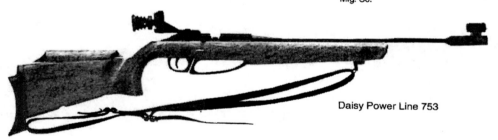

Daisy Power Line 753

DAISY POWER LINE 853
Caliber: 177 pellets.
Barrel: 20.9″; 12-groove rifling, high-grade solid steel by Lothar Walther, precision crowned; bore size for precision match pellets.
Weight: 5.08 lbs. **Length:** 38.9″ overall.
Power: Single-pump pneumatic.
Stock: Full-length, select American hardwood, stained and finished; black buttplate with white spacers.
Sights: Globe front with four aperture inserts; precision micrometer adjustable rear peep sight mounted on a standard ³⁄₈″ dovetail receiver mount.
Features: Single shot. From Daisy Mfg. Co.

DAISY POWER LINE 856 PUMP-UP AIRGUN
Caliber: 177 pellets (single shot) or BB (100-shot reservoir).
Barrel: Rifled steel with shroud.
Weight: 2.7 lbs. **Length:** 37.4″ overall.
Power: Multi-pump pneumatic.
Stock: Moulded wood-grain with Monte Carlo cheekpiece.
Sights: Ramp and blade front, open rear adjustable for elevation.
Features: Velocity from 315 fps (two pumps) to 650 fps (10 pumps). Shoots BBs or pellets. Heavy die-cast metal receiver. Cross-bolt trigger-block safety. Introduced 1984. From Daisy Mfg. Co.

DAISY POWER LINE 880 PUMP-UP AIRGUN
Caliber: 177 pellets, BB.
Barrel: Rifled steel with shroud.
Weight: 4.5 lbs. **Length:** 37³⁄₄″ overall.
Power: Multi-pump pneumatic.
Stock: Wood-grain moulded plastic with Monte Carlo cheekpiece.
Sights: Ramp front, open rear adjustable for elevation.
Features: Crafted by Daisy. Variable power (velocity and range) increase with pump strokes. 10 strokes for maximum power. 100-shot BB magazine. Cross-bolt trigger safety. Positive cocking valve. From Daisy Mfg. Co.

DAISY POWER LINE 922
Caliber: 22, 5-shot clip.
Barrel: Rifled steel with shroud.
Weight: 4.5 lbs. **Length:** 37³⁄₄″ overall.
Power: Multi-pump pneumatic.
Stock: Moulded wood-grained plastic with checkered p.g. and forend, Monte Carlo cheekpiece.
Sights: Ramp front, fully adjustable open rear.
Features: Muzzle velocity from 270 fps (two pumps) to 530 fps (10 pumps). Straight-pull bolt action. Separate buttplate and grip cap with white spacers. Introduced 1978. From Daisy Mfg. Co.

Airguns–Long Guns

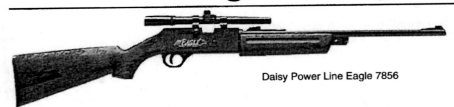

Daisy Power Line Eagle 7856

DAISY POWER LINE 2001 AIR RIFLE
Caliber: 177 pellets, 35-shot helical magazine.
Barrel: Rifled steel.
Weight: 3.1 lbs. Length: 37.4″ overall.
Power: CO_2.
Stock: Moulded woodgrain with Monte Carlo comb.
Sights: Ramp and blade front, fully adjustable open rear.
Features: Velocity to 625 fps. Bolt-action repeater with cross-bolt trigger block safety; checkered grip and forend; white buttplate spacer. Introduced 1994. From Daisy Mfg. Co.

DAISY POWER LINE EAGLE 7856 PUMP-UP AIRGUN
Caliber: 177 (pellets), BB, 100-shot BB magazine.
Barrel: Rifled steel with shroud.
Weight: 2³/₄ lbs. Length: 37.4″ overall.
Power: Pneumatic pump-up.
Stock: Moulded wood-grain plastic.
Sights: Ramp and blade front, open rear adjustable for elevation.
Features: Velocity from 315 fps (two pumps) to 650 fps (10 pumps). Finger grooved forend. Cross-bolt trigger-block safety. Introduced 1985. From Daisy Mfg. Co.

Daisy Model 95

DAISY YOUTH LINE RIFLES

Model:	95	111	105
Caliber:	BB	BB	BB
Barrel:	18″	18″	13¹/₂″
Length:	35.2″	34.3″	29.8″
Power:	Spring	Spring	Spring
Capacity:	700	650	400

Features: Model 95 stock and forend are wood; 105 and 111 have plastic stocks. From Daisy Mfg. Co.

EL GAMO 126 SUPER MATCH TARGET RIFLE
Caliber: 177, single shot.
Barrel: Match grade, precision rifled.
Weight: 10.6 lbs. Length: 43.8″ overall.
Power: Single-pump pneumatic.
Stock: Match-style, hardwood, with stippled grip and forend.
Sights: Hooded front with interchangeable elements, fully adjustable match rear.
Features: Velocity of 590 fps. Adjustable trigger; easy loading pellet port; adjustable buttpad. Introduced 1984. Imported from Spain by Daisy Mfg. Co.

FAMAS SEMI-AUTO AIR RIFLE
Caliber: 177, 10-shot magazine.
Barrel: 19.2″.
Weight: About 8 lbs. Length: 29.8″ overall.
Power: 12 gram CO_2.
Stock: Synthetic bullpup design.
Sights: Adjustable front, aperture rear.
Features: Velocity of 425 fps. Duplicates size, weight and feel of the centerfire MAS French military rifle in caliber 223. Introduced 1988. Imported from France by Century International Arms.

"GAT" AIR RIFLE
Caliber: 177, single shot.
Barrel: 17¹/₄″ cocked, 23¹/₄″ extended.
Weight: 3 lbs.
Power: Spring piston.
Stock: Composition.
Sights: Fixed.
Features: Velocity about 450 fps. Shoots pellets, darts, corks. Imported from England by Stone Enterprises, Inc.

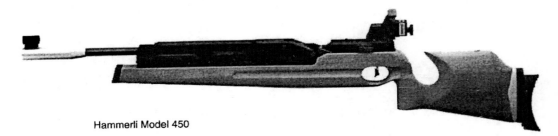

Hammerli Model 450

HAMMERLI MODEL 450 MATCH AIR RIFLE
Caliber: 177, single shot.
Barrel: 19.5″.
Weight: 9.8 lbs. Length: 43.3″ overall.
Power: Single-stroke pneumatic.
Stock: Match style with stippled grip, rubber buttpad. Beech or walnut.
Sights: Match tunnel front, Hammerli diopter rear.
Features: Velocity about 560 fps. Removeable sights; forend sling rail; adjustable trigger; adjustable comb. Introduced 1994. Imported from Switzerland by Hammerli USA.

MARKSMAN MODEL 28 INTERNATIONAL AIR RIFLE
Caliber: 177, single shot.
Barrel: 17″.
Weight: 5³/₄ lbs.
Power: Spring-air, barrel cocking.
Stock: Hardwood.
Sights: Hooded front, adjustable rear.
Features: Velocity of 580-620 fps. Introduced 1989. Imported from Germany by Marksman Products.

Airguns–Long Guns

MARKSMAN MODEL 40 INTERNATIONAL AIR RIFLE
Caliber: 177, single shot.
Barrel: 18³/₈".
Weight: 7¹/₃ lbs.
Power: Spring-air, barrel cocking.
Stock: Hardwood.
Sights: Hooded front, adjustable rear.
Features: Velocity of 700-720 fps. Introduced 1989. Imported from Germany by Marksman Products.

MARKSMAN MODEL 45 AIR RIFLE
Caliber: 177, single shot.
Barrel: 19.1".
Weight: 7.3 lbs. **Length:** 46.75" overall.
Power: Spring-air, barrel cocking.
Stock: Stained hardwood with Monte Carlo cheekpiece, buttpad.
Sights: Hooded front, fully adjustable micrometer rear.
Features: Velocity 900-930 fps. Adjustable trigger; automatic safety. Introduced 1993. Imported from Spain by Marksman Products.

Marksman Model 45

MARKSMAN MODEL 56-FTS
Caliber: 177, single shot.
Barrel: 19⁵/₈", rifled.
Weight: 8.8 lbs. **Length:** 47" overall.
Power: Spring-piston, break-barrel.
Stock: Ambidextrous hardwood with fully adjustable cheekpiece, stippling and soft rubber recoil pad.
Sights: No open sights.
Features: Velocity about 910-940 fps. Carefully engineered barrel weight improves stability, performance and accuracy. Imported from Germany by Marksman Products.

MARKSMAN MODEL 58-S
Caliber: 177, single shot.
Barrel: 16", rifled.
Weight: 8.5 lbs. **Length:** 42" overall.
Power: Spring-piston, break-barrel.
Stock: Ambidextrous hardwood with stippling and soft rubber recoil pad.
Sights: No open sights.
Features: Velocity about 910-940 fps. Conforms to NRA silhouette rules. Fitted with Rekord trigger. All-steel barrel sleeve adds weight for offhand shooting. Imported from Germany by Marksman Products.

Marksman Model 60

MARKSMAN MODEL 60 AIR RIFLE
Caliber: 177, single shot.
Barrel: 18.5", rifled.
Weight: 8.9 lbs. **Length:** 44.75" overall.
Power: Spring piston, under-lever cocking.
Stock: Walnut-stained beech with Monte Carlo comb, hand-checkered pistol grip, rubber butt pad.
Sights: Blade front, open, micro. adjustable rear.
Features: Velocity of 810-840 fps. Automatic button safety on rear of receiver. Receiver grooved for scope mounting. Fully adjustable Rekord trigger. Introduced 1990. Imported from Germany by Marksman Products.

Marksman Model 55 Air Rifle
Similar to the Model 70T except has uncheckered hardwood stock, no cheekpiece, plastic buttplate. Adjustable Rekord trigger. Overall length is 45.25", weight is 7¹/₂ lbs. Available in 177-caliber only.

MARKSMAN MODEL 70 AIR RIFLE
Caliber: 177, 20 or 22, single shot.
Barrel: 19.75".
Weight: 8 lbs. **Length:** 45.5" overall.
Power: Spring air, barrel cocking.
Stock: Stained hardwood with Monte Carlo cheekpiece, rubber buttpad, cut checkered p.g.
Sights: Hooded front, open fully adjustable rear.
Features: Velocity of 910-940 fps (177), 810-840 fps (20), 740-780 fps (22); adjustable Rekord trigger. Introduced 1988. Imported from Germany by Marksman Products.

Marksman Model 1710

MARKSMAN MODEL 1710 PLAINSMAN AIR RIFLE
Caliber: BB, 20-shot repeater.
Barrel: Smoothbore steel with shroud.
Weight: 2.25 lbs. **Length:** 34" overall.
Power: Spring-air.
Stock: Stained hardwood.
Sights: Blade on ramp front, adjustable V-slot rear.
Features: Velocity about 275 fps. Positive feed; automatic safety. Introduced 1994. Made in U.S. From Marksman Products.

Airguns–Long Guns

MARKSMAN MODEL 1740 AIR RIFLE
Caliber: 177 or 18-shot BB repeater.
Barrel: 15¹/₂", smoothbore.
Weight: 5 lbs., 1 oz. **Length:** 36¹/₂" overall.
Power: Spring, barrel cocking.
Stock: Moulded high-impact ABS plastic.
Sights: Ramp front, open rear adjustable for elevation.
Features: Velocity about 450 fps. Automatic safety; fixed front, adjustable rear sight; positive feed BB magazine; shoots 177-cal. BBs, pellets and darts. From Marksman Products.

MARKSMAN MODEL 1750 BB REPEATER RIFLE
Caliber: BB, 18-shot magazine.
Barrel: 15", smoothbore.
Weight: 4.7 lbs.
Power: Spring piston, barrel cocking.
Stock: Moulded composition.
Sights: Tunnel front, open adjustable rear.
Features: Velocity of 450 fps. Automatic safety. Positive Feed System loads a BB each time gun is cocked. Introduced 1990. From Marksman Products.

Marksman Model 1790

MARKSMAN MODEL 1790 BIATHLON TRAINER
Caliber: 177, single shot.
Barrel: 15", rifled.
Weight: 4.7 lbs.
Power: Spring-air, barrel cocking.
Stock: Synthetic.
Sights: Hooded front, match-style diopter rear.
Features: Velocity of 450 fps. Endorsed by the U.S. Shooting Team. Introduced 1989. From Marksman Products.

MARKSMAN MODEL 1792 COMPETITION TRAINER AIR RIFLE
Caliber: 177, single shot.
Barrel: 15", rifled.
Weight: 4.7 lbs.
Power: Spring-air, barrel cocking.
Stock: Synthetic.
Sights: Hooded front, match-style diopter rear.
Features: Velocity about 450 fps. Automatic safety. Introduced 1993. More economical version of the 1790 Biathlon Trainer. Made in U.S. From Marksman Products.

Parker-Hale Dragon Field

PARKER-HALE DRAGON FIELD TARGET AIR RIFLE
Caliber: 177, single shot.
Barrel: 25".
Weight: 10.7 lbs. **Length:** 40" overall.
Power: Single stroke pneumatic.
Stock: European walnut; high comb thumbhole with adjustable rubber buttpad. Right- or left-hand versions available.
Sights: None furnished. Action and front sight base dovetailed for scope or iron sights.
Features: Velocity about 800 fps. Very moderate cocking effort. Fully adjustable target trigger. Recoilless; vibration free. Previously imported from England by Beeman.

PARKER-HALE DRAGON SPORTER AIR RIFLE
Caliber: 22, single shot.
Barrel: 23".
Weight: 8.6 lbs. **Length:** 37.75" overall.
Power: Single stroke pneumatic.
Stock: European walnut; checkered grip and forend; rubber buttpad.
Sights: None furnished. Action and front sight base dovetailed for scope or iron sights.
Features: Velocity about 520 fps. Very moderate cocking effort; recoilless, vibration free. Constant power. Previously imported from England by Beeman.

RWS SM 100 AIR RIFLE
Caliber: 177, 22, single shot.
Barrel: 22", 12-groove Lothar Walther.
Weight: 8¹/₂ lbs. **Length:** 39¹/₂" overall.
Power: Precharged compressed air from diving tank.
Stock: Walnut-finished beech.
Sights: None furnished.
Features: Velocity to 1000 fps (177), 800 fps (22). PFTE-coated lightweight striker for consistent shots. Blued barrel and air chamber. Previously imported from England by Dynamit Nobel-RWS.

RWS NJR 100 Air Rifle
Similar to the SM 100 except designed for Field Target competition. Hand-picked Walther barrel for best accuracy. Walnut Field Target thumbhole stock has adjustable forend, cheekpiece and buttpad. Has lever-type bolt, straight blade trigger. Previously imported from England by Dynamit Nobel-RWS.

RWS TM 100 Air Rifle
Similar to the SM 100 except is target model with hand-picked barrel for best accuracy. Target-type walnut stock with adjustable cheekpiece and adjustable buttplate. Stippled grip and forend. Available in 177 or 22 (special order), right- or left-hand models. Variable power settings. Two-stage adjustable trigger; 22" barrel. Previously imported from England by Dynamit Nobel-RWS.

Airguns–Long Guns

RWS/DIANA MODEL 24 AIR RIFLE
Caliber: 177, 22, single shot.
Barrel: 17", rifled.
Weight: 6 lbs. **Length:** 42" overall.
Power: Spring air, barrel cocking.
Stock: Beech.
Sights: Hooded front, adjustable rear.
Features: Velocity of 700 fps (177). Easy cocking effort; blue finish. Imported from Germany by Dynamit Nobel-RWS, Inc.

RWS/DIANA MODEL 36 AIR RIFLE
Caliber: 177, 22, single shot.
Barrel: 19", rifled.
Weight: 8 lbs. **Length:** 45" overall.
Power: Spring air, barrel cocking.
Stock: Beech.
Sights: Hooded front (interchangeable inserts avail.), adjustable rear.
Features: Velocity of 1000 fps (177-cal.). Comes with scope mount; two-stage adjustable trigger. Imported from Germnay by Dynamit Nobel-RWS, Inc.

RWS/Diana Model 34 Air Rifle
Similar to the Model 24 except has 19" barrel, weighs 7.5 lbs. Gives velocity of 1000 fps (177), 800 fps (22). Adjustable trigger, synthetic seals. Comes with scope rail.

RWS/DIANA MODEL 45 AIR RIFLE
Caliber: 177, single shot.
Weight: 7³/₄ lbs. **Length:** 46" overall.
Power: Spring air, barrel cocking.
Stock: Walnut-finished hardwood with rubber recoil pad.
Sights: Globe front with interchangeable inserts, micro. click open rear with four-way blade.
Features: Velocity of 1000 fps. Dovetail base for either micrometer peep sight or scope mounting. Automatic safety. Imported from Germany by Dynamit Nobel-RWS, Inc.

RWS/Diana Model 52

RWS/DIANA MODEL 52 AIR RIFLE
Caliber: 177, 22, 25, single shot.
Barrel: 17", rifled.
Weight: 8¹/₂ lbs. **Length:** 43" overall.
Power: Spring air, sidelever cocking.
Stock: Beech, with Monte Carlo, cheekpiece, checkered grip and forend.
Sights: Ramp front, adjustable rear.
Features: Velocity of 1100 fps (177). Blue finish. Solid rubber buttpad. Imported from Germany by Dynamit Nobel-RWS, Inc.

RWS/DIANA MODEL 75 T01 MATCH AIR RIFLE
Caliber: 177, single shot.
Barrel: 19".
Weight: 11 lbs. **Length:** 43.7" overall.
Power: Spring air, sidelever cocking.
Stock: Oil-finished beech with stippled grip, adjustable buttplate, accessory rail. Conforms to ISU rules.
Sights: Globe front with five inserts, fully adjustable match peep rear.
Features: Velocity of 574 fps. Fully adjustable trigger. Model 75 HV has stippled forend, adjustable cheekpiece. Uses double opposing piston system for recoilless operation. Imported from Germany by Dynamit Nobel-RWS, Inc.

RWS/Diana 75 Model T01

RWS/Diana Model 100

RWS/Diana Model 75S T01 Air Rifle
Similar to the Model 75 T01 except has beech stock specially shaped for standing and three-position shooting. Buttplate is vertically adjustable with curved and straight spacers for individual fit, adjustable cheekpiece. Introduced 1990.

RWS/DIANA MODEL 100 MATCH AIR RIFLE
Caliber: 177, single shot.
Barrel: 19".
Weight: 11 lbs. **Length:** 43" overall.
Power: Single-stroke pneumatic.
Stock: Walnut.
Sights: Tunnel front, fully adjustable match rear.
Features: Velocity of 580 fps. Single-stroke cocking; cheekpiece adjustable for height and length; recoilless operation. Cocking lever secured against rebound. Introduced 1990. Imported from Germany by Dynamit Nobel-RWS, Inc.

Airguns–Long Guns

RWS GAMO DELTA AIR RIFLE
Caliber: 177.
Barrel: 15.73".
Weight: 5.3 lbs. **Length:** 37" overall.
Power: Barrel cocking, spring piston.
Stock: Carbon fiber.
Sights: Blade front, fully adjustable open rear.
Features: Velocity to 565 fps. Has 20-lb. cocking effort. Synthetic seal; dual safeties; grooved for scope mounting. Previously imported from Spain by Dynamit Nobel-RWS, Inc.

RWS Gamo Delta

RWS GAMO HUNTER 440 AIR RIFLE
Caliber: 177, single shot.
Barrel: 18".
Weight: 6.75 lbs. **Length:** 43" overall.
Power: Spring piston, barrel cocking.
Stock: Hardwood.
Sights: Hooded blade on ramp front, fully adjustable rear.
Features: Velocity 1000 fps. Monte Carlo stock with cheekpiece; scope rail; dual safeties. Previously imported from Spain by Dynamit Nobel-RWS.

SHERIDAN PNEUMATIC (PUMP-UP) AIR RIFLES
Caliber: 20 (5mm), single shot.
Barrel: 19³/₈", rifled brass.
Weight: 6 lbs. **Length:** 36¹/₂" overall.
Power: Under-lever pneumatic, hand pumped.
Stock: Walnut with buttplate and sculpted forend.
Sights: High ramp front, fully adjustable notch rear.
Features: Variable velocity to 675 fps. Bolt action with ambidextrous push-pull safety. Blue finish (Blue Streak) or nickel finish (Silver Streak). Introduced 1991. Made in the U.S. by Benjamin Sheridan Co.

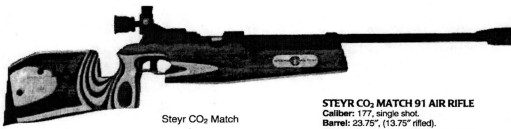

Steyr CO₂ Match

STEYR CO₂ MATCH 91 AIR RIFLE
Caliber: 177, single shot.
Barrel: 23.75", (13.75" rifled).
Weight: 10.5 lbs. **Length:** 51.7" overall.
Power: CO₂.
Stock: Match. Laminated wood. Adjustable buttplate and cheekpiece.
Sights: None furnished; comes with scope mount.
Features: Velocity 577 fps. CO₂ cylinders are refillable; about 320 shots per cylinder. Designed for 10-meter shooting. Introduced 1990. Imported from Austria by Nygord Precision Products.

Airgun & Equipment Manufacturers' Directory

A

Action Arms Ltd., P.O. Box 9573, Philadelphia, PA 19124/215-744-0100; FAX: 215-533-2188

ADCO International, 10 Cedar St., Woburn, MA 01801-2341/617-935-1799; FAX: 617-932-4807

Aimpoint, Inc., 580 Herndon Parkway, Suite 500, Herndon, VA 22070/703-471-6828; FAX: 703-689-0575

Air Arms, Hailsham Industrial Park, Diplocks Way, Hailsham, E. Sussex, BN27 3JF ENGLAND/011-0323-845853 (U.S. importers—Air Rifle Specialists; Air Werks International; World Class Airguns)

Air Rifle Specialists, 311 East Water St., Elmira, NY 14901/607-734-7340; FAX: 607-733-3261

Air Venture, 9752 E. Flower St., Bellflower, CA 90706/310-867-6355

Air Werks International, 403 W. 24th St., Norfolk, VA 23517-1204/800-247-9375

Airgun Repair Centre, 3227 Garden Meadows, Lawrenceburg, IN 47025/812-637-1463

Airguns-R-Us, 300 S. Campbell, Columbia, TN 38401

Airrow (See Swivel Machine Works, Inc.)

American Arms, Inc., 715 E. Armour Rd., N. Kansas City, MO 64116/816-474-3161; FAX: 816-474-1225

Anschutz GmbH, Postfach 1128, D-89001 Ulm, Donau, GERMANY (U.S. importer—PSI, Inc.)

Austin Sheridan USA, Inc., P.O. Box 577, Durham, CT 06422

B

B-Square Company, Inc., P.O. Box 11281, 2708 St. Louis Ave., Ft. Worth, TX 76110/817-923-0964, 800-433-2909; FAX: 817-926-7012

Baikal (See U.S. importers—Air Werks International)

Bausch & Lomb, Inc., 42 East Ave., Rochester, NY 14603/800-828-5423

Beeman Precision Airguns, 5454 Argosy Dr., Huntington Beach, CA 92649/714-890-4800; FAX: 714-890-4808

Benjamin/Sheridan Co., Crosman, Rts. 5 and 20, E. Bloomfield, NY 14443/716-657-6161; FAX: 716-657-5405

Big Bear Arms & Sporting Goods, 2714 Fairmount St., Dallas, TX 75201/214-871-7061; FAX: 214-754-0449

Birchwood Casey, 7900 Fuller Rd., Eden Prairie, MN 55344/800-328-6156, 612-937-7933; FAX: 612-937-7979

Brass Eagle, Inc., 7050A Bramalea Rd., Unit 19, Mississauga, Ont. L4Z 1C7, CANADA/416-848-4844

Break-Free, Inc., P.O. Box 25020, Santa Ana, CA 92799/714-953-1900; FAX: 714-953-0402

Brocock Ltd., 43 River Street, Digbeth, Birmingham, B5 5SA ENGLAND/011-021-773-1200 (U.S. importer—Airguns-R-Us)

Brownells, Inc., 200 S. Front St., Montezuma, IA 50171/515-623-5401; FAX: 515-623-3896

BSA Guns Ltd., Armoury Rd. Small Heath, Birmingham, ENGLAND B11 2PX/011-021-772-8543; FAX: 011-021-773-0845 (U.S. importer—Air Rifle Specialists)

Burris, P.O. Box 1747, Greeley, CO 80631/303-356-1670; FAX: 303-356-8702

Butler Creek Corp., 290 Arden Dr., Belgrade, MT 59714/800-423-8327, 406-388-1356; FAX: 406-388-7204

C

Cannon Safe, Inc., 9358 Stephens St., Pico Rivera, CA 90660/310-692-0636, 800-242-1055; FAX: 310-692-7252

Century International Arms, Inc., 48 Lower Newton St., St. Albans, VT 05478/802-527-1252; FAX: 802-527-0470

Champion's Choice, Inc., 201 International Blvd., LaVergne, TN 37086/615-793-4066; FAX: 615-793-4070

Component Concepts, Inc., 10240 SW Nimbus Ave., Suite L-8, Portland, OR 97223/503-684-9262; FAX: 503-620-4285

Crawford Co., Inc., R.M., P.O. Box 277, Everett, PA 15537/814-652-6536; FAX: 814-652-9526

Creedmoor Sports, Inc., P.O. Box 1040, Oceanside, CA 92051/619-757-5529

Crosman Airguns, Rt. 5 and 20, E. Bloomfield, NY 14443/716-657-6161; FAX: 716-657-5405

Crosman Products of Canada Ltd., 1173 N. Service Rd. West, Oakville, Ontario, L6M 2V9 CANADA/905-827-1822

CZ (See U.S. importer—Action Arms Ltd.)

D

Daisy Mfg. Co., P.O. Box 220, Rogers, AR 72756/501-636-1200; FAX: 501-636-1601

Daystate Arms, Newcastle Street, Stone, Staffs, ST 15 8UJ ENGLAND/011-0785-812473

DBI Books, Inc., 4092 Commercial Ave., Northbrook, IL 60062/708-272-6310; FAX: 708-272-2051

Diana (See U.S. importer—Dynamit Nobel-RWS, Inc.)

Dynamit Nobel-RWS, Inc., 81 Ruckman Rd., Closter, NJ 07624/201-767-1995; FAX: 201-767-1589

E

E.A.A. Corp., P.O. Box 1299, Sharpes, FL 32959/407-639-7006

Emerging Technologies, Inc., P.O. Box 3548, Little Rock, AR 72203/501-375-2227; FAX: 501-372-1445

European American Armory Corp. (See E.A.A. Corp.),

F

Famas (See U.S. importer—Century International Arms, Inc.)

FAS, Via E. Fermi, 8, 20019 Settimo Milanese, Milano, ITALY/02-3285846; FAX: 02-33500196 (U.S. importer—Nygord Precision Products)

Feinwerkbau Westinger & Altenburger GmbH & Co. KG (See FWB)

Firearms & Supplies, Inc., 514 Quincy St., Hancock, MI 49930/906-482-1673; FAX: 906-482-3822

Frankonia Jagd, Hofmann & Co., D-97064 Wurzburg, GERMANY/09302-200; FAX: 09302-20200

FSI, Inc. (See Firearms & Supplies, Inc.)

FWB, Neckarstrasse 43, 78727 Oberndorf a. N., GERMANY/07423-814-0; FAX: 07423-814-89 (U.S. importer—Beeman Precision Airguns, Inc.)

G

G96 Products Co., Inc./237 River St., Paterson, NJ 07524, 201-684-4050; FAX: 201-684-3848

Gamo (See U.S. importer—Daisy Mfg. Co.)

GFR Corp., P.O. Box 430, Andover, NH 03216/603-735-5300

Great Lakes Airguns, 6175 S. Park Ave., Hamburg, NY 14075/716-648-6666; FAX: 716-648-5279

Groenwold, John, P.O. Box 830, Mundelein, IL 60060/708-566-2365

GSI, Inc., 108 Morrow Ave., P.O. Box 129, Trussville, AL 35173/205-655-8299; FAX: 205-655-7078

GZ Paintball Sports Products, P.O. Box 430, Andover, NH 03216/603-735-5300; FAX: 603-735-5154

H

Hämmerli Ltd., Seonerstrasse 37, CH-5600 Lenzburg, SWITZERLAND/064-50 11 44; FAX: 064-51 38 27 (U.S. importers—Hammerli USA; Mandall Shooting Supplies, Inc.)

Hartmann & Weiss GmbH, Rahlstedter Bahnhofstr. 47, 22143 Hamburg, GERMANY/(40) 677 55 85; FAX: (40) 677 55 92

Hebard Guns, Gil, 125-129 Public Square, Knoxville, IL 61448

I

I.S.S., P.O. Box 185234, Ft. Worth, TX 76181/817-595-2090

Interarms, 10 Prince St., Alexandria, VA 22314/703-548-1400
International Shooters Service (See I.S.S.)

J

Johnson Gunsmithing, Inc., 111 Marvin Drive, Hampton, VA 23666/804-838-8091; FAX: 804-838-8157

K

K.B.I., Inc., P.O. Box 5440, Harrisburg, PA 17110-0440/717-540-8518; FAX: 717-540-8567

L

Laseraim, Inc. (See Emerging Technologies, Inc.),
Leupold, P.O. Box 688, Beaverton, OR 97075/503-526-1491; FAX: 503-526-1475
List Precision Engineering, Unit 1, Ingley Works, 13 River Road, Baeking, Essex 1G11 0HE/011-081-594-1688
Lyman Instant Targets, Inc. (See Lyman Products Corp.)
Lyman Products Corp., Rt. 147 West St., Middlefield, CT 06455/203-349-3421; FAX: 203-349-3586

M

Mac-1 Distributors, 13974 Van Ness Ave., Gardena, CA 90249/310-327-3582
Mandall Shooting Supplies, Inc., 3616 N. Scottsdale Rd., Scottsdale, AZ 85252/602-945-2553; FAX: 602-949-0734
Marksman Products, 5482 Argosy Dr., Huntington Beach, CA 92649/714-898-7535, 800-822-8005; FAX: 714-891-0782
Maryland Paintball Supply, 8507 Harford Rd., Parkville, MD 21234/410-882-5607
MCS, Inc., 34 Delmar Dr., Brookfield, CT 06804/203-775-1013; FAX: 203-775-9462
Merkuria Ltd., Argentinska 38, 17005 Praha 7, CZECH REPUBLIC/422-875117; FAX: 422-809152

N

National Survival Game, Inc., P.O. Box 1439, New London, NH 03257/603-735-6165; FAX: 603-735-5154
Nationwide Airgun Repairs (See Airgun Repair Centre)
Norica, Avenida Otaola, 16, Apartado 68, 20600 Eibar, SPAIN (U.S. importers—American Arms, Inc.
Nygord Precision Products, P.O. Box 8394, La Crescenta, CA 91224/818-352-3027; FAX: 818-352-3378

O

Oakshore Electronic Sights, Inc., P.O. Box 4470, Ocala, FL 32678-4470/904-629-7112; FAX: 904-629-1433

P

P&S Gun Service, 2138 Old Shepardsville Rd., Louisville, KY 40218/502-456-9346
Pardini Armi Commerciale Srl, Via Italica 154, 55043 Lido Di Camaiore Lu, ITALY/584-90121; FAX: 584-90122 (U.S. importers—MCS, Inc.; Nygord Precision Products)
Park Rifle Co., Ltd., The, Unit 6a, Dartford Trade Park, Power Mill Lane, Dartford, Kent DA7 7NX/011-0322-222512 (U.S. importer—Air Werks International)
Parker-Hale (See U.S. distributor—Beeman Precision Airguns, Inc.)
Pelaire Products, 5346 Bonky Ct., W. Palm Beach, FL 33415/407-439-0691
Penguin Industries, Inc., Airport Industrial Mall, Coatesville, PA 19320/215-384-6000
Precision Airgun Sales, Inc., 5139 Warrensville Center Rd., Maple Hts., OH 44137-1906/216-587-5005
Precision Sales International, Inc., P.O. Box 1776, Westfield, MA 01086/413-562-5055; FAX: 413-562-5056
Premier Reticles, 920 Breckinridge Lane, Winchester, VA 22601-6707

Q

QB air rifles (See U.S. importer—Sportsman Airguns, Inc.)

R

Ravell Ltd., 289 Diputacion St., 08009, Barcelona SPAIN

Redfield, Inc., 5800 E. Jewell Ave., Denver, CO 80224/303-757-6411; FAX: 303-756-2338
Ripley Rifles, 42 Fletcher Street, Ripley, Derbyshire, DE5 3LP ENGLAND/011-0773-748353
Rossi S.A., Amadeo, Rua: Amadeo Rossi, 143, Sao Leopoldo, RS, BRAZIL 93030-220/051-592-5566 (U.S. importer—Interarms)
Rutten (See U.S. importer—Air Werks International)
RWS (See U.S. importer—Dynamit Nobel-RWS, Inc.)

S

S.G.S. Sporting Guns Srl., Via Della Resistenza, 37, 20090 Buccinasco (MI) ITALY/2-45702446; FAX: 2-45702464
Savana Sports, Inc., 5763 Ferrier St., Montreal, Quebec, CANADA/514-739-1753; FAX: 514-739-1755
Shanghai Airguns, Ltd. (See U.S. importer—Sportsman Airguns, Inc.)
Simmons Outdoor Corp., 2120 Killearney Way, Tallahassee, FL 32308-3402/904-878-5100; FAX: 904-878-0300
Skan A.R., 4 St. Catherines Road, Long Melford, Suffolk, CO10 9JU ENGLAND/011-0787-312942
Smart Parts, 1203 Spring Street, Latrobe, PA 15650/412-539-2660; FAX: 412-539-2298
Sportsmatch Ltd., 16 Summer St., Leighton Buzzard, Bedfordshire, LU7 8HT ENGLAND/0525-381638; FAX: 0525-851236
Steyr Mannlicher AG, Mannlicherstrasse 1, P.O.B. 1000, A-4400 Steyr, AUSTRIA/0043-7252-896-0; FAX: 0043-7252-68621 (U.S. importer—GSI, Inc.)
Stone Enterprises Ltd., Rt. 609, P.O. Box 335, Wicomico Church, VA 22579/804-580-5114; FAX: 804-580-8421
Swivel Machine Works, Inc., 167 Cherry St., Suite 286, Milford, CT 06460/203-926-1840; FAX: 203-874-9212

T

Theoben Engineering, Stephenson Road, St. Ives, Huntingdon, Cambs., PE17 4WJ ENGLAND/011-0480-461718 (U.S. importer—Air Rifle Specialists)
Tippman Pneumatics, Inc., 3518 Adams Center Rd., Fort Wayne, IN 46806/219-749-6022; FAX: 219-749-6619
Trooper Walsh, 2393 N. Edgewood St., Arlington, VA 22207

U

Uberti, Aldo, Casella Postale 43, I-25063 Gardone V.T., ITALY (U.S. importers—Uberti USA, Inc.)
Uberti USA, Inc., 362 Limerock Rd., P.O. Box 469, Lakeville, CT 06039/203-435-8068; FAX: 203-435-8146
UltraSport Arms, Inc., 1955 Norwood Ct., Racine, WI 53403/414-554-3237; FAX: 414-554-9731
United States Shooting Team (USST) Sales, Inc., 1565 Vapor Trail, Colorado Springs, CO 80916/800-395-5991
United States Olympic Shooting Center, One Olympic Plaza, Colorado Springs, CO 80909/719-578-4670

V

Valor Corp., 5555 NW 36th Ave., Miami, FL 33142/305-633-0127
Venom Arms Co., Unit 1, Gun Garrel Industrial Centre, Hayseech, Cradley Heath, West Midlands B64 7JZ ENGLAND/011-021-501-3794 (U.S. importers—Mac-1 Airgun Distributors, Trooper Walsh)
Vortek Products, Inc., P.O. Box 871181, Canton, MI 48187-1181,

W

Walther GmbH, Carl, B.P. 4325, D-89033 Ulm, GERMANY (U.S. importer—Interarms)
Wayland Precision Wood Products, P.O. Box 1142, Mill Valley, CA 94942/415-381-3543
Weatherby, Inc., 3100 El Camino Real, Atascadero, CA 93422/805-466-1767; FAX: 805-466-2527
Webley and Scott Ltd., Frankley Industrial Park, Tay Rd., Rubery Rednal, Birmingham B45 0PA, ENGLAND/011-021-453-1864; FAX: 021-457-7846 (U.S. importer—Beeman Precision Airguns, Inc.)
Weihrauch KG, Hermann, Industriestrasse 11, 8744 Mellrichstadt, GERMANY/09776-497-498 (U.S. importers—Beeman Precision Airguns; E.A.A. Corp.)
World Class Airguns, 2736 Morningstar Dr., Indianapolis, IN 46229/317-897-5548
World of Targets (See Birchwood Casey)

Airgun Associations

American Airgun Field Target Association
5911 Cherokee Ave.
Tampa, Florida 33604

American Paintball League
P.O. Box 3561, CRS
Johnson City, Tennesee 37602
Phone: 800-541-9169

Dutch Paintball Federation
c/o Aceville Publications
Castle House 97 High Street
Colchester, Essex, England C01 1TH
Phone: 011-44-206-564840

European Paintball Sports Federation
c/o Aceville Publications
Castle House 97 High Street
Colchester, Essex, England C01 1TH
Phone: 011-44-206-564840

International Paintball Field Operators Association
15507 S. Normandie Ave. #487
Gardena, California 90247
Phone: 310-323-1021

International Paintball Players Association
P.O. Box 26669
San Diego, California 92196
Phone: 619-695-8882; FAX: 619-695-6909

National Professional Paintball League
540 Main Street
Mount Kisco, New York 10549
Phone: 914-241-7400

North American Paintball Referees Association
584 Cestaric Drive
Milpitas, California 95035

Stock Gun Players Association
6038 Appian Way
Long Beach, California 90803

Airgun Publications

Action Pursuit Games Magazine
CFW Enterprises, Inc., 4201 W. Vanowen Pl., Burbank CA 91505/818-845-2656. Single copy: $2.95 U.S., $3.50 Canada. World's leading magazine of paintball sports.

AAFTA News
5911 Cherokee Ave., Tampa, FL 33604. Official newsletter of the American Airgun Field Target Association.

Air Gunner Magazine
4 The Courtyard, Denmark St., Wokingham, Berkshire, RG11 2AZ, England/011-44-734-771677. One-year subscription to U.S.: $44.00. Leading monthly airgun magazine in U.K.

Airgun Ads
Box 33, Hamilton, MT 59840/406-363-3805. One-year subscription: $35.00 for first mailing, $20.00 for second mailing, $35.00 for Canada and foriegn orders. Monthly tabloid with extensive For Sale and Wanted airgun listings.

Airgun Letter, The
Gapp, Inc., 4614 Woodland Rd., Ellicott City, MD 41042-6329/410-730-5496. One-year subscription: $18.00 U.S., $21.00 Canada, $24.00 Mexico and $30.00 other foreign orders. Monthly newsletter for airgun users and collectors.

Airgun World Magazine
4 The Courtyard, Denmark St., Wokingham, Berkshire, RG11 2AZ, England/011-44-734-771677. Call for subscription rates. Oldest monthly airgun magazine in the U.K., now a sister publication to *Air Gunner*.

IPPA News
International Paintball Players Association, P.O. Box 26669, San Diego, CA 92196-0669/619-695-8882. Call or write for subscription rates. Newsletter for members of the IPPA.

Paintball Consumer Reports
14573-C Jefferson Davis Highway, Woodridge, VA 22191/703-491-6199. One-year subscription: $19.95 U.S., $27.95 foreign orders. Product testing for the paintball industry.

Paintball Games International Magazine
Aceville Publications, Castle House, 97 High St., Colchester, Essex, England CO1 1TH/011-44-206-564840. Call or write for subscription rates. Leading magazine in the U.K. covering competitive paintball activities.

Paintball Hotline
American Paintball Media and Marketing, 15507 S. Normandie Ave. #487, Gardena, CA 90247/310-323-1021. One-year subscription: $50.00 U.S., $75.00 Mexico and Canada, $125.00 other foreign orders. Weekly newsletter that tracks inside industry news.

Paintball News
PBN Publishing, P.O. Box 1608, 24 Henniker St., Hillsboro, NH 03244/603-464-6080. One-year subscription: $35.00. Bi-weekly newspaper covering new product reviews and industry features.

Paintball Players Bible
American Paintball Media and Marketing, 15507 S. Normandie Ave. #487, Gardena, CA 90247/310-323-1021. One-year subscription: $12.95 U.S., $19.95 foreign orders. Bi-monthly publication with profiles of guns and accessories, as well as a manufacturers' index.

Paintball Sports Magazine
Paintball Publications, Inc., 540 Main St., Mount Kisco, NY 10549/941-241-7400. One-year subscription: $24.75 U.S., $32.75 foreign orders. Monthly magazine covering the competitive paintball scene.

U.S. Airgun Magazine
2603 Rollingbrook, Benton, AR 72015/501-778-2615. One-year subscription: $22.00 U.S., $24.00 Mexico and $32.00 other foreign orders. Quarterly magazine covering all aspects of airgunning.